Indigenous Religions

Indigenous Religions

A Companion

Edited by
Graham Harvey

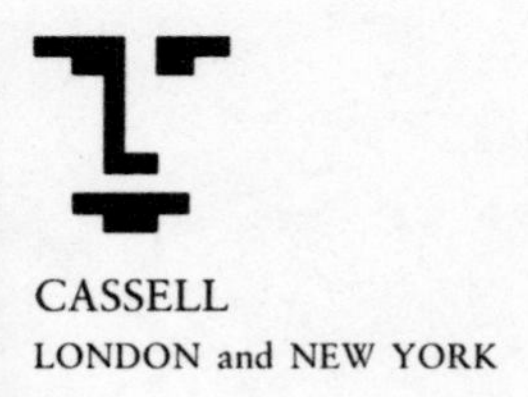

CASSELL
LONDON and NEW YORK

Cassell
Wellington House, 125 Strand, London WC2R 0BB
370 Lexington Avenue, New York, NY 10017-6550

First published 2000

British Library Cataloguing in Publication Data
A catalogue record for this book is available from the British Library.
ISBN 0-304-70447-4 (hardback)
0-304-70448-2 (paperback)

Library of Congress Cataloging-in-Publication Data
Indigenous religions: a companion/edited by Graham Harvey.
p. cm.
Includes bibliographical references and index.
ISBN 0-304-70447-4 (hardcover).—ISBN 0-304-70448-2 (pbk.)
1. Indigenous peoples—Religion. I. Harvey, Graham.
BL380.I56 2000
299–dc21 99-41462
CIP

Typeset by Paston PrePress Ltd, Beccles, Suffolk
Printed and bound in Great Britain by Bookcraft (Bath) Ltd

That the people might live

Contents

Part III Gifts

Contributors

Dr Raoul R. Andersen, Memorial University of Newfoundland, Canada

Dr Fiona Bowie, University of Wales Lampeter, UK

Dr Teri Brewer, University of Wales Glamorgan, UK

Sean M. Connors, University of California, Santa Barbara, USA

Dr James L. Cox, Edinburgh University, Edinburgh, UK

Dr John K. Crellin, Memorial University of Newfoundland, Canada

Dr M. A. Jaimes Guerrero, San Francisco State University, USA

Dr Charlotte E. Hardman, University of Newcastle upon Tyne, UK

Dr Graham Harvey, King Alfred's College, Winchester, UK

Dr Lynne Hume, University of Queensland, Australia

Misel Joe, Saqamaw, Conne River band, Mi'kmaq Nation, Canada

Berel Dov Lerner, University of Tel Aviv, Israel

Peter J. Mataira, Massey University, New Zealand

Dr Kenneth M. Morrison, Arizona State University, Arizona, USA

Dr Jan Platvoet, Leiden University, The Netherlands

Olu Taiwo, King Alfred's College, Winchester, UK

Dr Charles D. Thompson, Jr., University of North Carolina, Chapel Hill, USA

Dr Piers Vitebsky, Scott Polar Research Institute, Cambridge, UK

Dr Mark R. Woodward, Arizona State University, Arizona, USA

Preface

Indigenous religions are co-operative activities in which individuals often have considerable freedom. In theory at least, academia is also a communal activity which values individual effort, interpretation and maybe even vision. There are many differences as well as many similarities between these two domains – as is true of all human activities. The position and authority of elders is but one of these differences, demanding great care from researchers moulded by their tradition to question, challenge, refute and always 'improve'. All but one of the contributors to this volume work within the privileges and stresses of contemporary academia – as professors, postgraduate research students or somewhere in between. Several contributors, including the only non-academically employed contributor, are members of the indigenous nations about which they write here. Other contributors have engaged with particular people(s) in various ways, as will be clear in what they write. Many of us are honoured to participate in continuing conversation and dialogue with the people whose lifeways are of vital interest and inspiration to us. It has been an additional privilege for me to edit the work of this team of friendly and expert collaborators. Several potential contributors had to drop out of the project for one reason or another, their absence is deeply regretted. Publishing is also a collaborative enterprise and I am grateful to Janet Joyce and the team at Cassell Academic for their enthusiasm and expertise in producing this Companion.

The intention of this Companion is to aid and abet the collaborative engagement in dialogue – with its central emphasis on respectful listening and joyous participation – that is the essence of the study of indigenous religions. Contributors have been asked to write about particular themes in which they have shown great interest. They do so in relation to (and relationship with) nations, communities, peoples and/or traditions with whom they are intimately familiar and often passionately involved. Their chapters reflect the various approaches and methodologies applied in their research. As such, each chapter can be studied not only for information about a theme or people, but also about academic approaches and methodologies. Readers are encouraged to explore each theme in relation to other indigenous religions, and to ask whether insights gained here might cast light elsewhere in the study of religions. Happily, the current phase of the study of indigenous religions is committed to the self-determination and vitaility of indigenous peoples. The authority to define what is true, correct or worthy of celebration resides not in distant disengaged academics but among the people themselves. Researchers – wherever their place is – should be respectful listeners before they are careful speakers.

Introduction

Graham Harvey

Health, wealth and the pursuit of happiness are central concerns of religions. Even in the credal religions that insist they (alone) are divinely revealed, and in those recently formed religions that locate everything of value in the individual 'self', these goals are sought communally. In larger or smaller groups or networks, people express their desire for a better life. How 'better', 'healthy', 'wealthy', or 'happy' are understood varies from one community to another, and from one individual to the next. The ways in which it is legitimate to express one's desire or possession of a 'good life' also vary. Religions are structured, orderly, socially sanctioned ways of reaching out to those things, or that thing, which people most want. Sometimes religions are defined by authoritative teachers who assert that 'what people really want' is something that only they can mediate, organize and offer. Sometimes it is asserted that the 'good life' is defined not by human desires but by divine dictate. But this is not always so, and it is a mistake to think that 'true religion' is 'what God says it is', or that it is solely or primarily concerned with a future life. People do religion, just as they make music. They may gladly do what someone else (a divinity, ancestor, priest, or buffalo) says. They might adjust their mannerisms, desires, actions, diction, and even world views to what is acceptable to their source of authority and to their community, culture or society.

Religions are far from static, they change like everything else in this world. People experience something that forcefully validates what has until now been a marginal part of their lifeway. Or they meet someone who has a more dramatic or more humbling way of expressing a similar intuition about that which is desirable. Sometimes events overwhelm a group of people and their lifeway is irrevocably damaged or otherwise made obsolete (un-do-able at least as often as untenable). Perhaps aspects of their old lifeway can be subsumed into a new, seemingly more empowering religious tradition – or at least one that provides hope for future improvement. There are lots of possibilities open to people.

Politics and catering are also ways in which people express or reach for health, wealth and happiness in orderly, socially structured ways. The fact that religions do not only involve humans (but also divinities, ancestors, plants, animals, and a host of others) is also true of politics, catering and other facets of human life. Religions are not defined by 'belief in God', or even 'doing the will of God (or the ancestors, etc.)'. This would be equally true of politics and catering to a considerable number of people. All of this is to say that we must take seriously the fact that most languages have no word for 'religion'. Most people do not separate bits of their lives into neat boxes which can be labelled 'religion', 'politics' or 'catering'. People live lives in which these are inter-linked, meshed, blended, and generally inseparable. They do not say, 'we've done religion, now let's cook'. Rather, the preparation of a favourite food might be both enjoyable and also honour the ancestors – which could bring more of what is needed to be considered healthy, happy, wealthy and wise (knowledgeable or useful politically) in a society.

On the other hand, just because most languages do not have a word for 'religion' does not mean that their speakers are not religious, or that they do not do religion. Nor does it mean that English speakers do something unlike people whose languages do not have a word like 'religion'. The particular history of Europe led to the word 'religion' being used in the way it is now. The Study of Religion as an academic discipline is well aware that religion is not best understood as a discrete category, a label for bizarre or archaic activities that are of no significance to politics, catering and other 'secular' pursuits. Religion is no more 'odd things people do on Sundays' than it is 'belief in God'. A careful discussion of a lifeway will recognize that in particular ways and at particular moments (of temporal space), people express their foundational desires, truest intuitions, and most profound understandings of the way things are, or could or should be.

None of this is true only of indigenous religions. It may even be a peculiar way to begin this book about such religions. Instead, it could have begun with information about the global spread, diversity, richness, vitality or otherwise of indigenous religions. However, exploring some of the meanings and uses of the word 'religion' (and the thoughts, desires and actions expressed by that word), enables a more adequate approach to the realities of the lifeways of interest here. This book will refer to deities, ceremonies, beliefs and practices that will be new, and maybe even bizarre, to some readers. But this is no more true than that the climate and environment in which people do these religions are different to the ones which some readers inhabit. It is also probably true of a good book about any religion. It is a considerable mistake, however, to see beliefs and practices about deities as definitive of or central to religion. When dealing with indigenous religions there is the added complication that some people become obsessed by the differences, or 'curiosities' as Victorian museums labelled some of their displays. So, while this book will discuss 'foreign' (to some) concepts, it will not mystify them as 'alien', 'primitive', 'prehistoric' or 'fantastic'. Religions are human activities. Humans approach that which is of considerable, and sometimes ultimate, significance for them, by means of ceremonies, identification, and other expressions of reciprocal or hierarchical relationships. Exploration and explanation of such human engagements require a holistic, interdisciplinary, multi-perspective conversation between engaged participants, observers, participant-observers and others committed to dialogue.

It is the very ordinariness and unexceptional regularity of (religious) lifeways that make them powerful or empowering. One desire underlying this book is that indigenous religions should receive similarly respectful treatment to that considered appropriate to the larger 'World Religions'. Underlying this desire is the understanding that indigenous religions reveal much that has not otherwise been noticed about other religions. What makes indigenous religions important in the Study of Religions is not that they are necessarily different from – and especially not more 'simple', 'primitive' or less complex than – other ways of being human, but that they are similarly human. There are, of course, plenty of other good reasons for studying indigenous religions. The disciplines engaged in, and methodologies applied to such study are many and various (Anthropology, Sociology, Native American Studies, Maori Studies, Politics, Art, History, and many more). This Companion demonstrates some of these good reasons and valuable approaches. An overview of the diversity of indigenous religions will provide an introduction to the structure, contents and contributors of the Companion.

Indigenous diversity

Indigenous religions are the majority of the world's religions. They are as diverse as the languages spoken, the music made, and the means of subsistence employed by the many and various people who live them in a wide variety of environments, in all continents of the Earth. The number of 'indigenous religionists' may not account for the majority of the world's religious people – some of these religions exist only in one small village – but they are far from insignificant either numerically, taken altogether, or in many other ways. Given the growth and spread of transcultural or global religions (e.g. Buddhism, Christianity and Islam), some indigenous religions have been rejected, abandoned or destroyed. Others have accepted the arriving religion on their own terms, slotting it into an indigenous understanding. Many have adapted to the presence of more powerful or dominating religions, and continued with considerable vitality and creativity. Indeed, many people are returning to their 'traditional religion', or engaging in both 'indigenous' and another, newer religion. For at least some such returners the tradition is found to have remained vitally alive, against all odds, and it is human people and communities who are revitalized by returning to such lifeways. Their return is often experienced as welcomed and affirmed by other-than-human people who also engage in these indigenous religions.

Indigenous religions happen everywhere. Some are certainly limited to small, rainforest villages only minimally in contact with other villages let alone the 'global village'. Most are the fruit of considerable sharing and blending arising out of contacts with neighbours, trade partners, enemies and many others. Some are now as globally visible as some 'World Religions'. Maori tohunga purify auditoriums before Maori opera singers perform there. Aboriginal Australian didjeridu players or First Nation Canadian drum groups play their religious (though not necessarily sacred) musics to a wider audience at WOMAD and other festivals. Yoruba funerals reincorporate the dead as 'ancestors' in their London-centred community. Traditions that some label 'syncretistic' (as if all religions did not learn from and share with others) root that which is indigenous to one place into many other places or diasporas. Santeria, Vodun, Candomblé and other West African rooted traditions exist or flourish not only in the Caribbean and South and Central America, but also in New York and elsewhere in North America and Europe (see, for example, the chapters in Clarke 1998). Indigenous religions have contributed words to European languages (e.g. 'shaman' and 'tabu'). Admittedly, the horticultural, culinary and medical knowledge gained from indigenous peoples has usually been dislocated from its 'religious' context. ('Religious' should not be read as 'spiritual' or 'supernatural', see Green 1999). Tobacco is only rarely smoked 'in a sacred way' now. Potatoes are planted, tended and harvested without much ceremony (cf. Arnold 1989). But even rare respect and uncommon ceremonies are something. Indigenous religions may not have the profile of some larger religions, but size and profile may be the only significant differences between such lifeways.

Since some studies of religion focus exclusively on deities and (allegedly) 'unseen superhuman controlling powers', we can note too that some indigenous religions are deeply interested in the activities and desires of such beings. There are indigenous religions in which 'God' is perceived similarly to the way 'he' might be in the larger monotheisms. Even male gender is attributed to this 'greatest of all beings' – not often with dogmatic insistence or great concern. Similarly, the assertion of divine singularity is not always dogmatic, the 'one and only creator' may have many divine children. Indeed, such (lesser?) deities may be the focus of more attention and generate more aspects of an indigenous religion than their (greater?) progenitor or creator. Meanwhile, 'polytheistic' religions rarely make this question of numbers central to the dissemination and inculcation of their religion. The number of deities is typically indeterminate, even uninteresting, and it is perfectly possible to know that many exist while venerating only one – or none. Divine beings can be left to get on with their own lives, while religion concerns itself with more straightforward relationships between humans and those other-than-human people regularly encountered in daily life: plants, animals, rocks, clouds, and so on. So, while some indigenous people do pray, praise, sacrifice to, and otherwise 'make sacred' particular exalted beings, others do not. Religion, then, is not simply about such activities and beings. It can be concerned with reciprocal relationships between humans and all the other people we encounter – especially those we eat or cut down in order to build dwellings. Some of these other-than-human people may be more powerful than humans. Then it is possible to wish to obtain power or empowerment from them. It is just as possible, as with deities, to try to keep the power from overwhelming us and our regular lifeways. There are many different ways in which religions can approach and apprehend the various powers considered to be available or intimidating.

Ancestors, ghosts and other 'dead' people can also be central and welcome, or central and unwelcome except at special feasts where they are 'bought off' (somewhat like the Mafia perhaps), marginal but welcome, or marginal and unwelcome. Facing mortality has generated a wide diversity of beliefs about post-mortem existence, and can be an excellent context in which to explore the entire religious system. It is equally possible that strongly held ideological positions about death and the dead may generate nothing beyond eloquent funeral speeches and enchanting ceremonies.

In addition to interest in deities, ancestors, 'spirits' and other other-than-human people, some studies of religion are deeply interested in underlying energies, life-forces, or powers held to exist by particular indigenous religions. These mysterious powers have been mistaken for personal Creative beings (deities, or God) – and sometimes this has led to the evolution of a new (theistic) tradition. However, some indigenous understandings entail a diffuse, universally available and impersonal energy that wells up in 'health, wealth and happiness' which is to be drawn on (by humans, deities, plants, animals and everyone else) in particular ways. The orderly tapping or directing of such energy might be the preserve of particular religious officials or ceremonies.

In various ways, the succeeding chapters will explore such matters – the point here is to note the considerable diversity of indigenous religions. How could there not be diversity? Even if we were to break down our large category 'indigenous religions' and explore only those of one continent there would still be great diversity. For example, as Jace Weaver says:

> No universalized essence can encompass the six hundred different tribal traditions, eight major language families, and probably three distinct racial strains lumped together under the collective construct *Native American* or *American Indian*. (1998a, x).

Just as there is no single reality (apart from that of stereotypical racist clichés) that is identifiable as 'the Native American', there is no single 'Native American religion'. There may be broad levels of agreement between people living in similar places – we might, for example, talk about a High Plains religious culture – but even this is only adequate at the level of generalization. When different Lakota groups do and see things differently, it becomes necessary to be careful to identify just who is being spoken about – and who is speaking. This book does not homogenize all Native American, let alone all indigenous religions, into one single indigenous religion.

It is a fact, however, that the academic Study of Religions has adopted three broad categories for religions. It has been most interested in the 'World Religions'. Not only are there books and courses devoted to particular members of this elite club, but there are also books and courses that discuss the rites of passage, for example, of all six or seven 'World Religions'. The second category is 'New Religious Movements'. There are books that discuss a single religion from this category, but typically movements so labelled are discussed together. Like 'World Religions' these movements have little or nothing in common other than this labelling process. In such a context, the use of a third inclusive category 'Indigenous Religions' is not surprising. Until recently such religions have received little attention in Study of Religions scholarship. Anthropologists, of course, have devoted considerable energies to understanding and discussing indigenous 'cultures' (but see Masuzawa 1998). Recently Native American Studies, Maori Studies, and other departments and programmes have been established (not primarily devoted to the study of religions, but almost always including such an interest). These are usually geographically near to the relevant indigenous communities, and the impetus for such developments has often come from indigenous peoples themselves – either as faculty or as students. There has also been considerable interest in indigenous religions from missionaries of one 'World Religion' or another. Considerable popular interest in some of them is exemplified in Sting's introduction of a Yanomamo elder to environmentally concerned music fans in Britain and North America.

Recognizing the diversity of human activities labelled 'religions', and of that which is considered 'indigenous', what justification is there for continuing to write about 'indigenous religions'? Can nothing more positive be said than that 'we are stuck with it'? First, it is possible to find considerable common ground that justifies the use of the label. This will be argued more fully below, and illustrated by the successful cohesion of the chapters of this book. Second, it is possible to draw the wrong conclusion from the diversity, and from the broadness of the categories. Confronted by the many ways in which 'religion' can be defined, students often conclude that it is 'impossible to define religion'. 'Not at all!', says Jonathan Z. Smith, 'The moral ... is not that religion cannot be defined, but that it can be defined, with greater or lesser success, in more than fifty ways' (1998, 281). Smith further notes the validity and utility of the term 'religion' in the study of religions, concluding 'there can be no disciplined study of religion without such a horizon [as is established by such a generic concept]' (Smith 1998, 282). Just so, if we wish to establish the study of indigenous religions near the centre of the Study of Religions (or other academic study), then we can celebrate the label. Of course, we will not forget that it remains an imprecise tool, a broad category and a wide, generic term. Disciplined study has plenty of these, generally uses them carefully, and does not object to the refining of terms and critical approaches. This is at least part of what is happening in this Companion to the study of indigenous religions. The value of studying such religions is heightened by the exciting challenge they offer to prevalent (Western) academic concepts of and approaches to 'religion'.

The process of refinement is itself reflexive, dynamic and (in recent years at least) dialogical. Various other terms have been applied to 'indigenous religions'. Discussion of some of them provides further clarity about what we are studying here.

Rejected terms

More is revealed about the writer who considers these religions 'primitive' than is usefully said about the religions so labelled. Indigenous religions are neither simple nor mere fossils from the earliest evolution of humanity. Their dynamic complexity is in no way exhausted by this book, the main chapters of which illustrate the elaborate and satisfying ways in which people live religiously. The fact that these religions do not have professional bodies of theologians to define them, or to assert authoritative 'final' versions of them, might have led some to the mistaken idea that this is a fault. In fact, even religions which do have theologians are better understood as dynamic and diverse lifeways made visible in what non-theologians do and think rather than in what some (dogmatic) theologians attempt to insist on as orthodoxy or orthopraxis. Meanwhile, the idea that humanity's earliest religion could have survived without change, or with minimal change, is ludicrous. (This is true too of the more polite, but equally fallacious 'archaic'.) Indigenous peoples may or may not live technologically simpler lives than Western industrialized peoples, but if they do it is because they have chosen (for various interesting reasons) to live in particular ways. No group of people has ever lived in complete isolation from all other people – except perhaps when they are about to become extinct. Sharing, exchange, borrowing, learning and choice are ubiquitous human activities. When we observe religions we are seeing human agency, not human stagnation, expressed.

Another category sometimes applied to these religions is 'pre-literate' or 'non-literate'. There is some truth in this designation, in that writing systems are rare and few indigenous peoples write down ceremonies, practices, rules or meditations. There are (at least) four problems with the label. First, Nations like the Maya did write (about) their religion, and this religion did not become totally different to neighbouring non-literate religions. Second, the privileging of writing unnecessarily dismisses the power and adequacy of oral/aural, artistic, dramatic and other means of communication. Indigenous people frequently celebrate 'tradition', which is indicative of the strong links to remembered past activities, and intimates various interesting ways of encouraging memory, acknowledgement and observance. This negative term is, therefore, empty: it says nothing about the actual means by which people communicate or the content of their religions. Third, the privileging of written literature overplays the significance of texts in 'World Religions' in ways that legitimize the hierarchical authority of 'experts' above the lived experience of 'ordinary' people. Conversely, given the persuasiveness of Protestantism in Enlightenment culture, it unduly hints at an alleged lack of individuality in indigenous religions which do not encourage the 'priesthood of all believers', each free to proffer their own interpretation. Fourth, this label refers only to the past. Not only have indigenous people written plenty of invaluable books about their lifeways, or aspects of them, but they have also disseminated information via web pages, e-mail and the full panoply of World Wide Web technologies. Many of these religions are now fully literate.

Their continuing resistance to the encoding of 'scriptures' (universally authoritative texts) is matched by the diversity of the literary forms which, to one degree or another, replicate oral/aural and ceremonial/performance transmission of tradition. Whether the changes following this use of literature are developments or deteriorations could be interestingly debated, but should not be prejudiced by use of the labels 'pre-literate' or 'non-literate'.

'Primal religions' suggests something like 'archaic', especially in that it is usually meant more positively than the term 'primitive'. However, the term compromises efforts towards understanding, dialogue and mutuality between people. If you are considered to represent something foundational beneath all other 'developed' religions, your concerns with life today will hardly be heard. 'Primal' is evocative of those museums in which indigenous artefacts are displayed alongside 'Natural History', i.e. stuffed animals. Native peoples, plants and animals are all presented as part of the scenery awaiting 'discovery', 'exploration', 'civilization' and 'progress' (which are represented elsewhere in these museums by such things as settlers' houses). 'Primal religions' is a 'non-empirical theological construct' which is supposed to provide understanding of that which is about to be replaced either by Western rationality, or one of the missionizing 'World Religions' (Cox 1998, 15–31). It is difficult to use it without prejudice, so it should be abandoned.

'Traditional' clearly labels something of significance to many indigenous religions, i.e. those that honour what previous generations did as formative and of abiding significance. However, not only is this also true of most other religions, it can also mask a polemic in which indigenous religions are berated for being backward-looking and static. The label 'African Traditional Religions' can be used to identify something positive, i.e. that the 'traditional' indigenous religions remain vital alongside the missionary religions Christianity and Islam. Furthermore, links between the diverse traditions have been established and identified, not without problems, as 'African Traditional Religion' (singular). Clearly, there is considerable ambiguity in the use of a label that can suggest something like 'primitive/static' and also something like 'authentic' and deep-rooted.

These major terms applied to indigenous religions are problematic. There are some other terms that require notice because their use in the study of religions, especially indigenous ones, has been formative and not always helpful.

Other difficult terms

The Study of Religions approaches its subject matter, religions (or perhaps 'religion') without assuming that this is a self-evident or obvious piece of life separate from anything else. The discipline is as dynamic as religions are, and applies a wide variety of methodologies to the many and various ways in which people do things that can be labelled 'religions' or 'religious'. This book illustrates what can be achieved by some of those approaches. But if 'religions' have been misconstrued as systems of peculiar ('meta-empirical', 'supernatural' or 'spiritual') theories or 'beliefs' divorced from real (secular?) life, need we adopt the opposite, totalizing, approach in which we are required to study an entire 'culture'? On the one hand, religious people do not isolate 'religion' from catering or politics. On the other hand, no one experiences culture 'as a complex whole'. Only outsiders trained in the art/science of 'participant observation' (i.e. adopting a particular way of looking at what other people do) could possibly think to formulate something as systematic as a description of a 'culture' (cf. Masuzawa 1998). Somewhere between these two academically and ideologically constructed positions is the messy diversity of real life. The words 'religion' and 'culture' are part of our lexicon, but they are often imprecise, messy, everyday generalizations rather than sharp precision tools.

The regular borrowing, sharing, blending and development of religions (as everyday human activities) can be opposed by some experts who insist on established, correct and authorized ways of understanding, doing or being. The word 'syncretism' (and its relations) implies a God-like view of how religions should be, rather than a human celebration of how they are. Certainly we can pay attention to the fascinating ways in which religions are created, encounter others, and respond to new situations. We could stress the associations of 'syncretism' with confederation, fusion or with a dialectical growth, but more often it is negatively associated with confusion or that which is synthetic rather than 'natural'. Clearly the term requires considerable care in its use, and considerable critical clarification before we can be certain that it points to anything of value.

Despite the efforts of anthropologists to convey a sense of the 'complex wholes that are cultures', the West continues to insist on indigenous people being 'tribal' – that is, defined by tribes rather than by any larger community. Myriad forms of political and social organization are regularly reduced to 'tribes', providing a comforting (to the colonizers) image of small and only minimally organized groups. The colonizers can civilize the tribes, and aid their evolution towards participation and incorporation in more complex and modern systems. (This can be attempted as aggressively by missionizing 'World Religions' as it can by 'rational' modern states bent on assimilationist policies.) There are, of course, small aggregates of families (whatever that means) which can be labelled 'tribes'. Equally, there are indigenous terms for such groups that might appropriately be translated 'tribes'. Careful use of such terms will be rooted in awareness of larger social structures, and will not define a community simplistically by one of its constituent parts. Native Americans are typical in their preference for 'Nations' as a label for the various conglomerations and confederations which negotiate treaties with other sovereign nations (not only conquering Euroamerican ones, but also neighbourly indigenous ones).

Underlying the great diversity of life and lifeways of this world may be a single energy, force, source or power. While some indigenous religions identify a divine creator responsible for the way things are, many more understand life to have arisen, and to continue to arise, out of something impersonal and diffuse. There are many ways in which such a power can be apprehended, drawn on, avoided or conceptualized. To the extent that this is part of a religion it could appropriately be labelled 'animist'. Although the label valuably points to the ontological similarity and relatedness of everything that is animated by some such vitalizing power, it is problematic. It still bears a heavy burden given it by those who thought such understandings of the world were 'primitive' (foundational and simplistic). Careful use in relation only to those traditions that are centrally concerned with 'animating powers' is possible (Bird-David 1999; Harvey forthcoming).

A variety of other contested, difficult or debatable terms – such as 'spirits', 'Spirit', 'magic' and various words for 'deities' – will be noted, discussed, problematized and sometimes rejected in the following chapters.

Indigenous?

This survey of some of the problematic terms used to categorize and link the diversity of indigenous religions cannot conclude without noting that the term 'indigenous religions' is itself problematic. If the term indicates belonging to a particular place and people, perhaps it includes European Christianity, which has existed for longer than some 'indigenous people' have lived where they now belong. Also, perhaps 'indigenous' labels an absence rather than a distinguishing characteristic. In comparison with the 'World Religions' and the 'New Religious Movements' these 'indigenous' ones may seem to lack universality. Perhaps they apply to only a few people in remote places, and have little to say to 'outsiders' beyond 'behold how curious we are'. These are, of course, limited, patronizing and erroneous views. Indigenous religionists have always spoken with their neighbours, visitors and others. Their continuing vitality (and, perhaps, revitalization) shows, at least, that they are relevant to people in the contemporary world. The presence of indigenous religions on the Internet demands a reconsideration of their obscurity. Their forceful presentation in law courts in many countries (for example, arguing for the fulfilment of treaty obligations or recognition of land-rights) demonstrates that they remain thoroughly part of the contemporary world. The adoption of indigenous religious terminology (e.g. tabu), and Western interest (albeit flawed) in at least aspects of indigenous religions, is also evidence of their universality. That they do not engage in evangelism is not a unique characteristic, few of the 'World Religions' are concerned to gain universal assent. More importantly, this is to miss the point that indigenous religions are inculcated in various ways. Visitors are expected to respect elders, places, ceremonies and traditions; they are encouraged (subtly maybe) to find something of value, and graft it, somehow, into their existing lifeway. This might not be evangelism, but it certainly does not show a lack of interest in the religious engagement of others.

What the label 'indigenous religions' valuably points to is more than merely existing in a particular place, it is the celebration of the experience of continuity of peoples and places. The label respects the almost ubiquitous centrality of elders and ancestors as holders and sharers of tradition. It respects the almost ubiquitous veneration of particular lands. This is a theme that recurs in the living and study of indigenous religions, and therefore will be a leitmotif of this Companion.

The label also rides precariously on the undertow that is the equally ubiquitous experience of colonial genocide and expulsion that has confronted and continues to confront indigenous people everywhere. Precisely these aspects of Western 'contact' bring central characteristics into sharp relief. Intimate reciprocal relationships between human people (ancestors, living and yet-to-be-born) and all other-than-human people are destroyed by genocide. (Genocide usually refers to the mass murder of human groups, but is here widened to include what might otherwise be called ecocide, the mass murder of other-than-human persons.) The centrality or sacredness, perhaps, of lands and places which, as persons in their own ways, also participate in relationships with other people, is destroyed by the process which treats them as resources or commodities to be bought, owned and sold. Thus for example, strip-mining of a mountain's 'living rock' (no mere metaphor here) is another act of genocide. For most indigenous people it is far too early to speak honestly of postcolonialism (see Weaver 1998b), except as a worthy ambition.

This bleak picture of the West might perhaps be (not entirely) balanced by a note that the academic tradition might encourage a very different relationship to the world. Its critical and humanistic stance celebrates or at least encourages respect for diversity, agency and self-determination. If this sounds too idealistic it is because academia does not always live out its foundational principles. This book exists within that context of mutual conversation, celebrating the important diversity of ways of being human, and the ways of being alive. In various ways it arises from, expresses and contributes to dialogue and other conversations.

Persons, powers and gifts

Structurally, this Companion is divided into three Parts which are entitled Persons, Powers and Gifts. Chapters are placed within these parts for good reasons, but some might have been placed elsewhere. For example, if masks and drums are alive (in some sense, and perhaps only when worn or played) then they are 'persons' and discussion of them belongs among the 'Persons' chapters. An overview of the book should clarify what is significant about the three headings.

Each contributor has been asked to discuss a particular theme with reference to an indigenous people or to peoples of an area. Themes include various significant people, their characters, activities and roles; the powers underlying the way things are, and how they are dealt with; and gifts of art, music, well-being, ceremonies of various sorts, and some of the relationships between indigenous and other ways of being human. The intention is to illustrate both diversity and complexity. As only a sample of the world's indigenous religions can be introduced in the space of a single (non-encyclopaedic) volume, and as little or no prior knowledge is assumed, the contributors have not attempted to say the last word about their topic or the people(s) they are discussing. Readers will gain understanding of various important issues in the study of indigenous religions and be in a better position to build on this knowledge. They will see how various academics approach, engage with, or represent indigenous religions, and they will be referred onwards to other valuable studies.

The Companion does not seek to be only an introduction to the study of indigenous religions, but also to enhance continuing dialogue with and between indigenous religionists. It takes up Kenneth Morrison's suggestion that 'the existential principles of person, power, and gift invite a new humanistic discourse [about 'religion'], striving for a holistic conversation that might be at once interdisciplinary and, perhaps, cross-cultural' (1992a, 204). The Companion uses these principles as section labels in a suggestive and evocative way rather than dogmatically or systematically. They are part of a conversation, sometimes of an argument, never an absolute conclusion.

Part I ('Persons') begins with Kenneth Morrison's discussion of Native American other-than-human persons. Given the way religions are often studied, it is important at the outset to be clear about references to deities, spirits, 'supernatural' or 'spiritual' beings. Morrison expands his discussion of 'the existential principles of person, power and gift' with particular reference to those persons often, but erroneously, labelled 'spirits' and considered 'non-physical'. He synthesizes more recent developments in research building on Hallowell's (1975) 'dialogical anthropology' entitled 'Ojibwa ontology, behavior, and world view'.

A.J. Guerrero's chapter is an eloquent and empowering exploration of Native Womanism. She deals with the ramifications of various sacred traditions (of cosmology and kinship in particular) among Nations indigenous to the Southwest of what is now the USA. Beginning with Changing Woman and other-than-human persons of significance – especially to women – she discusses the implications of taking seriously indigenous and womanist understandings. The chapter integrates ethnography with activism, and shows how women's lives have been, are, and might be affected by indigenous and colonial systems of kinship, governance, land use and respect.

Piers Vitebsky's considerable expertise and intimate knowledge of the world views and activities of shamans, particularly among the Sora of Eastern India, are clear in his invaluable contribution. Once again we encounter human people being empowered in their encounters with other-than-human people in various dynamic activities. Other contributors will deal with different ways in which religious leadership – and human agency in the face of difficulties and dangers – are evident. Shamans play roles in their communities unlike those typical of Western religious leadership, and if nothing else, provide one more proof of the value of studying indigenous religions. Without them our vocabulary and our understanding of human diversity would be much poorer. In fact, there is much more to learn from them.

Fiona Bowie challenges Western notions of the stasis and isolation of indigenous peoples and their religions. Drawing on her fieldwork notes, she highlights the danger of turning the diversity of Bangwa views into something highly structured and less 'slippery'. She insists that 'witchcraft' among the Bangwa of Cameroon is a 'flexible and adaptive phenomena'. Her chapter is placed here among 'Persons' because witchcraft is 'part of the way in which contemporary Bangwa conceive of themselves as individuals and as social beings'.

Continuing the theme of human and other-than-human persons encountering one another (and perhaps defining one another in the process), Jan Platvoet applies scholarly approaches to the study of 'spirit possession' rituals among the Bono of West Africa. These are events in which 'one, or a few, or even several, of the participants in a public ritual behave in ways which believers interpret as signifying that "spirits" have taken "possession" of them'. Using a well-documented historical event – an earlier encounter between an anthropologist and the Bangwa – he illustrates various different kinds of analyses that can be derived from ethnographic case studies.

In one way or another, the chapters in Part I explore the persons of significance in particular indigenous religions. Human and other-than-human persons (including those some would call deities and/or spirits, but also including plants, animals, winds and rocks) encounter one another. These chapters also illustrate ongoing dialogues between academics and those they study (in various ways), and between different academic approaches.

Part II is devoted to various Powers which enable people to act. Morrison notes that

> Persons are powerful in various degrees, but significantly some human beings, particularly those who have ritual knowledge, exercise power equal to, if not superior than, other-than-human persons ... In effect, power is the existential postulate which accounts for those personal decisions which make for both human and cosmic order and harmony. (1992a, 203).

The following four chapters are devoted to particularly significant powers and the ways people draw on them or are constrained from abusing them.

Peter Mataira forcefully argues that *mana* has been misconstrued as positive 'power' or force to be manipulated, and *tapu* as a negative consequence of ritual transgression. Clearly, the colonial mindset was deeply influenced by the obsessions of Protestant Christianity. Mataira roots himself within a cosmic and intimately human lineage, in which he expertly and evocatively discusses *tapu* as 'the sacred state of the endowed person or thing under the patronage of the Gods' and *mana* as 'the endowment process through which spiritual power was given by the indwelling spirit that presided over it'.

Berel Dov Lerner also explores the challenge offered by indigenous world views to those taken for granted in the West. In this case the question is whether 'magic' is really religious, or whether societies that engage in what the West calls 'magic' are deeply spiritual. Might they not, rather, be engaging in a thoroughly secular practice? Is magic predicated on hidden, 'occult', forces or on the regular workings of nature? This chapter also engages with a classic moment in anthropological study of indigenous religion, namely Evans-Pritchard's works on the Azande and Nuer.

If there are powers available or avoidable (and open to misunderstanding), they might well derive from what the West categorizes as Nature. Indigenous perceptions of their environment might more appropriately be seen as relationships with particular places, bioregions perhaps. Two chapters are devoted to indigenous perceptions of and dealings with the lands which animate and maintain them. Lynne Hume's discussion of 'the Dreaming' resists the timeless abstraction of much that claims to be discussion of this vital foundation of traditional and contemporary Aboriginal Australian lifeways. She 'explores the ways in which various Aboriginal groups have come to terms with both their traditional culture and the encroachment of imported beliefs'. The expression of the Dreaming in ceremony ('business') is predicated on Dreaming as 'Law' binding on all, and as a 'speciated and individuated' power experienced by all. That is to say, all who know their connection to the land(s). The relationships between indigenous people and lands in which they are indigenous are discussed in Sean Connors' exploration of the 'thicker understanding [that] obtains from imagining Native traditions as emerging from a dialectic between religions, traditions and particular bioregions – between people and place'. Much of this careful discussion of the diversity of traditions and the particularities of place deals with ecosystem management. It is placed here (rather than in 'Gifts') because it stresses that 'people and place are integrated through a reciprocal relationship'. Indigenous Nations are empowered by their rootedness in particular places.

Part III is entitled 'Gifts'. The 'existential principle of Gift' (singular) labels 'the moral processes through which the dangerous neutrality of power can be moderated' (Morrison 1992a, 203). It names interpersonal agency or relationships expressed in giving, sharing and participating. 'Gifts' (plural) here names the various activities in which indigenous people express their relationships and exercise power. It is of the essence that gifts do not have to be given, that they are not always given, and certainly not given equally to all. Selfishness and acquisition are just as possible as selflessness and reciprocity. This is what makes the principles of 'person, power and gift' dynamic rather than trite. This is what generates morality, notions about what is good or bad: generally sharing is good, withholding is bad. The chapters in Part III discuss the various performances and activities in which indigenous religionists do their religions, express or empower their relational personhood.

The permeability of the boundary between 'person', 'power' and 'gift' is clear when we ask whether a mask is 'alive' or not. In many indigenous ceremonies masks act, they cause change, express themselves, communicate. My own contribution is a visitor response to what might be considered the finest expression of Maori art, *marae* and their associated buildings. As well as being a medium for the display of ancestral and family history, the *marae* is a work of art that works. It converts strangers (potential enemies) into guests, and converts the dead into ancestors. The full panoply of arts is significant in this treasure which is itself an ancestor.

Olu Taiwo devotes greater attention to the performing arts of music and movement, without ignoring the carved and decorated drums and masks that do far more than facilitate human performance. He offers an exceptional engagement with the 'return beat', a rich evocation of the 'ontological experience of the tempo within any given rhythm. It draws attention to the spaces between the beats, which are personally experienced as a curve that leads back to the self, echoing the metabolic rhythm of the heartbeat.' He shows that this 'feeling of returning is fundamental to the artistic and experiential viewpoint in the cultural traditions in Africa and the African Diaspora'.

Charlie Thompson also engages with dance. Like other contributors, he challenges the perception that indigenous religions are 'static', exploring the dances in which Jakalteko Maya dance their conquest, their survivance (a term coined by Vizenor 1994) and their continuity. This is not only a powerful discussion of the layered nature of the performing arts of ceremony and dance, but of steps taken towards self-determination, liberation and perhaps post-colonialism. It also contributes to debates about syncretism and the permeability of boundaries (whether geographical or cultural).

Rites of passage are among the most common rituals performed and undergone. Charlotte Hardman applies van Gennep's analysis of such rituals to the Lohorung Rai of eastern Nepal. She shows that this helps to make sense of some of their 'transition' rituals. Rai birth and marriage rites demonstrate the importance of Durkheim and van Gennep's view of ritual as being primarily of social importance to indigenous societies. Among other things, she concludes that 'rites of passage are not just about changes in individual status and the dynamics of human society but also about the dynamics of their relations with ancestors'.

Similarly, Mark Woodward shows that sacrifices are rooted in the social order and also in indigenous systems of cosmological and metaphysical postulates. His discussion of sacrifice – and head hunting – among the Naga of Burma and Assam is therefore 'predicated on the assumption that the meanings of sacrifice and other modes of ritual action are determined by the cosmological and social orders in which they are located'. However, he notes that such postulates and orders are also among 'the theoretical constructs employed by anthropologists, historians of religion and others in the study of cultures'. Once again, the study of indigenous religions demands reflection on scholarly theorizing. Woodward also shows that lines drawn between indigenous religions and Christianity (or other non-indigenous religions) are far less secure than some have asserted.

Similarly, Jim Cox contends 'that the main characteristics of African indigenous religions persist in and through the variety of Christian denominations and movements found throughout the country, in syncretistic new religious movements and through contemporary expressions of traditional observances'. With reference to an interview with a medium (in the course of which the medium became possessed) and a New Religious Movement of African origin, he concludes that 'the essential features of African indigenous religions' are determinative of the way other religions are received, adopted, adapted and eventually transformed in contemporary Africa. In short, indigenous religiosity (and whatever else is now growing from this root) is largely 'pragmatic, unanalytical and multistranded'.

The collaborative chapter of Raoul Anderson, John Crellin and Misel Joe about the revitalization of the Mi'kmaq Community at Conne River, Newfoundland, provides an excellent example of what dialogical research can achieve. It becomes clear that indigenous health is a holistic matter, engaging every facet of an individual and a community's life. A much less ambivalent relationship between this indigenous community and both the Catholic Church and the state had led to considerable problems. The revitalization process tackled (and is tackling) communal, individual, historical and contemporary aspects of such dis-empowerment. Spirituality is central to what can easily be seen as the re-formation of a gifted and gifting community.

One aspect of the revitalization at Conne River has been a series of annual, non-competitive powwows. In the final chapter of this Companion, Teri Brewer discusses the way that powwows 'touch the past and teach ways forward'. She notes that powwows are 'periodic short festive events which American Indians organize for social and celebrative, competitive, educational, political, benevolent and sometimes commercial purposes'. While they could be relegated to the margins of the study of religions (one function of labels such as 'syncretistic'), Brewer's chapter shows what a potent blend of music, ancestral traditions, contemporary needs and desires, pan-Native American and specifically 'tribal' (or National) identities contribute to the vitality of Native identities.

Last words

This Companion is not intended to be the last word on the themes or the Nations discussed. Certainly, it cannot be the last word about indigenous religions, far too few of them are mentioned here. There is more to study. Those indigenous religions that continue to survive or flourish do so in changeable ways, so what is said here can always be improved upon.

The contributions to this volume are rooted in different approaches and methodologies. They exemplify the range of scholarly interaction with indigenous religions. This will repay careful consideration, as of course, will a study of the themes and Nations that are the Companion's chief focus. If it needs to be said that indigenous religions are in many ways like all other religions, this point might well be reinforced by comparing topics raised in the following chapters with other books published by Cassell concerned with the so-called 'World Religions'. For example, Cassell's series 'Themes in Religious Studies' includes volumes devoted to *Making Moral Decisions*, *Worship*, *Myth and History*, *Attitudes to Nature*, *Sacred Writings*, *Women in Religion*, *Human Nature and Destiny*, *Picturing God*, *Sacred Place* and *Rites of Passage*. The series 'Issues in Contemporary Religion' will include volumes on *Conversion*, *Animal Rights*, *Social Calling*, *Authority*, *Salvation*, *War and Peace*, *Sexuality*, and *Medical Ethics*. Indigenous religions have something to say about most of these issues.

Science is now clear that the act of observation changes that which is observed. It has long been the understanding of the human sciences and arts that observers are changed by what they observe. Sadly, many scholars have attempted to resist change in either their 'subjects' or themselves. This Companion is full of scholarly excitement about the dialogues and conversations that they have had, and the changes that have resulted so far. Readers are invited to participate in this process, hopefully they will find it as exciting and rewarding as we do.

Finally, this introduction has rather clumsily suggested at times that 'religions' do things (such as encounter one another). In fact, of course, it is people who do religion, do the encountering, and so on. The following pages are snippets of ongoing discussions, conversations, dialogues between people and other people.

Last words

This conclusion is not intended to be the last word on the [illegible] of the [illegible] almost indigenous [illegible] mentioned here. There is [illegible] These indigenous [illegible] [illegible] ways [illegible] upon [illegible]

The contributors to this volume are [illegible] in different approaches and [illegible]ologies. They exemplify the range of scholarly [illegible] with [illegible] with a study of [illegible] and [illegible] that indigenous religions are to [illegible] all other religions [illegible] this point might well [illegible] the following [illegible] with other [illegible] the so-called 'world religions' [illegible] Moral Issues [illegible] Women [illegible] Sacred Place and [illegible] The series [illegible] will [illegible] Rites of Passage [illegible]

Scholars [illegible] that the [illegible] change [illegible] has [illegible] readers are invited [illegible]

Finally, this introduction has [illegible] people who [illegible] and [illegible] between people and other [illegible]

Part I
Persons

1. The cosmos as intersubjective: Native American other-than-human persons

Kenneth M. Morrison

Any study of those Native American beings often called 'spirits' meets difficult problems of interpretation. From first contact, Europeans recognized that Native American worlds are populated by a vast array of apparently nonphysical entities. I say 'apparently' to challenge the ways non-Indians oppose matter and spirit. A. Irving Hallowell observed that, encountered in dreams and visions, as well as in everyday situations, such beings are always perceived as having physical bodies (1975, 153–8). Sometimes, as in the Ojibwa shaking tent rite, such beings are not seen, but they are heard. Europeans identified these beings as demons, claimed that Native Americans were religiously deluded in 'worshiping' them, and began immediately an enduring effort to replace them in Indian peoples' hearts and minds. European Christians also blamed such beings for post-contact troubles – particularly epidemic illness, the socially devastating effects of alcohol, and massive depopulation – and they promised that their Christian God offered protection in times of trouble. Until the 1930s, European Christians and their governments made every effort to convert Native American peoples, or at least to outlaw their religious practices which link human welfare and that of the 'spirits'. Coupled with this hostility from the Christian Churches and American and Canadian governments, the development of anthropological science tended to relegate Native American religions to the subjective, emotional and irrational dimensions of human life. Ethnographers noted the existence of the 'spirits', but largely failed to understand them, or to examine their importance to Indian life (Martin 1987; Parkhill 1997; Mihesuah 1998).

I address this ongoing misunderstanding in a limited but focused way. Rather than survey all these beings and their relations with Native peoples (Gill and Sullivan 1992), I explore how these 'spirits' ... be comprehended in ways appropriate to their own nature. I re-examine the theoretical perspective that A. Irving Hallowell articulated nearly forty years ago. That study – 'Ojibwa ontology, behavior, and world view' (1975 [1960]) – broke new ground which has remained nearly fallow (but see Wallace 1980; Hallowell 1992; Smith 1995). In what follows, I outline Hallowell's argument to capture its enduring importance, and I do so to create a synthesis from the perspective of interpretive changes that have developed since.

Hallowell anticipates what Dennis Tedlock and Karl Mannheim (1995) call dialogical anthropology, a view that seeks to understand cultural reality as it emerges in engaged and embattled conversation. In center-staging such a conversation between humans and cosmic beings, Hallowell rejects a spiritual view of religion. He favors, instead, locating religious life in the world as a matter of responsibility between human and other kinds of being. Hallowell also prefigures current concerns for understanding human reality in terms of its sensual character, particularly in relationship to the body, and the externalization of self which occurs in acts of breath, song, dance, and gesture (see Classen 1993a and b). In demonstrating that religious life transpires in the ethical acts of powerful persons (Lee 1959), Hallowell points to the provocative insight that Native American religious life is negotiated between humans and other kinds of personal beings (Fienup-Riordan 1983).

Hallowell lays out interpretive principles which are still poorly understood. He examines what he called 'a relatively unexplored territory – ethno-metaphysics' (1975, 143), and should have launched a skeptical reappraisal of Native American studies. It is telling that Hallowell stresses that the Ojibwa people lived within what scholars were just then giving the technical term 'world view', an understanding of cultural order which highlights indigenous ways of understanding reality. For Robert Redfield (1952), upon whom Hallowell relied for the concept of world view, cultures are made up of both a technical and a moral order. Neither he nor Hallowell worked out the implications of such a cultural distinction. Hallowell can be said to have established the interpersonal and therefore ethical cast of Ojibwa reality, to have denied the operation of impersonal modes of causality, and, in effect, to have pointed to the ways in which the Ojibwa subsume the technical with the moral. Indeed, it could be argued that Ojibwa culture derives from mythic other-than-human persons who establish a technical order which has moral purposes in mind. Unlike other studies then and since, Hallowell appreciates that the Ojibwa must be understood in terms appropriate to their cosmology – the ways in which they think about their world. Hallowell lays out a radically humanistic way of thinking about the Ojibwa, and one which draws nonhuman entities into the linguistic, perceptual, cognitive, ethical and behavioral fields of Ojibwa life. In demonstrating that humans, plants, animals, and cosmic beings share the same nature and socio-religious motives towards each other, Hallowell moves beyond an anthrocentric view of Ojibwa reality. Hallowell insists, moreover, that social-scientific methodologies in their own right, and in their complicity with non-Indian metaphysical and theological categories, seriously distort the actuality of the Ojibwa's world (1975, 143–4).

Hallowell realizes that non-Indians assume ethnocentrically that their cosmological system is universal. He also understands that western ontology holds that a hierarchical dissimilarity exists between categories of being – divinity, humanity, and nature – which simply does not fit the Ojibwa's cosmology (cf. Miller 1955). Hallowell writes: 'In this paper I have assembled evidence ... which supports the inference that in the metaphysics of being found among these Indians, the actions of persons provides the major key to their world view' (1975, 143).

Before Hallowell, such 'person objects' (1975, 144) – an unhappy phrase because, given the thrust of Hallowell's argument, the Ojibwa perceive such entities as intentional beings whose character and purposes can be understood in their actual behavior – were usually called spirits because they seem to exist on a plane, in a dimension, or a realm separate from, and greater and more powerful than, everyday existence. In religious terms, scholars often think of these beings as the focus of visionary mysticism and magic, belief or faith (Hollenback 1996). In scientific terms, claims about the reality of these beings' existence were ascribed to superstition, imagination and psychological projection. Without empirical evidence, these beings' existence could not be verified, and Native American views about them could not be proven (Trigger 1991). It follows that both religious and scientific perspectives hold that Native American reality systems are supernaturalistic (Hultkrantz 1983).

Hallowell learned empirically, and to the contrary, that humans and those entities he came to call 'other-than-human persons' share with human beings powerful abilities, including intelligence, knowledge, wisdom, the ability to discern right from wrong, and also the ability to speak, and therefore to influence other persons. In Ojibwa thought, persons are not defined by human physical shape, and so the Ojibwa do not project anthropomorphic attributes onto the world (1975, 154–7). Hallowell insists, rather, that the Ojibwa world is a behavioral system, a social system, in which powerful persons are remembered, and they themselves emerge, in myth and lore. Moreover, other-than-human persons address and empower human beings in dreams and visions, present themselves as kinfolk and engage humans in daily life, and empower humans to embody them in ritual performances.

Hallowell shows that, because the Ojibwa do not recognize the cosmic dimension that non-Indians define as nature, their cosmology does not proceed in terms of the non-empirical domain called the supernatural (1975, 151). Ojibwa people recognize that animals, plants, the Sun, Moon, and stars, and even 'objects' are persons because they themselves behave as such. In this behavioral distinction, Hallowell contends that real-world, daily life transpires in the interactions of persons, human and otherwise. Ojibwa people experience themselves as being at the center of world order, not as pre-eminent beings, but certainly as essential to vital cosmic relations which make persons interdependent. Hallowell reveals a world in which both the Ojibwa and other-than-human persons express mutual responsibility, and thus give structure, pattern, and coherence to the multiple centers and related boundaries of cosmic life. At the same time, the Ojibwa understand that antagonistic relations among persons create disorder, including hunger, illness and social estrangement. (There are no studies which deal with Native American health and sickness in the relational terms Hallowell suggests – not even by his student Wallace 1966; see Hultkrantz 1992). In Hallowell's view, the Ojibwa do not recognize a cosmic hierarchy running from the least to the most perfect being. The Ojibwa emphasize the ontological similarity, rather than the dissimilarity, of all beings.

Hallowell recognizes, as did seventeenth-century Jesuit missionaries (Thwaites 1959, VII, 21–33), reality assumptions encoded in Algonkian languages, of which Ojibwa language is a typical dialect. Hallowell observes that Algonkian languages distinguish between the 'animate' and 'inanimate' character of the world (1975, 146). At the categorical level, Hallowell shows that this distinction, especially associated with the power concept *manitou*, has perceptual, cognitive, ethical and behavioral implications for the Ojibwa's way of life in the world. The animate identifies the potential presence of intentionality (desire, need, purposefulness, selfishness, selflessness), and thus the existence of self-conscious and other-oriented beings whose actions must be taken into account in the course of daily life. Hallowell rejects an older, evolutionary view which claimed that an impersonal stage of reality, defined as an electrodynamic view of reality called animatism, preceded an animate view. He argues, to the contrary, that, when the power concept *manitou* is understood as knowledge and influence, the term embodies (that is to say is given presence, rather than abstract representation) an awareness of the social interdependence of all persons. Far from being impersonal, then, *manitou* describes a world emerging from the intersubjectivity of various beings' self-oriented and other-oriented purposes.

Much of 'Ojibwa ontology' reconstructs the ways in which the Ojibwa's interactions with animals, plants, and even 'natural' objects derive from the animate linguistic category. The Ojibwa address not only the Master of the Animals, whose cosmic purpose is animal well-being, but also the particular being (Luckert 1975; Ridington and Ridington 1975; Tanner 1979; Harrod 1987). Hunting is an act of communication between human and animal persons because humans need to persuade animals to give their bodies, and to assure animal persons that humans will give back to ensure animal reincarnation. The animals also have their own languages, and their empowering gifts of animal language to some human beings make another level of communication (here ontological correspondence) possible: in sharing power, persons share being. At this level, Hallowell documents not simply interspecies communication, but interspecies similarity in which affirmations of mutual kinship go beyond metaphoric analogy to behavioral responsibility between humans and other-than-human persons. Every day (one should also say every night), human beings and animals communicate in dreams, a state of consciousness which bridges cosmological dimensions, including objective time and space (1975, 164–8). In such dream states, human beings are not only addressed by entities who live in other space–time dimensions; they also respond in kind, acknowledge mutual responsibility, and so motivate everyday behavior. (Compare, with reference to Plains Indian dreaming life, Irwin 1994; and to dream in the Huron encounter with the Jesuits, Irwin 1992.) Hallowell concludes that Ojibwa reality consists of interpersonal encounters with other-than-human persons, and not in the objective or supernatural character of a world upon which non-Indians insist for reasons of both science and faith. (Hallowell does not separate himself uniformly from the Western world view he criticizes. He uses the term belief, for example, and thus undercuts his argument that Ojibwa reality has perceptual and behavioral, as well as cognitive actuality. In time, Rodney Needham (1972) would examine the category belief and demonstrate that the term has no technical precision; to say that people believe in such and such is, in effect to say nothing about how they constitute their world.)

Hallowell's conclusions can be productively contrasted with those of folklorist Thomas Blackburn (1975), who evaluates the rich stories from the California Chumash. Although Blackburn does not cite Hallowell's 'Ojibwa ontology', his examination of what he calls the Chumash's existential and normative postulates complements Hallowell's world view argument. I do not wish to say, or even to imply, that Ojibwa and Chumash cultures are the same. Although they share 'person' as an ontological postulate, their cultures differ. Just as the Ojibwa case resembles closely that of other Algonkian-speaking peoples, Blackburn notes the greatest similarities in world view occur between the Chumash and other Californian groups, including the Cahuilla, Luiseno, Pomo, and Wintu. Blackburn also draws analogies between the Chumash and the Navajo and the Pueblos of the Southwest (1975, 65–6, 68). However, the Chumash's foundational postulate, which Blackburn calls the 'assumption of a personalized universe', aligns Chumash and Ojibwa realities. Blackburn discusses this existential assumption as a personification (1975, 66) (thus an act of projected imagination), a view that Hallowell rejects (1975, 152), but notes that the Chumash 'attribute to the beings thus depicted the same qualities of sentience, will, rationality, and emotionality that characterize man himself' (1975, 66).

Blackburn also sustains Hallowell's interpretation in several other ways. First, the Chumash cosmos is composed of an 'interacting community of sentient creatures' (1975, 66). Hallowell's most compelling evidence demonstrates that the Ojibwa orient to other-than-human persons as kinfolk, as Blackburn does for the Chumash. Both scholars agree that kin status defines power, privilege and responsibility for both human and other-than-human persons. Blackburn notes that persons in the Chumash cosmos 'share reciprocal rights and responsibilities . . . reinforced by bonds of kinship and mutual dependency' (1975, 66). Second, like the Ojibwa, the Chumash understand causality in interpersonal, rather than impersonal, ways. As Blackburn puts the case, 'success or failure in any endeavor depends upon the relative power and knowledge of the participants – there is neither luck nor accident' (1975, 67).

Third, like the Ojibwa, the Chumash posit that power, which they understand as 'sentience and will' (1975, 67), characterizes all animate beings, although to different degrees. Fourth, since human and other-than-human persons share causal agency, and exercise power in both negative and positive ways, the Chumash perceive the cosmos as a dangerous and unpredictable place (1975, 69). Thus, as Hallowell shows for the Ojibwa, an inherent ambivalence derives from the interaction of persons because, as Blackburn develops for the Chumash, interpersonal influence can proceed in terms of cajolery, entreaty, insult, pity, anger, and pride (1975, 70). (On 'percept ambiguity' among the Ojibwa see Black 1977.) Fifth, Blackburn documents for the Chumash a temporal and spacial plasticity which Hallowell (1975, 163–4) calls the power of metamorphosis: the ability of persons to shift physical form. As one mode of metamorphosis, the Chumash and the other-than-human persons of their cosmos experience reincarnation, as do the persons of the Ojibwa world-system (1975, 72). In this way, again, neither an objective nor supernaturalistic view explains the ways in which both the Ojibwa and the Chumash conjoin personal intentionality and physical bodies. (The recent publication of *Amerindian Rebirth* (Mills and Slobodin 1994) suggests that cosmology, kinship, naming, mortuary practices, identity, self, gender, ideas about psychology, education, and child-rearing are all closely associated with Native American person concepts (Mills 1994, 13). None of the essays in that volume make such an argument about interpersonal cosmic process directly, and none refers to Hallowell's 'Ojibwa ontology'. Various essayists note human to human, animal to animal, human to animal, and animal to human reincarnations.)

Surveying the 'psychological unity of the Ojibwa world' (1975, 168–73), Hallowell examines the ways in which notions of causality and power, and disease and well-being, derive from the interpersonal relations between humans and other-than-human persons. In his treatment of the interpersonal character of the Ojibwa cosmos (a system of eight dimensions, each with its characteristic persons (see Landes 1968, 21–41, and Smith 1995)), Hallowell stresses that the Ojibwa temper pragmatism with a moral responsibility that they exercise towards other persons. Hallowell, in other words, recognizes that Ojibwa religious life concerns itself with moral and cosmic meaning in the mutual obligation that exists between humans and other-than-human persons. In all these ways, the Ojibwa and the Chumash seem to share cosmic existential principles.

When Blackburn begins to discuss what he calls 'normative postulates' (1975, 74–80) – the ethical principles of Chumash life – comparing the Chumash with the Ojibwa, and Blackburn with Hallowell, becomes more difficult. The difference has to do with the range of evidence that Hallowell and Blackburn bring to bear. Hallowell's data cover several related fields: the formative actions of heroes in a beginning time, the oral tradition by which their actions are remembered and legitimated, dream, visionary, and everyday encounters between the Ojibwa and other persons, empowering gifts compassionate persons bestow on Ojibwa relatives to empower success in hunting, gathering, war, love, and in curing disease, and, finally, ritual encounters in which the advice of the spirits is actively sought. Furthermore, Hallowell's discussion of Ojibwa life is far from complete, particularly in terms of the ways in which the Ojibwa exercise their obligations to meet the needs and desires of other-than-human persons. Three examples come immediately to mind: 1) the human responsibility to ensure the reincarnation of game animals; 2) offerings in which other-than-human persons are fed, and given tobacco for their pleasure; 3) meeting the social needs of other persons for companionship, friendship, and kinship.

On the other hand, Blackburn does not describe Chumash relations with other-than-human persons in any of these ways. In part, he is handicapped by the nature of the stories he has available. These largely concern the Chumash tradition of a time of the First People, a Flood and the transformation of the First People into present-day plant and animal persons (1975, 25). In addition, Blackburn's sources for nineteenth-century Chumash religious life reflect both the cultural loss of a pre-Spanish ritual tradition, and the syncretism associated with Spanish Catholic missionization (1975, 26). Consequently, Blackburn's discussion of the normative postulates of the Chumash world view proceeds without any reference to everyday Chumash relations with other-than-human persons, although their existential postulates imply such a moral orientation.

There is another reason Hallowell and Blackburn cannot be compared easily. Unlike Hallowell, Blackburn contends that Chumash cosmology works in terms of causal assumptions which are natural and supernatural (1975, 14–15, 22–6), although his mythological evidence suggests that it does not. We learn, for example, that the Chumash cosmos consists of three (or five) vertically organized dimensions (1975, 30), with the Chumash's domain, like the Ojibwa's, at the center. Blackburn also reveals that persons from the upper and lower domains interact on the Chumash plane, but the stories do not permit a detailed understanding of their actions and purposes, or of the Chumash's posited responsibility toward them. But the telling difference is that Hallowell rejects both a naturalistic and a supernaturalistic explanation of such a system. Blackburn relies on magic and the supernatural to characterize Chumash causality. Although all beings of the Chumash cosmos are persons, and therefore alike in nature if not in power, Blackburn categorizes other-than-human persons as the 'First People, supernatural beings, and nunasis or monsters' (1975, 25). Blackburn does not define supernatural, and he uses the term to describe a wide variety of persons and phenomena not only as other-than-human, but as superhuman as well. In other words, Blackburn's supernaturalism denies the ontological similarity of the Chumash and other-than-human persons.

Hallowell's work remains foundational because he anticipates both the interpretive confusions which have continued to trouble Native American religious ethnography, and newer, more productive lines of thought. Hallowell himself was more interested in reconstructing the cognitive and behavioral details of Ojibwa life than in theorizing about their religious ideas and ritual practice. Although his evidence is drawn from several complementary cultural domains – myth, dream and ritual – he focused on mapping the philosophical foundations of Ojibwa life. In all these areas, and especially the comparative ontological status of human and other persons, much work still needs to be done. Hallowell points the way, at least in identifying appropriate directions for future research. For example,

Hallowell does not detail the philosophically and morally formative gestures of the Ojibwa's culture heroes and their antagonists. Then, too, he only suggests that other-than-human persons were motivated actors in Ojibwa life, and that the Ojibwa were also intentional presences in theirs. He realizes that he did not have significant access to the Ojibwa dream world. He does not reconstruct either the range of Ojibwa ritual life, or its underlying rationale. He does not formulate a coherent critique of non-Indian objective and spiritual views of reality. He does not compare the Ojibwa world view with others, not even other Algonkian cultures. For all of that, Hallowell articulates hypotheses which have the potential of transforming a myriad of misunderstandings between Euramerican and Native American peoples.

For example, the concept of other-than-human person seems closely associated with Native American power concepts (Fogelson and Adams 1977). Hallowell outlines aspects of Ojibwa thought that defy both impersonal and objective social-scientific methodologies. As one would expect in a cosmos constituted by persons, the Ojibwa think precisely in relational, rather than objective, terms (Detwiler 1992; Morrison 1992b; Pflug 1992; 1998). For them, as for other Native American peoples, causality and personal intentionality are synonymous, particularly since they invariably locate power – here understood as the ability to influence other beings – in the interplay of all sorts of persons. Such a relational view shapes the ways in which the Ojibwa conceive of a wide range of interpersonal phenomena. They understand prominent features of the land as having emerged from the intentional acts of Nanabozho, their culture hero. They think of the course of the seasons, and of day and night, as related to the purposes of Winter and Summer, the Sun, the Moon, and the stars. Bird and animal behavior reveal a similar purposefulness as these persons interact with each other, and with Ojibwa individuals. In all these ways, personal intentionality shapes every aspect of life (Smith 1995). Purposefulness informs substance, and thus embodiment becomes a way of practical life. Nor do the Ojibwa think of powerful knowledge as an impersonal product of an objectifying intelligence. Indeed, while the Ojibwa learn from personal interactions in everyday life, the relational knowledge they acquire is also not objectifying. Hallowell writes that the Ojibwa are not at all interested in dominant non-Indian modes of thinking. They do not ask: *What* causes? They ask instead: *Who* causes? (1975, 169–72). Thus, in recognizing that the Ojibwa philosophical system requires a shift from impersonal to personal and interpersonal modes of causality, Hallowell defines an enduring interpretative need to balance non-Indian and Indian modes of causal explanation.

Hallowell's understanding of the interactions of human and other-than-human persons is not at all typical of Native American studies, not even recent work. Particular ethnographic cases seem to support the main tenets of Hallowell's view of other-than-human persons, even while their interpretation departs from his conclusions about the Ojibwa case. Stanley Walens' study, *Feasting with Cannibals: An Essay on Kwakiutl Cosmology* (1981), is a vivid case in point. In Walens' reconstruction of the Kwakiutl cosmos, humans share being with non-human entities, expressed in the understanding that life consists of eating and being eaten. Walens writes that

> Food provides for them a model of the nature of life; the act of eating provides a model of assimilation that recurs through every aspect of their culture; and the food chain itself provides the link between one human and another and between humans and the rest of the world. (1981, 12)

Walens cites Irving Goldman to demonstrate that the entities of the Kwakiutl cosmos are interdependent: 'Each possesses a portion of the sum of all the power and properties of the cosmos; each must share with all or the entire system of nature would die' (Goldman 1975, 177; Walens 1981, 24).

At one level, then, Walens describes Kwakiutl cosmology in ways that are comparable to the Ojibwa's:

> the Kwakiutl believe that animals and spirits lead lives that are exactly equivalent to those of humans. They live in winter villages, perform dances, wear masks, marry, pray, and perform all other acts that humans perform . . . In fact, since animals are considered to be human beings who have donned the masks and costumes that created their animal forms, people are united with the animals by virtue of the fact that they are all actually human beings. (1981, 23)

In recognizing that the opposite is also true – 'because humans are really animals' (1981, 23) – Walens seems to recognize Hallowell's cardinal insight that all beings are persons.

At this point, however, Walens introduces cosmological ideas which are alien to Kwakiutl thought and ritual practice, notions which also contradict his understanding that all beings share a need and desire for food which can be satisfied only temporarily. Walens understands that Kwakiutl chiefs incarnate those entities who Hallowell calls other-than-human persons; in this way a line distinguishing humans from others disappears. Kwakiutl leaders embody in their names, persons, and houses, the founding ancestral beings who are themselves animals as well as persons.

Like the ancestors they make present, Kwakiutl chiefs are both givers and receivers of food. They give not only to their human inferiors, but also to other-than-human persons in their turn. Although it seems that the Kwakiutl combine what non-Indians think of nature and the supernatural in a single whole, Walens treats them as separate categories:

> Kwakiutl conceptions of the characteristics of supernatural power are complex and varied. Even human activity and characteristics are in some way participant in the world of power; similarly, every animal, spirit, and plant being participates to some degree in the possession and exercise of supernatural power; and finally, all world events are the consequences of the exercise of supernatural power. In brief, the entire world is directly involved in the acquisition, the use, and the experience of supernatural power. (1981, 28)

While Walens uses problematic terms which do not seem to fit the interpersonal Kwakiutl system – mechanistic causality (1981, 18), magic (1981, 22), the numinous (1981, 27–8), the sacred (1981, 28), and divine being (1981, 29) among them, he also discusses an interpersonal causality which is remarkably similar to that which Hallowell describes for the Ojibwa:

> For the Kwakiutl all events result from the conscious exercise of power by some human or spirit agency. Events whose every characteristic cannot be traced directly to a human action are explainable only as the result of spirit action. This means that there are no unexplainable acts, no events that are not the result of well-known mechanistic forces acting through ritual channels, no 'miracles' that can be differentiated in principle from normal acts. (1981, 28)

This statement recognizes that Kwakiutl people and 'spirits' share the same nature and so contradicts the other-worldly emphasis of the supernatural category Walens applies. (Similarly, Goldman (1975, 8) declares that the Kwakiutl do not distinguish between the natural and the supernatural, but applies those terms regardlessly.) Walens thus seems not to understand Hallowell's insight that Native American ways of life have a relational character whose power cannot be understood either in objective or supernaturalistic ways. Native American religious sensibilities focus on the ways in which reality is interactive, rather than substantial, fixed, mechanical, or magical. The same behavioral rules apply to humans and other-than-human persons alike. Kinship is paramount.

The notions of person and power are related in another purposeful way. Thomas Blackburn emphasizes that power is, by its intentional nature, entropic; in Walens' terms, hunger always returns. Understood in relational terms, power's entropy plays itself out in the intimate (and sometimes threatening) details of interpersonal encounter. In Native American religious life, power is always understood as a gift which forges solidarity, or, in being withheld, destroys it. Good will between persons has to be won, is often tested, is sometimes shared and enjoyed, and always requires renewal. As one example, Native American prayer acts are commonly invocations of kinship, at once earnest petitions and reminders of interdependence (Gill 1977; 1981; Loftin 1986). Indeed, ritual forms as various as green corn and harvest rituals (Witthoft 1949), first salmon rites (Gunther 1926), buffalo renewal ceremonies (Harrod 1987), and bear ceremonialism (Hallowell 1926), all revolve around relational concerns in which human well-being is achieved only in gifting acts which ensure the well-being of other persons. Such rites recognize and work with the intersecting needs and desires of all persons, but, it needs to be said, all such ritual forms need to be re-examined with Hallowell's intersubjective concerns in mind: ritual contextualizes human and other-than-human interaction.

Indeed, innovative approaches to the study of Native American religions are related at least implicitly to Hallowell's insight that these traditions recognize the ontological similarity and the interdependence of all beings. Sam D. Gill has shown, for example, that Native Americans think of 'religion' in performative terms, as transformative speech acts in which communication shapes all ethical purpose (1982, 11; 1987b). In these terms, ritual modalities like song, dance, smoking, and drumming imply acknowledgment and mutuality. Ritual processes draw human and other-than-human persons into active communities, particularly in rites in which names, masks, costumes, bundles, sand paintings and pipes embody cosmic persons in forms with whom humans can interact, feast, and celebrate solidarity (Crumrine and Halpin 1983; Frisbie 1987; Paper 1988; Lokensgard 1996; Ridington and Hastings 1997). Such ritual systems are poorly interpreted in the credal, dogmatic, textualized and institutionalized forms of religion that characterize church-based religions.

In fact, as has been demonstrated amply for the Navajo (Gill 1977), Yaqui (Yoeme) (Evers and Molina 1987), and Lakota (Bunge 1984; Powers 1986), Native American languages encode the insight that speech is a power all persons share. As Gary Witherspoon (1977) has shown, the Navajo think of language as generative rather than, as in European convention, representative. Navajo speech does not encode realities which might exist independently, objectively apart from itself. In Witherspoon's interpretation, Navajo words do not mirror reality. Words do not stand for or, as is often said, symbolize any reality apart from themselves. On the contrary, Navajo speech embodies the speaker's intentionality, and extends the self beyond the body, to shape a reality coming into being in the field of interpersonal dialogue. Speech influences and motivates a cosmos of relationships and social processes (Witherspoon 1977).

Such a view of language has revolutionary importance for the study of Native American religions in terms of the personal entities who constitute them (Morrison 1992a, b). A generative view of Native American languages requires scholars to recognize that non-Indian languages assume that words have a representative character in relation to an external reality which is objective. One major consequence has been the pervasive misunderstanding of Native American symbolism as encoding and representing a reality that is otherwise unseen, non-empirical, and 'spiritual' in character (Lakoff and Johnson 1980). Sam Gill partially addresses this misrepresentation in arguing that Native American symbols have a performative significance which their use evokes (Gill 1982, 59–82). But Gill does not go quite far enough.

Native American 'symbols' are generative because they themselves are persons. So-called 'sacred,' 'symbolic' objects are intentional beings. Walens, for example, documents the complex ways in which Kwakiutl feast dishes have distinctive lives of their own, and link 'the household of the chief who owns them and that of the spirit who gave them' (1981, 57). In the Southwest, for another example, Kachina masks are embodiments, in which a human person gives physical form to cosmic persons encountered in dreams. Embodied as well in dance, what appears as a 'spiritual' difference between human beings and the kachina merges as an essential truth of cosmological correspondence (Gill 1982, 71–2). Similarly, at both Zuni and Hopi, prayer-sticks extend the life-bearing breath of human beings, and thus extend human intentionality towards non-human others. The being of the prayer-stick is inhaled by cosmic kachina persons who, thus nourished, extend themselves in rain. Rain in turn nourishes corn, who in turn feeds human beings. In these ways, Kachina masks, rain, corn and prayer-sticks are not 'sacred' in the sense of referring to, or revealing, another, pre-eminent order of reality. On the contrary, they are each intentional beings, whose needs are bound up with the desires and needs of all persons (Fulbright 1992).

A. Irving Hallowell establishes that an understanding of other-than-human persons is foundational for the study of Native American religious traditions. In rejecting cosmic hierarchy, ontological dissimilarity, impersonal, objective, mechanical, and supernaturalistic modes of causality, Hallowell locates Native American religious thought and behavior in the freighted dialogue of various types of personal beings. Hallowell relocates the religious in the actual relationships which constitute the everyday world. Hallowell also anticipates recent understandings that have come to recognize that Native American life proceeds in terms of a gifting principle which shapes the ethical character of both tribal and cosmic life. Human and other-than-human mutuality can thus be understood as both the social and cosmic ideal, and the goal of ritual action. In all these ways, Hallowell points to the possibility of understanding Native American religious realities in the ways in which they are grounded in the interpersonal engagement of human and other-than-human persons.

2. Native Womanism: Exemplars of indigenism in sacred traditions of kinship

M.A. Jaimes Guerrero

> The Navajo People of the American Southwest tell of a spirit named *Changing Woman*. She is enigmatic, young at one time, old at another, and then young again. She is the mystery of reproduction and birth; sometimes she is the earth's mother. Changing Woman decrees fertility and sterility and has elaborate mythic ties to Sun, Moon, the Holy People and to the power of rainmaking ... The ceremony for Changing Woman at her first menstrual period was the first ever performed and the model for all to follow. The great epic tale about the creation of the world instructs the Navajo how to honor menstruating girls in a four-day ritual called *Kinaalda*.
>
> (Ward 1999, 70)

Ward also states that the Navajo, the largest group of Native Americans in the USA, practice matrilineal kinship, tracing descent through the female or mother's line. She surmises that this may be one reason why they honor the biological beginnings of womanhood with a celebration (Ward 1999, 70). My own research in this area indicates that almost all indigenous peoples, if not all at one time, were matrilineal societies before the European conquest and colonization. Today, however, most tribes are seeing a kind of 'trickle down patriarchy' that has eroded women's traditional roles of authority and leadership, and which has especially impacted tribal membership that favors patrilineal over matrilineal traditions. Ward does not note that the Navajo/Dine people are relative newcomers to the Southwest, among more ancient indigenous peoples of Pueblo cultures. Why this is important is that even though they are recognized as an indigenous people who migrated across the Bering Strait (as popular theory says) much later then those Pueblo peoples already in the area (as in the case of the ancient Hopis), they adopted many ideas and images of the already established cultures to contextualize within their own Navajo cosmology and belief systems. Hence it may be that Changing Woman may have been one of those adaptations (as in the case of Kokopelli, a Pueblo trickster god), with her original cultural source among the more ancient cultures of the Southwest.

Native Womanism

This chapter is concerned with 'Native Womanism', conceptualized in the context of *Indigenism* among Native American peoples. First, it is important to note that the concept 'Womanist' was inspired by Alice Walker, the well-known literary writer and author of the novel, *The Color Purple*. She prefaces her *In Search of Our Mother's Garden* (1983) by defining *Womanist* as 'women loving women' and as 'women who appreciate women's emotional flexibility and strength'. She also states that womanists are 'committed to survival and wholeness of entire people, male *and* female', which reflects the need for respect to our greater humanity. Hence, Walker's concept is in response to a prevailing patriarchal and colonialist society at large, and one that still denigrates women in many ways. I also connect her meaning to what I refer to as *the Female Principle*, which is not essentialist but rather essential to comprehending our secular existentialism as a result of this gender inequity. This principle is connected with the indigenous image of the Earth as Mother, or what many of us call *Our Mother Earth*, and as an enspirited presence as well as metaphoric in one's Native Spirituality. It is also said that 'Everything begins in the womb of Earth herself' (Leeming and Leeming 1994, 13), which reflects an image of what most, if not all, indigenous peoples refer to as 'Mother Earth', or 'Earth Mother'. This interpretation recognizes that:

> The Earth Mother takes many forms in creation myths. She is sometimes the generating earth itself, sometimes the unseeded primary waters out of which creation will emerge when affected by the male Supreme Being. In emergence myths the other world is her womb, from which the people emerge. (Leeming and Leeming 1994, 79)

One such sacred female image for our times is Changing Woman, known among several Southwestern Native cultures, and symbolized by the Moon (Leeming and Leeming 1994, 13; in Lipan Apache, Acoma Pueblo, and Navajo/Dine creation stories). This creatrix is not only about present-day change in these fluctuating and transitional times for indigenous peoples and others, she is also about the restoration and renewal of Native women's rightful authority and leadership for a universal indigenous world view. Such a world view also respects and practices biodiversity in bioregional spheres of auchtothonous homelands among traditionally oriented indigenous peoples in their respective ecocultures. These are the topics with which this chapter is concerned.

Native geomythology and consciousness

On the subject of mythos and cosmology, Vine Deloria, Jr. has written on his conceptualization of what is meant by geomythology in a Native cultural context of creation/origin stories (Deloria 1995). I take this contextualization further for an indigenous interpretation of what is being called biodiversity in bioregionalism in a Native Genesis. But first there is a need to comprehend what is meant by 'myth' in metascientific terms. Primack and Abrams write about 'quantum cosmology' that:

> To experience the human meaning of the scientific story, we must translate it into myth, the traditional form for stories about the origin of the world. In common parlance [however], 'myth' has come to connote the opposite of reality, or the simplistic fare of the hopelessly backward or quaint. But myths, as they function in human societies, actually are explanations of the highest order: the stories a culture communally uses in order to connect with and give meaning to its universe. Every traditional culture known to anthropology has had a cosmology – a story of how the world began and how human beings took their place within it. A functional cosmology grounds people's everyday expectations of each other in the larger patterns of the universe. Such a shared cosmology may be essential to successful human community and even to individual sanity. The understanding doesn't have to be scientifically accurate ... The map is not the terrain. What we humanly need is to know the truest story of our time. Unlike other myths, however, a scientific myth never stands still. As long as the universe of knowledge expands, the myth must absorb, be tossed out, or else be enfolded in larger understandings. No myth is for all time, but myth-making is an ongoing human pursuit. (1968, 72)

In illustrating cases-in-point of geomythology there also has to be a discussion of what anthropologists call 'animism'. Animism is a concept first articulated by Sir Edward Tylor in his anthropological work, *Primitive Culture* (1871). The Leemings state that the term is:

> derived from the Latin word for soul, and the concept assumes the existence of a universal soul or spiritual power that is reflected in the existence of the spiritual aspect of all living things, especially in the existence of souls in human

> beings. Any creation myth that stresses the spiritual or godly essence of each element of the creation might be called animistic. (Leeming and Leeming 1994, 8)

These authors illustrate the connection between mythos and animism in the case of one among many Apache Creation stories, that of the Jicarilla in northeastern New Mexico, whose

> emergence myth, with *creation from chaos* and animistic characteristics, gives a prominent role to kachina-like personifications of the basic natural powers ... These beings, called Hactin, existed before creation, when there was only dark, wet, chaos – the world womb, as it were. Being lonely, Hactin created the essential elements of the universe and also created Earth Mother and Sky Father ... Once there was only the Great Spirit. He created the world in four days. He made Father Sun, Mother Earth, Old man Thunder, Boy Lightning, and the animals. Then on the fourth day he made the People, the Tinde. (Leeming and Leeming 1994, 8–10)

On an historical note, they state:

> The Tinde (People) were named Apache (the enemy) by the Pueblo people they raided. The Apaches are related to the Athabascan-speaking peoples such as certain Eskimos and Navajos (Dine). They came to the Southwest relatively late compared to the Pueblo people – perhaps as late as 1000 C.E. The Apaches are now divided into five basic groupings ... (in Arizona, New Mexico, and Texas). Not surprisingly, given the scattering of the tribe and its tendency to breakup into still smaller sub-groups, there are many Apache creation myths. (Leeming and Leeming 1994, 8)

However, there is a eurocentric bias evident in their treatment, which does not acknowledge what I refer to as their 'indigenous transference' to the Southwestern states, and that is about enculturation (cultural adoption) in contrast to acculturation (cultural appropriation); to use anthropological terms. The Navajo/Dine are also an example of this indigenous transference to the Southwest, which is about respecting biodiversity in a particular bioregion when a tribal people can assert indigenous self-determination with a healthy degree of autonomy in the face of Euroamerican modern-day encroachment.

Another illustration of a creation story, incorporating the Trickster/Coyote motif, is that of the Yuma Indians of southern Arizona in an 'emergence/earth-diver creation story that stresses the natural and original struggle between good and evil in creation':

> At first there was only water and emptiness. Then mist from the waters became sky. Then the Creator, who lived without form deep in the maternal waters, was born of those waters as the twins, Kokomaht, the good one, and Bakotahl, the evil one . . . The first man and woman made by Kokomaht were the Yuman ancestors. Kokomaht went on to make the ancestors of other tribes as well – the Diguenos, Apaches, Pimas, and others. He made 24 pairs of humans before he finally made white people . . . Komashtam'ho continued with creation (after Kokomaht's death). First he made the sun and then wood. With the wood he made a funeral pyre for his father. He sent Coyote to get a spark from the sun, but as soon as Coyote was gone, the good twin made fire with sticks and lit the pyre . . . As the body was burning, Coyote stole its head. For this theft, he was condemned to be a wild man and a thief . . . Komashtam'ho sent a flood to rid the world of some of the wilder animals, but good animals and human died too. (Leeming and Leeming 1994, 300–2; summarizing Erdoes and Ortiz 1984, 77–82)

The Trickster appears in many cultures, and is often referred to as Coyote among Native peoples and their indigenous cultures. The Leemings cross-culturally state:

> Hermes in Greece is a trickster of sorts, and so is Brer Rabbit in the folklore of the American South. The figure is especially popular among Native American and African peoples. He usually plays an important role in creation . . . because he represents the amoral, creative power that exists in the preconscious stages of human development. Often he uses his wiles to steal things, such as fire, for humans [as in this Yuman case]. He has what might be called the creative power of dream. Thus, the trickster is often highly erotic and apparently immoral. He is almost always funny and is frequently the butt of his own tricks. (Leeming and Leeming 1994, 272)

Challenging Jung

In *Creation Myths* (1995), Marie-Louise von Franz, a Jungian collaborator, writes:

> Coyote in the mythology of many tribes is the trickster god *par excellence*. Whole cycles are told of his deeds. You can find this material in the book Paul Radin, Karl Kerenyi, and C. G. Jung published together on the divine trickster. You will see from Jung's comments [based in studies of the Pueblos in New Mexico] that he interprets Coyote as a shadow figure whose function it is to undo the consolidation of consciousness. Consciousness has the unfortunate tendency, inherent in its functioning, of solidifying, and affirming itself and maintaining continuity – its very essence must be like that if it is to function; but

> it has the disadvantage of constantly excluding the irrational, the primitive, the unwanted. So it needs a counterfunction in the unconscious, something which constantly breaks the consolidation of collective consciousness and thus keeps the door open for the influx of new creative contents. (1995, 95)

I would add that this lends itself to 'creative change agents' who seek balance between these two spheres, consciousness and subconsciousness (I don't care for the word 'unconscious', since one would have to be dead). This is stressed in the creation stories, origin mythos, and spiritual images of traditionally oriented indigenous people of the Americas.

Von Franz also adds to her Jungian analysis that:

> Jung's comment about the figure of Coyote does not refer only to creation myths. It is striking that in (the) Achomavi cosmogony the Trickster God is there from the beginning ... The duality, namely a tendency toward ordered consciousness and a basic tendency toward a counterposition, something that acts according to emotion, moods, and momentary disturbances, a semi-animal figure, is there from the very beginning. It comes up at the same moment as a double movement of the birth of consciousness ... So you can say that from the very beginning of consciousness, if there is that yes toward consciousness, there is also the no, the tendency toward undoing and creating a counterposition. (1995, 97)

I have difficulty with this last statement since it seems to set up yet another polarity or dichotomy, 'consciousness versus unconsciousness', that does not get to the heart of indigenous thinking and knowledge, which is more cyclical and spiraling in its cultural manifestations of creative expression. This is what I call 'indigenous dialectics'.

In this indigenous vein, therefore, consciousness would be recognized as functional, productive, and practical, but it would not be at the expense of the inner realm of one's subconscious that is as yet unrealized or potential creativity. To contextualize this with a gender distinction, the female is often connected with the shadow figure (what Jung calls the alchemy of *anima/animus* in gendered relations and interactions between males and females in Eurowestern society) and unconsciousness in the eurocentric world view, while the male is perceived as fully conscious in his egotism, and therefore the maker of 'civilization' with the woman as subordinate helpmate. Merchant (1980) shows that women generally are seen as connected with Nature and therefore share Her unpredictable and chaotic ways which threaten men. I have also added to this equation that early Christian colonizers also projected the same xenophobia on Native peoples. In the name of religion they attempted to 'civilize the savage heathen' who was linked to Nature and the denigrated 'feminine wiles' of all women – clearly linking 'masculine fears' about Nature, Natives, and Women. I think it can also be argued in this context that in the indigenous world view(s) the female, as a Feminine Principle in both genders but prevailing in women, is respected and even revered for her 'intuitive' or introspective powers; without denigrating one's inner realm of individual and collective consciousness. Her more cooperative and relational powers are also meant to curb the conscious competitive inclination of males, as a Masculine Principle among both genders but prevailing among men, in their building of society for gender egalitarianism. The feminine and masculine energies, as gendered principles, are distinct to traditionally oriented indigenous peoples and their respective cultures, which manifest their relationship with their bioregional homeland as an ecoculture for biodiversity. Hence, such engendered energies recognize the fluidity of 'femaleness' and 'maleness' with regards to one's subjectivity and erotic agency; the latter in the case of one's individual sexuality. This analysis is made in contrast to the fundamentalist notions in Eurowestern society of fixed genders and biodeterminism that are being challenged by feminists and others as essentialist thinking.

Womanism and indigenous kinship

I conceptualize 'Native Womanism' within a broader understanding that means women connected to kinship and activism for both subjective/ sexual (personal and individual) and historical (communal or collective) agency. This metaphor is, therefore, a concept rather than a construct. It has similarities with other conceptual writings in decolonialist dialogue in the context of post-colonial womanist deconstruction and cultural differences – such as Ada Maria Isasi-Diaz's (1996) *mujerista* work, and Ana Castillo's (1994) *xicanisma* and *mestizaje* writings. This anti-colonialist discourse also addresses hybridity among mixed bloods, *mestizas*, *metis*, and *mulattas*, and respects what is being called biodiversity (bioregions influence cultures; biology is nurtured by biodiversity). However, there is a need to distinguish what is meant by 'culture' today. The globalizing, hypermodernist, abstract society abounding with virtual realities is in contrast to societies of more indigenous and organic times. In this vein, 'Native Womanism' is primarily premised on kinship traditions and 'birthrights' tied to indigenous homelands, and, more often than not (to use anthropological terms), matrilineal. Matrilineality was, therefore, more advantageous to women in these early indigenous societies, as economic inheritance primarily derived from the mother's descent lines. These indigenous social systems held Native Nationhoods together with the strength of clan mothers, as in the case of the Iroquois Confederacy in the Northeast, Pueblo Societies in the Southwest, as well as others. Kinship traditions in all tribes determined relationships between members, especially if a Native society practiced matrilineality as most of them did in precolonialist times. Yet, a tribal people could be patrilineal and still be considered egalitarian, with the advantage going to the father's family and clan moieties in this indigenous kinship system. However, both matrilineal and patrilineal societies practiced matrifocal (women-centered) and patrifocal (men-centered) spheres of authority, with the elders among both genders having the final authority in decision-making in important leadership matters. There is evidence that these Native Nations valued 'gender egalitarianism' in pre-colonialist times, i.e. there was a balance of power between women and men. However, this also had to do with the fact that Native women often outlived Native men, and that meant when women rose to clan mother status in the tribe, they had more influence and authority as elders.

There was also a high degree of exogamy, intermarriage avoiding incest, rather than endogamy, which permitted marriage with close kin. In these elaborate kinship systems, matrilineal authority usually prevailed regarding the status of any outsiders or newcomers, and that included the offspring of these liaisons as members of the tribe. Consequently, there is a profundity of 'mixed bloods' (i.e. *mestizos*, *mulattos*, *metis*, etc.). Native exogamy was about inclusivity instead of exclusivity, and was considered necessary for health and survival. However, today this has caused conflict in terms of 'Indianness', and in regards to what is often referred to as divisive 'Indian identity politics', which would not have been a problem in stronger matrilineal times (Jaimes 1992).

I do not mean for this concept of 'Native Womanism' to undermine the gains of feminism and the more mainstream women's movement, which has focused on righting gender inequities. And I do recognize that not all Native women would be comfortable with the term 'womanism'. However, I put forth 'Native Womanism' as an indigenous metaphor that can make a broader conceptual distinction from the narrower feminist agenda. It pays attention to Native women's experiences and perspectives that are tied to Native spirituality and indigenous models of family, community, and nationhood. This idea of nationhood is distinct from what is meant by nationalism today, since the latter is built upon both patriarchal and colonialist structures that subordinate both women and people of color and culture. Conversely, in pre-patriarchal and precolonialist indigenous nationhoods, Native women were voices of authority in traditional kinship relations and especially within a matrilineal social system.

Womanism and indigenous governance

One significant way in which Native women's lives and visions are different is in how they value the sacred traditions in kinship. This is manifested in the establishment of indigenous governance for the making of nationhood that enables 'participatory democracy' and gender egalitarianism, in contrast to the problems of 'representative authority' in modern-day nationalism (see Jaimes 1992). Also connected to this vision is a bioregional homeland that respects biodiversity by acknowledging reciprocal relations among humans and non-humans (among four-legged animals, plants, etc.), as well as natural entities that are designated as sacred sites in auchtothonous geomythology. Hence, Native women, in the past as well as present, are concerned with land restoration for cultural preservation of indigenous lifeways, which requires economic self-sufficiency and an environmental ethic of ecological sustainability.

'Native Womanism' also honors the historical legacies of indigenous societies, past and present, with ancient roots in the Americas. In this vein, indigenous knowledge and wisdom, as acquired over a long time, can contribute significantly to humankind's atonement for its mistreatment of the Earth as our planetary habitat, by providing indigenous models of ethics, health, and well-being in sustainable Native lifeways (in contrast to hypermodernist lifestyles). However, as Newcomb notes:

> The root problem that indigenous nations and peoples face is that they are still being deemed irrelevant by nation-states, based on having been historically nullified under Christian international law ... As a result, the laws and policies of the dominant society treat Indigenous homelands and environments as a readily available supply of 'natural resources' and 'commodities' that are simply waiting for 'development'. (1994, 20)

In the context of our 'environmental crisis', he concludes:

> If 'law' is defined as a set of rules that establishes standards for proper conduct or behavior, then we must also say that every Indigenous cultural paradigm is therefore a system of law. This conceptual form of governance is rooted in the people's perception of the sacred, and actually pre-determined the people's way of life (as indigenous lifeways). (1994, 23)

Mander (1991, 217) writes that, compared to modern-day 'hierarchical political forms', Native peoples' models of governance, generally speaking, take the following forms:

1. mostly non-hierarchical, and chiefs have no coercive power;
2. decisions are usually based on consensual process involving all tribal members, rather than by executive power, majority rule, and dictatorship;
3. a direct participatory democracy, with rare examples of autocracy;
4. recognizable operative political modes are anarchist, communist, or theocratic (however, I would make the distinction between indigenous communalism and what Karl Marx called 'primitive communism'); this is in contrast to eurocentric ideologies and praxis of socialist, monarchist, capitalist and fascist regimes;
5. decentralization, where power resides mainly in community, among peoples (exceptions were the city–states among Aztec/Mixtecas, Mayans, and Incas, who are purported to practice a kind of militaristic feudalism);
6. laws are transmitted orally with no adversarial process, and interpreted for individual cases. In this process, 'natural law' explaining 'taboos' is used as a basis to settle 'criminal' cases by groups or peers. This is in contrast to euroamerican codified and written law, that is adversarial, anthropocentric, and inherently imperialistic (as in the USA, Western Europe, and the Soviet Union);
7. it is the indigenous concept of identity as 'nation' (my preference is 'nationhood' premised on kinship) which is distinct from the eurocentric construct of the 'State' (or nation–state) and its operant statism.

What Mander has formulated here, despite the self-limiting scope of his stereotypical generalizations, is the basis for 'participatory democracy' in indigenous governance. This is in contrast to 'representative government' that has led to concentrated wealth among the elite class, corporate monopolies, and even fascistic rules as a result of elitist corruption among 'elected' politicos who are above the law in the USA and elsewhere.

As an illustration of 'indigenous governance', the founding fathers of American democracy, most notably Thomas Jefferson and Benjamin Franklin writing in their memoirs, were influenced by the Iroquois model of governance, which was made up of seven Native Nations. They adopted many ideas in the establishment of their plan for federalism (see Grinde and Johansen 1991; Lyons and Mohawk 1992). However, they left one very important component out, and that was the leadership and authority of the clan mothers. One can only surmise that this was because these European fugitives were already established Aristotelian chauvinists and even misogynists – subordinating women's status to that of male property, along with children and slaves.

However, this raises an issue that requires attention, whether it is an intentional or non-intentional propensity of some writers to insist that indigenous nationhoods were 'matriarchies'. In her work, 'Is equality indigenous? The untold Iroquois influence on early radical feminists' (1996), one such feminist writer, Roesch Wagner, cites Paula Gunn Allen, a recognized Native woman writer, in the use of this term. There is also Foster (1995) in her 'Lost women of the matriarchy: Iroquois women in the historical literature'. Yet there is no actual evidence of this among any communal peoples, and this notion insults the egalitarian relations practiced in indigenous kinship, in both matrilineal and patrilineal societies as Native Nationhoods. Even so, the work of these women should be commended, in illustrating the importance of Iroquois clan mothers in their authority to nominate and select their leaders, as well as pointing out the empowering responsibilities of all women in reciprocal kinship relations.

In such humanitarian societies, there was no notion of an 'illegitimate' child or a 'bastard', as it is punitively put in eurocentric societies, for all children were born among the people and all members, both men and women, were responsible for his or her upbringing and well-being. This was the essence of extended family traditions, which has been attacked as (a eurocentric notion of) nepotism, while at the same time it is tragically lacking in today's fragmented modern families, in a global new world order. Ironically, transnational mega-corporations have their own kind of feudalistic surrogate nepotism in Western capitalist enterprises, which enables them to indenture their employees while exploiting consumers and oppressing laborers in rapacious profit-motive schemes.

The Yaqui peoples, located in both the US Southwest and northern Mexico, at one time had eight pueblos that operated as a political alliance with each other, much like we think of 'federalism' today. This socio-cultural system has also been referred to as a 'confederacy' model. The term confederacy is still sometimes used to refer to the 'Iroquois Confederacy', the 'Blackfoot Confederacy', and others among quasi-existing indigenous societies. The point made here is that indigenous societies, in pre-patriarchal and pre-colonialist as well as pre-capitalist times, had sophisticated models for social and political organization, that involved intertribal alliances and coalitions where women made significant contributions among their peoples. Yet a distinction should be made between patriarchal confederacy models (as in the case of the southern 'Civil War' states) and more egalitarian social systems in the case of the earlier indigenous confederacies.

Indigenism

The literal meaning of 'to be indigenous' is to be born of a place. Yet, Indigenism in a broader scope also has to do with how you live in relationship and reciprocity to that place. This distinction can be made in terms of indigenism with a lowercase 'i' and Indigenism with a capital 'I'. What I mean by being Indigenous, in this context, is not necessarily inherent in any race or creed among Native peoples. Yet it is about cultures among land-based peoples who lived in reciprocal relationship with their environment, habitat, or indigenous homeland. This can also be conceptualized as 'ecocultures' that respect how culture is derived from bioregions for biodiversity, and which in turn nurture cultural diversity for health and well-being among indigenous peoples. These Native societies were not perfect models of humanity, but they held people together for responsibility and accountability via kinship traditions; this is in stark contrast to today's Darwinian economics and Newtonian scientism. Indigenous peoples also derived a sense of identity from a sense of place, with the goals of economic self-sufficiency and environmental sustainability working in tandem. The essence of Native Spirituality is that peoples lived in reciprocity with each other and with their environment in ecological balance (comparatively speaking) with other living entities (i.e., plant, animal, non-human). Indigenism is also upheld by the principles of 'Native Womanism' in the reverence for places where one's ancestors are buried and where one's children are born. These are often called 'the navel of our existence' which is why is it still a traditional practice, among many Native people, to bury a child's birth aftermath near the site of where they are born, and preferably to nourish a tree or plant, and for this person to always know their familial origins on her/his life journey. In the case of my own Yaqui ancestry, among the Pueblo Nations of the Southwest, these societies had ancient traditions that enabled their peoples to live in relative good health and well-being, and to always know where one's indigenous roots were, as the center of one's universe (see Kelley 1978).

I deem it important to also mention the controversy that is presently being waged in challenging the popularized 'Bering Strait' theory that all Native populations of this hemisphere, called the 'Americas', (im)migrated from Asia. This heated debate, among mainstream scientists and Native scholars and activists, has been triggered by the discovery of 'Kennewick Man', found on a Columbia riverbank in the state of Washington, on 28 July 1996. A case is being made by these so-called experts that his features are 'European' and therefore comparatively distinct from Native populations who claim ancient indigenous rights to the Americas. In a recent issue of *Discover* magazine, Karen Wright's article, 'First Americans' (1999), reinforces this theory of an early immigration by Europeans as far back as 20,000 BCE, possibly by boat. This is not actually a new theory, since other writers on the subject have also contended this as probability. But now Kennewick Man seems to support this notion as well, even though the Umatillas in the state claim his remains. However, Wright's article does conclude that such theories actually raise more questions and problems than answers to who the 'First Americans' were after all.

The problem with these myopic theories, that also counter early indigenous peoples' creation stories and origin myths from oral tradition, is that they do not take into account a sacred belief among Southwestern Pueblo societies, mainly in Arizona, New Mexico, and Southern California, that these cultures with ancient roots to Uto-Aztecan ancestry have been in this hemisphere from time immemorial. These beliefs cannot be proven by conventional theories of methods for origin dating. But it is my prediction that genetics will play a key role in sorting out what indigenous groups have been here longer than other later arrivals. However, right now the emphasis is on who came over first to the 'New World' as earlier founders (Asians/Siberians or Europeans, etc.?) – at the expense of any notion of a 'Native Genesis' among the ancient ancestors of the Southwestern peoples in the USA with their strong cultural ties to what is now called Latin America.

Such academic conflicts do have repercussions with regards to Native cultural rights for ownership of indigenous knowledge that involves burial sites and artefacts in what is being called repatriation cases. In 1990, the US Congress passed a law, the Native American Graves Protection and Repatriation Act; it was intended to protect these repatriation rights, but has instead caused much infighting among competing tribes as well as with the mainstream scientists. These cases also involve basic human rights as well as civil and legal considerations, which threaten Native/tribal self-determination and autonomy for indigenous knowledge claims. And this is mainly premised on the eurocentric view that the longer a tribal people and their culture can claim residency to a landbase, the more rights they can exercise in territorial ownership of an indigenous landbase. Of course, these theoretical ideas have not held in practice: early indigenous peoples have had to contend with the European invasion by conquest, colonization, and enforced assimilation that has threatened their indigenous lifeways. Hence the gist of this discourse, and including the Wright article, is to undermine even further the auchtothonous claims of today's Native/tribal peoples to land restoration, cultural preservation, and other indigenous rights.

Ecoculturalism versus biocolonialism

In broadening the concept of 'biodiversity' and its connection with Indigenism and the natural environment, this concept recognizes the relationship between biology (including genetics) with cultural diversity in a particular bioregion. However, this is a far cry from what some would criticize as 'biological determinism'. This connection is also manifested in indigenous kinship, which is about relationships with non-human species – not only four-legged animals, plants, etc., but also natural features in the ecological habitat. Hence, these reciprocal relations within these given ecocultural spheres determined what a clan ate and in what season (in ritual mode compared to daily activities), when the seasonal rituals and ceremonies took place, where and what clans participated, and so on. Such ecocultural practices can be illustrated in numerous examples and cases-in-points in what is being called 'indigenous knowledge systems', and that is now raising issues of 'intellectual property issues' around 'patent law'.

In this arena, there is a lot of interest in indigenous knowledge today, but this is being exploited and even appropriated by non-Indians in the name of the new sciences and biomedicine and at the expense of Native peoples. The vehicle for this theft, in what some are calling 'biocolonialism' and 'biopiracy' (Shiva 1997), is the Human Genome Diversity Project (HGDP) that is interested in sampling human DNA among targeted indigenous peoples worldwide. This Project is what I call 'the Great Spiritual Ripoff', since it is about genetic engineering and biotechnology that links the genocide (biological economic erosion) of indigenous peoples with their ethnocide (cultural erosion) and even ecocide (ecological or environmental erosion). Those indigenous peoples targeted by the HGDP are not meant to live out the twenty-first century; they are even termed 'threatened peoples', with over 700 targeted worldwide, including about 70 in the North American countries of the USA and Canada. Hence, Indigenism is concerned both with challenging this biocolonialist agenda that has dire portents for a 'new age eugenics', and also with ecological alternatives that seek to live in reciprocity with the land. Native women have always been the stewards of 'indigenous knowledge' in their homelands and in kinship, which are Native Womanist principles in the building and holding together of indigenous nationhood that is humanitarian and egalitarian between the genders.

Feminine organic archetypes

I have also linked 'Native Womanism' with what I call 'feminine organic archetypes'. These are sacred images of powerful female 'deities', as entities, that are represented in all indigenous cultures in reverence to the image of 'woman as sacred'. They are often connected to matrilineal kinship and agrarian traditions of sustenance and survival, as in the case of Corn Daughter among the Hopi and other Pueblo peoples in the Southwest. They are manifest in oral traditions of regeneration, in creation stories and cosmologies, as in the case of Changing Woman and Spider Woman among the Navajo/Dine, Buffalo Calf Woman among the Lakota and other Great Plains tribes, Sky Woman among the Abanaki in Vermont, and Manitou among the Great Lakes tribes. There is also the more secular Cherokee's Beloved Woman; the latter was personified by 'real' woman among them who was chosen to be representative of this sacred tradition (see, for example, Mankiller and Walls 1993).

As sacred images of these archetypal configurations, and in what I conceptualize as 'female organic archetypes' among Southwestern Native people and their early indigenous cultures, the Leemings write about:

> Spiders in Creation: Spiders, as spinners (spinsters) or weavers – that is, natural creators – are popular in creation myths, especially those of the American Southwest (among the Hopi, Navajo/Dine, To'Odom Odo/Papago, Zia Pueblo peoples and cultures, among others). The spider can be male in the myth but is usually female (as Spider Woman in the Southwest). The spider figure often has a trickster aspect ... The basis for the metaphor is the spider's ability to weave a clever, beautiful, intricate, and dangerous web ... [Hence] Spider Woman is a popular creatrix among the Hopi and other Southwestern tribes (also related to Thinking Woman). She is either the assistant to the supreme creative power or the personification of that power ... She is sometimes Spider Grandmother, as in the Hopi Village of Old Oraibi, and she has a human counterpart in the old women of the various Pueblo clans, who weave the stories of the creative past for the children even as the Spider Fathers and Spider Grandfathers weave the ceremonial shawls in their underground kivas. (1994, 256–7)

In the Hopi Pueblo Creation story is the central figure of Hard Beings Woman, who symbolizes the spiritual basis for the matrilineal system in this ancient indigenous culture. This sacred image is also identified as similar to Spider Woman and Thinking Woman (Leeming and Leeming 1994, 111).

> In this relationship to Spider Woman, Thinking Woman is also known as Thought Woman or Prophesying Woman (Tsitctinako or Sus'sistinako and various other spellings), is the creatrix of the Keresan pueblos of the Rio Grande Valley in New Mexico (as among the Tewa, Acoma, Keres, and Laguna Pueblos). She is of the fertile underworld and projects her thoughts outward in creative acts of lifegiving. (Leeming and Leeming 1994, 269)

> The Earth Mother is a major figure in the world parent type of creations . . . Typically, everything begins with a primordial union between the Earth Mother and the Male Force. (Leeming and Leeming 1994, 79)

However, the problem with this cross-cultural translation is that a eurocentric bias prevails to preserve the patriarchal views of 'male or masculine superiority'. This may be true for Eurowestern cultures (as in Greek mythology), but a distinction needs to be made regarding the conceptual meaning of a 'Supreme Being', also often referred to as the 'Great Spirit', which integrates both feminine and masculine energies, as an androgynous metaphor that counters the engendered binaries as polar opposites projected on these sacred images.

The Leemings contextualize the theme of 'creation by emergence,' by noting that:

> Emergence is a basic concept in creation myths that takes various specific forms, especially among the Indians of the American Southwest and Mexico. This type of myth describes the emergence of a people into this world by way of one or more underworlds. The underworld in such creations can be seen as a world womb, a place in the Earth Mother where humans, plants, and animals are conceived and gradually mature from a seed-like state in darkness until they are ready to be born through a sacred opening. In the underworld, the people, especially, undergo a process of development to prepare them for a new life under the sun. Sometimes the underworld 'people' are still animals, from which they later take clan names or around which they later develop totem traditions. They are taught by some agency of the supreme forces in nature. The world womb aspect of the myth suggests an earlier time when the earth itself was sacred, the source of all possibilities, when goddess as earth reigned supreme. In this connection, it is of interest to note the presence in many of the emergence myths of a creative female midwife such as Spider Woman or Thinking Woman. The male role in the emergence is slight or sometimes nonexistent (as in the case of Acoma Pueblo, Hopi Pueblo, and Navajo/Dine Creation stories). (1994, 58)

As noted above, Changing Woman is a central spiritual metaphor for our times (also see Anderson 1996, for whom Changing Woman provides a powerful/empowering title).

In such translations, I contend that these creation myths and origin stories provide language that can be interpreted as native knowledge on evolution (linked with animism). They also indicate the significance of 'indigenous genetics' in the determination of clan relationships in kinship, among humans (for intermarriage), animals (as totems), and plants (as subsistence), and in which matrilineal, matrifocal authority and leadership prevailed among Clan Mothers. A White Mountain Apache Creation Origin story on the Four Grandfathers and the sacred lodge states that:

> Four people started to work on the Earth ... This is the way they made the earth for us. This is the way all these wild fruits and foods were raised for us, and this is why we have to use them because they grow here. (Leeming and Leeming 1994, 10–12, citing Goodwin 1939)

This excerpt reflects the significance of bioregional cultures and the need for biodiversity, in that the people are meant to live with what the Creator and the Earth provides for them in a particular region. This is to be done in reciprocal relationships that defend against a parasitic symbiosis, and generate sustainable health and well-being for both humans and their natural environment as an indigenous homeland.

These images of the Female Principle are also tied to geomythology, which connects the people to the land as 'sacred sites', with these archetypal images of strong Native Women Entities endowed with a powerful spiritual presence. This concept can also be seen in terms of what I call 'organic materialism' in contrast to 'abstract/virtual materialism'. Among indigenous peoples in pre-capitalist times this had to do with the making of material items and products which had a sacred animistic significance, acknowledged in gratitude to one's Creator, rather than the crass commercialism and reification wrought by Western capitalism today. Hence, the material production of items, such as clothing and tools, was perceived as sacred as well as functional and aesthetic, and not devalued by an abstract monetary assessment. These activities were also individualized among the group's membership, since it was deemed significant that all members were productive and creative agents, for themselves as well as their contributions to their peoples and cultures. Trask, a Native Hawaiian woman activist and author, asserts:

> As in most indigenous societies, there was no money, no idea or practice of surplus appropriation, value storing or payment deferral because there was no idea of financial profit from exchange. In other words, there was no basis for economic exploitation. (1993, 5)

Conclusion

'Native Womanism' is manifested in Native Spirituality and ecocultural survival that advocate the protection and preservation of Mother Earth, and is reflected in the indigenous traditions of 'birthrights' for gender egalitarianism and our greater humanity among traditionally oriented Native peoples. Trask (1993) also shows that this reciprocity extends to an indigenous peoples' familial kinship with their homeland, as in the case of her own people, the Kamaka Maoli. Thus, she writes of an indigenous way of caring for the land, called *malama aina*. These traditions of indigenous womanhood linked with nationhood need to be reclaimed – especially in order to challenge what I call 'masculinear canons of authority' that prevail in a society of institutions today, as a legacy of colonialism and conquest. There is also a critical need to resist the 'trickle-down patriarchy' that still holds Native women back as a result of present chauvinist and misogynist conditions. However, there are many illustrative cases-in-point on how Native Women today are manifesting 'Native Womanism' in life and land struggles with a decolonialist agenda. This Indigenous Movement is one that is inspired by sacred kinship traditions that date back to pre-patriarchal, pre-colonialist, and pre-capitalist times, and is being re-envisioned by Red Warrior Women on the worldwide scene as a 'blueprint for a revolution'. It is a *tour de force* in the global theater that can be guided by the principles of 'Native Womanism' among us, as exemplars of Indigenism that the rest of the world urgently needs to follow – for the sake of 'Our Mother's Sons' as well.

3. Shamanism

Piers Vitebsky

The terms 'shamanism' and 'shaman'

From the Stone Age to the New Age, the figure of the shaman has continued to grip the human imagination. Being chosen by the spirits, taught by them to enter a trance and fly with one's soul to other worlds in the sky or clamber through dangerous crevasses into terrifying subterranean worlds; being stripped of one's flesh, reduced to a skeleton and then reassembled and reborn; gaining the power to combat spiritual enemies and heal their victims, to kill enemies and save one's own people from disease and starvation – these are features of shamanic religions in many parts of the world. And yet they are generally regarded by the communities in which they occur, not as part of some extraordinary sort of mystical practice, but as a specialized development of the relationship which every person has with the world around them.

'Shamanism' is probably the world's oldest form of religion. It is a name generally given to many hundreds, perhaps thousands, of religions around the world. These are thought to have something in common with the religion of the Tungus hunters and reindeer herders in Siberia from whom the word 'shamán' or 'hamán' was taken. (In English the word is widely pronounced 'sháy-man'. The ending has nothing to do with the English word 'man'. Whichever way one pronounces it, the plural is 'shamans'.) It could thus be said that there are many shamanisms (Atkinson 1992), just as there are many monotheisms.

Among the Tungus peoples such as the Evenki and the Even, a shaman is a man or woman whose soul is said to be able to leave their body during trance and travel to other realms of the cosmos. The term is thus named after a central figure and refers, not to a single religion, but rather to a style of religious activity and a kind of understanding of the world. The term was not traditionally used in any indigenous culture, for two reasons: first, every language has its own words for figures who correspond to the shaman, such as the female *udaghan* and the male *oyuun* among the Sakha (Yakut) of Siberia, the *kuran* among the Sora of tribal India, the *angakkoq* of the Greenlandic Kalaallit (Eskimo) or the *payé* in various languages of the upper Amazon. Second, the ending '-ism' carries an implication of formal doctrine which belongs to more systematized religions and ideologies from the 'western' world and is inappropriate for the fluidity and flexibility of these uncodified religions from largely non-literate societies. The word's usefulness therefore depends on our ability, and our need, to perceive parallels between these many different religions. Even if we accept these parallels, it has been suggested that, rather than shamanism as a systematic form of religion, we should speak of 'shamanship' as a skill or personal disposition which is manifested to a greater or lesser degree in various cultures and persons (Atkinson 1989; Vitebsky 1993, 21–2).

By a strict definition, 'shamanism' should perhaps be used only for religions of the non-European peoples of the circumpolar north, and especially of Siberia, where many other peoples have similar religions to those of the Tungus peoples. This view is taken by some scholars specializing in the religions and cultures of this region (for good overviews, see Siikala 1978; Hoppál 1984; Balzer 1990). A broader and more common approach (Eliade 1964; Lewis 1989; Atkinson 1992; Vitebsky 1995a) recognizes shamanic kinds of religion around the world, particularly among the Inuit (Eskimo) peoples,[1] in Amazonia, in Arctic and sub-Arctic North America, and underlying other more mainstream or 'world religions' in Mongolia, Tibet, Central Asia, Nepal, China, Japan, Korea, aboriginal India and Indonesia.

There is less agreement about how far the term should be applied to indigenous religions in Africa, Australia, the Pacific, North America south of the sub-Arctic, or ancient Europe. Such controversies generally concern the nature of the relationship between religious practitioner and spirits, and particularly the frequent absence of soul travel. In African religions, for example, with some exceptions (e.g. the !Kung Bushmen, see Katz 1982) the souls of specialists do not generally travel to the world of spirits. Rather, spirits more commonly visit this world and possess people here (de Heusch 1981). This is a reminder that, even if we believe that all early religions were based on direct relationships between humans and spirits, these can take many different forms.

In industrial or 'western' society today, people interested in spiritual revival sometimes use the word 'shaman' for anyone who is thought to have a special relationship with spirits. In this chapter I shall keep to the criterion of soul flight, since this constitutes a distinctive form of human religiosity with its own particular theological, psychological and sociological implications. This already contains enough diversity to make generalization difficult, but I shall try to highlight some widespread features which such religions have in common.

Prehistory and hunting

Broadly speaking, shamanic kinds of religion have tended to be marginalized or persecuted with the growth of urban civilizations, centralized states (Thomas and Humphrey 1994), and institutionalized priest-based religions (though their legacy can be seen, for example, in mystical experiences of ascent in Christianity and Islam). Their scattered distribution worldwide, mostly in small-scale societies outside the main orbit of these structures, raises the question of whether these religions could be relicts of some pan-human form of early religion.

Prehistoric paintings and petroglyphs, some dating to the paleolithic era, have been found in Europe, South Africa, Australia, Siberia and elsewhere, portraying figures which are part-human, part-animal. Though this is impossible to prove, some scholars have interpreted these as shamans undergoing transformation into animals. Less controversially, rock carvings in Siberia which are several thousand years old show recognizable modern Siberian shaman's costumes, complete with reindeer-antler helmets and drums stretched over a distinctive style of wooden framework. This at least suggests that, even if not unchanging, the religions of this region have a very ancient core.

Another possible link with prehistory is the close, though not exclusive, link between soul flight and hunting. In many societies the shaman's journey across the landscape or the sea echoes the movements and experiences of the hunter but also enlarges and intensifies them. Just as the hunter may try to share the mentality and being of his quarry by dressing in its skins and smelling, calling and moving like an animal, so the shaman may undertake a soul flight in order to locate game animals. But the shaman may also go further and experience turning into an animal, possibly even living for a while as a member of that animal's community and then using this knowledge to encourage members of the species to give themselves up to the community's hunters, or to become the shaman's own spirit helper. Such imagery is often quite male and contrasts with the more female shamanisms found in some agrarian societies in Asia (Kendall 1985).

Trance, cosmology and reality

Shamanic believers generally say that many features of the world, whether animals, trees, streams, mountains, heavenly bodies, even man-made objects like knives and drums, may be imbued with some form of spirit. These manifestations of spirit represent the very essence of these phenomena: the bearness of a bear, the treeness of a tree, the musical power of a drum. At the same time, they resemble human consciousness in that they are capable of experience and volition. They notice how we treat them and can give or withhold from us. They also represent a principle of causality in human affairs. Just as bears, trees and knives interact with us physically according to their qualities and powers of growing and cutting, so their spirits may have effects and cause events in our lives in accordance with their own nature and desires.

The shaman's journeys allow him or her to perceive the true nature or essence of phenomena, to understand how this is implicated in the causation of events in this world, and to act upon this understanding in order to change undesirable situations and sustain desirable ones.

This dimension of reality is not accessible to ordinary people, or in an ordinary state of consciousness. The shaman's switch to an altered state of consciousness is expressed as a journey in space. This imagery conveys the otherness of the spirit realm, but it also opens up a whole topography of mental or spiritual states. This topography is elaborated by different cultures in very different ways. Though the shaman may also fly around the known local landscape, it is also very common to travel up and down through a many-layered cosmology in which our world occupies a position somewhere in the middle. For example, in various parts of Siberia there may be several lower worlds as well as seven, eleven or more upper worlds, of which the higher ones can be reached only by shamans with appropriate skills and training.

Though the shaman's journey to another world suggests a theology of transcendence, the fact that that other world also animates the phenomena of this world shows that this theology is also deeply immanentist. Rather than occasional theophanies, shamanic religions tend to emphasize concentrations or intensifications of a divine presence which is continuously in the world, while humans are not separated from the divine but shade into it, or partake of it, through forms of shared soulhood.

This emphasis on immanence can also be linked to what may be called a shamanic view of time. Unlike the linear historical time of Semitic religions, with their strong concern with eschatology, shamanic thinking tends to conceive time as cyclical or steady-state. The Inuit shaman's journey to the bottom of the sea and the Sora shamans' journeys to the

Underworld described below are intended to ameliorate a situation, but they do not provide a permanent solution. The sea spirit may withhold whales from hunters again on another occasion, the Sora patient who gets better today may be ill again tomorrow and will eventually die. Similarly, the shamanic community's cosmos may contain a finite amount of soul-force, so that animals hunted must be paid for by trading in the lives of humans (the Tukano of Amazonia, see Reichel-Dolmatoff 1971) or parts of a seal must be honoured and thrown back into the sea to be reincarnated (some Inuit of the Arctic).

This is not because these religions are theologically undeveloped. Rather, it is because they regard the problematic nature of life as existentially given, rather than as a situation of ignorance or sin awaiting a historical redemption. Shamanic rites are based on an acknowledgement of the essences and processes of the world, combined with a willingness to use them to achieve one's goals.

Person, powers and initiatory experience of the shaman

In many societies there can be several kinds of shaman, who shade in turn into a range of other specialists such as midwives, diviners, exorcists, bone-setters or herbalists. Some shamans may use techniques of soul journey to fulfil any of these functions, as well as those of doctor, priest, mystic, social worker, psychoanalyst, hunting consultant, psychopomp, astronaut and many others. It often seems that a shaman has to encompass the totality of possibilities of being, transcending boundaries of gender, species and other categories. The ability to make a soul journey is linked to special skills at transformation. Shamans may be transvestite or sexually ambiguous, may speak languages of other peoples or other worlds, or may transform themselves into animals or other beings.

The trance of an experienced shaman is a technique of dissociation with a high degree of control, entered into more or less at will. It is often established with the aid of rhythmical drumming, chanting and dancing, or invocations describing the imminent journey, obstacles which will be encountered, and anticipated battles with hostile spirits and monsters. Other aids, especially in Amazonia, can include the ingestion of psychotropic plants which are said to teach the shaman by revealing what cannot be seen by other means (Reichel-Dolmatoff 1975; Schultes and Hofmann 1979).

The element of will and control in trance makes shamans very different from some other kinds of spirit mediums who stay in this world and are possessed or dominated by spirits which come to visit them and take over their body. Eliade (1964) and Shirokogoroff (1935) have emphasized the shaman's 'mastery' of spirits, but it should be remembered that the degree of this control is always precarious. The shaman's involvement with spirits is very dangerous and there is said to be a constant risk of insanity or death.

Though there is much variation across societies, shamanic power and practice are often inherited within a lineage or kin-group. But at the same time it is generally said that a future shaman does not choose his or her profession, but is chosen by the spirits themselves to serve them. The young candidate may be made aware of this through dreams or by other signs. Their first response is often to refuse to accept such a life of suffering and hardship. The spirits then torment them for months or years until they submit, threatening to kill them if they resist, driving them mad, dismembering them in visions, sending spirit animals to devour them, or forcing them to live up trees eating bark or rush crazily across mountains and snowfields.

The symbolism of transformation and rebirth is often very clear. The candidate comes to understand the true nature of things by being dismembered and reassembled as someone greater and more complete than before. These additional powers are represented by animal helpers whose properties of skill or strength the shaman acquires. Other power objects can include crystals, drums and costumes, melodies, spells, and parts of animals such as a deer's paw for swiftness or (in Nepal) porcupine quills to fire as darts at evil spirits.

Here is part of an account of his initiation in the lower world given by a Siberian shaman to a Russian anthropologist earlier this century (Popov 1936, 84ff., translated in Vitebsky 1995a, 58–61; for other shamans' narratives, see Halifax 1979):

> The Great Underground Master told me that I would have to travel the path of every illness. He gave me a stoat and a mouse as my guides and together with them I continued my journey further into the underworld. My companions led me to a high place where there stood seven tents. 'The people inside these tents are cannibals,' the mouse and stoat warned me. Nevertheless I went into the middle tent, and went crazy on the spot. These were the Smallpox People. They cut out my heart and threw it into a cauldron to boil. Inside this tent I found the Master of my Madness, in another tent I saw the Master of Confusion, in another the Master of Stupidity. I went round all these tents and became acquainted with the paths of various human diseases.
>
> Then I went through an opening in another rock. A naked man was sitting there fanning the fire with bellows. Above the fire hung an enormous cauldron as big as half the earth. When he saw me the naked man brought out a pair of tongs the size of a tent and took hold of me. He took my head and cut it off, and then sliced my body into little pieces and put them in the cauldron. There he

boiled my body for three years. Then he placed me on an anvil and struck my head with a hammer and dipped it into ice-cold water to temper it.

He took the big cauldron off the fire and poured its contents into another container. Now all my muscles had been separated from the bones. Here I am now, I'm talking to you in an ordinary state of mind and I can't say how many pieces there are in my body. But we shamans have several extra bones and muscles. I turned out to have three such parts, two muscles and one bone. When all my bones had been separated from my flesh, the blacksmith said to me, 'Your marrow has turned into a river' and inside the hut I really did see a river with my bones floating on it. 'Look, there are your bones floating away!' said the blacksmith and started to pull them out of the water with his tongs.

When all my bones had been pulled out on to the shore the blacksmith put them together, they became covered with flesh and my body took on its previous appearance. The only thing that was still left unattached was my head. It just looked like a bare skull. The blacksmith covered my skull with flesh and joined it onto my torso. I took on my previous human form. Before he let me go the blacksmith pulled out my eyes and put in new ones. He pierced my ears with his iron finger and told me, 'You will be able to hear and understand the speech of plants.' After this I found myself on the summit of a mountain and soon afterwards woke up in my own tent. Near me sat my worried father and mother.

The shaman in practice

A shaman's practice will vary enormously across numerous diverse cultures. It may also cover a wide range of domains which industrial society regards as very separate. In theological terms, it represents a communion with the divine; medically and psychiatrically, it can represent a movement from sickness to health; socially, it leads from a dysfunctional situation to one of communal harmony. So while it is reminiscent in some ways of mystical experience in the mainstream historical religions, shamanic journeying is at the same time extremely pragmatic and goal-oriented.

In many rites one can discern a re-enactment of the central experience of transformation from the shaman's initiation, but on a smaller and less drastic scale. Some rites, such as offerings, are performed regularly or seasonally to maintain order. Others are performed in response to a problem. When a person falls ill because their soul has been abducted by spirits, or the community begins to starve because animals refuse to give themselves to hunters, the shaman must go on a soul journey to visit the spirits concerned and persuade or coerce them to change their behaviour. This widespread format can be seen clearly in a classic example collected earlier this century from a community of Iglulik Inuit (Eskimo) in northern Canada (summarized from Rasmussen 1929, 123–9).

When there was an incurable sickness, a hunter was particularly unsuccessful, or an entire village was threatened by famine, this was thought to be due to the anger of the sea spirit Takanakapsaluk, who had become contaminated with the community's accumulated sins and breaches of taboos. She was a woman whose father had cruelly cut off her fingers, which then turned into the different species of sea creatures on which the Iglulik Eskimo depend and which she grants them or withholds from them at will. This immediately highlights a central dilemma of traditional Inuit life. Not only do they have to take the life of animals to live, so that those animals must be treated with respect and gratitude, but these animals are also part of the flesh of the sea spirit and humans are able to live only as a result of her suffering.

Anywhere in the world, a shaman's response to this kind of problem may be to enter a trance and go on a soul journey. In this case, the shaman prepares for a difficult journey to Takanakapsaluk's house on the sea-bed. The community gathers in a house and the shaman sits behind a curtain. After particularly elaborate preparations he calls his helpers, saying again and again, 'The way is made ready for me, the way opens before me!', while the audience reply 'Let it be so!' Finally, from behind the curtain the shaman can be heard crying 'Halala – he – he – he, halala – he – he!' Then as he drops down a tube which is said to lead straight to the bottom of the sea, his voice can be heard receding ever further into the distance: 'Halele – he!', until it is lost altogether.

During the shaman's absence, the audience sits in the darkened house and hears the sighing and groaning of people who lived long ago. These can be heard puffing and splashing and coming up for air in the form of seals, whales and walruses. As soon as the shaman reaches the sea-bed, he follows a coastline past a series of obstacles to the sea spirit's house. He has to dodge three deadly stones which churn around leaving hardly any room to pass. The entrance tunnel to the sea spirit's house is guarded by a fierce dog over which the shaman must step. He is also threatened by her father.

When the shaman finally enters the house he finds Takanakapsaluk with a great pool of sea creatures over the floor beside her, all puffing, blowing and snorting. As a sign of her anger, she is sitting with her back to this pool and to the blubber-oil lamp which is the only source of light. She is in a pitiful state. Her hair is filthy and uncombed and hangs over her eyes so that she cannot see. Her body is also filthy. This dirt represents the sins and misdeeds of the human community up above. The shaman must overcome her anger and slowly, gently turn her towards the lamp and the animals. He must comb her hair, for she has no fingers and is unable to do this for herself.

When he has calmed her, he tells her, 'Those above can no longer help the seals up by grasping their foreflippers', and she answers, 'The secret miscarriages of the women and breaches of taboo bar the way for the animals.' When the shaman has fully mollified her, Takanakapsaluk releases the animals one by one and they are carried out by a torrent through the entrance tunnel into the sea, to become available again to hunters.

Just as when a patient's soul has been kidnapped, a shaman will regain possession of it in preparation for restoring it to the patient's body, so here the shaman has moved the situation decisively towards a resolution. He has done this by precipitating, and winning, an encounter. Here, he achieves his goal by tender persuasion, though in other situations a shaman may have to beg a great spirit lord for mercy, or lead serried ranks of helper spirits in a pitched battle against armies of hostile demons.

Now the shaman starts to return. He can be heard a long way off returning through the tube which his helper spirits have kept open for him. With one last 'Plu – a – he – he', he shoots up into his place behind the curtain, gasping for breath. After an expectant silence, he says, 'Words will arise.' Then, one after another, people start to confess their misdeeds, often bringing out secrets which were quite unsuspected even in a small community living at close quarters. In particular, many women confess to a breach of taboo which the sea spirit finds particularly offensive, the concealment of miscarriages. (After a miscarriage, all soft skins and furs belonging to everyone inside the house must be thrown away. This is such a serious loss that a woman may try to conceal any miscarriage or irregular bleeding.) By the end of the seance there is such a mood of optimism about the next hunt that people may even feel grateful to the women whose behaviour caused the problem in the first place.

This example shows how intensely the community is involved, both in commissioning the shaman's soul journey and in participating in it from a complementary position as audience or congregation. The shaman's activities are intensely embedded in the local social structure. The entire practice of shamanism must therefore be understood with reference not only to indigenous theology, but also to local concepts of nature, humanity and the person, the meanings of life and death, and even the workings of the economy. Many writings about shamans ignore social context or even deny the shaman's social role, promoting an image of the shaman as some kind of solitary mystic (Eliade 1964, 8; Castaneda 1968). But as the earlier initiation narrative shows, a shaman may pass through eremitic or psychotic phases, but must always be re-socialized and psychologically reintegrated to serve a social function within the community. The mystic is also a social worker.

The public role of the shaman also emerges clearly among the Sora, an aboriginal tribe in eastern India (Vitebsky 1993). The Inuit shaman's trance, like that of the Siberian shaman, is a rare and highly dramatic occasion. But in every Sora village, almost every day, one of the many shamans will go into trance, allowing groups of living people to hold dialogues with the dead, who come one at a time to speak to them through the shaman's mouth. Here, instead of being called in for a crisis, the shaman is involved in a constant regulation of social relations.

The shaman (usually a woman) sits down and invokes her predecessors and helper spirits with a rhythmic chant. When she enters trance she experiences her soul clambering down terrifying precipices to the underworld like a monkey. This leaves her body vacant for the dead to use as their vehicle of communication and one by one, they begin to speak through her mouth. (Here, the technically distinct 'shamanism' and 'possession' are combined into one system.)

Every case of illness or death is thought to be caused by the dead. The living respond by staging dialogues in which they summon the dead persons responsible, interrogate them in an attempt to understand their state of mind, and negotiate with them. Closely related groups thus find themselves in constantly recurring contact: mourners crowd around the shaman arguing vehemently with the dead, laughing at their jokes, or weeping at their recriminations; family conversations and quarrels continue after some of their participants have crossed the dividing line between what are called life and death.

In this way, everyone engages in a continual fine-tuning of their mutual relationships and each dialogue is only a fleeting episode in an open-ended relationship which explores and ultimately resolves a range of emotional ambiguities in the lives of the participants.

After death, a person's consciousness becomes a form of spirit called *sonum*. Sonums are a powerful causal principle in the affairs of the living. But they are also a contradictory one. On the one hand, in certain moods or aspects, sonums nourish their living descendants through the soul-force they put into their growing crops, giving them their continued sustenance and their very existence; but on the other hand, they 'eat them up' and destroy them.

A person's susceptibility to the effects of sonums depends on a subtle interplay between their own state of mind and that of the numerous other living and dead persons who are caught up in the ongoing dialogue. Different categories of sonum are located in different features of the landscape. As a living person moves around this landscape, he or she may encounter sonums and become involved with them. But this happens not at random, but as a development of their long-term relationships with the various dead persons who now reside in those places. What seems at first sight like a person's medical history also turns out to be a comprehensive social and emotional biography.

Illness arises out of the playing out of an emotional attachment and healing consists in altering the nature of that attachment over time. When a dead Sora encounters a living one, it is said that the dead person's attachment can be so strong that, even without meaning to, they overwhelm and engulf the living. During the course of several years' dialogue, living and dead will discuss and develop their relationship to the point where the deceased is gradually persuaded to move into ever less unwholesome places on the landscape and less disturbed and threatening categories of sonum. Finally, the deceased becomes a pure ancestor, who is supposed to have no remaining aggressive impulses but to recycle his or her name into a new baby among their descendants and to watch over this baby. This is the final resolution of a range of ambivalences which can be emotional, sociological and even legal, concerning inheritance.

If the Inuit example directs us towards one aspect of a shamanic way of thinking, namely the intimate and complex relationship between humans, animals and morality, the Sora show us something else: a system in which shamans use their trance to act as conduits for a shifting and constantly renegotiated concept of personhood. It would be hard to conceive the Sora person without these dialogues since the Sora person seems not to have a unitary core but to be composed almost entirely of the confluence of the person's relationship with other persons.

Shamans have often been compared to psychoanalysts and psychotherapists, and here we see how both Inuit and Sora shamans not only engage with spirits, but also use dramatic enactment to conduct a form of psychotherapy and sociotherapy. The Inuit shaman makes a sharper contrast between the roles of shaman and audience, while the Sora shaman bows out as the dead arrive and leaves the living clients to face them unaided. Either way, however, there is a profound theological contrast with psychoanalysis concerning the presumed reality of spirits. In the Sora view, the dead not only exist but are equal partners in their encounters with the living. In Freud's model of bereavement, the dead have ceased to exist and the mourner who continues to speak with them is suffering from a 'hallucinatory wishful psychosis' (Vitebsky 1993, 238–47) – just as in zoology, marine mammals have no spirit keepers.

A shamanic revival?

In the West, there is a growing fascination with indigenous and synthetic forms of shamanism (see e.g. *Shaman's Drum: A Journal of Experiential Shamanism*). Forms of so-called 'shamanism' flourish in popular magazines and weekend workshops, under the guidance of a new profession of 'urban shamans'. As organized religion retreats ever further from the lives of millions and as institutionalized medicine is subjected to unprecedented criticism, increasing numbers are wondering whether what they call shamanism may offer an appropriate new way of thinking and acting in the industrial and post-industrial world. The evaluation of shamans themselves has shifted from their earlier dismissal as crazy and deluded, to a respect and awe for these people who are said to go to the edge of psychosis, perceive reality and return to serve society (see Walsh 1990 for a survey of shamanic and related states of mind).

However, such movements do not deal easily with the embeddedness of shamanic beliefs in their social structures, and some neo-shamanic practitioners advocate a composite form of 'shamanism' based on ideas of universal human spiritual potential (Harner 1982), arguing that shamanism is not a religion but a technique which anyone can learn. This contrasts strikingly with the claim in many traditional societies that a shaman is a rare person who has been specially chosen by the spirits.

While shamanic revival is a major strand in Western life today, it is also appearing among the people who were the world's earlier shamanists but who abandoned shamanic religions under colonial pressure. But revival cannot mean a return to an old way of life. Modern indigenous 'shamanisms' have become linked to ethnic identity, environmental protest, democratic ideals or a backlash against the militant atheism of communist regimes (Vitebsky 1995b). Moreover, even the remotest tribal shamans may now have relationships, not only with white people, but increasingly even with shamans from other, separate traditions of which they are only just becoming aware.

So, perhaps as in the paleolithic era, there is a possibility that shamanism may now become a sort of world religion. But this is most likely to come about only in a globalized form in which diverse shamanic ideas and practices are severed from their roots in numerous small-scale societies, largely at the hands of white outsiders. For the foreseeable future, the term 'shamanism' will be the subject of intense controversy centring especially on questions of definition, authenticity and appropriation.

Note

1. Each of the different peoples of this family in Greenland, Canada, Russia and Alaska has their own name for themselves. The name 'Eskimo' is now considered insulting among some groups such as the Inuit ('Real People') of Canada. However, other groups reject the name Inuit and there is currently no name which is universally acceptable for the peoples of this family.

4. Witchcraft and healing among the Bangwa of Cameroon

Fiona Bowie

It is common to hear generalizations concerning 'what Africans believe', or comparisons of African and European witchcraft that depend on a view of Africa, or at least sub-Saharan Africa, as a homogeneous unit. There is also a tendency to ignore African history prior to the colonial period, and to regard African societies as relatively unchanging and exotic. While there can be a place for generalizations, which may even contain an element of truth, the African continent has been subject to enormous and varied pressures, population movements and internal developments, not least through the impact of the trans-Saharan and trans-Atlantic slave trades.

In this chapter I argue that Bangwa notions of witchcraft (and methods for dealing with it) are best understood in the context of a specific cultural history. The Bangwa are not and have never been an isolated group, and their beliefs and practices have much in common with those of neighbouring peoples, which in turn reflect particular cultural and historical experiences. Witchcraft is a flexible and adaptive phenomenon. It is not a secret or hidden 'tradition', but part of the way in which contemporary Bangwa conceive of themselves as individuals and as social beings. Although concerned with the occult and forces of the night, witchcraft is at the same time a necessary concomitant of power and success, spoken of openly and acknowledged as a fact of life, as ordinary as breathing or eating. Nineteenth-century scholars such as Sir James Frazer, and even the father of fieldwork anthropology, Bronislaw Malinowski, assumed that belief in witchcraft and magic would disappear, to be replaced by scientific rationality. Numerous studies of witchcraft in Africa and elsewhere have shown that this is not the case. (See, for instance, the articles in Comaroff and Comaroff (1993), for the ways in which witchcraft beliefs adapt themselves to new economic and social realities.)

I have opted for an 'experience near' approach, using field notes as points of reference. As a postgraduate student of anthropology I was encouraged to 'write everything down' in the hope of later distilling a single, accurate, definitive account of Bangwa culture and society. While not unaware of the inevitable processes of selection, from the choice of a topic and area of study, to the people I met, questions I asked and interpretations I put on their answers, the final account of my efforts was nevertheless intended to be a generalized 'true' picture of the Bangwa (see Bowie 1985). By sharing with the reader some of the material on which this earlier, more polished account was based, I hope to convey some of the ordinary, everydayness of witchcraft discourses among the Bangwa, as well as the rather piecemeal way in which information is obtained. Most conversations were with relatively well-educated Bangwa or mission employees in English or Pidgin English, using Bangwa terms for clarification, or as a pivotal point for discussion.

Witchcraft and witch-curing in Bangwa

At the risk of oversimplifying, or of giving a normative account of an extremely slippery subject, we can start by identifying the following salient features of witchcraft in Bangwa, which emerge from the conversations recorded below (and other similar accounts).

1. The Nweh (Bangwa) word *lekang* (plural, *begang*) is variously translated into English as 'witch', 'spirit' and 'animal'. The term would also encompass the notion of sorcery, i.e. the direct and conscious manipulation of objects in order to harm others, as defined by Evans-Pritchard (1976) for the Azande of Central Africa. The term 'sorcerer' is used by Nweh speakers in English for the Bangwa word *nganga* (a term common to many Bantu languages) or *gambe man* in Pidgin English. The *nganga* is a diviner who identifies witches (using his own occult power). The English term 'witch doctor' translates the Nweh *nganga fu*. While I did not hear of female *nganga* among the Bangwa, there are some well-known and respected women native doctors (*nganga fu*). A French Jesuit priest, Eric de Rosny, who worked for many years in Cameroon's main town, Douala, wrote a fascinating account of his contact with Duala *ngangas* and of his own initiation into the world occult healing (de Rosny 1985). Geschiere (1997) paints a fairly negative view of *ngangas*, as did many of my Bangwa informants (admittedly mostly Christians, and therefore perhaps biased), whereas de Rosny is generous in his praise of their healing powers.

2. Everyone has a spirit animal that lives in his or her stomach, which can be 'sent out' in order to operate in the spirit world. The idiom used is one of shape-changing or 'transforming'. The witch transforms him or herself into their witch animal in order to harm others. This harm may be practical – a bush pig may trample the crops of a co-wife, or occult, usually 'eating' a victim. Witches and victims are usually patrikin (related through a man, but not through a woman) or inhabitants of the same compound (such as co-wives of a polygynist). Witches can be male or female and any age.
3. The spirit animal may be activated knowingly or unconsciously. Witches may try to entrap others to join them in their cannibalistic feasts. To join a coven a witch must sacrifice a member of his or her own family. The victim will be 'eaten' by witches in the spirit world, and the individual will sicken in the everyday world. Unless the spell is broken, either by stronger counter-magic, or by forcing the witches to confess and 'cool' the witchcraft, the victim will die.
4. Witches like dark places and operate at night. Electricity and clearing the bush are thought to frighten them away (which is one reason Europeans don't suffer from witchcraft). This view was changing when I returned to Fontem in 1995. Despite the increase in generators and bush clearance, witches continue to thrive, and people continue to sicken and die.
5. All deaths are suspicious (except possibly a peaceful death in old age, with many grandchildren to 'feed the skull' of the deceased). Autopsies, officially illegal, are still performed in order to discover whether the deceased is a witch – identified by substances in the gullet. If the dead person is a witch, the assumption is that their death was caused by anti-witchcraft medicines. As witchcraft is passed from a woman to her sons and daughters, maternal kin (male and female) of the deceased are also stigmatized as witches. A titled man passes his witchcraft substance to his successor. There is a sense therefore, in which female witchcraft is seen as 'bad' and harmful, whereas male (chiefly) witchcraft is legitimate and 'good'.
6. A chief (*fon*) has the authority to hear cases of witchcraft among his subjects. He may call on the services of a diviner (*nganga*). Recourse to external authorities is discouraged. Witchcraft matters should be settled 'within the family'. In Eastern Province (the equatorial forest zones to the south east of the country) state courts are increasingly hearing witchcraft trials, often convicting people as witches on the evidence of a *nganga*. In other parts of Cameroon this is rare, and in colonial times it would be the *nganga* rather than the accused who would suffer the force of the law. This led to the view that colonial and post-colonial courts,

by denying the reality of witches, were in fact protecting them, allowing witches to go free (Fisiy 1990).

7. A powerful chief is also expected to use his witch powers for the good of his people, operating together with his counsellors (the 'Night Society' or *tro*) and through the witch-finding *kungang* society.
8. The church provides a new and alternative means of opposing witchcraft. While the missionaries often encourage the people to dismiss witchcraft as superstitious nonsense, they also provide practical means to counter it in the form of sacred objects, prayer, and the belief in the power of God to protect people from the power of witches. Priests can sometimes act as an alternative to a *nganga*.

Entering the world of witches

The following extracts are taken from my fieldwork diaries covering the periods 1980–81 and 1995. While a striking picture of a particular view of the world emerges, it is not necessarily homogeneous or clearly articulated. As Robert Pool (1994) has demonstrated in his account of witchcraft among the Wimbum of the Bamenda Plateau, everyone has their own interpretation of witchcraft, which is contextual, depending on the situation and occasion. Contradictions and anomalies are not regarded as a problem, and may well go unnoticed by all but the inquisitive anthropologist who feels obliged to produce a coherent synthetic account of 'native beliefs'.

> Saturday 12th April 1980, Fontem.
> *Baby witches*: Recently in the hospital people told a mother that her baby was a witch and she didn't want the staff to give it injections. Margaret from Bamenda was really indignant that the mother called her own child a witch. The staff of the hospital had a real struggle to get the mother to agree that they could treat the child. Apparently they will still let their children die if they think they are witches.
>
> Monday 8th September 1980, Fonjumetaw.
> *Native Doctors*: This afternoon a young man came to see Father Luigi. He was from Fongo Tongo, near Dschang. He thought that he was bewitched and wanted a blessing. If he had gone to a native doctor (gambe man or *nganga*) he might have been told the name of the witch and would have been obliged to poison them (or have been accused of being a witch himself). He went to a priest nearer home, but the priest would have nothing to do with it, but told him he could try Father Luigi, so he came. Father Luigi gave him a holy card and the man went away relieved and happy. Father Luigi said it was not the first

time. One man in Dschang spent 300,000 CFAs because he thought he was bewitched. Father Luigi gave him a rosary and that was enough. He keeps a supply of holy pictures for such occasions.

Thursday 11th September 1980, Fontem.
Witchcraft: Pia (an Italian midwife) told me of a woman who died in the hospital when Giacomo, the married doctor, was here. She said that she would die that day because her witch animal had been killed in the forest. Her witchcraft and therefore she herself would die. Giacomo didn't take too much notice but that day she died – she said that if she fell asleep she would die and that is just what happened. Another boy very recently said that he had been bewitched and would die and he did.

Saturday 13th September 1980, Fontem. Interview with Justine Fomengia.
Witches/Spirits: Spirits/witches (*begang*) like dark places. If a place is cleared of bush the spirits go away. Until the ground was cleared people didn't like to cross the Begeh River where the bridge is, below the hospital. There used to be a hammock bridge there. When the road was built they cleared a *lefem* copse (a sacred grove, meeting place of spirits/witches). In many places spirits have been driven away by clearing the bush, so people can move more freely. Spirits like the dark so it is dangerous to travel at night. They like bushy places. Water spirits include hippos, crocodiles and water snakes. Land spirits include the elephant, leopard, snakes, porcupines, bush pigs and a type of deer. Owls are air spirits. 'Not all are spirits but it is believed that all leopards, crocodiles, hippos and owls are spirits.' People change into a bush pig or porcupine to eat the crops, cocoyams, etc. of others. There is a type of big wild deer with two horns that is a spirit. Every owl that you see is some individual transformed. You only have one animal spirit. If your spirit animal is shot you will die. The person who owns the animal spirit will fall sick. The native doctor (*nganga fu*) has to replace the animal in the patient's stomach with native medicine. The spirit lives in the stomach unless you send it out. You need to be able to get it back again. Witches can bewitch adults and children. At a post-mortem you sometimes find a 'baby' in the gullet, that was carried into the spirit world and killed. Each person knows his or her own spirit animal. You are not told by anyone, you feel it yourself. Witches and wizards start transforming from birth. A father gives all his internal powers to the son who will succeed him before the son is made his successor to see whether he can control them. The son will not be told but as he grows he realises himself. A man transfers his powers to his successor only when he is old or dying. He will introduce the child to the spirit house and show him where to sit. The child must be old enough to control the spirits.

Case of witchcraft: Justine recounted the following case of witchcraft reported in the last few days. A girl accused five persons of witchcraft. She is in her teens, fourteen or fifteen, but her growth is stunted (hasn't reached puberty?). The girl reported to the Fon (the paramount chief of Lebang village, Fontem Defang) that seven persons from her quarter had carried her into the witchcraft world and had given her a drug to turn her into an owl. They are living in a tree in a spirit house with eleven rooms. She has seven roommates (who were present in the place of the Fon). Each one had to give a contribution of human flesh. The five people had given their contribution and it came to the girl's turn. She was told to give the flesh of the first child of her eldest (or an elder) sister. She had refused and had run to the palace to report to the Fon. The Fon asked the seven people about it and they refused to talk. This was taken as an admission of guilt. Native doctors were summoned to take her out of the tree. If the tree is just cut down all seven and the girl will die. She identified the tree, which is in or near her compound. The girl will remain safely in the palace until she is taken out of the tree. The compound is at Atonga, on the way to Takwa, just the other side of the river that divides Bayang from Bangwa. The Fon asked money from the father to pay a powerful native doctor to take the child out of the tree and cut down the tree. As they have been warned, the other spirits will escape from the tree and enter another tree so the people will not die. [This incident is similar in many details to one recounted by Robert Brain during fieldwork in Fontem sub-division (now Lebialem Division) in the 1960s (Brain 1970).]

Thursday 25th December 1980 (Christmas Day), Fontem.
Rose Nkeng's father is convinced that he is bewitched by a witch/spirit from Mamy Water (*Lebialem*, a massive waterfall at the confluence of two rivers – a powerful *fuandem* or sacred site, considered by many as too dangerous to visit) and is going to die. In fact he is quite healthy. He will no longer sleep in his bedroom, which is bewitched. Cecile (a Dutch nurse) asked Rose if her grandfather, one of the first Christians in Fotabong (and in Bangwa as a whole), would have believed in witchcraft so. Rose said 'No', 'Never! He was very strong in his faith.' Cecile told Rose that her father was not free, not in the will of God, because he was a slave to witchcraft. She has to help him to have a strong faith. Rose said that she would go home and sleep in the room he says is bewitched so that they will see there is nothing there.

Tuesday 7th July 1981, Mbetta.
The catechist, Christopher, is a native of Foreke (a Bangwa village). He has just returned from a visit to his native village, and he told me that two days ago a very beautiful girl died so the people went to find the cause of death. A 'big man' came forward and took a leaf, divided it into four parts and threw it into the air to see how it would land. The pieces fell two up and two down, which he interpreted as meaning that his spell had taken effect. He called the people to look and verify the result. He said that he had put a spell in his compound, and that the dead girl had transformed herself and come to his compound and tried to eat his child. The spell had stabbed her to death, which was why she died. The only thing to do was for the family of the dead girl to pay him 30,000 CFA to 'feed' the spell, so that it didn't kill other members of the family. Christopher

said that they will pay, people were tense and frightened, both Christians and non-Christians.

Thursday 1st June 1995, Fontem (a visit to the Fon's palace at Azi).
A son of the late Fon (Fontem Defang), educated and well dressed, came to show us round and apologised that the Fon was not there. [Fontem Defang died on 7th April 1982, and was succeeded by one of his sons, Fontem Njifua, born in 1961. In 1995 he was living in Baffousam, in Eastern Province, but returned regularly to Fontem.] He managed to find some keys for the old palace which looks the same on the outside, but which is deteriorating with neglect on the inside. The fine central carved pillar is still there, and several leopard stools. Upstairs a modern carving of a hunter stood under a photo of Paul Biya (the President of Cameroon). In an inner upstairs room were some tatty feather head-dresses, a pile of dusty leopard ('tiger') skins (*ngui*) – probably the same ones illustrated by Brain and Pollock (1971, plates 6, 54 and 55); and which I had seen being worn at funerals or 'cry-dies' in 1980 and 1981. The headdresses probably belonged to the Fon's royal *Albin* society, a dance society for titled men and women, originating in the Bamileke grassfields. There were also a couple of *jujus*, one carved and one, which I was told was very powerful, a brass figure with a gong, probably from Fumban (to the northeast) . . . We then went to look at the half-built *lemoo* hall (a chief's meeting chamber, usually in the centre of a royal compound or 'palace'). It is a concrete block construction with a zinc roof, mainly occupied by goats at present. I gathered that there was some debate as to whether it should be built in the traditional style of the old *lemoo*, which collapsed in the 1970s, or 'modern'. The Fon opted for the latter. In front of the raised podium on which the Fon will sit to hear local disputes is a shallow depression in concrete, about three inches deep and twelve inches across, for people to pour water when swearing in witchcraft cases. I was told that it really works, even if they don't know how. Witchcraft cases seem to be the majority – someone accused of 'eating' someone else. The accused is asked to swear his or her innocence by pouring some water in the hole. If they are guilty both the person and their witch (animal) will die. In some instances they pour water out of shame and then die. In other cases their relatives and friends hold someone back and tell them not to risk their lives or to kill themselves in that way (tantamount to an admission of guilt). If someone refuses to pour water, guilt is assumed.

On the way back I was shown the place in the upper market square, not far from the slit gongs, where Conrau's head is buried. Charles (my Bangwa guide) knew the story but not the name. He knew him by his Bali nickname 'Manjikwara'. [Gustaf Conrau, a German trader, was the first European to enter Bangwa territory in February 1898. He returned the following year, but committed suicide (or was killed), which initiated several years of punitive raids against the Bangwa. See Dunstan (1965), Brain (1977) and Ndobegang (1983)]. Conrau continues to play an important role in Bangwa historical consciousness. In his interview with Michael Ndobegang, Fontem Njifua described the support he had received from the people by saying, 'They have told me that even if I ask for "Manjikwara's" head our fathers talked about in the past they would give me' (1983, 48)]. The stone marking the spot has gone. I was told that it is in the palace. I didn't see it, but did see another slab, which looked like marble, with a German inscription, 'Peter B?, b.1875' with the dates '1900–1904, *kaiserstorm-truppen*'. My guides didn't know this man's story, but presumably he was a soldier killed in Fontem (or who died there) during the punitive raids that followed Conrau's death.

The extracts above are typical of many conversations and observations made during my two periods of fieldwork among the Bangwa. They offer a glimpse into a world in which witches (spirits) are ubiquitous, in which notions of the human person and his or her constitution differ markedly from that of post-Enlightenment European rationalists, and in which occult power is an ambivalent force, both necessary but potentially deadly. The Bangwa live in a world that has witnessed precipitous changes. While the majority of those still living in their mountain villages are peasant farmers, many Bangwa live outside the area in neighbouring towns or overseas. Within a period of a hundred years they have witnessed the first European penetration of their hills, the arrival of Christian mission-aries, the construction of roads linking them to the outside world, and the establishment of the institutions of a modern state. Such changes should not be seen as incursions of Western and global forces into a 'traditional' way of life and indigenous belief system. There never was a static Bangwa traditional society, or ancient, unchanging belief system. The Bangwa exemplify the complex interplay of international political and economic forces with 'traditional' social beliefs and practices. If we want to find a society that lays to rest the old structural–functionalist paradigm (the view that 'primitive' societies are in a state of a-historical harmony with all institutions operating to maintain an integrated social whole) this is a good place to start.

The witchcraft of chiefs

The Bangwa area consists of a group of nine paramount chiefdoms occupying the mountainous rainforest that rises from the Cross-River Basin to the south and west, to the Grassfields to the north and east. Culturally and linguistically the Bangwa are similar to the Bamileke, one of the most prosperous and numerous linguistic and ethnic groups in Cameroon, whose societies are described as hierarchical, with powerful polygynous chiefs. The Bamileke cannot be described as a 'tribe' or single people (although they have come to be regarded as such). The term is probably derived from '*MbeLeku*', 'the people of the plateau'. There are many similarities between the Francophone Bamileke and Anglophone peoples of the adjoining Bamenda Plateau. Although they regard the Bamileke as their 'brothers' the Bangwa were separated from them by linguistic and colonial boundaries. The Bangwa hills were the easternmost part of the Cameroons under British Mandate, with its headquarters at Enugu in Nigeria. The Banwga were therefore Anglophone, and the regional centre was at Mamfe to the west, while the Bamileke grassfields formed part of the Francophone Western Province. In 1966 the Bangwa, and Mundani to the north, were linked administratively as Fontem Sub-Division, and in August 1992 the Nweh-Mundani area achieved full divisional status, taking the name 'Lebialem' from the sacred waterfall or *fuandem* on the border of Lebang village. The Bangwa also have links and almost certainly some common origins, with the forest peoples to the south and west, typically acephalous and 'egalitarian'. In terms of witchcraft beliefs and practices, the Bangwa exhibit characteristics of both these cultural areas. (See Ruel (1974) for a description of the Banyang, also referred to as Bayang or Byangi, the Bangwa's lowland neighbours to the west.)

The term 'Bangwa' was probably used first by the Germans at the end of the nineteenth century for the peoples of the mountains who spoke languages referred to as *Nweh*. It is unlikely that the Bangwa 'villages' ever thought of themselves as a single unit before this time. Differences between various Bangwa groups are still pronounced, and each has its own story of origin. Robert Brain (1967, 6) suggests that the peoples now referred to as Bangwa are of relatively recent origin, moving into their current territory no later than the middle of the eighteenth century as middlemen in the lucrative trade in slaves and European goods. They spanned the inhospitable, sparsely inhabited territory between the populous grassfields and the lowland coastal tribes who dealt directly with the European slavers. This interpretation is supported by Bangwa historians. Michael Atemnkeng Ndobegang (1983, 17) records a royal line for Lebang, the largest of the Bangwa paramount chiefdoms or 'villages', with nine patrilineal chiefs down to the present Fon, Fontem Njifua. Oral history records that the Lebang people were hunters and warriors who displaced the indigenous 'dwarf' (i.e. pygmy or pygmoid) inhabitants, the Beketchi. Lebang territory was later consolidated by the grandfather of the present Fon, Asonganyi (*c.* 1826–1951), who enlarged his country at the expense of the Mbo, who were driven further south. According to the Bangwa, the Mbo were cannibals who caught and ate Lebang people, so the Mbo war (*ncho Lebo*) was fought in self-defence (Ndobegang 1983, 9).

The history of the Mbo war exemplifies the Bangwa tendency to combine the witchcraft of chiefs, associated with grassfield societies, with forest cults (cf. Geschiere 1997). Asonganyi worked hard to acquire the wives, retainers and royal paraphernalia, such as leopard skins, masks, royal dance societies, titles and esoteric powers associated with grassfield chieftaincy. As women were the main source of wealth and status, warfare was a convenient mean of acquiring wives and concubines, as well as slaves for the domestic and long-distance markets. In the forests witchcraft depends on a zero-sum view of the world in which success depends on acquiring power at someone else's expense. Witchcraft therefore has powerful levelling tendencies – anyone who achieves something in life must have done so by 'eating' their kin. Those who are successful fear both the jealousy of their relatives, who might try to bewitch them, and accusations of having profited at someone else's expense. Witch finding is in the hands of secret societies and individual specialists (the *nganga*). In grassfield societies, on the other hand, the institution of chieftancy can channel and help to control witchcraft. The occult powers of the chief can be used for legitimate purposes, i.e. for the good of his people (their protection and the fertility of the land). The chief can also regulate anti-witchcraft activities and act as final arbiter in disputes concerning witchcraft.

Asonganyi was said to transform himself into a leopard to fight the Mbo in the world of witches, together with his Night Society (*tro*). He also relied on forest magic, as described below by Michael Ndobegang:

> Asonganyi knew that driving away the Mbos was not going to be an easy affair, so he consulted his nobles and they agreed to prepare some war charms and medicine. This was the famous '*Aziah*'. It gave Lebang people the ability to resist bullets, matchets (*proff*) and the rest of the war hazards. The war magic was prepared (*ndah*) with among other things, the heart and blood of a slave. A trench was dug in the ground and filled with water and a person had to go through it and on emerging at the outlet was fired at with a gun and he shouted '*aziah*' and then the bullets [appeared] in his palm. At first the people feared and hesitated to undergo this ceremony. Asonganyi then decided to go first. When the people [saw] that he had successfully gone over the ordeal without being hurt they then followed after him until all the warriors were initiated.
>
> '*Aziah*' was prepared by a Bayang man (*wuo-akap*), Nchancheu [from the lowland forest area to the west] . . . He was rewarded. But when he left to go it occurred to the people that he could prepare the same medicine for some enemy of Lebang. He was followed, caught and killed and his medicine bag (*aboh-afou*) taken away. (1983, 9–10, my italics)

In an interview with Ndobegang in 1983, the current Fon described his duties at the Palace. Fontem Njifua had succeeded his father in 1982, inheriting 37 wives (his father's widows) and 127 children; and was hoping to marry many more wives. He found that much of his time was taken with settling disputes – over land, property, between husbands and wives, witchcraft, indebtedness and so on (although he could no longer order that witches be summarily executed and their property confiscated as his grandfather, and even his father in earlier days, had been able to do). Fontem Njifua also stated that he remains in contact with his late father (in the spirit world), and hopes to learn something from Fontem Defang of his knowledge of herbs (medicines with both natural and supernatural powers).

Conclusion

Fear of witchcraft plays a prominent role in the lives of the Bangwa. As AIDS adds to the already high death toll from malaria and other tropical diseases, people will continue to regard witches as being active in their midst (cf. Lockhart 1994). Geschiere (1997) gives fear of one's family (i.e. of their power to bewitch) as a reason the new elites often keep their distance from their natal villages, and de Rosny (1985) cites fear of familial witchcraft as motivating young people to leave their villages for the relative anonymity of the city. To the Bangwa living in their mountain villages, however, the world outside can also seem a frightening place. Indians ('Hindus') may transform themselves into black men in order to lure them into their houses so that they can kill them and sell their heads to India for millions of francs (as recounted in the experience of one student, who described his narrow escape from such horrors in Baffousam). There is always the danger that one will be turned into zombie to work as a slave in someone's invisible plantations on Mount Kupe in Bakossi country. (For the development of ideas concerning the witch markets and invisible plantations on Mount Kupe, and links with the slave trade and plantation economy of pre-colonial and colonial times, see Ardener 1970; de Rosny 1985; Rowlands and Warnier 1988; Pool 1994; Geschiere 1997.)

Although witchcraft can have a levelling effect, and may follow lines of social tension, it does not entirely block the entrepreneurial spirit of the Bangwa and, as in the grassfields, witchcraft can also be controlled through chiefs who harness witch power for the good of the people, and see that the land is cleansed of witches. Diviners and native doctors (*nganga* and *nganga fu*) wield considerable power and are often disliked and distrusted (although the medical skills of some native doctors are widely acknowledged, even by the staff of the mission hospital). *Nganga* and *nganga fu* have gained quasi-official status via the Association of Traditional Healers (established in the 1970s) and some proudly display their credentials and advertise for business on painted signs outside their village compounds or city houses. 'Tradition' and modernity proceed hand-in-hand, reaching new forms of accommodation as circumstances demand. Witchcraft and healing have not been subsumed by Christianity, education or modern health care. For example, Paul Gifford (1998, 347) notes that Pentecostal forms of Christianity legitimize the accumulation of wealth by preaching that it is a blessing, desired by God, and that poverty is the result of a curse, or of satanic forces that can be exorcized, enables people to break out of the levelling circle of witchcraft accusations and ordeals, and feel confident in expressing their entrepreneurial ambitions. Among the Bangwa, witchcraft and healing remain an important idiom in which people express who and what they are, and explain the mechanisms of a market economy and their role within it.

Acknowledgement

The initial fieldwork on which this article draws was carried out for a D.Phil. thesis (Oxford 1985) and was funded by the ESRC and the Buttle Trust. The Radcliffe-Brown Fund helped with the production of the dissertation. The return trip in 1995 was supported by grants from the Pantyfedwen Fund and the Department of Theology and Religious Studies at the University of Wales Lampeter.

5. Rattray's request: Spirit possession among the Bono of West Africa

Jan G. Platvoet

In this chapter I deal with spirit possession as it was found among the Bono of West Africa. This chapter on this important and fascinating subject has four parts. In the first, I explain, by way of introduction, what spirit possession is, in what religions it is found, how it may be studied, and what theories have been developed to better understand, and explain, certain aspects of it. The second part serves to create the settings, geographical, historical, social and religious, for the main purpose of this chapter: an analysis of a spirit possession session which Captain Rattray, government anthropologist in the Gold Coast in the 1920s, witnessed at Tanoboase, a Bono village on the edge of the forests of West Africa. In the concluding part, I discuss how far theories on spirit possession help us to understand it better.

Spirit possession

Spirit possession is the standard label among anthropologists and scholars of religions for rituals in which one, or a few, or even several, of the participants in a public ritual behave in ways which believers interpret as signifying that 'spirits' have taken 'possession' of them. In that condition, they are for them the 'mediums' of unseen beings. In ancient Greece, such a person was termed a *prophetès*, 'mouthpiece'. The message that was received through the mouth of a 'possessed' person was called an *oraculum* – from *orare*, 'to speak' in Latin. Believers experienced these rituals as the manifestation of spirits among them and as 'face-to-face' contact with them.

The term 'spirit possession' is in one respect a happy term. It readily calls to mind the main feature of this ritual in nearly all religions: the belief that 'spirits' take possession of humans on certain occasions and/or in certain ritual settings. 'Spirit possession' is, therefore, what anthropologists call an *emic* term. It expresses a meaning which believers themselves attach to what they believe happens during a spirit possession ritual. 'Spirit possession' is, therefore, a religious, or theological, term. People who believe in spirit possession regard certain invisible realms, beings, qualities, actions and/or qualities as 'real' and assume that they are, or may be, active in the empirical world of humans. They conceive of them as belonging to either the meta-empirical world of 'the spirits', or to the empirical one of humans, in ways which we cannot empirically observe and cannot investigate with scientific tools. In that respect, their faith is basically similar to that of Christian believers who trust in the grace of God, the intercession of a saint or in the operation of sacraments.

The study of religions is, however, a scholarly enterprise. It is limited to what science can investigate. It can study only the empirical part of spirit possession rituals, i.e. those elements that are part of the history of the cultures of humankind in a verifiable, or testable, way. Scholars (of religions) have no means of investigating the meta-empirical part – if any – of spirit possession (or any other religious ritual or belief). They cannot verify, nor falsify, whether spirits actually 'take possession' of their 'mediums', and 'heal', or perform other 'work'. Not being able, on grounds of the methodology of scientific research, to either prove or disprove the claims of the believers about spirits and their activities, scholars of religions can neither support them as true, nor reject them as false. They can only take an agnostic position in respect of the truth or falsehood of the beliefs of faithful. They must, therefore, confine themselves to investigating what is empirical about these beliefs and rituals, i.e. to those elements and aspects of them that belong squarely to our own world and are part of its empirical cultural and historical realities. They need, therefore, to supplement spirit possession with another term, or set of terms which clearly expresses what can be investigated in them.

Now, the most empirical element of spirit possession is spirit possession behaviour. Spirit possession rituals are always performed in public, for the 'spirit', or possessed medium, needs an audience which it/he/she can address. The rituals can, therefore, be witnessed, recorded, and their meanings for the believers can be discussed with them. In these public rituals, spirit possession beliefs are acted out. Although they are notions in the heads of the believers and, as such, invisible, they are mental constructs about the 'unseen', and as such an important part of the cultures of the believers, and so of humankind. They are, moreover, not only expressed in behaviour, but also function as the religious institution by which spirit possession behaviour, of the mediums as well as of the other participants in a ritual, is governed, moulded and constrained. Their spirit possession beliefs determine which behaviour is proper for each of the participants. They teach them to behave in deferent ways – fitting the various roles participants have to play in a spirit possession ritual – and to avoid deviant acts. Spirit possession beliefs can, therefore, also be studied as a religious institution. In addition, scholars can investigate how that institution, its rituals as well as beliefs were moulded by the cultures of the societies of believers in spirit possession. In like manner, they can also study the many functions, religious and especially non-religious, which the institution of spirit possession fulfils in the societies of the believers.

As will become clear from the materials presented below, spirit possession rituals may be described in a preliminary way as those public rituals in which at least one participant enters into a trance, or altered state of consciousness (ASC). That special state of mind and body is usually marked by four features. First, the person who has entered into it, is 'dissociated' to a greater or smaller degree, i.e. he or she is to a certain degree 'out of (normal) touch' with his or her social environment. Second, that person often exhibits a certain loss of muscle and motor control. Particularly in certain kinds of spirit possession, or in the early phase in a spirit possession career, he or she may be in a state of considerable bodily agitation. That state is termed *hyperkinesis*. Third, in that state, he or she is acting out a character and role that are markedly different from those of his or her normal self. Finally, the person often does not remember what he or she has said or done during the period of ritual dissociation. That loss of memory is termed *amnesia*.

The trance behaviour displayed is interpreted by the other believers present as the manifestation of a spirit with the self, or character, that the 'possessed' person is acting out. He or she is the 'medium' of that spirit for the believers by the very fact of his or her acting out the 'personality' of a spirit in a state of dissociation from that person's normal self. They infer from that behaviour that a particular spirit is present among them, and communicating with them. The 'medium' displays numerous marked changes in his or her face, voice, body language, attire and actions during the period of the trance. By means of these clues in the behaviour of the possessed person, the believers identify which 'spirit' is present among them in the body, and through the mind, of the 'medium'. These clues are traditional in a society, and the believers readily recognize and interpret them. The possessed person, therefore, displays 'coded behaviour'. However wild and uncontrolled the behaviour of the 'possessed' may seem to Western observers, mediums always display the behaviour that is prescribed by their role in the possession ritual. Not only the believers, but also observers can verify that the 'possessed' person displays a personality other than his or her own. They can also establish that the faithful interpret it as the behaviour of the possessing 'spirit' from the way the believers behave towards the 'medium' during his or her 'possession'. That behaviour is clearly different from the one they direct towards him or her outside the ritual, when that person is not possessed and displays his or her own normal self.

Four elements have now been identified which can all be empirically investigated. They are, first, the public character of spirit possession rituals. Second, the hyperkinetic character of the trance behaviour of the 'medium'. Third, the coded behaviour displayed by the 'possessed' person from which the other participants infer that such and such a spirit is now among them. And finally, the beliefs of a society that spirits take possession of humans. Or, spirit possession is the public religious ritual in which the trance of a 'medium' is taken to signify that a meta-empirical being is present among the believers.

The task of scholars of religions investigating the empirical elements of spirit possession may now be summarized as follows. It consists in the accurate description of, first, the public ritual actions which believers perform on account of their beliefs, and second, of the meanings which spirit possession beliefs have for the believers who entertain them – without pronouncing on their truth or falsity. Third, showing how spirit possession beliefs function as an institution that assigns specific roles to specific believers and governs, moulds and constrains the role behaviour of each of them. Fourth, studying how a spirit possession event affects the state of mind, and the behaviour of the 'possessed' person(s) during the ritual. Fifth, researching how the culture of the participants (which includes their religion) has shaped these beliefs and rituals. And finally, investigating how they affect the relationships between the members of these societies.

Where may spirit possession be found?

Spirit possession, defined in this way, is found in virtually all religions of humankind from earliest times until now, from the religions of the bands of food gatherers since Neolithic times to the most modern religions of today. Its forms, and to a lesser degree its belief contents, show an amazing diversity. Important varieties of spirit possession are indicated by special labels. Some of them are shamanism (Arctic, Siberian and other), prophetic movements (e.g. in ancient Israel and several in other times and places), mantic oracles and dansomaniac cults in Mediterranean religions (ancient, medieval and modern), and *zar* and *bori* cults in Africa. Others are the many exorcist rituals (e.g. Buddhist, Christian, and Muslim) by which 'evil gods', 'demons', 'devils' and *jinn* are expulsed; spiritism and spiritualism; certain forms of ritual healing; glossolalia in Pentecostal and charismatic varieties of Christianity (see Goodman 1972; Samarin 1972; Malony *et al.* 1985); and channelling in New Age religions (e.g. MacLaine 1984). No less varied are its functions: apart from religious and cosmological functions they have psycho-hygienic, therapeutic, socio-structural, political, economic, and several other functions (much of this is surveyed in Lewis 1989).

The place spirit possession has in religions varies greatly. In most small-scale societies and their pre-literate, or indigenous, religions, spirit possession has, or had, a central position. It has been, and is, practised frequently in them, and is regarded as a normal and approved way of communication with 'the spirits'. It provides mediums at times with the option of an interesting career, income and influence. Spirit possession holds this central place in these religions, because these religions habitually practise ongoing communication with the 'world of the spirits'. They do so, because their believers are in constant need of revelations, of the pragmatic kind that will assist them, they hope, in improving the quality of their lives and warding off the disease, disaster, dissent, death and other evils that threaten their lives. Therefore, they regularly practise spirit possession, and other rituals, such as divination. They have, so to speak, an 'open channel' to the supernatural.

The missionary religions of Buddhism, Christianity, and Islam, however, have relegated spirit possession to a marginal place. They are in the habit of attempting to banish it from their congregations altogether, for three reasons. The first is that spirit possession, as a process of ongoing revelation of the pragmatic kind, does not sit well with their exclusivist soteriological claims. They base these on a Scripture that is held to contain the complete, unique, once-and-for-ever revelation, to which nothing may be added and from which nothing may be subtracted. That 'revelation' is, moreover, directed at 'eternal salvation', and not at well-being in this life. The second reason is that they regard spirit possession as the superstition of ignorant folk believers. They attempt to banish it by presenting possession in the theological terms of an absolute moral, and even cosmological, dualism. They represent spirit possession as believers being captured against their will by evil spirits, gods, demons and devils that seek the eternal perdition of the believers, and therefore, as an unmitigated evil, that can be overcome only by conquering and driving them out. Having been demonized, spirit possession, therefore, took the form of exorcisms in these religions: the evil spirit, devil, or *jinn*, etc., had not only to be thrown out from the possessed person, but also banned from the community of believers (from the Greek: *exorcizoo*, 'to ban beyond the borders'). The third reason is that they see 'possession by the devil' as radically different from, and squarely opposed to, the rituals of dissociation of which they approve. They are, in Buddhism, the disciplining of the mind in meditation through which enlightenment is sought. In Islam, they are the ecstatic experiences of (personal and/or collective) unification with 'God' in Sufi *dzikr* rituals and the dances of the dervishes. And in Christianity, they are the 'speaking in tongues' (glossolalia), and other ecstatic experiences, in the Pentecostal and Charismatic movements in mainly first-century and twentieth-century Christianity.

Finally, this demonizing of spirit possession by Christianity has made the general public and scholars with little knowledge of indigenous societies and religions in modern Western societies regard spirit possession as weird, occult, strange, 'primitive' and repulsive. Westerners habitually see spirit possession as a symptom of mental instability and even insanity, and are inclined to account for it in terms of psychopathology. Western psychiatrists in particular and psychologists have a long tradition of regarding it as the nervous disorder of hysteria, because mainly women were found to suffer from it in Europe in the nineteenth century. More recently, they regarded it as some other form of psychic lability, or as a folk ritual means to forestall, or cure, mental illness.

How may spirit possession be studied?

An example of the latter is the psychiatric theory of Walker that spirit possession rituals provide mediums with an opportunity for 'regression in the service of the ego'. During the time of the rituals, mediums relinquish, she says, control over their minds to a subsystem of their minds which hallucinates and recalls 'repressed material', i.e. the representations about the possessing 'spirit' and the clues about how to act its role. By thus using 'the [fictive] gods' as objects of transference for past traumas, mediums would gain improved control over themselves, and restore their mental health or maintain its balance (Walker 1972, 33–9, 154).

Other theories have been developed in the past few decades to account for spirit possession, or for certain aspects of it. Anthropologists, as social scientists, have mainly studied spirit possession as the ritual interaction between the medium and the other participants by means of which not only religious, but also important social, economic, political and other processes are transacted. An important example of this is the theory of the British social anthropologist I.M. Lewis. He distinguishes between 'central' and 'peripheral' forms of spirit possession. The former serve to legitimate and maintain the existing public (political and moral) order of a society, i.e. to keep the powerful in power, and to increase the wealth of the rich. The latter are found in far greater numbers. They flourish also in the major missionary religions of Buddhism (e.g. Kapferer 1991), Christianity (e.g. Goodman 1981; 1988, 52–63, 79–122) and Islam (see references in Lewis 1986, 1989 to *jinn*, *zar*, and *bori* cults). They serve as the rather ineffective means by which some of those situated in the periphery of a society in terms of prestige, privileges and pay, i.e. the poor and women, try to shift the uneven balance of power and possessions a little bit in their favour. As such, they are cults of protest and the religions of the deprived (Lewis 1989, 59–116; also Lewis 1986, 23–50. On Lewis, see Morris 1987, 231–3). Lewis argues that in a way that is true even of central possession cults: they are found in societies in which instability prevails because of acute external pressures, e.g. from the ecology (1989, 29–30).

Spirit possession usually takes the form of dramatic, expressive rituals with a great deal of role acting by the possessed and, in response, the congregation. They may, therefore, also be interpreted as discourses in which the identities, statuses, duties and aspirations of certain persons, or groups of persons, in a society are expressed, maintained, developed or reconstructed, especially those of the selves of the persons 'possessed'. Spirit possession discourses use the rich symbolic means which the spirit possession idiom offers for these purposes. Spirit possession then functions as a means for the 'possessed' and other participants to imagine themselves, to act out their problems, to comment, in often provocative ways, on issues they would not comment on in their ordinary selves, and to voice demands they would not, or could not, make themselves. In brief, they serve for the possessed and the congregation as a means of achieving some pre-theoretic awareness of their particular situation (usually a stressful subordinate one) in their societies, allowing them to reflect on it by means of the drama, symbol and story of spirit possession, and thereby reformulate it metaphorically. Janice Boddy (1989) has presented such a discourse analysis of a *zar* possession cult group of women in a village in Northern Sudan.

As spirit possession rituals are often performed to cure diseases, or to provide protection against the 'spiritual' agents that are believed to cause diseases and other misfortunes, the therapeutic function of spirit possession rituals may also be given special attention (ter Haar 1992).

The most distinctive part of spirit possession is, however, the trance into which the medium enters in order to serve as the vehicle and mouthpiece of some (postulated) intelligent being from a 'realm' other than our empirical one. The psychological and cultural mechanisms by which that altered state of consciousness may be achieved, and the marks of that state itself, demand neuro-biological and psychological analysis and interpretation. The studies of this crucial aspect of spirit possession are, however, as yet very few. The neurobiology and psychology of ASCs (altered states of consciousness) and trance have been dealt with by Ludwig and Lex (Ludwig 1967, 1968, 1972; Lex 1976, 1978, 1979).

Finally, spirit possessions rituals may be analysed as processes of (presumed) communication between humans and unseen beings, for the faithful believe that the unseen beings get in touch with them by taking possession of one, or several, of them. As with empirical communication between humans – and also between them and their pets and other domestic animals, and between all animals that live in groups structured by social relationships – the postulated communication between believers and possessing spirits cannot take place in a social void. It presupposes a postulated network of pre-existing relationships, or community, between those believers and the unseen beings that take possession, or may take possession, of some of them. That network serves as the field, or arena, within which the actual processes of communication take place, and as the institution by which they are governed and constrained. This may be studied in what I call the network or field analysis of the process of communication in a spirit possession ritual, as I will show below. Network analysis must be complemented by the analysis of the actual process of the (postulated) communication in what I call process analysis. It analyses not only the flow of the process, the content of the communication, the symbolic means used to convey the messages, but also several other elements, such as those relating to the time when, and the place where the ritual took place, who took the initiative in it, etc.

To these two analyses must be added the context analysis, in which the various contexts of a spirit possession ritual are examined: the geographical, historical, cultural, political, economic, etc., but also that of the entire religion of the society. Their purpose is to investigate how that ritual has been shaped by them, and how it presently functions in them. To these three, finally, an analysis of the trance of the 'possessed' must be added. It examines the means by which the trance was induced; how deep was it; whether there was hyperkinesis and/or amnesia; how the relationship between the possessing spirit and the possessed person began; with what status did it endow the possessed in his, or her, community?; what profits or suffering did it bring to the medium?; what ends did it serve?, etc. As is clear from the above, spirit possession is a very complex phenomenon that needs to be studied from many angles by quite a number of different disciplines.

The setting

The following discussion relates to the Bono of the forested coastal region of West Africa. In 1980 the Bono, or Brong, were an Akan society of some 520,000, with Takyiman (also Techiman) as its capital, in the Brong-Ahafo region of the modern state of Ghana. They are one of the fifteen different ethnic groups of Southern Ghana that speak a dialect of the large Akan language. The largest are the Asante (often written as Ashanti) in the interior, who speak Twi, and the Fante on the coast, who speak Fante. These Akan societies were not only a linguistic, but also a cultural unity because they all had an identical matrilineal social structure, political organization, and religion (see Platvoet 1982). I present data concerning a ritual that took place in 1921, therefore I use the past tense.

Rattray's request for a god

Robert Sutherland Rattray (1881–1938), who spoke Asante-Twi fluently, was government anthropologist in the Crown Colony of the Gold Coast from 1921 to 1930. (On Rattray, see Platvoet 1982, 57–68; von Laue 1975 and 1976; there is also an unpublished biography of Rattray by Machin.) He came to Bono-Takyiman in early May 1922, partly because he had been told often that much of the culture, religion and institutions of the Asante had originated there, but mainly because he had been told it was 'the home of the gods – and the factory, so to speak, of their shrines' (Rattray 1923, 146, 172). New gods were usually 'born' in an Akan town by a long process of incorporation into human society, which began, it was thought, by a new god seizing its future medium in a violent and mute possession, consisted mainly in that god and its medium being trained for a number of years until the god had been taught how to 'work' properly among men, and ended by it being installed ritually in its own shrine (*yawa*, brass pan), being given a residence, and being 'fitted out' with its means of divination and its 'medicines'. But gods might also be imported from elsewhere (see Platvoet 1973, 32–5). After Bono's incorporation into Asante, the fame of Tano – the river and god who was regarded as the 'first born' (*piesie*) son of creator god Nyame, and as the most senior god of the Akan pantheon – spread far and wide. Many Asante towns had sent delegations to the village Tanoboase ('Under Tano's Rock'), the 'spiritual capital' of Bono-Takyiman, to request that the priests of Tano produce an *atano*, 'son of Tano', for them and allow them to install him, i.e. his *yawa*, 'shrine', in their town. Shrines of *atano* gods had thus spread throughout the Akan region.

Rattray wished to witness the production of a new *atano* god. In addition, he meant to obtain an authentic *yawa* for himself. He had just been informed that he would be in charge of the sections on the Gold Coast in the forthcoming World Exhibition at Wembley in London in 1924. His pet project was to obtain permission from priests of an *atano* god that he be allowed to take a shrine of a 'son of Tano' with him to Europe in order to put it on show there, in an imitation Akan *bosombuw* ('temple'), as an authentic example of Akan culture and religion. Rattray had been encouraged to conceive this bold plan because the priest of the most important *omanbosom* ('state-god') of Bono-Takyiman, Taa Mensa Keseè, (Tano's 'third son', *miensa*, 'the great', *keseè*), had been inclined to permit that a shrine of a son of his god be made for Rattray (Rattray 1923, 172). But he was hesitant to allow him to take it to Europe. So Rattray decided to take his project to the highest level and to put it before the priest of Tano himself, Kofi Duro, the *ohene* ('leader') of Tanoboase.

He arrived at Tanoboase in the afternoon of Thursday, 4 May 1922. He put his request before the priest that very evening. His plea was strongly supported by his two Asante friends who accompanied him on this trip, and by the priest of Taa Keseè. Kofi Duro and his elders answered that this request was too extraordinary for them to grant or refuse. Only Tano himself could permit it. They informed Rattray also that the next day was a *Fofie*, 'Court Friday', the day in the 42-day Akan 'month' (cf. Bartle 1978) on which Tano was to be welcomed back in his temple after an absence of six days for his monthly 'retreat for prayers'. They would put the request before him first thing next morning.

That night a violent rainstorm broke over Tanoboase. A tree just outside the room in which Rattray slept was struck, the lighting splitting it from top to bottom, without, however, charring it (Rattray 1923, 176).

The possession rite

In the early morning of 5 May 1922, Rattray, his two companions and the priest of Taa Mensa Keseè were met by Kofi Duro, who was clad in a white cloth, and some six Tanoboase men in the courtyard of the temple of Tano. They entered the 'room of the gods' (*bosomdan*) barefoot. Most bared also the upper part of their body. The oblong room contained the shrines of Tano and eight of his 'sons', and five *apunnua*, 'black stools'. The wide and flat one of Tano stood on top of a raised, cloth-covered altar in the far corner in the right-hand part of the room (see Rattray's photographs and descriptions, Rattray 1923, 172–7, Figs. 74–8). Just below it were the smaller and slightly higher ones of Ateakosea and Taa Kwasi Kramo (the

'Muslim'). In the 'court' of Tano at Tanoboase, Ateakosea was believed to serve as Tano's *okeyame* ('speaker'), and Taa Kwasi Kramo as *kyidomhene*, 'commander of the rear of the army'. In Tano's absence, he 'ruled' the 'court'. The shrines of Tano's other six 'sons' stood, each on his own *akonnua*, 'stool', on the floor of the temple along the long rear wall to left of the altar, opposite the entrance to the room. Along the short wall at the rear in the left-hand part of the room stood the blackened stools of four predecessors in office of Kofi Duro, and that of a deceased *obaapanyin*, female elder.

Kofi Duro and his followers seated themselves on their low stools (*nkonnua*), or on the floor, in the right-hand part of the room, in front of the shrine of Tano. Rattray and his three followers did likewise in the left-hand part of the room, in front of the five blackened stools. A cloth was spread out between these two group in front of the six shrines of the 'sons' of Tano. One man from the group of Kofi Duro came forward, placed his stool in the centre of the cloth, and, facing the entrance, sat himself on it. The shrine of Ateakosea was now uncovered. A carrying pad, of twisted cloth, was taken from the altar and handed to Kofi Duro. He spat on it, pressed it to his forehead and breast and passed it under his left knee. Then he handed it to the man who sat on the stool in the centre of the room as a commission to 'carry the god', i.e. to serve as the medium of Ateakosea in this session of the consultation of Tano. The man set his heels firmly on the cloth, straightened his back, and put the pad on his head. The shrine of Ateakosea was at once put on his head. The medium sat perfectly motionless, holding a *bodua*, tail switch as a sign of his commission. An intense and deep silence reigned in the room.

In this silence, an old man with reddish hair and light complexion, who was seated between Kofi Duro and the medium, addressed in a soft voice, as the *okyeame*, 'speaker' or 'mouthpiece', of Kofi Duro, a prayer, full of praises and historical allusions, to Tano (see Rattray 1923, 178–9 for the Twi text and Rattray's translation; see also Platvoet 1983, 205–6, 214–15, for my analysis of this prayer). He ended the prayer with the request: 'Today is Court-Friday, and we wish to see your face; Therefore, come and listen to what we have to discuss with you.'

A minute of deep silence followed. Everyone in the room sat intensely alert. Their breathing could be heard. Then the medium began to twitch all over his body and to slap the side of the shrine on his head with the flat of his right hand. At once, all present, in one voice, greeted the god: *Nana, makye oo*, 'Grandfather, good morning'.

The priest with the red hair now addressed the priest of Taa Keseè and requested that he, as *okyeame*, spokesman, of Rattray, state the request to be put before Tano. The priest of Taa Keseè rose. Addressing the twitching medium, who now held the *bodua* between his teeth, he related that Rattray had come to visit the great Taa Koraa ('Preserver'), because he, Rattray, knew that Tano was the greatest of the gods, and also because he hoped that Taa Koraa would permit the priests of Tanoboase to construct the shrine of a 'son of Tano' for him. He knew well how they were made (Rattray 1923, 145–50), but had never actually witnessed the consecration of a shrine. If his request were permitted, Rattray would leave it to the discretion of the priests of Tano whether or not he could take the shrine with him to Europe.

The medium, quivering more spasmodically now with his heels on the cloth and still slapping the side of the shrine on his head with the flat palm of his right hand, took the *bodua*, switch, from his mouth into his left hand. Then he called out the names of the spokesmen of Kofi Duro and Rattray, and said that he had always come to the aid of the kings of Asante when they were in need of his help. But they never asked that he present them with one of his children. Being Taa Koraa, the Preserver, he was not an *akoraa*, an 'old man', who let things get spoiled. If Rattray had come to ask for help, he could, and would, have assisted him. But he could not present him with one of his sons.

The medium then paused for a moment. Then he added that he, Tano, granted permission that Rattray visit him 'in the [cave] where I live', and that he sprinkle himself with water from the source of the River Tano. He added that he had no quarrel with his many 'children and grandchildren' who went to school and now served God in the Christian way, but asserted that he was himself 'in truth a child of God'. He finished by saying: 'If my grandchildren say that the white European says that he loves me and has drawn near to me, then I will protect him also' (see Rattray 1923, 180–1; Platvoet 1983, 207).

After a brief pause, Rattray rose and said in Asante-Twi that he had understood the words of Taa Koraa. He thanked him for the permission to visit Tano in his cave and at the source of the river. He also complimented him on his liberal attitude to the Christian religion. It was, he said, as liberal as that of the English, who allowed freedom in matters of religion to all men. In school, the children would be taught about God, but that God, he said, was no other than Nyame, the creator whom the Akan had known and worshipped since long before the Europeans came to this country. When Rattray had finished, the priest of Taa Keseè repeated his words in Bono-Twi.

To this the medium answered: *Me da mo ase*, 'I thank you [all]'. Then he said: *Me kotenase*, 'I am going to sit down', a set formula for announcing the end of a consultation. The shrine of Ateakosea was removed from his head. The medium shook the pad from it. Kofi Duro and his *okyeame* closely watched how it fell to the ground. From the side it showed, they concluded, that Tano had indeed ended the consultation. The medium sat dazed for a few moments meanwhile, then passed his hand over his face as if he awoke from sleep. He later told Rattray that he had no recollection of what he had said and done during the trance.

In conclusion

In this conclusion, I distil a few important points for the study of religions, rituals and spirit possession from the particularities of this event by means of (elements from) the network, process, context, and trance analyses, which I set out in the first part of this article. But I make first a more general point.

It is clear from this spirit possession ritual that the Western analytical dichotomy of the 'supernatural', or 'spiritual', *versus* the empirical, or 'material' is not substantiated by the Akan religion. It cannot be applied, for the two, although conceptually distinct for the Akan also, were at the same time conceived by them as not only continuous realms but also as substantially overlapping, intermingling, and often even as identical. In Akan traditional religion Nyame is the (unseen) creator-god as well as the visible sky, and descends on earth as rain to become rivers and lakes. Tano, likewise, is both his 'eldest son', the greatest of the Akan *atano* gods, and *obomuhene*, 'king inside the rock', as well as that rock, the source of the River Tano, and the River Tano (Rattray 1923, 183–6, 191–2; Platvoet 1983, 208–11).

More important than 'being' a river or a rock, however, is that the usual hierarchy between the 'supernatural' and the 'natural' is inverted. For Akan religion the gods in nature must be 'tamed' by being immersed in, and restrained by, five additional, man-made forms that make them not only more visible, but also *fiebosom*, 'house gods', i.e. part of human society, easily addressable and even consumable. These five forms are: his medium-priest (*okomfo*) for meeting with people; his shrine (*yawa*) and shrine room (*bosomdan*) or 'temple' (*bosombuw*) for receiving their prayers and gifts of libation, food, and sacrifices; and also its means of divination (*nsuo Yaa*) and 'medicines' (*nnuru*) for assisting them in their problems in life (see Warren 1974). Only as part of the networks that constitute society are the gods manageable and trustworthy, to a degree.

Network analysis

That brings me to network analysis. Space does not permit that a full network analysis is made. I will only indicate one striking general feature, namely, that the network governing this ritual is isomorph with the hierarchical institution that is typical for this Akan society and governs other domains of it.

Rattray's consultation of Tano was pervasively structured after the institution central to Akan society: the king and his court. Three 'rulers' – Tano, Kofi Duro, and Rattray – were present in Tano's temple at Tanoboase, each with his own 'court'. As was proper to Akan 'kings', they communicated through their spokesmen (*akyeame*). Ateakosea was believed to have taken possession of the medium and to speak as the *alter ego* of Tano, the 'king within the rock'. The priest with the red hair acted as spokesman on behalf of Kofi Duro, *ohene* of Tanoboase. And the priest of Taa Keseè did so when he put forward the request of Rattray. As government anthropologist, he was clearly perceived as a highly placed representative of *aban*, the colonial government (Platvoet 1983, 211–14). Akan spirit possession of this kind fits in well with the general traits and sociological functions which I.M. Lewis postulated for 'central spirit possession' (1989, 29–30, 114–59). More recent Akan types of spirit possession, many of them imported from non-Akan areas, are not, or in a very limited degree, integrated into the Akan traditional political system (see Platvoet 1973). They belong to the other major type distinguished by Lewis, 'peripheral spirit possession' (1989, 27–31, 59–113).

Significantly, it was Rattray who offended against the rules of this institution by responding himself to Tano's 'decisions'. His response showed him also as the outsider in this ritual: he was permitted to speak himself, for, say the Akan, 'the stranger does not break laws' (*ohoho nto mmara*). (For Twi proverbs on the position of the 'stranger', *ohoho*, in Akan societies, see Akrofi n.d., 82–3). His position in this event was an anomalous one. On the one hand, the Bono had already nicknamed him *oburoni okomfo*, 'the white [traditional] medium-priest [of an Akan god]', because of his exceptional interest in traditional religion (Rattray 1923, 152), and he participated in this ritual as a (more or less) sincere supplicant to Tano. On the other hand, he was distinctively present also as an officer of high rank in the colonial government, who did the job they had commissioned him to do and had the full backing of the local DC (District Commissioner). As such, he was even the person with the greatest power present. Conflicting and contradictory hierarchies, traditional as well as colonial, were therefore shaping, constraining and, to some degree, confusing this communication event. It is significant that the priest of the state-god (*omanbosom*) Taa Keseé, and a resident of the political capital Takyiman, acted as Rattray's *okyeame* and had already assented to the request which Tano refused.

Process analysis

Here also no full analysis can be made. Process analysis is concerned with a ritual as a communicative event, and with the business transacted in it. In a spirit possession event, the communication is normally of the dialogical type, for it is believed that the spirit is present, can be 'addressed' 'face-to-face', and can respond by virtue of it 'possessing' the medium. Rattray's consultation of the god Tano is an excellent example of this dialogical conversation, be it that Tano, as Akan court etiquette demanded, did not speak himself but spoke through his 'mouthpiece', Ateakosea.

Context analysis

Here again I have to be very selective. A major subject to be studied in context analyses is what 'secular' (i.e. social, political, economic, etc.) functions spirit possession rituals or events have in the society of the particular time and place in which they are enacted.

The context of the ritual consultation of Tano on behalf of Rattray on Friday 5 May 1922 was that the Bono religious and political establishment with whom Rattray was negotiating before and during this event, was clearly internally divided, and not able, nor willing, to stage war, ritual or real, to regain full internal solidarity and cohesion. Moreover, the British colonial governments in West Africa were actively pursuing the policy of the Dual Mandate, of governing subject peoples through their own traditional rulers – often the puppets that had won the contest for the throne because they had the backing of the colonial authorities. The Bono political establishment at the capital, Bono-Takyiman, represented in this matter by the *okomfo* of Taa Keseè, the state-god, was quite subservient and willing to accommodate nearly every wish of Rattray, precisely because he was a high-ranking officer in the colonial government.

Context analysis also pays attention to elements in the context (ecological, economic, historical, etc.) of a spirit possession ritual which exert an important influence on its morphology or content. Such contexts may be endogenous and have shaped and constrained the ritual for a long time, or exogenous and have begun only recently to have an effect on a ritual, or more often, to produce new varieties of it. Of the former, examples have already been mentioned above, such as the court model in the consultation of Tano.

Of the latter, one example may be pointed out, that of the collusion between the colonial government of the Gold Coast and the Christian missions. By 1920, colonial rule was securely established, and a transformation of the economy under way. It offered new opportunities for many people, but on the condition that they had received some formal schooling. Education began to be massively offered by Christian missions at that time with the full backing of, but only limited financial assistance from, the colonial government. The several Christian missions were, however, quite eager to foot the bill for the schools (hospitals, and other means of modernization), for they were eager to use them as means for initiating mass 'conversion' to Christianity by offering literacy and the Christian religion in one package deal. The priests at Tanoboase were aware of these developments, as is clear from Tano's remarks on the shifting religious allegiances.

For broader discussion of Christian missions in Africa, see for Ghana, Platvoet 1979, 566–75; for Sub-Saharan Africa, see Platvoet 1996, 61–2; 1999. See also Platvoet 1996, 55–7 on the theory of Robin Horton (1971) and (1975) that the large numerical successes of Islam and Christianity in Africa in this century may be accounted for by the micro/macro shift in cosmology brought about by the colonization of Africa. It caused the limited space and time world of the 'African village world' to expand into the globalizing world of the colonial empires.

Trance analysis

I point to only two remarkable elements here. The first has to do with memory. The medium of Ateakosea 'suffered' *amnesia*. Loss of memory of what he had said and done was not merely a neurological event, but also a culturally conditioned, 'normal' trait in Akan possession. It served to strengthen the belief that mediums were 'really' possessed; and it exculpated them, and in this case also the priests of Tanoboase, from the unpleasant elements in the 'messages' they conveyed. Not only did amnesia strengthen belief, it was also a strategy for concealing the power, political and other, which the medium actually had and used.

The second has to do with entering into trance. The consultation of Tano was exceptional in that the medium of Ateakosea did not rely on otherwise common means for entering into public hyperkinetic dissociation, i.e. fierce, monotonous sonic drive of drumming, clapping, singing, rattles strapped onto stamping feet; the photic drive of the flames of dance fires; or even the exertion of the heavy dancing. Rather, it relied on cultural expectation, to wit that it was 'normal' for mediums to enter that altered state of consciousness under these ritual conditions. Instead of sonic and photic drive, the silence of intense expectation and the dignified quiet of diplomatic conversation reigned during the consultation of the Preserver and King-inside-the-Rock (Tano Taa Kora *Obomuhene*). In addition, the hyperkinetic state of his body did not prevent him from securely balancing the shrine of Ateakosea upon his head throughout the rite.

Part II
Powers

6. *Mana* and *tapu*: Sacred knowledge, sacred boundaries

Peter J. Mataira

Io ki te Atua, Atua ki te tipuna,
Tipuna ki te matua, Matua ki Au,

Au ki te whanau, Whanau ki te hapu,
Hapu ki iwi, Iwi ki te Ao,
Ao ki Io.

From the Creator derives the Gods, from the Gods derives my ancestors,
From my ancestors derives my parents, from my parents derives me,

I am a product of my family, my family is a product of my sub-tribe,
My sub-tribe is a product of my tribe, and my tribe a product of the world,
The world shaped by the Creator.

Life, to the Maori, is predicated on the understanding of connectedness, that all things have rhythm, shape and form, and are woven and patterned together in a pre-determined design created in the heavens. The traditions of the Maori embrace the acceptance that chaos and change, order and stability are conjoint processes held in tension by the existence of each other. Life as such is bound to the dynamic of shifting states between sacred and ordinary. Here the encompassing exchange of energies unleashes to create both potential and possibility. This process is called *wheiao*, which is the compelling paradox of nature's patterned movement.

Wheiao is the state between dark and light. This is a universal term used to describe the transitional condition between polar states: birth and death, night and day, sacred and profane, pleasure and pain. This is illustrated in Figure 6.1.

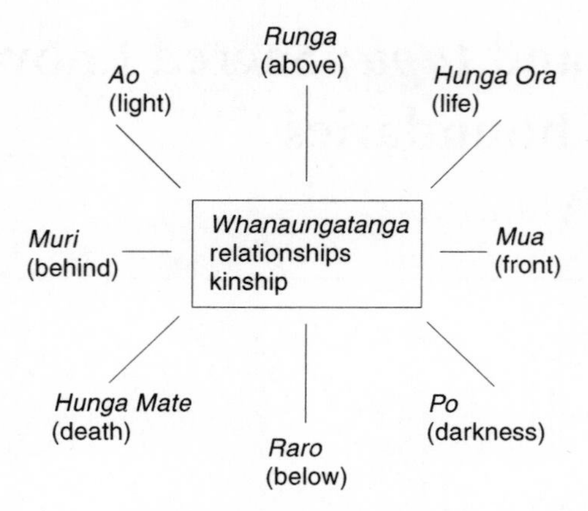

Figure 6.1 The concentric dualism of Maori thinking. Source: After Kawharu (1980).

The relational worldview of the Maori: 'Everything is connected'

The notion of movement, in and out of states, is indeed a profound and revealing understanding of the Maori world. A view that sees life as systemic, suggesting it ebbs and flows, forever evolving, seeking, re-balancing and moving (Spencer 1882) to exalted forms of order. It is through seeking, through human quest towards enlightenment along *te ara poutama*, that purpose and meaning are discovered. Maori understood the theoretical idea of dissipative structures by watching nature create, destroy and recreate herself. Illya Prigogine (1984) discovered the tendencies of non-equilibrium structures to fluctuate and dissipate as they propel away from a balanced state to reconstituting higher states of order. In her work with Maori concepts and ideas Dreardon (1997) developed a model fusing infinity and direction, *Awhiowhio-poutama*. This model constructed life around patterns of spirals, *awhiowhio,* and progression, *poutama*, in the transforming of sacred states. Her contention was that life is complex and dissipative, but above all, about developing strength from strength.

What is known and understood relating to the realms of the Universe and Humanity is, for Maori, explicated in terms of this connectedness. This is not contradictory as Maori consider life is not *in-itself* but *of-itself*. The Hegelian philosophical view of truth as an absolute whole shares a common thread with this Maori thought.

As an example, the World of Light (Earth) is not defined without reference to the World of Darkness (the Underworld); as such, life is not explained without understanding death; foresight is meaningless without hindsight. Life is in constant transformation and therefore connected to a greater profound pattern. It is arguable that 'science' and 'technology' cannot explain natural order without acknowledgement of its sacredness. Scholars and philosophers throughout the decades have all but pondered the fundamental question: Is God real? In order to contemplate the nature of God's existence, I believe it is necessary to examine the meaning and significance of *mana* and *tapu* within the traditional Maori context of spiritual power and authority.

> *Te Ara Poutama*: the stairway patterned into the side panels of the meeting-house, it represents the pathway to the heavens, towards knowledge and enlightenment.

Mana

It is important to stress that there are no words within the English language that fully reflect the essence and meaning of terms like *mana* and *tapu* (Pere 1991), and it is perhaps because of this that their definitive understanding may never be fully realized outside of the Maori world. However, for comparative purposes only, *mana* is similar to the English term, *charisma*. Maori understood the exceptional qualities of outstanding leaders in traditional society as ascribed through the predominance of aristocracy. They accorded due respect to those with such gifts and abilities (Webster 1979).

Weber defined charisma in part as: 'a certain quality of an individual personality, by virtue of which he [sic] is set apart from ordinary men and treated as endowed with supernatural, superhuman, or at least specifically exceptional powers or qualities' (1966, 358–9).

In his authoritative account, *Maori and the Universe*, Maori Marsden, a respected Maori *kaumatua* and scholar, qualified this further by referring to *mana* as the 'lawful permission delegated by the Gods to their human agents and accompanied by the endowment of spiritual power to act on their behalf and in accordance with their revered will' (1992, 119). According to this view, *mana* is defined in terms of an outcome of being directly descended of the Gods and the Universe.

The Creator gives spiritual authority to all things. This tells us that all things originate, genealogically, from the Gods. Marsden argues that since knowledge of the authority of the Gods is a treasured gift, *he taonga tuku iho*, humans remain by virtue of *whakapapa* under their dominion.

Inherent in this understanding is the acceptance that we are not the source of *mana*, but that this is given to us by the Gods. And as we are the youngest, *teina*, of the descendants in the *whakapapa* chart, our older deity siblings, *tuakana*, remain eternal.

Kaumatua refers to respected elders who act as spokespersons on the *marae* or at special occasions on behalf of a family, sub-tribe or tribe. They are the storehouses of traditional knowledge and protectors over families. In my particular tribe, Ngatiporou, where women have equal speaking rights, *kaumatua* refers to both respected men and women. Other Maori *iwi*, tribal groups, prohibit women from this role.

Whakapapa refers to the genealogical descent of all things from the Gods to the present time. *Whakapapa* means 'to lay one thing upon another'.

Marae commonly refers to the courtyard in front of the meetinghouse, including all other buildings associated with the tribal ancestors whose names are carried on the main buildings. The *marae* is a symbol of a tribal identity and solidarity and a common social and cultural gathering place.

Tapu

Tapu is perhaps understood most clearly in the use of the biblical term 'holy' or 'sacred'. It is possessed of both religious connotations and legal requirements. According to Henare (1988), *tapu* is a social-psychological state, of which *mana* is the manifestation.

Religious and legal elements of tapu

Tapu relates to the dedication of a person, place or thing to the God(s) concerned and by this arrangement are set apart for the exclusive purpose of use by a particular God. This process transcends the dedicated individual or thing from the world of the profane to that of the sacred, and, in so doing, is exalted to a 'higher order'. In this sacred station, profane use constitutes sacrilege and a violation of the law of *tapu*. It is this sacrosanct 'untouchableness' that lies at the heart of *tapu* (Marsden 1992).

The legal component of *tapu* is connected with the contractual relationship existing between human subjects and the Gods. This concerns the service we, as agents, render to the Gods, and, in reciprocation, the protection we receive against malevolent forces of evil.

It is said that the Gods also gave us the power to manipulate the environment appropriately for the purpose of meeting our needs. This understanding is premised on the view that four orders of reality exist (and must continue to exist): the physical/natural world, *te taha tinana*, the psychic world, *te taha hinengaro*, the spiritual world, *te taha wairua*, and the familial world, *taha whanau*. These interrelated orders require balance and maintenance throughout the cycles and challenges of life. They are in constant flux moving between states of balance and imbalance. To ignore or damage them in any way is to place oneself and one's family in peril. These orders are important to understanding the 'wholistic', connected thinking of Maori, and are therefore vital in this discussion of *mana* and *tapu*.

Te taha tinana: While the natural realm is subject to physical laws, these can be affected, modified and changed by the application of the higher laws of the psychic and spiritual realms. *Taha tinana* relates to the physical realm in terms of what we see, touch, smell and taste – referring to our physical bodies and to physical presence.

Te taha hinengaro: The application of psychic laws (intellectual and emotional consciousness) in a scientific way is the manner in which humans have learnt to manipulate their environment. To understand the concept of *hinengaro* we need to understand the importance of left brain and right brain activity. Maori accord functioning of the right brain to that of the God Tumatauenga, the God of War and Man. He is the rational, analytical and logical thinker and his skill is required to live and survive in a changing, hostile world. His activity is complemented and balanced by presence of Rongomatane, the Goddess of Cultivated Foods and Peace. (Early literature depicts Rongomatane as a male deity, however authoritative Maori writers claim Rongomatane is female, see Pere 1994). She is the nurturer and peacemaker, the carer – and related to the creative and imaginative aspect of human mental processes forming the left brain. Her skills are necessary to pacify the abrogating tendencies of Tumatauenga. In this respect her quality is in procreation, nourishment and continuance (Pere 1994; Orbell 1995).

Te taha wairua: The application of spiritual law is dependent upon human co-operation with the Gods. *Taha wairua* embraces feelings, compassion, love and caring for one another. Both the spiritual and physical worlds are intricately interwoven and this is captured in the proverb: *Whiringa a nuku, whiringa a rangi*, where everything that exists here on Earth has its blueprint in the Heavens and must be completed in the realm of the ancestors.

Taha whanau. Mau e ki mai, he aha te mea nui? Maku e ki atu, he tangata, he tangata, he tangata. 'If you were to ask what is the greatest thing? I will tell you: it is people, people, people.' This signifies that people are sacred and that one does not stand or walk alone. We, as individuals, carry our families, ancestors and future generations with us throughout our lives. As members of families we are not seen in isolation from our birthright or our *whakapapa*.

Violation of sacred boundaries: Its repercussions

To the Maori the domain of spiritual power is distinct (and supervised by the Gods) and to transgress its boundaries, as delegated by Io Matua, would constitute abusing the gifts provided.

Mana is the practical force of the Gods at work in everyday life (Salmond 1991) and as such to abuse what is sacred results in the withdrawal of power, or the enraged power causing harm to whom so ever transgresses it.

Mana Atua is perhaps most sacred as it is the divine right of Io Matua to exercise supreme authority (Barlow 1993; Shirres 1994). Maori believe people have this divinity and the power to perfect themselves through the living of sound principles, honesty in their dealings, virtuousness and the acknowledging of the Creator's presence. Mana Atua recognizes absolute uniqueness of individuality (Pere 1991) and in this context cannot be attained without the sacred endowment of the authority sustained through *tapu*.

The profanation, *takatakahi*, of the laws of *tapu* incurs vengeance of the Gods and, in this context, *tapu* refers to an accursed or unclean person or thing. By this understanding, the condition of *tapu* could conceivably be transmitted through contact, through touch, trespass or association, causing contamination to others. In situations where contamination occurs through such contact, cleansing rituals are performed to allow normal life to resume.

Contamination through transgression requires the transgressor, not just to be cleansed from the pollution, but neutralized from the ill effects of the *mana* brought into action by the act of transgression. It is in this way that *tapu* is classified as accursed or unclean – a state where one's character or autonomous identity becomes subject to the invasion of demonic spiritual forces.

Because *tapu*, as a condition in which one is set apart by dedication to the Gods, removes a person from all common use, and because this is secured by sanction and reinforced through endowment, the most common cause of transgression is ignorance and one's obliviousness of this authorized, sacred, use.

As mentioned previously, to counteract the effects of transgressing *tapu*, purification rites had to be performed to cleanse and neutralize *tapu*, or to propitiate the Gods. The most common sacramental element used for this purpose is water, and in cases of propitiation, cooked food is commonly shared. The water used in purification (*Te Wai o Rehua*, the sacred water of Rehua) is dedicated to *Rehua* who resides in the tenth heaven and is said to be the God of Kindness who cures disease and is able to raise people from the dead. It is used in much the same way as in other religions.

The act of dedication is followed by consecration, that is, by the extolling of the power of the Gods. Always invoked by name, the Gods are petitioned to endow the person with *mana*. This understanding of dedication is the obligation of human subjects and its consecration is exercised by the presence of the Gods.

Since dedication is sacrificial – in the sense that it is an offering or service to the Gods – it is acknowledged that the bestowal of *mana* confirms that the terms of the contract are carried out. To ensure this, the Gods place *kaitiaki* over people or sacred sites to ensure they are protected. *Kaitiaki* manifest as birds, animals or as natural objects, like trees or rocks, and serve the purpose of warning against transgression. The *pakeha* western notions of ghosts and haunting could perhaps describe the phenomena of *kaitiaki* manifestation.

Kaitiaki are guardian spirits who watch over people and sacred places. They are messengers and a means by which we are able to communicate with the spiritworld.

Pakeha refers to non-Maori, Caucasian people living in Aotearoa New Zealand, predominantly of European descent.

Transgression and the acceptance fault

In Maori law there is no forgiveness for the deliberate transgression of the Gods. All transgression is viewed as a direct challenge to their *mana*, irrespective of circumstance. And yet, as certain as people strive to learn and understand, they continue to transgress as almost an act of predestined *fait accompli*.

Where *mana* is directly challenged, ceremonial cleansing rites, *pure whakanoa*, are initiated to neutralize and ward off the malevolent or debilitating effects (Mead 1969; Henare 1988). A good analogy would be the administering of anti-venom to the snake bite victim who transgresses the domain and *mana* of the snake. The very poison used to kill or ward off potential threat is used to counteract the victim's encounter with the deadly toxins. Knowledge is important and serves as the link not just to saving life but propagating it as well. *Pure whakanoa,* as the ritualized process to administer cures for transgression, is a vital part of the process of Maori practice in maintaining physical and spiritual well being. It has been referred to as the 'live-giving constructive influences of Maori ritual' (Pere 1991: 56) that guide us through life.

The liminal state

In our modern times, sacred rituals are still important and employed, perhaps somewhat tokenistically, in the building and construction of new edifices (roads, commercial offices, sports stadiums, schools, parks, etc.). During the development stages, new and impending structures are placed under the *mana* and *tapu* of Tane Mahuta (God of the Forests) for protection. After completion and before any site could be opened and dedicated they need to be freed from the *tapu* and *mana* of Tane. This lifting of *tapu* requires the presence of a woman (Orbell 1995). A senior woman, *kuia*, of the local tribal group, accompanied by the *tohunga* and other members of her tribe, enter into, or onto, the completed site to trample under foot, *takahi*, the *tapu* under whose *mana* the building is placed. This process is to neutralize, decontaminate and importantly to ensure the protection of all those who enter onto its consecrated space. *Takahi* also is a central feature of the funeral, *tangihanga*. Important propitiatory rites are connected with the rituals associated with the dead. Death itself comes under the jurisdiction of the Gods of the Darkness, notably that of, the Goddess, Hine-nui-te-Po.

The *tapu* of the dead is particularly virulent. A living person contracting such a *tapu* through contact has to be purified and neutralized as a matter of priority by incantation, and the cleansing and washing of the transgressor with water. This cleansing rite is a preventative measure and is today practised as a matter of due course during sacred occasions. *Pure* is based on the principle that all things are unpolluted and are the property of the deities, and they, as the regents of Io Matua, are responsible for the department of nature over which they have dominion.

Kuia: The elderly women of a family. Their status is achieved after they have passed through menopause. They have particular roles in the welcoming call of visitors onto the *marae* and in nurturing.

Tohunga: sacred experts, specialists with priesthood powers and authority given by the Gods to act on their behalf. The *tohunga* are highly regarded by the family and tribe and act in cleansing and propitiatory rites.

He mana te matauranga: Knowledge is power

To have knowledge of all things is to have power over all things. Michel Foucault (1977) contends that knowledge is power and power is knowledge as his extension of Nietzsche's *Genealogy of Morals*, work shows. Foucault believed the crucial site of power is where people are willing to subject themselves to conformity and social norms. For Foucault the inseparable nature of knowledge and power defines who and what determines decisions and outcomes. To his argument we could add that since knowledge is sacred and of the Gods, power must accordingly be imbued with *mana* and *tapu* obligations.

In search of knowledge: Tane's journey to the twelfth heaven

According to Maori tradition, three baskets of knowledge, *wananga*, were held in the highest heaven. According to legend, it was Tane Mahuta's fate to journey to the heavens to retrieve them. It is also said his feat was the greatest undertaking during the time of the Gods. The baskets were significant to the ordering of the world and contained all sacred knowledge (P.S. Smith 1913–1915) required to sustain life.

Io Matua sent messages to the sons of Ranginui (Skyfather) and Papatuanuku (Earthmother) to select one of them to visit the highest heaven to seek knowledge. Tane Mahuta, chosen among his siblings, possessed the qualities deemed necessary to enter into the heavens. Whiro-te-tipua (the God of darkness, evil and death) objected to Tane's selection on the grounds that he was senior in birth and therefore should undertake the journey towards the heavens himself. In spite of Whiro's objection, Tane departed, and angered by this, Whiro sent a horde of insects, *Tini o Poto*, to attack Tane and kill him.

Accompanied by a number of his brothers, Tane was carried upward by the family of whirlwinds *Titimatakake*. When they reached the tenth heaven, Tane's siblings left him and returned to earth. The following army of insects overtook Tane at the eleventh heaven but because of the great gales stirred on by *Titimatakake*, they were unceremoniously blown away before they could get near him.

Tane passed through the entrance to the twelfth heaven, *Pumotomoto,* situated at the top of the eleventh heaven, *Tawhirirangi*, and entered into the guardhouse. There he was received by the guardians, *whatukura*, and cleansed and purified to enter into the house called *Matangi-reia,* to stand in the presence of Io Matua. Io asked Tane what the object of his visit was, to which Tane replied he had desired to obtain the sacred baskets of knowledge. Io escorted Tane to the courtyard where he was again purified to allow him to enter into the Treasure House of *Rangiatea*, whereupon the guardians gave him the three baskets of knowledge and the two accompanying sacred stones.

The three baskets in order of priority were called:

1. *Te kete uruuru matua* (knowledge of peace, goodness and love).
2. *Te kete uruuru rangi* (knowledge of prayers, incantations and ritual).
3. *Te kete uruuru tau* (knowledge of war, evil and darkness).

Today they are commonly referred to as *te kete tua aronui*, *te kete tua uri* and *te kete tua tea*, respectively. They contained the wisdom and knowledge of all seen and unseen, with directions as to how the world should be organized. The sacred stones, having been set apart, were used for the purpose of ritual in the teaching of esoteric knowledge. These stones, one male, *whatukura*, and the other female, *mareikura*, were charged in the heavens with companies of spirits that moved throughout the twelve heavens.

The three baskets were considered *tapu* having derived from the highest heaven and were accorded stringent laws of use concerning the manner in which the earth should be arranged.

The rank and priority in which the baskets were given were predestined, and therefore *te kete tua aronui*, the basket of peace, goodness and love, outranked all other baskets, including *te kete tua tea*, the basket of war and evil. This affirmed to Tane and his siblings that people were required, above all else, to be peace-loving and humane. Maori were a warrior race and this warrior quality has prevailed throughout the generations, and today is still not lost (Belich 1986; Duff 1991) yet, it is superseded by the virtue of service and compassion.

It is understood that without the sacred knowledge of what is good, right and moral, one is none the wiser as to what is evil, demonic and immoral, nor what is required to sustain and order life. Through Ranginui and Papatuanuku's separation came the creation of life, and the manifesting principle that sacrifice is a prerequisite to exalted life (Mead 1969; Pomare and Cowan 1987). Existence has no purpose without sacrifice.

The virtue of peace is paramount and today manifests itself on the *marae* and throughout the protocols of the *marae*. Rongomatane is said to reside inside the meetinghouse where all matters are to be resolved peacefully, while out on the courtyard, battles and contestations of Tumatauenga are waged and aired before people enter the house to commence the reconciling of difference.

Te kete tua aronui also outranks *te kete tua uri,* the basket of ritual. To supersede this, it follows, is to assume that peace and goodwill are held accountable to more refined, stringent laws of *tapu*.

The interpretation of sacred knowledge within the realms of the cosmos

Kete tua uri translates literally as that knowledge which is 'beyond the world of darkness' – a world which contains the 27 nights, each spanning eons of time. Here it is acknowledged that the corporeal world as we know it stands behind the world of sense and perception. *Kete tua uri* is the seedbed of all creation where gestation, evolution and refinement of all living things are manifested in the natural world. Beyond the world of darkness is where all cosmic processes originate and operate in a complex series of rhythmical patterns of energy upholding, sustaining and replenishing life.

For us to understand the significance of the three baskets of knowledge, discussion of four essential elements is required to show how order came about on earth. These are the elements of *mauri*, *hihiri*, *mauriora* and *hauora*.

Mauri occurs early in the genealogical table and penetrates all things as that which binds them together (Marsden 1992). It is the 'bonding agent' cementing unity to diversity and sacrality to profanity. Mauri is the sole possession of Io, who makes it possible for us and all living things to move, to take shape and to live in accordance with the conditions and limitations of our own existence (Barlow 1993: 83).

Every creation, from the innate to the living, possesses *mauri* and for us, as humans of a higher order, it is said that the Creator bound our bodies and spirits together in a oneness through the presence of *mauri*.

Hihiri is described as pure energy, a refined expression of *mauri* manifesting as a form of high intensity light, an aura projected from all matter and evident in living things.

Mauriora is defined as the life principle. During the commencement of speech making, *whaikorero,* the speaker uses the opening formula, *Tehei mauriora*! *Tehei* symbolizes the sneezing sound which attracts the attention of the audience and *mauriora* represents the acknowledgement of binding all people to that place, that time and that occasion. It is the acknowledgement of the ancestors past and future who connect everyone to the present.

Hauora as 'the breath of the spirit' infuses life itself into the process. *Kete tua atea* is knowledge expressed 'beyond time and space'. It is recited in genealogical incantations that *hauora* begat shape, shape begat form, form begat space, space begat time and time begat Ranginui and Papatuanuku. This time–space genealogy develops as the framework by which the heavens and earth were formed and remain bridged. For Maori, time and space are conjoined in that the universe is finite in extent, and relative in time (Marsden and Henare 1992). This is in contrast to the realm of *kete tua uri* in which universal processes are found in the time–space void, Te Po, and set into the timeframe of Te Po. *Kete tua atea* is the realm and archetype (see Jung 1939, 1963) of Io Matua represented as eternity, omnipresent, all-encompassing and all wise. *Kete tua aronui* relates to the world before us, that which is apprehended by our senses and is passed through by each generation by *whakapapa*.

Upon Tane's return to earth, he built his first learning house, *whare wananga,* calling it *Wharekura*. He placed the baskets and sacred stones at the far end of the house. He then took governance over the earth and placed the *kaitiaki*, *Poutiriao*, at each corner of the world so that order would prevail. Whiro, enraged by Tane's success, went down to *Taheke-roa* to live with Hine-nui-te-Po and from there waged his war against Tane, against nature and against humanity in his attempts to destroy all that was created (Orbell 1995).

Although Tane's quest to the heavens was shrouded in sacred rites pertaining to *mana* and *tapu*, humanity's quest for knowledge today seems more about contesting the will to control destiny. Maori believe truth and wisdom are not solely products of intelligence, but of revelation and service to the Gods. This is recalled in a heedful statement made by my *kaumatua*, 'Scientists broke the fabric of the Universe, but can they fix it?' That is, far from the splitting of the atom molecule being a great human achievement, it is dangerous to tinker with nature and the natural order, and most of all, with things we know little about. Their point was that what is important is the putting back together again without harming the predestined patterns organized in the heavens. Marsden (1992) outlined a range of hierarchies of knowledge where higher knowledge – the preserve of the *tohunga* – is most sacred.

Maori cautioned against providing open access to those not initiated into these roles and responsibilities, and the expectations of this corpus of intellectual and spiritual knowledge. Tane's quest, however, involved not just selection, approval and courage, but also purification, ordination and sacrifice.

Foucault made a related point regarding the shift from sacred to scientific knowledge:

> The moment that saw the transition from historic-ritual mechanisms for the formation of individuality to the scientifico-disciplinary mechanisms, when the normal took over from the ancestral, and measurement from status . . . is the moment when a new technology of power and a new political anatomy of the body were implemented. (1977, 193)

For the Maori, this transition came about largely due to the influential reign of missionaries in the nineteenth century, and caused disruption and adaptations to the intrinsically held beliefs hidden deep within the fabric of social, political and spiritual discourses.

> *Te Po*: Darkness and light were separated from chaos during the creation of the world. Te Po refers to the night, representing ignorance and misfortune. From darkness came light, *Te Aomarama*, from which came Papatuanuku (Earth-mother) and Ranginui (Skyfather), our Godly parents. They were separated by Tane Mahuta to create the world and all that exists.

The colonial (mis)conception

The doctrine of early settler missionaries and British anthropologists (prior to, and following on from the signing of the 1840 Treaty of Waitangi) perpetuated two misleading views about Maori and their understanding of the psyche, cosmos and spiritworld. At the time missionary views were influential as one of their roles was to protect and mediate theological thought that established a Western theological discipline against pagan Maori beliefs.

The first misleading view was the assumption that *mana* was the manifestation of a 'positive' force pertaining to ritual enrichment, and that *tapu* was a negative consequence of transgression of a primitive understanding of the spiritual forces of nature. Conversely, however, Maori held the term *tapu* to be the sacred state of the endowed person or thing under the patronage of the Gods; and that *mana* was the endowment process through which spiritual power was given by the indwelling spirit that presided over it. The colonial view characterized an ethnocentric Christian interpretation, ignoring the fact that Maori had a sophisticated understanding of human nature and the place humanity occupied as channels through which the Gods worked.

The second colonial view expressed the sentiment that Maori – as a somewhat primitive culture with an allegedly limited technological and intellectual advancement – saw nature in an animistic way. This corresponds with a view of the past as antiquated, ancient and primitive, and of the present as valued, important and advanced. To suggest that Maori viewed natural objects as animated was contrary to the belief that there was a clear distinction between the essence of a person and the realm of those spirits that stood over natural order. Since the natural order is not a closed system it is subject to infiltration and interpretation by higher order spirits. Further to this, Maori distinguished between the essence of inanimate and animate objects. While all created order possessed mauri by which they cohere in nature, human beings – as united body/spirits – are of a higher order requiring the acknowledgement of *mauriora* (life-enhancing principles), which in turn entailed greater responsibilities.

Uncertain certainty: The future

Through the actions of the Gods, all living things are given their opposites and the potential to procreate their own species. We are subject to the dichotomy of opposing forces: pleasure and pain, vice and virtue, good and evil, health and sickness. As verified in *whakapapa* and incantations of old, were it not for the separation of Rangi and Papa and the presence of all opposing forces, life would be void of learning, and thus absent of choice (agency) and experience.

It follows that Eve's beguilement by the serpent and Adam's consequent partaking of the forbidden fruit, as recorded in the Bible, were somehow predestined – in the Maori context, that is.

Conclusion

This chapter has attempted to explore the complex nature of *tapu* and *mana* in relation to humanity's quest for knowledge and in relation to the Gods existing within the realms of the spiritworld. It is only an elementary account of how Maori view the sacred elements of life and the creation of these elements. *Mana* has been expressed as the endowment of spiritual power given by the grace of the Creator. *Tapu* represents sacred boundaries within which power is used for purposes of good virtue. To transgress, knowingly or unknowingly, the *mana* and *tapu* laws as set by the Gods incurs their inevitable wrath. However, it is important to remember that rituals were set in place to cleanse and sanctify all those who transgress these laws. The Maori understanding of life is that all things are connected and that transgression is part and parcel of life's journey.

The knowledge obtained by Tane from the twelfth heaven was used to bring order to earth. As such, it is humanity's purpose to continue restoring earth's balance and maintaining sacred ties to the spiritworld. Through understanding the sacred knowledge of all things and knowing that all things return to the Creator, one remains conscious and in awe of the sacred laws pertaining to *mana* and *tapu*. It is this knowing and the close connection Maori have to the Gods that remain central to the sacred practices of the Maori of Aotearoa.

7. Magic, religion and secularity among the Azande and Nuer

Berel Dov Lerner

Debates over the application of terms such as 'religion' and 'magic' are often too easily dismissed as sterile academic exercises or as mere 'semantics' (Hammond 1970; see also Hamilton 1995, Chapter 3). In fact, such controversies may involve fundamental issues that are relevant to many aspects of the study of religion. By identifying a particular cultural practice as religious rather than as belonging to another distinct cultural category (e.g. magic), I invite two general kinds of consequences. On the one hand, I predispose myself to interpret and explain the practice in the light of what I have already learned about other religious traditions. On the other hand, I commit myself to modifying my general view of religion in the light of the newly admitted specimen of religious activity. If I *inappropriately* label a practice religious, I risk distorting my understanding both of the particular practice as well as of religion in general. The danger of such mislabelling becomes acute in the case of practices belonging to indigenous, non-Western societies, since these are likely to pose special challenges to classic academic (*Christian*) notions of religion.

In this chapter I examine some problems surrounding the distinction between religious practices and magical practices in relation to the cultures of two East African peoples, the Azande (singular Zande) and the Nuer. While I shall say something about latter developments in these cultures, most of my account will be drawn from the work of Sir E.E. Evans-Pritchard whose writings on these peoples have become great classics of modern anthropology. They have not only been the subject of continued discussion by anthropologists and philosophers, but are also 'the standard example for use in discussions' about understanding a society radically different from our own (Barnes 1974, 27). Therefore, Evans-Pritchard's work offers an interesting example of how the same ethnographic materials may be understood in the light of different interpretive assumptions.

The Azande

According to Evans-Pritchard, the Azande use their mystical ideas to make seemingly chance events (especially misfortunes) more intelligible and controllable. In Western rationalist culture, misfortunes are often analysed in terms of predictable, causally explicable processes, working in combination with largely unpredictable factors, which are, for all practical purposes, random. The Azande account for these random factors in terms of 'witchcraft'. One of Evans-Pritchard's own examples should clarify these ideas:

> In Zandeland sometimes an old granary collapses. There is nothing remarkable in this. Every Zande knows that termites eat the supports in course of time and that even the hardest woods decay after years of service. Now a granary is the summerhouse of a Zande homestead and people sit beneath it in the heat of the day and chat or play the African hole-game or work at some craft.
>
> Consequently it may happen that there are people sitting beneath the granary when it collapses and they are injured, for it is a heavy structure made of beams and clay and may be stored with eleusine as well. Now why should these particular people have been sitting under this particular granary at the particular moment when it collapsed? That it should collapse is easily intelligible, but why should it have collapsed at the particular moment when these particular people were sitting beneath it? . . . The Zande knows that the supports were undermined by termites and that people were sitting beneath the granary in order to escape the heat and glare of the sun. But he knows besides why these two events occurred at a precisely similar moment in time and space. It was due to the action of witchcraft. If there had been no witchcraft, people would have been sitting under the granary and it would not have fallen on them, or it would have collapsed but the people would not have been sheltering under it at the time. Witchcraft explains the coincidence of these two happenings. (Evans-Pritchard 1937, 69–70)

A Western-educated engineer might say that the collapse of the granary at a certain particular moment resulted from the interplay of incalculably numerous parameters; the microstructure of various segments of the supporting beams, wind speed and direction, shifting and settling of the stored grain, etc. Azande make sense of the apparently chance aspects of misfortunate events by blaming them on witchcraft.

To what does the term 'witchcraft' apply in the Zande setting, and what does it mean to be a 'witch'? A Zande witch (or *Boro mangu*) is a seemingly normal man or woman who secretly exercises evil, psychic powers which do injury to, or cause problems for, other people. The physiological seat of these powers is 'witchcraft-substance', a material substance whose presence may be discovered by autopsy in the bodies of dead witches. Furthermore, the presence of witchcraft-substance (i.e. being a witch) is a condition inherited by men from their fathers and women from their mothers.

Although post-mortem examination is considered an accurate method for the identification of witches, it is obviously of little practical usefulness. A witch who is responsible for someone's death must be identified while still alive in order to be killed in vengeance. (I should emphasize that I am writing in the timeless 'anthropological present'; even by the time of Evans-Pritchard's study, such vengeance was itself executed through magical means.) A witch who is merely causing problems must be identified and pacified. The Azande, as is their custom in dealing with otherwise unsolvable dilemmas, turn to their oracles to identify troublesome witches. In particular, the most prestigious oracle, known as the *benge* or poison oracle, is used for locating the perpetrators of witchcraft. The poison oracle begins with the asking of a question; the death of a fowl is declared as indicating the truth of one possible answer, its survival points to a different answer. A special poison is then administered to a fowl, and how the bird copes with being poisoned determines the oracle's message in the way previously specified. Next, the oracle's response is verified by repeating the whole procedure on a different bird, this time letting the death of the bird indicate the answer previously associated with its survival and vice versa. If the trials are consistent, the oracle is a success. If the answers indicated are not consistent, it is assumed that some technical difficulty (e.g. the breach of a taboo, poor quality of the poison) has interfered with the workings of the oracle.

Protection against witchcraft is available to the Azande in the form of special whistles, medicines and other magical devices and techniques. Sometimes Azande will consult ritual specialists whom Evans-Pritchard calls witch-doctors. These are not as awe-inspiring as their name would suggest; they do not enjoy special social status and their abilities to identify witches and neutralize witchcraft are hardly held to be infallible. Besides counteracting witchcraft, Zande magical practices may be directed towards other practical goals: travellers may use magic to keep the sun from setting before reaching home and there is even a simple technique that allows one to appear in someone else's erotic dream! Furthermore, while magic in general is held by the Azande to be somewhat effective, different techniques enjoy quite different reputations for reliability, and individuals may select techniques in accordance with their own opinions and practical experience.

Consider the predicament of a scholar who has set about studying Zande religion. Should she treat their complex of magical beliefs and practices as constituting a religion, or should she reserve the term religion for other aspects of Zande culture? Or perhaps she should conclude that the Zande are not particularly interested in religion and that their culture is best characterized as *secular*? In order to deal with these questions, I must first introduce a pair of concepts: instrumental action and expressive action. By *instrumental action* I refer to actions performed in order to achieve practical results and benefits. For instance, when farmers irrigate their crops in order to produce a better yield they are involved in an instrumental activity. Obviously, not all action is instrumental. Many activities associated with art and ritual are not directed towards practical ends but are concerned instead with the expression and contemplation of human emotions, values and attitudes towards life. I shall call these *expressive actions*. Of course, most actions are of variously mixed types and possess both instrumental and expressive aspects. (For example, a completely rational action can bear deep expressive significance: a 'heroic' medical procedure such as a liver transplant may be the most practical course of action while simultaneously expressing the kind of symbolic closure associated with the cliché, 'we have done everything in our power'.)

Differing attitudes towards the instrumental orientations of magic and religion have been associated with different interpretations of Zande culture. Some contemporary scholars, including philosophers and theologians who have been influenced by the celebrated philosopher Ludwig Wittgenstein (1966, 1979), have denied religion any instrumental value whatsoever. They claim, for instance, that worship is an expressive practice. People who pray to God in order to improve their chances at succeeding in business confuse religion with superstition (see Phillips 1981). One such Wittgensteinian philosopher is Peter Winch, whose controversial essay 'Understanding a primitive society' proposes an essentially religious interpretation of Zande witchcraft and magic. Winch claims that 'Zande magical rites' should be viewed as comparable to 'Christian prayers of supplication' in as much as both 'are alike in that they do, or may, express an attitude to [life's existential] contingencies, rather than an attempt to control these' (1964, 321). Perhaps overplaying the mutual exclusivity of instrumental and expressive intentions, Winch wants Azande oracles and magic to be understood as expressive activities 'dealing (symbolically) with misfortunes and their disruptive effect on a man's relations with his fellows' (1964, 321) rather than as a hopelessly inaccurate method of prediction and an irrationally inefficient technology. By consulting an oracle before embarking on a hunting expedition, an Azande is not behaving like a European who checks the weather forecast before visiting a ski resort. Rather, he is using symbolic means to contemplate the fragility of his human life which weighs heavily on him before the undertaking of a possibly dangerous journey. If it is difficult for us to understand how magic adds an extra spiritual dimension to Zande life, this only reflects our own deadening materialism and 'alienation': 'Our blindness to the point of primitive modes of life is a corollary of the pointlessness of much of our own life' (Winch 1964, 321).

Winch's interpretation of Azande magic involves a number of ideas which fit together well: that religion is a purely expressive category of activity, that 'primitive' societies are endowed with profound religious sensibilities, and that it is unfair to view indigenous magic as geared towards the same *instrumental* goals as are Western science and technology. Scholars proposing different interpretations of Zande culture have challenged each of these theses. Let us begin with non-instrumental nature of religion.

The philosopher and anthropologist Robin Horton has repeatedly argued that, despite Wittgensteinian doctrine (on Winch in particular, see Horton 1976), African religions are, in general, greatly concerned with the pursuit of fundamentally instrumental goals:

> In work after work [of African ethnography], we find that explanation, prediction and control are the overriding aims of religious life. People want a coherent picture of the realities that underpin their everyday world. They want to know the causes of their fortunes and misfortunes in this world. They want to have some way of predicting the outcomes of their various worldly projects and enterprises. They want, above all, to have the means of controlling events in the space-time world around them. (Horton 1993, 177)

According to Horton, the contemporary Western tendency to distance religion from instrumental concerns is a historically recent development that occurred in reaction to the rise of modern science. The explanatory power of the scientific world view turned traditional religious descriptions of the universe into intellectual liabilities for modern theologians. The phenomenal success of modern medicine and technology reduced feelings of dependence on religious interventions. Prior to these developments (and even today among believers undaunted by the rise of science), Christianity did not shy away from claiming to serve the instrumental interests of its adherents through prayers of supplication, etc. Thus, the interpretive assumption that religion is a purely expressive category of activity distorts our understanding of traditional Western religion (see also Schneider 1970, Chapter 7) as well as of African religion. Furthermore, when introduced to Africa by missionaries, European forms of Christianity usually undergo a process of 'Africanization' in which their instrumental elements are brought to the fore. Many Africans expect Christian faith and prayer to produce tangible benefits for the faithful. Clearly, according to Horton, recognition that the Azande practice magic in order to further their own practical ends should not keep us from viewing it as a religious phenomenon.

Winch's next assumption, the idea that the members of 'primitive' societies unfailingly possess strong religious sensibilities, has also had its critics. In her programmatic essay, 'Heathen darkness', the anthropologist Mary Douglas has called upon anthropologists to free themselves from what she calls the 'myth of primitive piety', that is, the assumption that all traditional societies are universally religious. Douglas demands that we recognize the broad range of different attitudes towards religion held by different traditional peoples:

> Unless we can think of tribes as secular, or given to mystery cults, dualist philosophies, or heterodoxies about the nature of grace and the godhead, the questions that have unleashed historic wars and mass executions, we have hardly begun the anthropology of religion. (1975, 81)

Evans-Pritchard's original work on the Azande avoids Douglas' 'myth of primitive piety'. His tendency to emphasize the 'spiritual' nature of religion (which led Horton to count Evans-Pritchard, along with Winch, among the 'devout' scholars who are unmindful of the instrumental nature of African religion) allows Evans-Pritchard to deny religious significance to purely instrumental magic. Evans-Pritchard found much to praise in the Azande character: he found their commoners 'unusually intelligent, sophisticated, and progressive', their noblemen 'charming' and 'frequently talented' (1937, 13). However, given the practical bent of their magic and their lack of theistic tendencies, he characterizes the Azande as largely irreligious, 'As a rule [Zande] conduct rests upon quite other than religious foundations' (1962, 327). In fact, it is precisely the Zande fascination with magic which prevents them from developing the kind of religious sensibility associated with theistic religion: 'Both [witchcraft ideas and magic] are incompatible with a theocentric philosophy, for when both fortune and misfortune come from God they cannot also come from human powers, whether innate or learnt' (1956, 316–17). Azande magic does not invite pious meditation on the finitude of the human condition, rather, it is viewed by its practitioners 'as a tangible weapon of culture deriving its power from the knowledge of tradition and the abstinence of living men' (1929, 20).

I would go so far as to say (Lerner 1995a) that the key to understanding Azande religious life is to accept that they (writing once more in the 'anthropological present' of Evans-Pritchard's writings) simply do not have much in the way of religion. Availing themselves of their knowledge of witches and magical techniques, the Azande, like modern Western secularists, prefer to take matters into their own hands rather than nurture feelings of dependence on higher, spiritual, powers.

Some early writers (Philipps 1926; Lagae 1926) claim that, in fact, the Azande are devoted to the worship of a 'Supreme Being' known as *Mbori*. On the one hand, this kind of strong theistic element would allow us to regard the Azande as possessing a religious culture, regardless of the secularity of their magic. On the other hand, it would be easier to consider Zande magic and witchcraft as religious phenomena if they were shown to be somehow connected with *Mbori* (something like this was attempted by Arewa 1978). In any case, Evans-Pritchard is quick to point out that in his own experience *Mbori* plays a negligible role in Zande life and thought:

> There are no shrines or other material evidences of [*Mbori*] worship; there is but a single public ceremony associated with his name and this is performed on rare occasions (1962, 289)

> As a fieldworker I must record that I have never heard a Zande pray and that I have seldom heard people utter his [*Mbori*'s] name, and then only as an ejaculation of emotional intensity and with only the vaguest suggestion of doctrinal significance. I must confess also that I have found the greatest difficulty in obtaining either information about *Mbori* or arousing any interest in him. (1962, 299)

All in all, *Mbori* was of quite marginal importance to Zande thinking at the time of Evans-Pritchard's studies. The occasional reference to *Mbori* in Zande speech offers us no more evidence for theistic piety than does the use of the expressions 'go to hell' and 'it was heavenly' by present-day Europeans offer evidence of their belief in the traditional 'three story' universe of Christianity.

Paradoxically, Singelton (1972) tries to build upon *Mbori*'s very absence as a personal God in order to claim that the Azande posses a non-theistic religious world view comparable to that of the so-called 'death of God' theologians who rose to eminence in the West during the 1960s. This suggestion seems odd since 'death of God theology' draws much of its power from the very fact that Western religion has traditionally been overwhelmingly theistic. One of its leading representatives writes:

> The death of God radical theologians ... are men without God who do not anticipate his return. But it is not a simple not-having, for there is an experience of loss ... The loss is not of the idols, or of the God of theism, but of the God of the Christian tradition. (Hamilton 1966, 22)

The West's long adherence to Christianity has created particular cultural needs and expectations which, even (especially!) in God's purported absence, radical theologians still find themselves trying to address. There is no evidence that the Azande ever attributed much importance to *Mbori* in the past. Neither have they experienced the kind of traumatic break with a thriving theistic tradition which breathes emotional life into 'death of God' theology.

Before leaving *Mbori*, mention should be made of his ultimate, ironic, triumph. Acting from necessity and 'near idiocy', Christian missionaries latched onto the name *Mbori* as a Zande translation of the Christian notion of 'God' (Evans-Pritchard 1976, 249). Margaret Buckner has recently reported that in apparent reaction to decades of such missionary activity, the Azande have developed a 'native' theistic religion, called Nzapa Zande, whose doctrines often parallel those of Christianity. The new God of the Azande is none other than *Mbori*, who 'today is indeed perceived of as not only morally just and good, but also as omniscient' (1995, 110).

Finally, let us consider what I have identified as Winch's third thesis, i.e. that it is unfair to view indigenous magic as geared towards the same *instrumental* goals as are Western science and technology. This thesis can be understood as founded upon an argument from *interpretive charity*. Simply stated, interpretive charity requires that when we try to understand the words and actions of other people, we should avoid making them out to be stupid or irrational. Lacking such a principle, we would never be able to guess at people's intentions on the basis of their actions. For instance: holding Mary to be rational, I can assume that she lit a campfire in order to warm herself. If I eschew interpretive charity and allow for the possibility that Mary is completely irrational, there is no limit to her possible reasons for lighting the fire; she may even be trying to cool herself off: see Davidson's classic presentation (1980, 1984). Henderson (1987) examines Winch's own somewhat different brand of interpretive charity. The argument from charity against the instrumentalist interpretation of magic is discussed in Lerner (1995a, 1998). Assuming that magic constitutes a hopelessly inefficient technique for the achievement of practical ends, the instrumentalist interpretation of magic seriously offends against the charitable assumptions which undergird all interpretive projects. (How can we view the Azande as foolish enough to believe in the instrumental efficacy of their magic?) Once the instrumentalist interpretation of Azande magic is rejected, the way is clear to view magic as expressivist and religiously oriented.

The claim that an instrumentalist interpretation of magic makes out its practitioners to be unbelievably stupid must dismiss what Mary Douglas identifies as the principal theoretical goal of Evans-Pritchard's book, i.e. to show 'how Azande, clever and sceptical as they were, could tolerate discrepancies in their beliefs and could limit the kinds of questions they asked about the universe' (1970, xiv). Evans-Pritchard achieves this goal by demonstrating how Zande beliefs, intellectual tendencies and practices work together to form a self-reinforcing system. For instance, the Azande always have many ways to explain the ineffectiveness of any particular attempt at magic. Only careful experimentation, which controlled for these disruptive influences, could possibly prove that a magical technique was in itself impotent. Consider, too, that the full weight of tradition recommends the usefulness of magic; and that magic is never required to produce results which are in themselves unlikely. All told, Evans-Pritchard lists 22 such factors which predispose the Azande to continue believing in their magic (1937, 475–8). In their light, it becomes understandable how, in the appropriate social milieu, Zande mystical beliefs and practices can appear entirely reasonable. Or, as Evans-Pritchard wrote in regard to Zande belief in witchcraft and oracles,

> Their blindness is not due to stupidity ... it is rather that their intellectual ingenuity and experimental keenness are conditioned by patterns of ritual behaviour and mystical belief. Within the limits set by these patterns they show great intelligence, but it cannot operate beyond these limits. Or, to put it in another way: they reason excellently in the idiom of their beliefs, but they cannot reason outside, or against, their beliefs because they have no other idiom in which to express their thoughts. (1937, 338)

The Nuer

The religious attitudes of the Nuer contrast strongly to those of the Azande. In the preface to his book *Nuer Religion*, Evans-Pritchard recalls how quickly he became aware of their profoundly different orientations:

> I had previously spent many months among the Azande people of the Nile–Uelle divide. From my earliest days among them I was constantly hearing the word *mangu*, witchcraft, and it was soon clear that if I could gain a full understanding of the meaning of this word I should have the key to Zande philosophy. When I started my study of the Nuer I had a similar experience. I constantly heard them speaking of *kwoth*, Spirit, and I realised that a full understanding of that word was the key to their – very different – Philosophy. (1956, vi)

Unsurprisingly, the notion of *kwoth* stands at the center of Evans-Pritchard's treatment of Nuer religion. His theistic interpretation of *kwoth* is also the subject of substantial controversy. Often, Evans-Pritchard will emphasize the monotheistic bent of Nuer religion by translating *kwoth* with the English word 'God'. This is certainly not an *unconscious* eurocentric blunder, since Evans-Pritchard expressly adopts the hermeneutic strategy of comparing Nuer religion with that of ancient Israel (1956, vii). Bible scholars have mobilized the Nuer/Israel analogy for their own ends (Fiensy 1987). However, Evans-Pritchard must contend with the presence of lesser spiritual entities such as the *kuth nhial* (spirits of the sky) and *kuth piny* (spirits of the earth) who would appear to contaminate the pristine monotheistic belief in *kwoth,* or more specifically in *kwoth nhial*, Spirit of the sky. (See Hutchinson (1996, 306) for a dualistic account of the *kuth nhial*/*kuth piny* distinction.) Evans-Pritchard openly admits that: 'On one level Nuer religion may be regarded as monotheistic, at another level as polytheistic; and it can also be regarded at other levels as totemistic or fetishistic' (1956, 316).

Much of *Nuer Religion* is devoted to explaining how these seemingly antagonistic tendencies coexist within a single cultural system. In a nutshell, it contends that all of the various spiritual entities may be ultimately regarded as constituting different 'refractions' and 'modes' in which God as Spirit has become known to the Nuer, thus sustaining Evans-Pritchard's fundamentally monotheistic interpretation of their beliefs. Comparison between this description of Nuer religion with that of the closely related Dinka people, as studied by Lienhardt (1961), has raised concern that Evans-Pritchard's own Christian faith had led him to read monotheism into Nuer (see Meeker 1989, Chapter 5).

Numbering the entities referred to by the term *kwoth* is not essential for the purposes of this chapter – nor is the significant religious role of the Nuer prophets (for which see Johnson 1994). Hardly anyone would deny that polytheistic as well as monotheistic systems can be properly categorized as *religions*. It is more important to consider Nuer attitudes towards *kwoth*, especially in terms of the instrumental/expressive distinction which I developed above. According to Evans-Pritchard, *kwoth* is thought of as having created all things from nothing through the power of his thought, and is creator, protector and friend of human beings. Although 'God is sometimes felt to be present here and now, he is also felt to be far away in the sky' (1956, 9). This transcendent aspect of *kwoth* is reflected in the Nuer's feelings of insignificance relative to the overwhelming reality of Spirit as expressed in the Nuer saying, 'all of us are like little ants in the sight of God' (1956, 12). Such humility before Spirit is all the more impressive in light of the Nuer's reputation as fierce warriors and their generally proud bearing towards other people. This profound sense of human frailty combines with a feeling of absolute dependence on God to form a religious sensibility which gives rise to frequent and often spontaneous prayer. They also imbue the Nuer with a stoic attitude towards hardships, which they view as representing God's rightful exercise of His prerogative. After all, hardships may likely result from divine displeasure with improper human behavior. (For an important critique of Evans-Pritchard's use of the term 'sin' to refer to actions which the Nuer believe result in misfortune see Beidelman 1981.) All in all, Nuer religion is interested in expressing trust in Spirit and resignation to its power rather than with somehow harnessing Spirit for the accomplishment of practical human objectives.

Even this very short discussion of the Nuer must mention the role of sacrifice in their way of life. Cattle are of central importance to traditional Nuer culture, and the sacrifice of cattle may fairly be said to constitute the most important ritual of their religion. According to Hutchinson (1996, 299–301) the lack of cattle sacrifice in Christianity is seen by many Nuer as its most salient difference from their own traditional religion. Sacrifice is a means to purification and atonement, and affords some protection from the dangers associated with the interventions of Spirit, especially those resulting from misdeeds. Sacrifices may also serve to solemnize changes in personal status and the creation of new social units by 'making God and the ghosts [of the dead] ... witnesses' to them (Evans-Pritchard 1956, 199). The protective value of sacrifice obviously points to an instrumental aspect of Nuer religion, which may have been played down by Evans-Pritchard. Hutchinson (who, it must be recalled, studied Nuer society as changed by decades of tragic history since Evans-Pritchard's own field work) quotes a Nuer with whom she discussed *Nuer Religion* as saying: 'Ours is a very pragmatic religion – either the sacrifice is judged successful and the person cured or it is not, in which case further reflections and sacrifices will take place' (1996, 306).

Conclusions

Evans-Pritchard depicts the Nuer and the Azande as occupying polar extremes of religious life. Nuer religion seems practically devoid of crassly instrumental elements. The pious Nuer, who know little of magic and lack theurgical techniques to force God's hand, are left to surrender themselves to the workings of Spirit. Though prayer and sacrifice may be addressed to Spirit, at the end of the day a person 'cannot get to God but God can get to' a person (Evans-Pritchard 1956, 318). At the other extreme stand the Azande, who have developed magical practices and beliefs in a way that leaves little room for a recognizably *religious* way of life. Although such polar oppositions may be useful in the earliest stages of mapping the terrain of religion, we should not lose sight of the enormous complications forced upon us by the sheer variety of human cultural practices. Horton's insistence on the instrumental aspect of religion should not be forgotten. It may be tempting to adopt the Nuer as the paradigmatic example of a traditional religious culture, yet Evans-Pritchard himself clearly realized that the religion of the Nuer is unusual in the African context. He even mentions (1956, 316) magic and 'witchcraft ideas' as *typical* features of African religion. On the other hand, one must be careful to remember that just because some belief or activity may be a *feature* of some religions, that does not mean that in other contexts it will not lose its religious significance. Evans-Pritchard is careful to distance himself from the conceptual identification of magic with religion. In his *Theories of Primitive Religion*, he opposes the hybrid expression 'magico-religious' (1965, 33) and counts 'the differences between magic and religion' among a list of 'topics which appear ... to be still in a very confused state' (1965, 110).

Historical narratives, public celebrations and the plastic arts may all play essential roles in various religions. This does not preclude the possibility of secular historiography, secular celebrations and secular art. As secular activities, they may even work to *weaken* the position of religion. Similarly, in the Azande case, magic disconnected from a larger religious context (perhaps, for instance, genuine *Mbori* worship) becomes an essentially secular affair, which serves to facilitate an essentially irreligious way of life.

8. The Dreaming in contemporary Aboriginal Australia

Lynne Hume

Jacob Pandian wrote that 'cultural coherence and appropriateness are achieved by learning to deploy the structures of meaning embodied in the public symbols that constitute a culture or way of life' (1997, 507). All cultures have symbols of the self that convey the meanings of being human, signifying 'who I am' or 'what I am'. However, these are arbitrary associations of meaning, and individuals have to learn the meanings associated with human identities in specific cultural contexts or within the boundaries of the historical, cultural configurations of meaning. Non-remote (urban) Aborigines who, for one reason or another, have been displaced from their places of origin and their traditional religious and social contexts have had to learn what being 'Aboriginal' is within a newly configurated system of meaning – one that has placed them within a European historical and cultural context. The creation of a pan-Aboriginality that has emerged as a result of history has resulted in some interesting syntheses of ideas with regard to traditional cultural heritage and to the way some urban Aborigines speak about Aboriginal spirituality.

This chapter explores the ways in which various Aboriginal groups have come to terms with both their traditional culture and the encroachment of imported beliefs. It will be seen that, while in some areas of Australia, 'tradition' appears to have continued with little noticeable input from outside, in other areas Christianity has been adopted either partially or wholeheartedly. In yet others, a synthesis with more contemporary Western spiritualities such as the New Age has been created. This chapter in no way covers all aspects of Aboriginal spirituality, rather, it only serves to highlight some of the different ways in which Aborigines nowadays have incorporated the Dreaming into their own contemporary lives.

Traditional Aboriginal cosmology and the Dreaming

Aboriginal cosmology centres upon what has been translated as the Dreaming, or Dreamtime, which refers to both a creative period (or rather, a founding drama as there was no doctrine of creation *ex nihilo* (Keen 1986, 26) and a continual, atemporal metaphysical reality. The term 'Dreaming', being the first attempt at documentation of the Aranda words *altjiranga ngambakala*, does not adequately translate their full significance. When Aboriginal people search for an English equivalent they often use 'Law', or sometimes 'power'. 'Eternal Law' has been suggested as a more appropriate interpretation (Swain 1989). Nevertheless, 'Dreaming' still continues to be used and does, at least, convey the mystery, if not the complexity of Aboriginal culture and spirituality. The Dreaming's eternal nature has been referred to as 'everywhen' to articulate its timelessness.

During the founding drama, the Ancestors arose from beneath the earth, journeyed from place to place, gave shape to an existing, yet amorphous world, imbued all things with their own essence, and laid down the Law for all living Aborigines to follow. A power or energy was a part of the primordial scene, a power both speciated and individuated (Stanner 1998, 8–9). For example, a particular species, such as kangaroo, and those men totemically associated with kangaroo, could release from the sacred site (having gained, ritually, the right to do so), the life essence stored and potential in that site. As the Ancestors travelled, they left tangible expressions of themselves in the shape of some site or rocky outcrop, tree or waterhole, metamorphosing an essence of themselves into some feature of the environment or imprinting themselves onto cave walls or into ritual objects. When they had finished their work, they returned back into the earth. The Ancestors are therefore intrinsically part of the land over which they moved. All things – land, humans and that which is both living and non-living – are interconnected through these Dreaming beings. Via conception and initiation rites, an Aborigine becomes identified with certain areas of land, and with certain objects that are imbued with ancestral essence. Land is the mediating agency between the world of the ancestors and the world of living human beings (Munn 1984). Land, spirit and the living are inseparable.

A Yanyuwa man, Mussolini Harvey, from the Gulf of Carpentaria tries to explain the significance of the Dreaming:

> White people ask us all the time, what is Dreaming? This is a hard question because Dreaming is a really big thing for Aboriginal people. In our language, Yanyuwa, we call the Dreaming Yijan. The Dreamings made our Law or narnu-Yuwa. This Law is the way we live, our rules. This Law is our

> ceremonies our songs our stories; all of these things came from the Dreaming. One thing that I can tell you though is that our Law is not like European Law which is always changing – new government, new laws; but our Law cannot change, we did not make it. The Law was made by the Dreamings many, many years ago and given to our ancestors and they gave it to us. (Harvey, quoted in Bradley 1988, xi)

And in another part of the continent, a Pitjantjatjara woman, Nganyintja Ilyatjari, from the country around Mt Davies, explains:

> Our country, the country out there near Mt Davies, is full of sacred places. The kangaroo Dreaming has been there since the beginning, the wild fig Dreaming has been there since the beginning, many other women's Dreamings are also there. In other places men and women's Dreamings were together from a long time ago ... These places have been part of the sacred Dreamtime since the beginning of time, they were made then by our Dreamtime ancestors – like the kangaroo. Our country is sacred, this country is sacred. (Nganyintja Ilyatjari quoted in Gale 1983, 57)

Living Aborigines are tied to land and spirit in the most complex way which includes their kinship with the Ancestors, the land for which they act as caretakers and guardians, and their inextricable connection with all that exists on the land. Everything is interconnected in a vast web of sacredness. Ancestor tracks and sites, and the Dreaming stories associated with them, make up the sacred geography of Australia. The entire continent is criss-crossed by tracks that the Ancestors made on their travels. An entire myth complex might traverse several linguistic groups which each 'own' that tract of land for which they are guardians and caretakers. Those responsible must take care of country by periodically following songlines pertaining to these myths, thus maintaining their connections to the land and keeping the land. The Dreaming Ancestors are evidenced in paintings and engravings, in body painting and sacred objects, and in the songs that are handed down over generations. Some places belong to women's Dreaming (women's business), some to men's Dreaming (men's business), others to both genders. Both residence and myth link Aborigines to country in a deeply significant spiritual sense. As anthropologist, W.E.H. Stanner wrote, Aboriginal people moved 'not in a landscape, but in a humanised realm saturated with significations' (1979, 131). Aboriginal people are situated within their own country emotionally, psychologically and metaphysically (Rose 1996, 38–9).

Dreaming stories (myths) contain no notion of original sin or moral corruption, though some myths contain moral content. The recounting of myths and their meanings is part of the importance of knowledge as ownership. The more a male progresses in both age and the process of initiation, the more knowledge is revealed to him by older and fully initiated men. Likewise, in women's business, certain information is communicated through ceremonial activity and women learn progressively more the more they participate in women's religious life. In secret rituals which are closed to men, women also celebrate their relations to the land, its sites and its myths. While women's 'business' is complementary to the 'business' of men, the dominant theme of women's ceremonies is that of woman the nurturer, and their focus is on health, emotional management, resolution of conflict and matters that benefit the whole of society (Bell 1998).

Even a small segment of myth can have multiple meanings. In fact, there are layers upon layer of meanings in merely one short myth sequence. The following short sentence from a Yolngu (northern Australia) myth, demonstrates this multiplicity: 'Mosquito [particular species name] thrust his proboscis into the ground at [place name] where the mound now exists.' From this scant piece of information, the enculturated Yolngu person would know that 'Mosquito' is a spirit-being whose journey in the distant past took him to the particular place named, and that several other places visited by mosquito are linked through myth narrative. Other information would include the knowledge that Mosquito beings vested land in certain patrilineal groups which have ties with all the people at the places where Mosquito performed a similar act, that Mosquito's proboscis was transformed into a spear, which Mosquito people carry in rituals commemorating Mosquito's journey, and that the mound of land was caused by the proboscis being thrust into the ground, just as a swelling is caused in the human body by a mosquito bite. In addition, by meditating on Mosquito's spear, Mosquito people make themselves angry enough to carry out hostile acts such as a revenge expedition (Williams 1986, 23–4).

The Yolngu assume that a great deal of information exists in symbolic forms and at different levels of reality (Williams 1986, 23–4). They speak of meanings 'multiplying' and this has implications for what is regarded as the most important category of knowledge, and for the contexts, conditions and means of transmittal. The most important category of knowledge comprises history, ritual, and myth that relate to rights in land. What is most important is equated with what is most sacred and is always hidden from public view. Thus, the safest repository of all is inside one's head, and knowledge acquired by older men in the course of a lifetime earns them respect and a certain amount of power. Such knowledge is only accessible with permission, and is slowly gained through ritual when an initiate is considered to have attained the appropriate level to receive highly valued information. Similarly, Aboriginal art and song have multiple levels of meaning depending upon how well advanced an individual is in years and the initiation process.

Aboriginal Law is land-based. That is, knowledge about the Law is specifically associated with particular tracts of land. Knowledge is not universalized but is localized. The actual information which people hold, teach, exchange and inherit constitutes intellectual property (Williams 1986, 32). Information is valued over material wealth, which is de-emphasized. Thus, information is stored in the minds of living Aborigines and is encoded in dance, designs, stories and songs. Ownership and transmission of knowledge are the prerogative of specific people in local areas. It is not freely available to all and must be earned.

Aboriginal people in remote Australia (one could say 'traditional' Aborigines, as opposed to those who have been displaced from 'country' and grown up without a traditional education) emphasize culture and knowledge about the Law that is learned cognitively, under instruction from elders who have passed through various stages of initiation. This is a long slow process which is tied up with the structure of Aboriginal society. Knowledge of the Dreaming, or Law, is in the hands of the elders, particularly older men, who impart their knowledge piece by piece, with each step of the process shrouded in secrecy. A good example of this is given by Ian Keen (1994) who describes the politics of religious knowledge employed by Yolngu (north-east Arnhem Land) men in the dissemination of knowledge. This is a complex process which involves age and gender relations, social networks centred on patrifilial group identity, as well as relationships with people of a wider region. Knowledge is not given out lightly and is acquired over very long periods of time within a framework of cultural immersion.

Aborigines who have been denied access to such enculturation and instruction such as those of the 'Lost Generation'[1] or those who were brought up on Christian missions, or entire communities that underwent displacement from their own 'country', have little knowledge of the complexities of the process. Nevertheless, some are explicitly declaring that in spite of this, they can re-establish connection by drawing on their innate capacities of Aboriginality. There is a shift from the acquisition of knowledge gained through complete immersion in Aboriginal Law pertaining to locale and 'looking after country' by being there, to a type of distanced affective intuitive knowledge. The connection, or spiritual continuity, is now being professed through blood links, intimating a kind of intuitive, or genetic, transmission of spiritual knowledge. The following statement demonstrates this shift:

> We've all got that spiritual contact inside us. Because of our blood: no matter what colour we are, whether we are fair or creamy or black or blue. Aboriginal people are in all colours ... They think we've lost our spiritual contact but we haven't; it's all inside us; it can come out of us. (ABC Television 1989, 'spirituality' episode on *Blackout*, quoted in Swain 1992, 128)

In spite of this reference to spirituality as 'being in the blood', as Swain points out:

> While there is a sense of spiritual awakening through affirming one's Aboriginality and asserting one's connection within the Aboriginal world, it cannot be denied that 'blood', whatever it might transmit, does not transmit those stories and ceremonies which provide the Absolute link between specific people and specific places. 'Blood' might feasibly be said to give one a sense of orientation of Aboriginality, but it cannot be expected to offer detail of the old Law. (1992, 129)

Aborigines and the New Age

Some Aborigines are now engaging in a mixture of their own ideas of a traditional cultural heritage and what is clearly New Age rhetoric. It is therefore not surprising to discover that many become interested in New Age workshops and ideas as well as the lesser known Neopagan groups who seek to discover a spiritual oneness with the earth through corporeal, experiential awareness – a somatic philosophy that goes beyond cerebral knowledge to a 'knowing' based on gut feeling. In this discovery of self, it is no wonder that contemporary Aborigines who have not been traditionally enculturated, especially those in urban and coastal areas, might turn to, and find compatibilities with, religious groups that are earth-based yet non-locative-specific, and that employ intuitive knowledge to achieve spiritual harmony with land.

Books such as Lawlor's *Voices of the First Day* are being endorsed by some urban Aborigines as being 'the way it [Aboriginal Dreaming] is', in spite of some of the reductionist approaches employed by their authors. Comments by Lawlor such as, 'the Dreaming has no religious, racial or cultural boundaries, no governments or social castes ... perception and Dreamtime are the two worlds of the Aboriginal people' (Lawlor 1991, xvi), have been highly criticized by researchers such as Jane Jacobs and Julie Marcus. Jacobs accuses Lawlor of conflating difference and denying history in the search for eco-spiritual rebirth, and creating a 'newly crafted Australian eco-philosophy' (Jacobs 1994, 308). Julie Marcus argues that the ways in which Australian Aboriginal culture is incorporated into New

Age cosmologies is 'clearly appropriative' and yet another manifestation of the colonization of Aboriginal culture by Europeans (Marcus 1988, 272). Like Jacobs, Marcus is particularly scathing about Lawlor's *Voices of the First Day* which incorporates, even equates, his own New Age ideas with Australian Aboriginal culture:

> With Lawlor's help, and the shamanic practices he will unfold within the text, you the reader will be able to go to sleep and dream your way into a new awakening which will be inside the Aboriginal Dreamtime.
>
> This is, I believe, a clear example of the imperial refusal to accept limits on either intellectual or physical space, and of, having taken away the land, refusing Aboriginal people even their last retreat, their religion. You too, can enter this formerly secret and hidden world. The promise is that you will thus regain the first day, the dawn of mankind, the paradise of the world, the universe. You will get back all that you have lost in the long climb out of the primaeval swamp to civilisation. (Marcus 1996, 41)

In spite of such well-deserved criticism, however, it is not only Westerners who are making connections between the New Age and Aboriginal world views. Some individual Aborigines are offering New Age-style workshops of self-discovery, using New Age rhetoric and practices. For example, a weekend workshop for men, organized by a group called Circle of Men, was held near Lismore, New South Wales from 6 p.m. Friday, 18 November, to 4 p.m. Monday, 21 November, 1994. The advertising flyer called the workshop 'Everyone Standing Up Alive' (from David Mowaljarlai's book of the same name) and offered 'creativity, indigenous wisdom and the masculine spirit' as its theme. The highlight of the weekend was that David Mowaljarlai (billed as 'an elder from the Ngarinyin people of the Kimberley region of Western Australia, and 1991 Aborigine of the Year') would share his knowledge of community life with special emphasis on the initiation of young men and the importance of male community. The flyer stated 'this gathering is a unique opportunity for men to experience the wisdom of an elder of the oldest culture on earth', and that it would be using 'story, music, poetry, drama and art to bring forth and nourish the potent, creative core of the masculine spirit'.

In a similar vein, Tjanara Goreng Goreng, who claims to be a traditional Aboriginal healer dancer and songmaker, says that she connects two ancient philosophies – Hindu and Aboriginal. Tjanara talks about breath healing, channelling, chakras and energy centres of the body – all New Age concepts. She talks about drawing people closer to the essential force of energy which Aborigines call the Dreaming because it is 'a place which is beyond space and time, beyond the physical body and this physical world':

> It [the Dreaming] is a place where your spirit goes without your body, where your spirit is just free to be out in the Universe beyond. It is beyond form. The Dreaming is a place that you can go to, but it is a place in the future, the past and in the now. Your Spiritual life is your Dreaming but it is not disconnected from you, you are in a physical form. Once you are in touch with your spirit you are in touch with who you really are, your own being. (Goreng Goreng 1997, 23)

Tjanara works with groups and practises healing at the Latrobe Healing Centre in Brisbane, a centre offering information and teaching on a range of New Age notions such as Reiki, past lives, spiritual healing and aromatherapy.

In 1998, a public two-week camp-out in New South Wales, which consisted of a series of workshops under the title 'Renewing the Dreaming' was advertised in the *Pagan Times* (the newsletter of the Australian Pagan Alliance):

> Renewing the Dreaming
> 1998 Dreaming Camp
> Blue Gum Flat, on the Clyde River, 4 hours South of Sydney
> With Guboo Ted Thomas, Elder of the Yuin Tribe, who turns 89 on the 27th January.
>
> Since 1980, Guboo has been spreading the message of Love, inspiring us to work together for Mother Earth. He will be holding several workshops, sensitising people to the Dreaming and their innermost feelings. He will take people to the Aboriginal burial site, and on walks to discover bush tucker. Each morning and evening Guboo leads traditional ceremonies culminating in the uplifting 'Humming Bee', which will open our hearts to the deep wilderness as it weaves its magic over the group, connecting everyone with Nature, and helping us to discover truths about ourselves, our lifestyles, and each other.
>
> For more information, contact *Pagan Times*. (Summer 1997, issue 22, 19)

In 'Reinventing the eternal: Aboriginal spirituality and modernity' (1992), Tony Swain suggested that Aboriginal religion had been 'reinvented' and that a new image – Mother Earth – was at the heart of this reinvention. Mother Earth, wrote Swain, provided 'a new, radically transformed, spiritual continuity' for Aborigines who had been denied a place. He then concluded that Mother Earth was compatible with the widespread phenomenon of Aboriginal Christianity. I have suggested elsewhere (Hume 1996) that the reinvention is much more compatible with the Neopagan spiritual ecology movement than with Christianity, because of the emphasis both place on the sacredness of the earth, non-Western methods of healing, and the belief in psychic phenomena. As well, both are engaged in a search for spiritual identity through a lost heritage.

Aboriginal references to Mother Earth allude to an emotional attachment to the land. The appeal calls upon affections which lie deep within a pan-Aboriginal soul, rather than an embedded and enculturated esoteric lore where myths are revealed and pedagogical instruction is received from elders. The poetry of Oodgeroo Noonuccal (Kath Walker) shows: 'I will always come back to this place to share the feeling of the land with all living things. I belong here where the spirit of the Earth Mother is strong in the land and in me' (Noonuccal 1988).

Anne Pattel-Gray (Executive Secretary of the Aboriginal and Islander Commission, Australian Council of Churches) is even more explicitly political in her references to Mother Earth, condemning Her destruction by (White) mining companies. She also identifies a pan-Aboriginality ('my people') along with spirit of the earth sentiments: 'My people became more and more distressed at the sight of the White men raping, murdering and abusing their Mother Earth through mining. We knew the price they would pay for abusing Mother Earth' (Pattel-Gray 1990, quoted in Swain 1992, 134).

The Mother Earth concept articulates the contemporary Aboriginal view of attachment to land in a generic sense. Similarly, the spiritual ecology movement regards the earth as sacred, a living entity with its own indwelling spirit. The expression of relationship with the Earth is one of 'deep connection, of stewardship, and of reverence for the Earth as Mother Goddess' (Hume 1997, 44). As well, both Aborigines and modern religious movements such as the Pagans believe in psychic phenomena such as thought-reading and thought-transference, shape-shifting, communication with spirits, and out of body experiences ('fast travelling' for Aborigines and 'astral travelling' for those in the West). All these have been reported as common characteristics of both the Aboriginal 'clever man' ('man of high degree') (Elkin 1997) and the Western psychic. T.G.H. Strehlow, who grew up among Aborigines at the Hermansburg mission in central Australia where his father was a Lutheran missionary, carefully documented Aboriginal beliefs and practices and in his 1971 book *Songs of Central Australia* repeatedly pointed to similarities between Aboriginal practices and pagan European magical practices.

In spite of some compelling similarities, some New Age extremists point to an idyllic, pre-colonial pristine past for Aborigines. Some, such as American, Marlo Morgan, even invent an Aboriginal perfect world in the present. Morgan's book, *Mutant Message Down Under* (1995) recounts her own putative adventures with a tribe of Desert Aborigines whom she calls the 'Real People'. The book portrays Aborigines as living in love and peace according to their own ancient wisdom, leading exemplary lives of communion with nature. A people who are, at heart, vegetarians (a curious notion, given that Aborigines were nomadic hunter–gatherers). They had sent for Marlo Morgan so that she could relay their message to the world and carry on their work of nurturing the Earth Mother. Although *Mutant Message* is a tall tale told as fact, it was nevertheless lauded, when it first came out, by Burnum Burnum, a Wurundjeri elder and a well-known activist for Aboriginal rights. He also studied law in Tasmania. Apparently, from his comments, Burnum Burnum saw positive aspects in *Mutant Message* – principally that the book portrayed Aborigines as 'the regal and majestic people that we are', and that it 'uplifts us [Aboriginal people] into a higher plane of consciousness' (Burnum Burnum, quoted in Hiatt 1997, 40).

This type of comment reflects both New Age rhetoric and a 'noble savage' picture of Aborigines. Other Aborigines also take this position. The following comment by Kevin Gilbert, of an idyllic past time prior to contact, mirrors that of Marlo Morgan:

> Our laws governed the sharing of resources, caring for every member of our society, the sanctity of ALL forms of life and the earth from whence we came and continue in sanctity as part thereof. Our people, our land, are based upon justice and universal humanity within our sovereign domain. (Gilbert 1987, 83)

In fact, the pre-colonial period of 40,000 years ago until 1788 is one that is invariably depicted as an idyllic past without strife or conflict – one which consisted of a life of simplicity, nobility and non-violence. Such romanticism denies any factual intra- and inter-community strife, blood revenge, and the normal conflicts that occur in any human community. And, although it must be emphasized that the advent of Europeans to Australia disrupted families, wreaked havoc on Aboriginal culture, irrevocably changed the Aboriginal way of life and resulted in some deplorable treatment of Aboriginal people, prior to this disruption, an idyllic Eden, it was not. However, instead of dismissing all New Age adoptions of indigenous cultures as yet another example of cultural imperialism, as some have done, we might heed Hiatt's suggestion:

> The emancipation of indigenous peoples, not only from colonial subordination but from the constraints of tribalism in both its modern and traditional forms, may ultimately depend less on rational, coordinated and centralised policy-making than on shifting alliances between strange bedfellows. (Hiatt 1997, 40)

Aborigines and Christianity

Another 'strange bedfellow', as far as traditional Aboriginal cosmology goes, is Christianity. Although there have been many valiant attempts at an Aboriginal hermeneutic of the Bible, these bedfellows do not have an easy sleeping arrangement. Aboriginal responses to Christian missionary messages have varied from outright rejection to syncretism in varying degrees and, lastly, acceptance. Some Aborigines have even become priests and ministers themselves. Aboriginal theologians now are attempting a biblical hermeneutic that is culturally relevant to Aborigines. Two major themes become apparent in this endeavour, namely, Aboriginal powerlessness and racial inequities (Hume 1994). However, little attention is paid to theologically important issues such as how Christianity might hold certain keys that could somehow be equated with the Dreaming. For instance, the inseparability of land–human–spirit, the kinship connection between all things, both sentient and non-sentient, as well as the land-based nature of spirituality and mythology, and the notion of an intrinsic spiritual 'energy' that is present in the land.

The central importance of 'place' and land to Aboriginal spirituality is just not present in Christianity, no matter how hard Aborigines (and others) might try to find it. Many would like to find equivalencies in order to make Christianity more compatible with the Dreaming, and the following few examples highlight these attempts. Guboo Ted Thomas (mentioned earlier), in addition to being an Elder of the Yuin Tribe, is also a spokesperson for Aboriginal rights and has published articles on an Aboriginal understanding of the Bible (see especially Thomas 1987). For Thomas, sacredness, power and energy emanate from nature, and, as he says, rocks take on meaning the more you dwell on them: 'Seeing these faces in the rocks is what I call the spirit. When you are there you get a feeling of our ancestors roaming all through the area thirty of forty thousand years ago' (Thomas 1987, 90). Thomas says that some places are so powerful that if you touch them 'your hand will be pushed to the ground', and that is 'Koorie power'. Even Thomas's valiant attempts to locate this sense of land and spirituality within a biblical context (noting, for example, that Moses was given the commandments when he went up on a mountain, that water gushed out when Moses struck a rock, that Jesus went up into the mountains to pray, and that most churches have been built on top of hills), fail to convince any but the most willing, that there are real comparisons. The sharp distinction between Aboriginal and European views of land sacredness was clearly demonstrated when Thomas took some members of the Department of Forestry to some of the sacred areas of his own 'country' in south-eastern New South Wales. He said:

> I took representatives of the Department of Forestry down to our valleys and into our mountains and told them where the areas sacred to my people were, even the place where young initiates sit and learn about our culture, have Dreamtime, everything. But they did not really understand, and I could see in their eyes they had no clue as to what I was talking about. They wanted to see stained-glass windows or statues of angels – something like that would make a place sacred. (Thomas 1987, 92)

An Aboriginal Lutheran pastor, George Rosendale, uses Aboriginal symbols and metaphors to translate Aboriginal mythology into Christian terms, in order to convey certain moral messages that are contained in both. Even this proves difficult:

> I have been able to understand and communicate Western Christianity [to other Aborigines] because I have been trained in European culture. But it was still very painful for me when I noticed that my people were straining desperately as they attempted to understand and grasp the deep meaning of the gospel. Only when I began to learn their stories and customs and used them as pictures to see and understand the gospel did I notice their faces light up. To hear comments such as, 'Aah! It's like our story!' made me very happy to share the gospel with my people. (Rosendale 1989, 2)

The major (but not sole) stumbling-block to a valid synthesis of the Dreaming (at least in logical terms) with any other, imported beliefs is the crucial component of sacred land/place exegesis. Because of this, there will always be attempts to gloss over the true significance of Aboriginal cosmology, even for those who find it important to achieve a synthesis. In a publication entitled *Rainbow Spirit Theology*, several Aboriginal people from Catholic, Anglican, Lutheran and Uniting Church backgrounds, joined in a dialogue to explore their Aboriginal culture as a source of mystery, meaning and theology. Yet, as one person wrote:

> Aboriginal culture is spiritual. I am spiritual. Inside of me is spirit and land, both given to me by the Creator Spirit. There is a piece of land in me, and it keeps drawing me back like a magnet to the land from which I came. Because the land, too, is spiritual.
>
> This land owns me. The only piece of land I can claim a spiritual connection with – connection between me and the land – is the piece of land under the tree where I was born, the place where my mother buried my afterbirth and umbilical cord. The spiritual link with that piece of land goes back to the ancestors in the Dreaming. This is both a personal and sacred connection – between me and the land, me and my ancestors. (Rainbow Spirit Elders 1997, 12)

This quote explicitly demonstrates that any non-land-based belief system will never be an adequate substitution or synthesis for Aborigines.

Pan-Aboriginality

Just as attempts are being made to forge some sort of link between imported religious or spiritual beliefs, the notion of a pan-Aboriginality is also being put forward by some to forge a link between all Aboriginal people, and to point out distinctions between Aborigines and non-Aborigines. Those who follow this line of thinking posit the theme of Aboriginal oneness in a more political fashion. Pan-Aboriginality defines Aborigines against the Western 'Other', creates an Aboriginal nationalism that was non-existent prior to contact, and in fact, has a very recent history. The construction of a pan-Aboriginal identity was created within a climate of racism and the Aboriginal fight for equality, autonomy and land rights. The subsequent projection of a pan-Aboriginal past is often accompanied by the view of pre-contact Aboriginal life as simple and noble, ultimately superior to the decadent Western material values of the colonists and post-colonists. This new self-image seems to be particularly important for displaced persons who have lost their spiritual connection with specific land locations, but who nevertheless feel that there is an intrinsic spiritual connection.

Sugirtharajah (1996) suggests that homelessness is increasingly becoming a new framework for hermeneutics. He discusses two categories of uprooted people who raise special questions for national identity. Although Sugirtharajah speaks of national identity in India, his categories have applicability for the Aboriginal situation in Australia. One category is 'voluntary exiles', the other is 'internal exiles'. Both voluntary exiles and internal exiles are united, says Sugirtharajah in their longing for a home. Voluntary exiles are 'de-localised transnationals' who are part of a diasporic culture which moves across borders and feels at home everywhere and nowhere. Internal exiles are 'de-rooted nationals who find themselves refugees in their own countries'. We could apply the term 'internal exiles' to those Aborigines who, as a result of their position in a colonial and post-colonial Australia, have been uprooted and transported from their locale-specific country to other regions. They are exiles from their land-based spiritual homes due to missionary and government influence, political policies on Aborigines, and mining interests.

Sugirtharajah further proposes that minority communities are engaged in ethnonationalist struggles invoking various kinds of age-old tribal and indigenous sentiments. Like their Sri Lankan counterparts, contemporary (urban) Aborigines have overlapping and multiple axes of identification. Two (conflicting) negotiating options for Aborigines of mixed descent are to say that there is no such thing as Aboriginality, or to fashion a very narrow and one-dimensional notion of Aboriginality. Sugirtharajah proposes a third option, one that is between and betwixt cultures and countries and which engages in a processual hermeneutic. Quoting Jan Mohamed, this is called the 'interstitial cultural space', which is a vantage point from which those who are caught amidst several cultures and groups can come up with unlimited alternative forms of group identity and social arrangement (Sugirtharajah 1996, 427). It is a space in which a contemporary heremeneutical praxis has the freedom to mix and harmonize, change and retain various ingredients.

It is this interstitial cultural space which is perhaps the best vantage point from which to view contemporary Aboriginal spirituality. Social and political changes inevitably lead to religious change. We have already seen how the Dreaming is being reinterpreted as a consequence of the Aboriginal interface with modernity. Aborigines are engaged in deploying structures of meaning in order to make sense of evolving cultural contexts. They, like everyone else, have been affected by historical and cultural impacts that have consequently changed their ways of viewing the world. If pre-contact Aborigines were suddenly catapulted into the 1990s they might find little compatibility with their modern descendants. But one could say that about any religion or world view. The Dreaming will not be lost altogether, but will undergo a transformation.

Note

1. The 'Lost Generation' refers to the children who were taken away from their Aboriginal parents during early government policies of assimilation. It was thought that 'half-caste' children should be given the opportunity to be educated and assimilated into a European way of life. Many adults are now trying to locate their Aboriginal kin through programmes such as Link Up.

9. Ecology and religion in Karuk orientations toward the land

Sean M. Connors

Much has been made in American popular and academic publications of the essentially harmonious orientation of Native American religious beliefs about nature. As public concern over the increasingly rapid pace of environmental degradation in America coalesced in the 1960s and early 1970s, the image of 'the Indian' living in harmony with nature was proffered as a paragon of right living with the earth. American Indians, it seemed to many, had deeply felt connections to the bosom of their Earth-Mother; they understood that they were at one with nature; and they were ardent conservationists – utilizing out of sheer respect all that nature had provided them; they lived in harmony with the earth, upon which they walked lightly, for subsistence was a holy occupation with them.

That is, just as the image of the Indian as the 'red man' had served the purposes of the American colonizers in the past, a greener image of the Indian as an 'original' ecologist came to serve the purposes of Americans again in the midst of their own ecological problems in the relative present. In both past and present cases, Native Americans have been imagined to suit non-Native interests (see Berkhofer 1978 and Gill 1987a). But to say that Native Americans have *not* lived with a concern for their interactions with natural environments is also less than tenable (see Vecsey 1980 and Callicott 1989). Certainly Native people today are quite vocal about sacred relationships with the land (see Martinez 1996); many, however, are also quite vocal about their ambitions to economically exploit the natural resources of their tribal lands (see Bordewich 1996). Attempts by non-Natives to imagine the nature of relationships between religion and ecology in Native America are always challenged by a history of imagining Native Peoples for non-Native reasons and by a vast diversity of Native perspectives and traditions. Even so, many are still asking whether Native Americans have some sort of special relationship with the natural world and, if so, whether anything in this special relationship can inform contemporary environmental policy and philosophy.

Approaches to answering such questions are typically veiled by the blanket concept of 'the Indian'. Discussions of the supposed 'environmental religion' (Vecsey 1980), 'land ethic' (Callicott 1989), or 'nature religion' (Albanese 1990) of Native Peoples typically obfuscate reliable and valid answers to such questions by reducing the unimaginable variances of Native American religious traditions to a homogenous template. Most scholars warn against such blanket concepts, yet many slip back into them. Well-known historian of American religions and author of *Nature Religion in America*, Catherine Albanese illustrates this tendency. Albanese acknowledges that North America prior to Columbus's voyages was home to peoples speaking well over five hundred languages, of nine radically different language families as diverse as Chinese from German, or Arabic from English. And while admitting that 'to speak collectively of native North American tribal cultures is to do violence to the subjective sensibility of many different peoples', she suggests that, 'cast beside the European invaders, Amerindians and their religious ways shared much in common' (1990, 19–20). As a generalized understanding, Albanese writes:

> in short . . . with correspondence as controlling metaphor, they sought their own versions of mastery and control through harmony in a universe of persons who were part of the natural world. Nature religion, if it lived in America at all, lived among Amerindians. (1990, 25)

Generalizations of this sort about Native American traditions are inevitably as false as they are true; even worse, they border on stereotyping. Far more can be learned about the dynamics between religion and nature in Native American traditions by focusing on the bioregional nature of Native religious traditions. There is no more a homogeneous Native American nature religion than there is a homogeneous North American environment. It is in particular places that Native Peoples struggle to maintain traditional relationships with their ancestral lands. In other words, rather than imagining an abstract set of Native American religious ideas concerning human relationships with the natural world, a thicker understanding obtains from imagining Native traditions as emerging from a dialectic between religious traditions and particular bioregions – between people and place. Particular environments have heavily influenced various Native American religious traditions, even as their religious traditions have oriented many of the ways in which they, in turn, have shaped their environments.

From this perspective, Native American religious orientations toward the natural world can be no more homogeneous than the environmental diversity of the North American continent. The North American continent is a generalization itself comprised of widely variant ecosystems – from woodlands to plains, desert basins to high mountain plateaus, arctic tundra to tropical wetlands, temperate to tropical forests, chaparral to swamp – widely different resource bases, and widely different population densities, languages and traditions of social organization. Eighteenth-century Lakotas, for instance, had a special place in their religious traditions for the buffalo because they lived in the Great Plains where buffalo were a primary resource for survival. Likewise, coastal peoples had special traditions relating them to coastal aquatic life, and agricultural peoples had a special reverence for cultivated staples such as maize. Similarly, many traditions indigenous to the northwest coast of contemporary California had special religious traditions concerning salmon, deer and acorns, among other regionally prevalent fauna and flora. Few scholars, however, have taken such a grounded approach to understanding the relationships between religion and ecology in the history of Native American traditions.

While generalizations of Native American orientations toward nature abound, there are few studies of Native religious traditions in relation to traditional bioregions. The most significant works have all been advanced by anthropologists. Richard Nelson (1983) broke important ground in this area of scholarship in his ethnographic work with the Koyukon people of Northern Alaska in *Make Prayers to the Raven*. Nelson describes an expansive Koyukon knowledge of the workings of their boreal forest environment and a rich narrative tradition oriented by stories of 'the distant time'. In the Koyukon culture, conservation practices are oriented by both ecological knowledge *and* religious tradition, as neither one is subsumed by the other. Keith Basso's (1996) *Wisdom Sits in Places* has also made a major contribution to understanding the place-based nature of Native American traditions. Basso elegantly describes the use of one genre of oral tradition among the Western Apache of Arizona. These stories concern places and their histories – things that have taken place, and continue to take place as the stories are remembered. There is an intimate relationship between language and landscape in the Western Apache culture which orients traditional social ethics in the community; Western Apache traditional ethics, that is, are inseparable from the places themselves. The first major work by a Native scholar in this area has been recently advanced by Yupiaq anthropologist Oscar Kawagley. Kawagley's ground-breaking work *A Yupiaq Worldview* (1995) approaches environmental science from a Yup'ik perspective, illustrating systems of complex technical knowledge of survival on the Kuskokwim River delta and their orientation in Yup'ik religious traditions. Kawagley, both science teacher and anthropologist, has established a summer fish camp where Yup'ik students learn environmental science through their own language and traditions. In this way, Kawagley offers both an ethnographic description of the dynamics between ecological knowledge and religious traditions in the culture of his ancestors, and a pragmatic application of such ethnographic work continuing to engender relationships between culture and environment. Both Nelson and Kawagley explore ecological knowledge and religious traditions, while Basso is somewhat more restrictive in his explorations of place and historical narratives; all of them, however, suggest intimate connections between oral tradition and local environment in the traditions they represent. Each is different from the other and from common generalizations because of particular relationships engendered in particular regions. Each, I believe, gives us a richer way of imagining Native American religious orientations toward the land.

Rather than explore generalizations about Native American 'nature religion', then, this chapter explores the relationships between religion and environment in a particular place among a particular people. A brief survey of the religious traditions of the Karuk people of the upper Klamath River in what is now known as Northwestern California will suggest the place-based character of Native American religious traditions and their dialectical relationship to particular environments; the land has shaped Karuk people's religious traditions even as their religious traditions have oriented the ways in which they, in turn, shaped the Klamath landscape.

In their own, soft-sounding, Hokan language (rather like Portuguese to a foreign ear), these people call themselves the *Karuk araara*, the 'Upriver People'. They live upriver from the Algonkian-speaking Yurok, or in the Karuk tongue, *Yuruk araara*, the 'Downriver People', and adjacent to the Athabaskan-speaking Hupa on the Trinity River, a confluence of the Klamath which marks the natural divide between Karuk and Yurok territories. Though these peoples speak radically different native languages, they share remarkably similar cultures oriented by and toward the Klamath River and the steep mountain slopes and drainages surrounding it.

The primary directions in the Karuk language illustrate the prominence of the river in their environment and culture: *karuk*, 'upriver'; *yuruk*, 'downriver'; *maruk*, 'uphill – away from the river'; and *saruk*, 'downhill – toward the river'. The topography is very steep and flat spaces are rare, hence village sites are ancient (some houses have been empirically dated to be 8–10 thousand years old). The forest environments range from redwood forests on the coast to oak, pine and fir further upriver. The river itself once coursed rhythmically with salmon, stealhead and eel. The watershed was home to bears, beavers, eagles, deer, elk, coyotes, salamanders, lizards and snakes, as well as humans and many other species. All of these aspects and inhabitants of the Klamath River region have had deep influences on the religious traditions of the Klamath River peoples, and likewise, their religious traditions have had important effects on the Klamath River environment in turn. From the forests and fields, Klamath River Peoples gathered acorns, brodiea (a starchy, onion-like bulb) and a wide variety of herbs and basketry materials. Hunters also culled the deer and elk herds. From the rivers and creeks, the people harvested enormous quantities of salmon, stealhead and eel. Though resources were extracted and the environment was shaped to maximize the abundance of them, none were depleted and biodiversity was maintained at a far greater level than is the case today under the stewardship of the United States Forest Service.

The most widely employed technique Native Californians utilized to manage resources was the complex use of burning in a variety of microenvironments for a variety of purposes. For instance, one Karuk colleague of J.P. Harrington's explained to him that:

> our kind of people never used to the plow . . . All they used to do was burn the brush at various places, so that some good things will grow up . . . They do not set fire for nothing; it is for something that they set fire. (Harrington 1932, 63)

Similarly, Emily Danahue, one of William Bright's Karuk colleagues, explained to him some twenty years later that in the preparation of basketry materials: 'first we went and set fires . . . Then, after two years, we picked the hazel twigs . . . We burned the bear-lilies [too]. Then we picked them [as well] . . . Then we dug up pine roots' (Bright 1957, 299). After an area had been burnt it provided a rich environment for a wide variety of vegetation that the Karuk actively managed.

Techniques like those of the Karuks of burning to increase the productivity of the ecosystems with which they lived was a widespread technique throughout what is now California. This was one of the most far-reaching ways peoples indigenous to this region of the continent interacted with their local environments, employing techniques which fostered both the health and the renewability of the resources upon which the people depended. Kat Anderson has argued that:

> a survey of the ethnohistoric literature regarding burning by California Indian tribes shows that the major purposes for the burning included (1) keeping the country open; (2) managing game; (3) stimulating the production of food crops;

> (4) decreasing insect pests and diseases; and (5) facilitating food gathering. (1993, 165)

In fact, the use of fire by the Klamath River peoples was so extensive, it had nothing less than a dramatic effect on the Klamath River landscape. As Yurok elder Che-na-wah Weithch-ah-wah, also known as Lucy Thompson, explained back in 1916, the Klamath River peoples 'took the greatest of care of the hazelnut flats', for not only were the nuts used for a variety of purposes, the shoots of the plant were foundational for their basket-making:

> In taking care of the hazel flats, they go out in the dry summer or early in the fall months and burn the hazel brush; then the next spring the young shoots start up from the old roots. On the following spring in the month of May, when the sap rises and the shoots start to grow, the women go forth and gather these young shoots, which are from one to two feet in length ... They gather these sticks by the thousands and take them home, where the women, children and men all join in peeling the bark off the sticks. (Thompson 1991, 31–2)

The use of burning to increase the abundance and quality of hazel nut yields and basketry materials was but one of the methods Karuks and other Klamath River Peoples employed to shape the landscapes which they inhabited. Fire was also used to clear the ground surrounding groves of oaks to reduce pest populations and increase the ease with which acorns could be gathered. The largest of these pests, ironically, was the Douglas fir – the timber most valued by the US Forest Service and the Interior Department. From the perspective of the Klamath River Peoples before their confrontation with the Americans, for example:

> the Douglas fir timber ... ha[d] always encroached on the open prairies and crowded out the other timber; therefore they have continuously burned it and have done all they could to keep it from covering all the open lands. (Thompson 1991, 33)

That is, far from living passively with nature and lightly on the land, Klamath River Peoples employed a heavy hand in shaping their environment to suit their own cultural preferences. They preferred oaks and hazel to Douglas firs, so 'many of the prairies were set on fire and burnt off every year during the dry season, which kept [the firs] from growing up very fast' (Thompson 1991, 85). However, even Douglas firs were not exterminated, for as Donahue explained to Bright, 'the best hazel twigs are those where it is sort of a fir forest' (Bright 1957, 299). Though hazel was favored, firs were still necessary in the general milieu of the Klamath River ecosystem.

Burning practices were not derived from purely mechanical or functional motivations, however; they were understood to be a part of the deep structure of the Karuk world. Fire was understood to be a force not at odds with the land or the people, but one with which the people could co-operate and participate. Johnny Bennett, lifelong resident of the Salmon River country and a nephew of renowned Karuk 'Squirrel Jim', discusses his sense of the appropriate relationship of humans to natural processes, as informed by traditional Karuk orientations:

> I'd like to know what the fire's for. I'd just like to know what was the fire for in lightning, why did it have to burn? It's for some cause now. It could storm without that y'know, but it had to burn. I think about it many times. The old Indians say the creator made it that way to clean out the forest. In places where it hit there would be a burn out, y'know, and they never put it out. They'd push it back up the mountain and it would burn, let it go. They wouldn't bother it because they claim it was put there for some cause, and they said it was good because they could sneak up on their game, pick up their acorns, and it generally never damaged much, because you could go to a forest, great big old trees, like redwoods, been burnt once, the bark is black. (quoted in Hillman and Salter 1997, 21)

Fire made the land vital and enabled the people to prosper; it was understood to fit into the order of things. Fire was created for a good reason; it was productive. However, it was productive only if the people saw how it fit into the workings of their environment and could be used for the prosperity of the people and for the health of the land that they depended upon for survival.

The millennia-old tradition of burning and its role in the dialectic between what the land provided and how the people enhanced this bounty were abruptly interrupted by the intrusion of Euro-Americans into the Klamath River region in the 1850s. First, the Americans came in pursuit of gold, but no sooner had they won most of it than they set their sights on other resources the Klamath watershed might offer. From an American perspective, the Douglas firs were seen as a valuable resource, a cultural preference that set them again at direct odds with the peoples indigenous to the Klamath River watershed. Traditional burning practices were forced to a halt. According to Bessie Tripp, granddaughter of renowned Karuk leader New-poss in 1876, the interruption of burning practices had profound social and ecological consequences:

> Sets fire, that's the way they do. There all time fire and everything grow then like they used to eat here. All those things that they used to eat, y'know, you get in the ground. Now I don't think there is any, too much brush growing ...

> There's something that used to grow, looked like parsley. Where there are fire[s], it great big, great big plant. They used to set fire for everything, acorns too. They set fire, more acorns came back ... Nothing grows now because no fire. They grow but they not good to eat, I don't think. (quoted in manuscript by Karuk tribe for the Department of the Interior, II-2)

The modern American perception of what constitutes a forest has dramatically altered the Klamath River ecosystem along with the traditions and lifeways of the Klamath River Peoples. Today, Karuks often describe the state of the forest from their perspective as rather like a garden grown over with weeds. The American preference for harvestable timber above all else in the forest has dramatically tipped the scales of biodiversity in the Klamath watershed and forcefully challenged traditional Karuk orientations to their ancestral territory.

Both Karuks and Americans have manipulated the Klamath watershed according to their own cultural preferences. However, as Robert Bunting (1997) argues, Native peoples in the Pacific raincoast not only interacted extensively with different geographies and microenvironments to shape distinct landscapes and cultures, they harvested no plant, animal, or fish exclusively enough to endanger its existence. For example, Henry Lewis notes that:

> in order to gather sufficient suitable branches for making the many kinds of baskets produced by adolescent and adult females in various villages, Native [Californians] had to manage and maintain abundant populations of certain plants at what was virtually an industrial level. (1993, 162)

Furthermore, recent estimates of the number of salmon taken by Native people indicate that the scale of Indian fishing among Northwest coast cultures 'was fully comparable to the [American] commercial fishery during its heyday in the late nineteenth century' (Taylor 1992, 59, 63–4). Despite the healthy magnitude of Native peoples' consumption, however, no species' population was ever endangered. Northwest coast peoples apparently had the numbers and skill to decimate plant and fish populations, yet they did not. And they did not, Bunting argues, because of cultural prescriptions:

> Although Northwest Indians adjusted their economic and cultural patterns to nature's abundance and seasonal offerings, they were not passive to an environmental determinism. Nor were they proto-[conservationists] who left the ecosystem unaltered ... Nature may have framed the choices people made, but the conscious ways that people shaped the environment to enhance their physical well-being were in accordance with cultural prescriptions. (1997, 12)

Similarly, Sean Swezey and Robert Heizer suggest that co-ordination of indigenous fishing techniques with the seasonal rhythms of the salmon migrations and the management of this important resource 'may have been accomplished through large-scale ritual organization and management of salmon fishing' (1993, 307).

Throughout the Northwest coastal region, American Indian peoples conducted elaborate, annual, communal fishing efforts involving the construction and maintenance of elaborate weirs (fish dams) as well as the delicate and precise timing of such ventures. More importantly, individuals who held specific and technical knowledge of such resource management practices and supervised the harvesting of resources also directed the ceremonies. That is, the co-ordination of salmon harvesting was organized and managed by ceremonial directors who possessed the ritual and ecological knowledge necessary to most efficiently manage the shared resource. In an analysis of northwestern California Indians' harvesting of salmon resources, Swezey and Heizer note that a careful study of the ethnographic record concerning the first salmon ceremonies reveals 'a remarkable similarity of form and function throughout Native California, particularly with respect to the seasonal occurrence of these rites and the central regulatory role assumed by various ritually empowered personalities' (1993, 300). In this way, ceremonial directors ritually marked the beginnings of the harvest, directed it, and limited its duration so that other groups upriver could share in the annual runs, and plenty of salmon could still reach their spawning grounds. The ritual specialists of the Karuks, who directed the building of the weirs and the harvesting of the salmon, marked off a ten-day period by visiting certain ritually significant sites, praying, fasting and sometimes crying, during which time the salmon were allowed to run freely upriver. Taking even a single salmon before the ceremonial director had completed the elaborate sequence of rituals was impermissible and certain to ruin one's luck and even endanger one's life. Even to accidentally glance at the smoke of the fire built to cook the first salmon dangerously disrespected the sacrality of the ceremony. For this reason, the people would leave the banks of the river and retreat to the mountain slopes, and the ceremony is often called *iduramva*, roughly, 'the people run away and hide'. While in hiding, the stories and traditions concerning the origins and travels of the first salmon would be told to honor it and encourage it in its ascent of the powerful river. The first-salmon and fish dam-building ceremonies

> were essentially ritual activities arising from the need to carefully manage the anadromous fish resources and to regulate the fishing activities of large human

> populations which intensively utilised this resource on major Northern California streams during a limited seasonal interval. (Swezey and Heizer 1993, 325)

Lucy Thompson's testimony corroborates the conclusions of contemporary ethnohistorians such as Swezey and Heizer. She describes the elaborate procedure of constructing the fish weirs as orchestrated by the ceremonial director, and she explains that the harvesting of fish was governed by 'very strict laws' handed down to the people by the spirits of the land – the potent beings who inhabited and shaped the land before the era of human beings.

> In these traps there gets to be a mass of salmon, so full that they make the whole structure of the fish dam quiver and tremble with their weight . . . After all have taken what they want of the salmon, which must be done in the early part of the day, [the ceremonial director or his assistant] opens the upper gates of the traps and lets the salmon pass on up the river, and at the same time great numbers are passing through the open gap left on the south side of the river. This is done so that [others] on up the river have a chance at the salmon catching. But they keep a close watch to see that there are enough left to effect the spawning, by which the supply is kept up for the following year. (Thompson 1991, 177–8)

As is still the case in Native Northern California, ritual specialists have historically held their culture's repertoire of technical knowledge regarding resource management. Technical knowledge of harvesting and conserving resources, however, was and continues to be guided by a religious orientation, one which recognizes that just as the environment shapes the religious traditions of the people, so do the people's religious traditions influence their interaction with the environment.

This dialectic between the religious orientation of the people and the shape of the natural environment can be seen in a starker contrast when compared with the cultural orientations of the Americans when they came to the Klamath region in the mid- to late-nineteenth century and the resulting effects this had on the Karuk people and the Klamath River watershed. By the turn of the century, Lucy Thompson – and many others – observed that while the Klamath River Peoples observed laws limiting the extension of the fish traps to two-thirds of the width of the river:

> The whites [also] have laws that no one is allowed to let a net extend more than two-thirds of the distance across the river, and wardens are paid to see that the law is obeyed. Yet the whites set one net from one side two-thirds across, and then just a few steps up another net from the other side, and which extends two-

> thirds across in distance. And in a distance of sixty yards, there will be from eight to ten nets, making so complete a network that hardly a salmon can pass. (Thompson 1991, 179)

The Americans had laws rather like those of the Klamath River Peoples, but they did not have a ritual or sacred orientation to harvesting the salmon runs. The result might be described as a classic case of following the letter of the law rather than the spirit of the law, an orientation quite common among Americans recently turned 'Californian'.

The Karuk, Yurok, and Hupa Peoples had, and continue to have, a deeply rooted history of dwelling in the Klamath watershed – at least ten thousand years as measured by empirical dating methods – since the beginning of time in their own reckoning. Their relationship, dependency upon, and gratitude for the salmon were as deep and strong as the waters of the Klamath River itself at the time the Americans arrived. The Americans had *just* arrived, though, and they had arrived with a cultural history of harvesting the resources of the 'New World', as they called it, in a spirit of 'Manifest Destiny' and a sense that the continuing growth and 'progress' of civilization were 'inevitable'. The salmon were perceived as a resource, not as a gift, and certainly not as part of an ancient and sacred relationship. The Klamath River Peoples had oriented themselves toward the annual arrival of the salmon as a reciprocal relationship and style of being which was given to them since before the beginning of time; the American arrivals to the Klamath River watershed saw a commodity – a resource with a market value – apparently free for the taking. Back in the first decade of this century Lucy Thompson wondered whether 'the whites [will] preserve the salmon through all the ages, as the Klamath Indians have done, if *they* [the whites] should last so long?' (Thompson 1991, 179). By the time Lucy Thompson's book was republished in the last decade of the century, salmon no longer packed the course of the Klamath as they had in her childhood years. By the time this piece I am now writing is published, 30 species of salmon, including those native to the Klamath, will have been added to the endangered species list in the United States.

The Klamath River Peoples and the Klamath River watershed have seen drastic, often violent, changes over the past century and a half. The salmon are endangered, the forest is overgrown here and clear cut there, the first salmon ceremony is no longer performed, the people have been hunted down, overpowered, and now face increasingly complex socio-economic problems. Leaf Hillman (Director and founder of the Karuk Tribe's Natural Resource Department and hereditary owner of the White Deerskin Dance) explains that:

> in recent decades the land and people have suffered from reckless over-reliance on herbicides, massive clear cuts in areas of highly unstable soil, the forced cessation of controlled tribal burning practices and the resultant development of frequent cycles of catastrophic wildfires. (Hillman 1997, 3)

As great as this impact has been, though, Hillman still asserts that 'in these times of rapidly changing conceptions of land management, the Karuk people have at their command the knowledge and traditions necessary to rehabilitate and sustain this landscape' (Hillman and Salter 1997, 25). Natural resource managers under Hillman's direction are committed toward resource management policies and projects which integrate ecological models with traditional Karuk systems of knowledge – including ritual knowledge and the cultivation of a spiritual orientation toward the rehabilitation of the Klamath River ecosystem. Similarly, rejuvenation of the Klamath River watershed is seen as fundamental to the continuing vitality of Karuk culture. The Karuk natural resource managers understand people and the landscape as being in a complex and dynamic system of relationships in which the land and the people continually recreate and perpetuate each other. Hillman and his colleague, Karuk Tribal Anthropologist, John Salter explain what they call 'the spiritual connection' in their work as Karuk natural resource managers:

> Among the Karuk, the spiritual emerges from a contemplation of the nature of Nature. This is not a sense of nature which is a narrow projection of rich and powerful mentalities. It is nature understood as a corrective process. With us the relationship to the land is an inclusive way of life in which the spiritual link is constantly reemerging and making clear consequences which cannot be ignored. That linkage is part of every consideration. (1997, 25)

They explain that: 'This perspective requires a concentration on the nature and needs of the whole system, and the links between that larger system and human beings with a unique potential for affecting the system – positively as well as negatively' (1997, 24). Ecological perspectives and traditional Karuk orientations are blended in contemporary Karuk approaches to forest and fisheries restoration and their co-operative ventures with the US Forest Service. Although they must often swim against strong currents of opposition from the commercial and political interests of others, they assert that:

> indigenous land management knowledge and philosophy has much to offer the non-tribal world. Recognition of this ... becomes increasingly necessary as the issues of sustaining humankind as one of the many species sharing life on this earth assumes global proportions. (Hillman and Salter 1997, 26)

The Karuks most certainly have had and continue to have an intimate relationship between their religious traditions and the landscape out of which their traditions have emerged. However, their religious traditions do not *necessarily* inform an understanding of traditions indigenous to other regions of the continent. Also, although contemporary Karuk tribal resource management is oriented by traditional systems of knowledge, this is not always the case with other contemporary American Indian Nations. Each Native Nation has its own regional, cultural and historical issues with which to contend. The Karuk Tribe of California on the Klamath River, however, has been able to draw on their own ancestral religious traditions for living in the Klamath watershed in their efforts to create a new paradigm for natural resource management. This 'new paradigm' is deeply influenced and informed by an ancient orientation which understands that people and place are integrated through a reciprocal relationship. In this the Karuk have much in common with other rural Indian and reservation communities, for whom, as Lee Irwin explains: 'preservation (or reclamation) of the land is coextensive with cultural survival because of the ways in which native spirituality is tied to specific places, seasonal activities, and narrative perspectives' (1998, 140). Although all this may still lend itself to the idea that Native American religious traditions are oriented toward living in harmony with the earth, it should also suggest that ancestral Native American religious traditions emerge out of relationships engendered between particular peoples and particular places.

The issue is a matter of focus and agendum. A wide focus on Native American religious orientations toward the land necessarily traffics in generalizations and tends to suit Non-Native interests. A tighter focus affords greater resolution. This greater resolution emerges from greater understanding of particular peoples in particular places; it means *learning from* particular peoples in particular places. And regional knowledge is more likely to suit the agenda of regional interests, even as it relocates the centres of scholarship to the peripheries of academia. For many rural and reservation Indian peoples, religious orientation toward their ancestral territories is not an issue of generalized representations; it is a matter of the cultural and economic survival of real people in real places. For scholars of religion this is an opportunity to learn from Native paradigms of people and place. It might also afford an opportunity to be socially responsible in our scholarship.

Part III
Gifts

10. Art works in Aotearoa

Graham Harvey

Cameras are problematic because they tend to prevent the photographer from participating in that which they observe. Or, rather, they turn the photographer into a problematic type of participant: a voyeur. Voyeurism is a qualitatively different sort of participation from that expected, encouraged and moulded by many ceremonies, rituals, performances and traditional understandings. Also, the distance between the photographer/ voyeur and that which they photograph/see is qualitatively different to the distance created between an object, event or person and the uninitiated whose 'absent presence' is often vital to the establishment and maintenance of 'secrecy' (cf. Taussig 1998, 354–7). The same problem of presence/full engagement or distance/observation has led to the development of various methodologies by missionaries and anthropologists in their encounters with indigenous and other researched groups. Most resolutions of this question of how to participate in order to achieve full understanding constellate around versions of 'participant observation' (see Masuzawa 1998; Cox 1998). Clearly, the goal here is to avoid 'going native' – precisely what the work of much art is intended to achieve. The camera re-reveals the Enlightenment fascination with sight (equally strongly encoded in text), establishing relationship by distance/ difference: subject/object, viewer/viewed. The inner I relates to the outer you – dangerously close to 'it' – through the eyes ('my' eyes not the mutual gaze of eye-to-eye contact, so near to touch). The camera aids the individuation process at the heart of the Western attempt to achieve 'progress'. To photograph is to do something to that which becomes scene/seen, observed/preserved (again much like literary encoding of events as 'history' or encounters as 'scripture'). It objectifies by reifying absence, distance, past, fixedness, universality. This is a far from passive process, but its end result is a sort of passivity to the present just as it is an absence from that which is present. In the act of photographing/ observing, the photographer/observer is most fully engaged with a future in which 'I/eye' will observe this past, finished event. The observer's present absence and distance will be consummated in the transcending of temporal space, embodiment and relationships that is the viewing of a photograph of a (mere) object. And this is why it is truly said that cameras steal soul(s).

There are, of course, other ways to use a camera. Grace Lau, for example, struggles with her engagement in the intimate encounters she photographs (1997). Perhaps somewhat more accessibly, the camera work in the TV series *NYPD Blue* deliberately reveals the engaged presence of the camera crew and director. There is, however, a pretence that this is not so in nature documentaries which allege that camera crews (being 'simply' observers and recorders of 'nature') cannot participate by making warning sounds that would save the life of the gazelle stalked by the lion. Meanwhile, there are also other ways to observe and participate in indigenous events, other ways to encounter people, other ways to engage with soul.

This chapter is concerned with indigenous art work and works of art, especially that of the *marae*, finest exemplar of Maori lifeways. It began with a rant about cameras so that I could express something of my intention to contribute to the processes of (re-)discovery of ways to build relationships with living art. Instead of seeing objects (whether as museum artefact, tourist spectacle, or indigenous ceremony), we meet with intentional agents, active beings. That is, masks, costumes, drums, carvings, paintings, statues, buildings, and so on are far more than objects to be used by people. Often they are people themselves (in senses familiar to readers of Hallowell 1975, and Kohák 1991, 1993). Meeting them requires a rich interplay of appreciation of craft skills, materials, symbolism, local cultural meanings, historical awareness, and openness to multiplicities of meaning, reference, understanding, use and access. More than that, it requires willingness to engage in appropriate protocol, forms of etiquette, modes of meeting, greeting and parting. Some indigenous art works act as signposts to something or somewhere else – usually a place that human people should or should not go now. But much of it encounters us in more open relationships, we are confronted and met with – and we are not always in a dominant position. None of this is to say that indigenous people do not make and decorate things for the pleasure of seeing them. Even if everything (shape, colour, texture, function, context, ownership) might be symbolic and revelatory of something else (power, relationships, value, place, meaning), it can also be what it appears to be: aesthetically pleasing. This adds to the beauty and power of encounters with indigenous art work.

What is 'art'?

Like religion, 'art' might be another of those Western categories sought out but not self-evident (and maybe not required) in indigenous and other contexts. The category helps Western visitors see what is there, but indigenous modes of experience, relationship and understanding enable full engagement with what is encountered. Indigenous art, like so much else, is almost always integrated with the rest of indigenous lifeways rather than being a separate domain, category, activity or experience.

Dictionary definitions of 'art' refer to a wide variety of uses of the term. Art is associated not only with appreciation of beauty (whatever that might mean!), but also with the making of artefacts (useful ones as well as decorative ones). It incorporates notions of energetic work as well as more passive enjoyment. Art can do a host of things, including be decorative, expressive, representative, symbolic and much more. It can refer to the making, display and appreciation of objects (paintings, carvings, etc.) and to performed actions such as dance, music and oratory. For further insight into uses of the word 'art' I consulted the index of an ethnography randomly picked from the library shelf. This reads:

> Art. *See* Batik; Body art, Carvings, Chromo-lithographs; Dance; Ijala; Iremoje; Iron, art; Oriki; Praise poetry; Sculpture; Songs; *Vèvè*. (Barnes 1997, 373)

Other entries widen the possibilities of discovering the richness of artistic activity and expression in a variety of West African traditions. These include alterations and adornment of the human body, the transformation and shaping of metals, woods, stones and other materials into usable, displayable or secret objects, and the performance of music (instrumental and vocal) for a variety of purposes including pleasure, worship, life-increase, edification and education. In no way does this exhaust the possibilities. This index entry also points to the need for indigenous guidance: some things are only knowable when indigenous words point them out. Other languages may not be able to express what is known to particular indigenous people, or may confuse matters by suggesting alien understandings – or, rather, misunderstandings.

Accessible expert introductions to indigenous religious art, and arts, which engage with and interact with indigenous aesthetics and categories, are provided by Albert Moore (1995) and Rosalind Hackett (1996). The opening chapters to these books admirably explore diverse views of all those activities and things that can be labelled art. Just as the study of indigenous religions will challenge Western (academic and popular) notions of what 'religion' is, so encounter with indigenous art challenges

Western understanding of art. There is, for example, a sneaking suspicion that 'art' refers to that which has no use beyond being looked at, or, at best, that which decorates objects which do have a function. So, a house could be functionally complete without decorative carving, it does not need to be painted (outside) and adorned (inside) with paintings of other places. Such carving, painting and paintings might be 'art', here understood to be part of luxury or leisure, and therefore carrier of little meaning or power. To say this is, hopefully, to realize the folly of such views. Even 'decoration' arises from agreed-upon cultural understandings and expresses values, identities and other 'meanings'. Luxury and leisure – if that is what art is – express, maintain and impose power relationships. Far from the assertion of leisure and luxury diminishing the significance of art in identity formation and maintenance, it might rather make it more central. In the end, we engage in all the seemingly separate but in fact inseparable aspects of life – politics, religion, work, leisure, etc. – precisely because we find them gratifying (to extend the argument of Beit-Hallahmi 1989).

The remainder of this chapter is concerned with the expression of creativity, autonomy, agency and relationships in objects that people make, wear, display, inhabit, exchange, view, and perhaps venerate or honour. Some of these objects are worn or otherwise used during the performing arts of dance, music, speech-making, ceremony, and perhaps war. The *marae* (meeting place and its associated buildings) provides the prime example of art-work (art that works) and is the context for discussion of the performed arts of oratory, dance and singing.

Rosalind Hackett's observation about African art is perhaps true of all art, certainly of indigenous art:

> It is affective – it causes, transforms. Many things happen, not just what one can see, hear, or think at one time. Ordinary items and objects used in everyday life are transformed into art forms, lending themselves to a virtually unlimited range of interpretations and applications. (1996, viii)

This range is unlimited not only for the Western observer (collector, tourist, art historian, anthropologist or scholar of religion), but also in the home context of indigenous manufacture and use. This is part of what it means to acknowledge that we are encountering 'living art' and 'living religions'. Indigenous religions and indigenous art(s) have always been changeable, this is part of what 'traditional' means in many traditional, indigenous contexts. Certainly people expect to see certain things, they associate particular shapes with particular objects and occasions. However, it is that epitome of modernity, the production line, rather than the indigenous artist, that produces precisely identical objects every time.

Reinforcing the need to approach indigenous art from indigenous perspectives, Hackett also invaluably notes that:

> In judging the efficacy and affectiveness of such objects or artifacts, however, considerations of technical skill, design consciousness, and familiarity with culturally relevant aesthetic concerns become paramount. It is at this point that the focus shifts to the artists – their creative genius, their deep esoteric knowledge of things and events around them, as well as their intellectual power of vivid expression. (1996, viii)

The following discussion is rooted in my (somewhat serendipitous) encounters and the generosity of those who have taught me the required protocols of such meetings. Paaka Tawhai writes of the sense of danger with which he narrates his people's flexible *korero tahito*, ancient explanations (1988, 857). My own misgiving is that I may have been insufficiently attentive to my hosts or breached a protocol binding on a grateful guest. Happily, Maori art consists not principally of 'objects' but of living beings with a story. In addition to explaining some of the *korero* of that which I encountered in Aotearoa – particularly that of Ngati Porou – my hosts pointed me towards a number of books by Maori experts amplifying key issues. My narration is therefore less ethnographic than it might have been: it is more of a dialogue with far from non-literate and, certainly, richly expressive people. This (and the fact that this is an introductory dialogue) might, at least in part, mitigate the limited sensuality of much of what follows. Any discussion of art ought, of course, to deal with the look, touch, sound, feel and sometimes the smell and taste of the thing (see Blake 1997, 125). Happily, the word 'soul' now encompasses the fully sensual realm of (earthy, gutsy, sexy) food and music arising from and vividly expressing people's identity, relationships and cosmology. An attempt to discuss such things ought to do so with soul, rather than the more refined, abstract, intellectual, (perhaps) spiritual but not spirited, and distant discussions to which we are sometimes treated.

Maori *Taonga*

Sidney Moko Mead summarizes some of the variety of Maori arts:

> large decorated meeting-houses and their various pieces such as centre-post figures; storehouses and some distinctive carvings that are associated with them; canoes and especially canoe prows and stern pieces; fishhooks; personal ornaments such as the well-known tiki, dog-shaped pendants and combs of

> various shapes and sizes; weapons of bone, stone and wood; items of costume such as the dogskin cloaks from the 1844 period, kaitaka cloaks with their taniko borders or decorated thrums; hafted adzes especially the toki-pou-tangata; burial coffins; bowls shaped like dogs; treasure boxes, both oval and oblong in outline; and so on. (Mead 1997, 159)

A full catalogue would require an extensive volume, especially if it did justice to the lived context of art works. Instead I offer here a visitor-response to *marae* (and their literary *korero*) because this is the context in which the most significant features of Maori arts are visible. Such arts are better labelled as *taonga* which might be translated as 'treasures' as long as we engage with indigenous appreciations of why and how 'objects' are treasured (see Mead 1997, 179–89), including (re)cognition of their intangible (or more than tangible) aspects (Walker 1990, 268). Or, as Mead puts it: 'a major difference between "artifact" and "taonga" is that there is a taha wairua [spiritual aspect, or soul] to the Maori concept' (1997, 184).

Te marae

A *marae* is a combination of an enclosed space and several buildings. The *marae* proper is the space in which people gather and meet – abiding by particular protocol and aided by traditional ceremonies. The buildings facilitate the normalizing of friendly relationships and permit a community to engage with issues that concern them. The arts of carving are evident in the manufacture and maintenance of the buildings; those of weaving and painting are significant in their further ornamentation. The arts of oratory, singing, dance and cooking are central to the functioning of the *marae*. People on the *marae* display some arts (e.g. carved pendants and tattooing) and perform others. These arts are alive not only in the sense that they are contemporary, or that they affect people, but in that they express relationships. A greenstone pendant, for example, is not only a ornament or an expression of Maori identity. Each piece of *pounamu*, greenstone, is alive, gendered and deserving of respect. Aside from whatever takes place between the stone and its quarrier or carver, only men should wear male greenstone, only women should wear female greenstone, they should know the name of the stone, and make sure that if it leaves its native land it will, sometime, return. (For a discussion of *pounamu* as a natural and spiritual resource, and thus an issue for the Waitangi Tribunal, see Durie 1998, 37.)

Despite the impression that buildings make, especially when carved and painted, it is the space that is most significant, and on which the most significant actions take place. In some respects the buildings simply complete what the space achieves. They earth the actions achieved on the open ground that is the *marae*. (The ambiguity of referring to both the whole complex and only the courtyard as the *marae* is now generally solved by calling the latter the *marae-atea*.) The creation of space is vital as it allows potential to be realized, it gives room for encounter and for normalization of that which is new and exceptional, or neutralization of that which is threatening. Of course, just as potential and possibility are unremarkable, so the space and all that it means generally go un-remarked. This is to echo what I think is implied in Paaka Tawhai's eloquent discussion of Maori religion (1988), that while the foundational realities, energies, existences (or potentialities) and ambiguities of the universe can be named (Te Kore and Te Po), little more notice is taken of them in daily life. They are taken for granted as the context in which everything of interest happens. They generate everything except attention to themselves. None the less, for the purposes of engaging with Maori *taonga* we must pay attention to that which is open and, at least initially, empty. Soon we will explore the buildings which call us, attract us, demand our attention by their ornate presence. But we can only do that when we have spent time in the space. This is difficult to do in narrative form. Here I can only assert that the first work of art (one that works) is the formation of space. The *marae-atea* space is bounded by a gated-fence and by buildings which appear more significant. But, attempting to emulate Maori art, we will spiral back to the space to note that it is the context for the performative arts, especially of oratory and music, after describing the buildings. Another turn of the spiral will note that decision-making in the buildings also spirals in towards consensus or resolution.

Meeting house

The most obvious building opening onto the *marae-atea* and facing the gateway is variously named the *whare nui*, large house, *whare tipuna* or *whare tupuna*, ancestral house, *whare whakairo*, carved house, *whare hui*, meeting house, *whare moe* or *whare puni*, sleeping house, or *whare runanga*, council house (Tauroa and Tauroa 1986, 90–1). Traditionally these were – and are again – carved from wood, some are also now painted. Basically such *whare* are rectangular (longer at the sides than at the front and back), with a roof sloping down from a ridge-pole to lower side walls. With appropriate *karakia*, invocations, at every stage, wood has been taken from among the trees and then shaped, formed, transformed into a culturally recognized, accepted or celebrated treasure, *taonga whakairo*, i.e. 'a taonga (highly valued object of culture) whakairo (to which the transforming process of art has been applied)' (Mead 1997, 184). This transformative process meets the lifeforce, *mauri*, which exists in potential within the wood, bone, greenstone and so on, and brings it into form by the transfer of *mana* carried by the *kaitiaki* from the heavens to the carver's hands. This too is what is meant by the insistence that Maori artwork lives (Mataira, personal communication).

At the front apex there is a carved figure, *tekoteko*, of the ancestor after whom the building is named, or who the building symbolizes. Although this is what most books about *marae* say, it appears to be a weakened version of *korero tahito*, traditional understanding, made palatable to the Western observer (art critic, tourist or scholar of religion). Everything else that is said about the *marae* requires that the *tekoteko* does more than represent the head of the ancestor symbolized, memorialized or honoured in the *marae*. The *marae is* the ancestor, the *tekoteko is* the ancestor's head. The ancestor's arms are seen – outstretched in welcome – in the gable ends or barge boards, *maihi*, which end in finger marks, *raparapa*. The strong ridge-pole, *tahuhu*, is the ancestor's spine, supported internally by two wooden pillars, *poutokomanawa*, which include a heart-post and also symbolize Tane's (creative and continuing) separation of Sky-Father, Ranginui, from Earth-Mother, Papatuanuku, which allows light and space for life to grow (see Tawhai 1988, 858–60, and Barlow 1991, 179). This expansion of horizons further alludes to the quest for knowledge, to which light metaphorically refers, as *maramatanga* in *te reo maori* as much as in English (Mead 1997, 512). The diversity of both life and knowledge are enriched and increased in human reciprocal relationships, which it is the work of the *whare* to enable and enhance. The ridge-pole also refers to the line of descent from the ancestor portrayed as the *tekoteko*, while the centre-support is the chief who now embodies the ancestor(s) and upholds their continuing lineage in the present generation. The front window, facing the rising sun, also engages with the *korero tahito* of how light and space were achieved at the cost of the separation of the first lovers. The door is not only a necessary entry point into the building, it is also the mouth of the ancestor – or perhaps that too is a polite rendition for those ill-at-ease with human embodiment. According to Barlow:

> The door symbolizes a change of state as one emerges from the main body of the house and enters the world outside. It is the threshold separating the sacred and the profane, and the door lintel is often carved in motifs representing the vagina, thus emphasizing the passage from the world of confinement into the world of light. (1991, 179)

An alternative perspective is offered in Walker's discussion of the chief's house Kaitangata as painted by Angus in 1844:

> The window and the doorway are carved, with the lintel carving depicting two female forms flanking the spiral design. The female vulva are inimical to tapu, and their function is to neutralise any residual tapu on strangers entering the house. (1996, 42–3)

Further ancestral figures are carved on the supports, *amo*, at either side of the front porch, *paepae*, which separates the *whare* from the *marae-atea*, but is not simply a space to cross. Or, as might be expected, its function is to be crossed after protocol is followed for the removal of *tapu*. That is, crossing is more significant than simply passing over, it requires considerable attention. The local community, *tangata whenua*, hosts of any meeting, sit on the *paepae* while their visitors are welcomed across or barred from crossing the *marae*. (*Tangata whenua* has wider resonances as it more appropriately names Maori as 'people of the land', but can also be used by them to refer to other indigenous peoples in their own lands.)

Inside the *whare* the ancestor's ribs are visible in the carved and decorated rafters, *heke* or *wheke*. The walls are decorated by carved panels, *poupou*, which depict other ancestors and significant events for the *tangata whenua*. 'One's link to the house thus may be a general one through the main ancestor, or a more particular one through connection to an ancestor figure inside the house' (Mead 1997, 163–4). An understanding of *whakapapa*, genealogy, permits the visitor to identify the relationships between the *poupou* and the *tangata kainga*, people of the place. Between such panels might be weavings and paintings representing elements of Maori spirituality, *wairua*. Many of these depict growth in various ways, especially in unfurling curls and spirals derived from the growing frond of the indigenous tree fern, *pitau*. Such forms distinguish Maori art from that of the rest of Polynesia where geometric patterns are more common and spirals are only found in the Marquesas as 'conventionalised ears, insect antennae and on the knees of the tiki' (Walker 1996, 39). In writing about the way Maori art 'expresses the unifying world-order' (1995, 176–7) Moore quotes Schwimmer:

> To the abstract patterns of these carvings the Maori artist brought his consciousness of the tight genealogical interlinking of all parts of the universe – the opulence and denseness of the spirals showing how in his view the world was a potent, convoluted unity. (1966, 97)

That unity and inter-relationship are not only portrayed in such spirals, but are also expressed in the craft of tree felling, and the arts in which wood is transformed into buildings, carved into the form of ancestors, and decorated to communicate *korero tahito*. Central to all of this art work is *whakapapa*: the right to use Earth's natural resources derives from genealogical descent from Papatuanuku and Ranginui, which makes people *tangata whenua*, i.e. 'an integral part of nature ... [with the] responsibility to take care of the whenua (land), and tangata (people)' (Dreardon 1997, 6). So everything about the *whare* concerns human relationships with their ancestors from the beginning, with their contemporaries among family, *whanau*, sub-tribe, *hapu*, tribe, *iwi* and outwards to the rest of humanity and the related realms of 'nature', and with those yet to be born, especially (but not only) those who continue the *whakapapa*.

Traditionally, the human form is not represented 'naturalistically' (as in the convention of much Western art since the classical Greek celebration of the athletic body as the embodiment of perfection). Maori art accentuates particularly significant features understood in the *korero tahito* to be full of vitality and/or *mana*, the foremost among these being the head. Even under the influence of European-introduced styles, carvers and painters still tend to draw greater attention to the head of ancestral and other figures. The carving of patterns on the human body replicate those on wood, stone and whalebone. Spirals and curves predominate in the tattoos, *moko*, that were chiselled into faces, thighs and buttocks of men of rank (chiefs, experts, *tohunga*, and warriors) or the chins and lips of powerful women. *Moko* are now tattooed rather than chiselled into human flesh, but traditional patterns continue to be seen in both flesh and wood. Typically, cosmic order

> is symbolised in the almost symmetrical designs of either side of the face separated by the split down the middle; as Schwimmer points out, left and right reflect the cosmic dualism of earth and sky. Here then tattooing serves to link the individual to the tribal, ancestral and spiritual dimensions within a sacred cosmos. (Moore 1995, 173)

Similarly, hands are typically given three fingers, which 'represents a useful, because balanced, piece of anatomy', comparable with other uses of the number three, e.g. in the three baskets of knowledge obtained by Tane. Among other things these represent 'a balance of knowledge to enable one to live a balanced life' (Tawhai 1988, 862; also see Peter Mataira's chapter in this volume). Such cosmic and relational symbolism is all the more obvious when the *moko* adorned face and body, and the efficiently balanced hands, are replicated in the carved or painted tribal/family ancestral figure in the *whare*.

Whare kai

Before discussing the activities for which the complex exists, it is important to note that it also includes the *whare kai*, a building for the preparation and provision of food, *kai*. Again it is named for an ancestor, often one associated with hospitality or links beyond the local *tangata whenua*, *hapu* or *whanau*. It stands behind or to one side of the *wharenui* depending on local *korero* about which side is more *tapu* than another. Some *marae* complexes combine the *whare kai* into the main *whare* building. *Whare kai* might also be full of ancestral and local symbolism. The chief art here is, however, the preparation and provision of food. This is supported by the art/science of production and preservation, e.g. of the kumara tuber which also migrated in the canoes and would neither grow nor last without human help (see Walker 1996, 31–2, 178). From agriculture to hospitality, food is at the centre of human relationships, and such arts either increase reciprocity or purposefully exclude outsiders (a point made obvious by the work of Mary Douglas, see especially Douglas 1992).

Performing arts

The purpose of the preceding paragraphs has been to introduce art or *taonga* on *marae*. Much of this could be picked up from looking at photos, visiting museums, looking over a fence or reading books (preferably illustrated). But such distant observation of the art of *marae* does not do it justice. *Taonga* needs to be treasured actively rather than stored away and objectified. It requires engagement and performance before our understanding of the treasuring of Maori art-work is adequate. Until now we have only dealt with part of the *kaupapa* of *marae* and their *whare*, i.e. *kaupapa* as 'conceptual plan'. The *whare*, for example, has been illustrated as a structure, the purpose of which includes 'to conserve tribal history and genealogy, so that they would be communicated from generation to generation' (Walker 1996, 45). The following extensive quotation from Ranginui Walker encapsulates the lived reality of the *marae*. It uses the past tense as it refers to activities in and around the chief's house as the precursor of the contemporary communal *marae*. With very little change it is entirely adequate as a description of a *powhiri* – the process by which *tangata whenua* greet their guests, *manuhiri* – today (see Tauroa and Tauroa 1986).

> As visitors entered the marae, the courtyard in front of the ancestral house of the chief, they were welcomed by the high-pitched karanga (call) of a kuia [female elder]. The reason for the first voice to be raised in welcome being that

> of a woman was because of her power to negate tapu and evil spiritual influences. Visitors from afar came as waewae tapu (strangers with sacred feet), and with them came the accompanying spirits of their own ancestors. The tapu and spirits that came with the guests had to be neutralised in case they conflicted with those of the tangata whenua, and so the woman's voice was the first step in the process that allowed the guests to come closer. On entering, a kaumatua [male elder] among the visitors recited a waerea, a chant, to counter any negative spiritual influences among the host tribe. The manuhiri (guests) maintained a spatial separation from the tangata whenua by stopping short of crossing the marae. At that point both paid homage to their mutual dead, while the kuia keened their sorrow for the departed with the haunting melodic tangi. After a while the hosts signalled the guests to come forward and be seated on the marae, thereby diminishing the distance between them. The kaumatua then made their mihi (formal speeches of welcome). After the visitors replied with their whaikorero, the distance between the visitors and guests was closed at a signal from the latter for the guests to come forward and hongi (press noses).
>
> The sharing of food which followed was the final negation of the alien tapu of the guests. The manuhiri and the tangata whenua were then able to intermingle freely. But as a precaution against some possible negative spiritual influences being retained among the visitors, a female figure was carved on the door lintel of the guest-house. Any residual spirits and tapu were discharged and negated by mana wahine, that is the dual generative and destructive power of the female sex. This binary opposition in the female genitals is conceptualised as te whare o te tangata (the house of men) and te whare o aitua (the house of death). The womb and the female sex are the house that both created and destroyed the culture hero Maui. (Walker 1990, 73–4)

Elsewhere Walker surveys the development of the meeting house from its precursors, particularly chiefs' houses and the ornate storerooms of earlier artistic periods (1996, 31–51; cf. Mead 1997, 157–66, 179–89). The availability of new (metal) tools and the proximity of many new 'guests' (the colonizing/invading Europeans) were among the factors responded to in the development of larger guest houses and, more recently, the revitalization of carving traditions in contemporary meeting houses. Each development met the needs of Maori for an expression of their identity as *tangata whenua*. (See also Walker 1990, 174, for a discussion of pragmatic reasons for some aspects of *marae* evolution.)

Dualities

The performing arts on *marae* respond to the built and carved art of *marae* and their *whare*, together they create life. The (pro)creation of life requires female and male co-operation in generative and cultural realms.

> The women's karanga on the marae is likened to the cry of a woman when she gives birth to her child, when the child leaves the womb and enters the world of light. This is implied in the words of the expression:
> He wahine te kaitohu i te tapu;
> He wahine hoki te kaiwhakonoa i te tapu.
> A woman instigates the sacred; a woman dissipates the sacred. (Barlow 1991, 38–9)

In their speeches, *whaikorero*, men – and women among Ngati Porou – offer what ought to be seminal words derived from (and explicitly honouring) a strong and long lineage and offered to the present and future generations (see Tawhai 1988, and Metge 1998). It is also men's cultural role to protect the *tangata whenua* (past, present and future as manifest in the land, its people, and their 'standing place', *turangawaewae*). Differences of male and female roles reinforce their interdependence, and eloquently exemplify the inseparability of seeming opposites, e.g. dark and light, spirit and matter, past and future, visible and invisible, earth and sky, local and visitor, insider and outsider, friend and foe, elder and child, cause and effect, potential and actual, and so on. (Perhaps this point could be more strongly made by replacing 'and' with a hyphen in these phrases.) The foundational interplay of *tapu* and *mana* is also evident and central in all the arts of the *marae*. Visitors bring their newness and are confronted by the abiding tradition of the *tangata* and the *whenua*. All newness is experienced as *tapu* which, unquestionably and unexceptionally, requires removal or transformation into ordinary regularity, normality, *noa*. Newness and difference are not extinguished, visitors do not become *tangata whenua*, but welcome friends.

The art-work of the *marae* is this transformation: the new is taken into the regular and made normal. It is prevented from irrupting and interrupting, rupturing the genealogy displayed in architecture, carving, performance (especially of oratory, *whaikorero*, and songs, *waiata*), participation, procreation and provision. *Korero tahito* further displays this vital(izing) interplay by insisting that the *marae-atea* is the domain of the war deity, Tu Matauenga, while the *wharenui* is the domain of Rongomatane, the peace deity. Again, these two modes of engagement only appear to be opposites, rather, they also complement and complete one another in the cause and creation of normal genealogy.

Ancestral cannibalism

Once, not so long ago, Maori engaged in cannibalism, the eating of human flesh. This has nothing to do with protein and everything to do with *mana*.

There are people with considerable skill and ability in areas that are so greatly valued that when they die (in whatever way they die) someone else wishes to incorporate such abilities into themselves. *Mana* is manifest in such skills and abilities, and in other noble, valued and visible/displayed forms. One quick way to continue the embodiment of *mana* is to ingest the corporeal remains of the *mana*-full person. On the other hand, skill possessed by an enemy bars, confronts and diminishes their opponents. What more effective rendering down to normality is there than that provided by the digestive system transforming the defeated opponent into excrement? Both these trends are narrated in Maori *korero* (Walker 1990, 72) – but rarely valued today (Mead 1997, 160). My purpose in mentioning cannibalism here is not to belittle Maori ancestors or tradition, nor to encourage the revitalization of the practice. (I am grateful to Peter Mataira for reminding me that that the taking of lives was a sacred act intrinsically related to *mana*, here to be understood in the context of *mana tangata*, '*mana* of the people/humanity' and *tangata Atua*, '*mana* of the divine originating realm/heaven'.) I have brought up the subject of cannibalism because the *kaupapa* of the *marae* complex suggests that something akin to cannibalism takes place.

The cannibal eats the ancestor. The *whare tipuna* as ancestor-ancestral house, eats the visitor. The cannibal incorporates the ancestor and the ancestor's *mana*. The *whare tipuna* incorporates the visitor. The cannibal transforms the *tapu*-newness of the ancestor's death into the *noa*-normality of a meal, of 'my' life, and of excrement. The *whare tipuna* transforms the *tapu*-newness of the visitor's arrival into the *noa*-normality of guesthood or neighbourly friendship. Neither cannibalism nor friendship become daily realities or needs. The cannibal does not rely on human flesh for protein. The visitor does not become *tangata whenua*, they remain people from elsewhere. Their potential hostility is met by a warrior who offers a challenge – generously (and potentially self-destructively) providing the visitor with an opportunity to remain an aggressive 'other'. Precisely in the challenging offer, *wero*, of a symbol of Tu Matauenga, war deity, i.e. the *taki*, challenge dart laid before *manuhiri* on full ceremonial occasions, is the visitor accorded great honour. Not only their *tapu* but also their *mana* is recognized. 'You are worthy to be an opponent', the *taki* says. But in accepting the challenge as a gift, the visitor increases the *mana* of both sides by agreeing to be transformed into a part of the lore of this ancestor and this *tangata whenua*. Picking up the *taki* affirms the visitor is honoured rather than insulted by the actions of the *haka* (a posture song integral to conflict resolution and guest-making more than it is a provocation of war). On the *marae*, especially in the space of the *marae-atea*, the visitor becomes guest.

Picking up the *taki* is, of course, only a preliminary matter. The process of normalization, incorporation and transformation is complete with the mingling of breath when *tangata whenua* and *manuhiri hongi*, when they share food after entering the body of the *whare tipuna* via the ancestral mouth/vagina. They eat having been eaten. They are given birth into their new status, but only because the vagina aggressively-lovingly and earthy-spiritually (soulfully?) strips them of all remaining *tapu* brought from a distance. They are not reborn into immortality in this world (Maui found that route barred to him, and lost his life in the process, see Mead 1997, 161–2). Maori tradition offers rich mortal-vitality dependent on lengthy *whakapapa* and wide *whanaungatanga* (family relationships), and wider neighbourly relationships. The *whare tipuna* offers a this-worldly engagement of honoured hosts and guests. The technology and performance of greeting (all that has been said so far) spiral inwards until, inside the *whare runanga*, council house, discussions can turn towards decisions.

Decision-making

In discussions hosts and guests confront each other under the tutelage of the peace deity, Rongomatane. One is not defeated by the other: Maori tradition endorses William Blake's aphorisms 'opposition is true friendship' and 'without contraries is no progression' (Blake 1793). Ema Dreardon quotes Chief Judge Durie as explaining:

> When we use the old way we sit around the hall looking to an empty space in at the centre and confronting one another. We emulate the circle. When we discuss the topic ... we talk around it ... It is rude to come too quickly to the point ... slowly, gradually ... taking on board everyone's thoughts en route, but circling inwards until eventually a consensus point is reached ... the koro says that the authority is in ourselves to make our own decisions affecting our own affairs, our own future and own children ... the decisions we make must be made in a way that upholds group harmony. (Durie in Dreardon 1997, 7)

In the *whare* the enchantment continues by the expert recollection and application of traditional understandings, lore touches law, new situations confronting the *tangata whenua* are considered in the light (and shade) of ancient wisdom. The *marae* continues to work its art.

Christianity and *utu*

This understanding of the process by which new situations and visitors are located within the story and lives of *tangata whenua* parallels the Maori acceptance of Christianity (or, given the conflicting diversities they were presented with, Christianities), and more recently of a variety of other religious traditions. For the most part, Maori have incorporated incoming traditions into what was already normal (not only *noa*, but also *maori* which itself means 'normal'). In this way, this discussion of what happens on *marae* today has ignored the fact that many (perhaps most) Maori are adherents of one Christianity or another. That omission can be rectified (in an introductory manner) by noting that generally the recitation of *karakia*, prayers/incantations, refer to a personalized 'Creator' more than was the case prior to European visitation, and often end with reference to Karaiti, Christ. Similarly, many church-based *marae* incorporate Christian motifs into their carving, but tend to follow the pattern of ancestral *marae*. For the most part, Maori Christians (and Maori of other religions) have less problem with reference (in word and carving) to ancestors and deities than they have to the absence of such reference. In other words, Christianities have crossed the *marae* and entered the *whare tipuna* and *korero tahito* far more than it has replaced them.

For example, the missionaries offered a further turn to the spiral by which conflicts and imbalances might be resolved. As with most words in *te reo maori*, *utu* can mean many things from equivalence to payment or revenge (Walker 1990, 69–70). An insult or a victory by one person or group required a reply by the insulted. In the acts of repentance and forgiveness, a pacifist (or at least pacific) form of Christianity provided yet another means to deal with *utu* to the satisfaction of all concerned. That this is no simple capitulation to European hegemony or an acceptance of a supposedly more advanced ideology is clear not only in explicitly negative Maori views of missionaries, but also in the parallel rejection of cricket in favour of rugby as a sport to adopt. Just as repentance and forgiveness found their place in the spiral of *utu*, so rugby had a closer affinity with Maori expressions and expansion of *mana* (see Walker 1990, 175).

Constructing reality

Construction and participation in the life of a *marae* require the combined skills of many experts, *tohunga* – expert carvers, expert singers, experts narrators of traditional or contemporary lore and law. The development over the last two hundred years of the *marae* complex builds on a strong foundation of traditional lifeways. As an expression of the vitality and resourcefulness of Maori tradition the *marae* is incomparable. They have been constructed to support and enliven all the social modes in which Maori now build and maintain their identities (rural or urban, tribal or elective, political or religious, etc.). The building and sea-craft of canoes, *waka*, may display equal skills in carving and in communal co-operation, and might also generate enlightening understandings. That can be safely left to others.

It is now commonplace to consider *marae* to be 'customary social and cultural centres' (e.g. Durie 1998, 57), and sometimes to say that these are not 'religious'. It is certainly true that *marae* do not represent a single religious ideology or dogma. *Marae* can be constructed and operated by Maori of many different perspectives. However, the underlying mechanism of *marae* protocol, *kaupapa*, and its artistic representations, are founded in profound spiritual understandings of the nature of life. The preference for honouring the dead by conducting *tangihanga*, funerals, on a *marae* is rooted in appreciation of this spiritual richness (Barlow 1991, 120–4).

Central to Mason Durie's discussion of Maori autonomy, governance and nationhood, *mana motuhake*, is the affirmation that 'there are many facets to the expression of Maori autonomy and authority, though probably the most illustrative of these is the marae' (Durie 1998, 221). In many museums, Maori art works/treasures (*waka*, store houses, *whare*, etc.), like those of many other indigenous peoples, have been placed alongside 'natural history' exhibits. Far from being a celebration of human relationships with the rest of life, this expressed a eurocentric vision of a 'primitive' world awaiting 'civilization' and 'progress'. Maori autonomy and prestige were diminished. A very different trend is now evident, flowing from the expression (or construction) of re-emerging Maori cultural vitality. Visitors to museums are now often encouraged to appreciate various overlapping dimensions of what they see. Reference can now be made to the spirituality as well as the shape and skilful design of artefacts. Wellington's Te Papa Tongarewa (museum) has recently constructed a *marae* and *wharenui* not only, or even principally, as an artefact for display, but as a forum in which identity can be explored. (The *tekoteko* of this *wharenui* is illustrated on the cover of this volume.) Among the other exciting implications of such a project, is the recognition that art is alive, has agency, or – simply – works.

Acknowledgement

Research for this chapter was undertaken in 1999 during a sabbatical awarded and financially supported by King Alfred's College, Winchester.

11. Music, art and movement among the Yoruba

Olu Taiwo

> Chernoff makes it clear that Africans do not improvise, at least not the way we think of improvisation in the west. Most of the rhythms and songs are traditional, allowing very little latitude for individual experimentation. The ideal, here as elsewhere in African culture, is to fit one's own personal rhythm seamlessly into the flow of the whole. You might call this rhythm sharing. Musically the rhythm of each drum in an ensemble is comparatively simple, consisting of endless variations on duple and triple time. It's only when these rhythms are combined that the complexity becomes impressive, threes beating against fours, throbbing and pulsing, creating a kind of bodily tension in listeners that is best released by dancing. (Hart 1990, 198)

Chernoff's statement provides us with an interesting perspective of a living musical tradition, which responds to change within a shared rhythmic context. I intend in this chapter to enlighten some of the ontological suppositions that epitomize the Yoruba perspective with regard to music, art and movement, in an attempt to share and express some of the issues, ideas and beliefs of a rich and diverse culture from a contemporary point of view. Before I start, I would like to clarify my methodological approach and contextualize my cultural position. First, my predominant method will be phenomenological, that is I am drawing from all my cultural experiences, with a distinctly intercultural approach.

My ethnic Yoruba heritage and British nationality are my foremost cultural influences, but growing up in Deptford, southeast London, between 1969 and 1984, meant that I was exposed to Caribbean, Indian, Chinese, British working- and middle-class perspectives, to name but a few. This unique intercultural position throws up ontological differences that co-exist within my psychological and physiological makeup. This is why I have chosen to write mainly in the first person, highlighting the experience from my own point of view. So I do not claim to speak for all Yorubas in Nigeria and the Diaspora, but I do hope to highlight some of the contemporary complexities that arise in cultures that are familiar with assimilating outside influences.

Second, my father is an Ijebu Yoruba, an older tribal group within the western region of Nigeria. My mother is from the Oyo tribal group, who by the seventeenth century had established a strong kingdom in the region approximately 100 miles to the north of Ife, an important city for the Yoruba nation (Ajayi and Smith 1964, 3).

When I ask my elders, 'How long have we lived in the western region of Nigeria?' the answer that comes back is 'From the beginning of time'. Archaeological evidence suggests that our ancestors have lived in this region since prehistoric times, but the evolution of our culture is more complex than that. The reasons for this are that migrants from the east arrived in waves bringing with them new practices and perspectives. A common language and culture emerged over time as a result, and this is reflected in the many tribal groups that make up the Yoruba peoples.

By 1903 Nigeria was officially part of the British Empire. With its strategy of divide and rule the British created a country that contained three distinct, though internally complex, cultural groups: Yoruba, Hausa and Ibo. These differences are complex because Nigeria, the political boundary, is a British construct created when the European powers agreed on colonial ownership of different parts of Africa. Nigeria gained independence from Britain in 1960. What resulted from these cultural divisions haunts post-colonial Nigeria, and one can argue, are major contributors to Nigeria's instability today.

My father was an engineering draftsman who worked for the Nigerian Railway, a legacy of British occupation. In 1963 he came to England to further his studies in drawing design, my mother came to join him in early 1964. I was born in 1965 in Clapham, London. Thanks to the Yoruba community in south London, centred on the Celestial Church of Christ, and the constant cultural contact with my immediate and extended family at home, I am able to enjoy gifts that emerged from the complex perceptions of a culture that has undergone and is undergoing major transformations. One of these many gifts is the experience and perception behind Yoruba rhythm. This phenomenon is what I refer to as the 'return beat' (Taiwo 1998, 159). The return beat deals with an ontological experience of the tempo within any given rhythm. It draws attention to the spaces between the beats, which are personally experienced as a curve that leads back to the self, echoing the metabolic rhythm of the heartbeat.

This creates an outgoing (centrifugal) and a returning (centripetal) aspect to the experience of temporal-space between beats that are perceived to emerge from a non-linear dimensional environment. This 'feeling' of returning is fundamental to the artistic and experiential viewpoint in the cultural traditions in African and the African Diaspora. This spiritual perspective underpins every aspect of our cultural life, especially in music and movement. By movement I include all gestured signs that are consciously constructed and shadow expression (i.e. unconscious movements that are habitual patterns performed just before conscious actions) that are not. In other words, all the para-linguistic, idiosyncratic behaviour patterns intrinsic to the aesthetics of our culture (Elam 1993). But these semiotic perceptions are inherently different from my grammar school education, where many of these nuances were signified with the use of a vast number of words, underpinned by reason (*spoken literal verbal text*). This replaced many of the nuances expressed in the use of gesture and posture, underpinned by metaphor (*the non-verbal and poetic*).

Christianity is one of the many beliefs and practices inherited from the British colonizers. The Yorubas broke into two main groups regarding Christian worship, those that adopted the Church of England method and those that created a new mode of worship incorporating the essence of Yoruba tradition. This is true in the African independent Churches, such as the Celestial Church of Christ which has a distinctly Yoruba cultural feel, using Yoruba rhythms in dancing and singing as an essential part of worship. The cultural experience behind Yoruba rhythm embodies a deep expression of spirituality and is the predominant theme of this chapter.

The Yoruba rhythmic and artistic sensibility has a Diaspora of its own. It can be found in Cuba, Brazil, parts of North America and in the Caribbean Islands. The return beat deals with the experience of rhythm from the point of view of participants and how they culturally perceive the spaces between beat and how they encounter the beats themselves. As I have pointed out, the spaces between the beats in the above perspective are subjectively experienced as a curve that leads back to the individual. This creates an outgoing and incoming aspect to the internal pathways of experience. The cultural resistance of African slaves helped propagate the return beat in the Western world through expressions of music and dance. The cultural information inherent within our ancient artefacts, situated in museums and wealthy homes around the world, introduced this implied aesthetic into the western representational consciousness. African art along with photography helped liberate the western artist from the Greek, Roman, Renaissance tradition of art as literal-poetic text, and enabled art as emotional-perceptual experience (Soyinka 1993, 28). Picasso expressed this perceptual liberation with African Art acting as a prism to reflect new ways of portraying European sensibilities. In a sense, the African mask is one of the faces behind modernity, but only as a reflection on the object, the artefact; because in the west, the older an object becomes, the more financial value it has. For African mask-makers the object, the mask, has a ritual life span and it is this ritual life span, not only the mask, that has value (socially and spiritually rather than financially). With the rise of the tourist industry in most of the now independent African nations financial value has gained prominence due to international market forces (Soyinka 1993, 168).

The mask acts as an interface between the event and the many tendencies that coexist in the virtual and actual realms of individual and communal life. So, the term African Art reveals more about Western (Enlightenment) perceptions in relationship to the making of artefacts than it reveals about the original artistic and symbolic intentions that the mask represents. However, in this chapter I do not wish to focus on the politics of the region, my intention is to look at the spiritual roles and parameters within the rhythmic sensibility of the Yoruba both at home and in the Diaspora.

The role the return beat plays in Yoruba religious practice whether traditional, Christian or Muslim, is fundamental to the meta-structure of Yoruba society, as it helps to shape the aesthetic, philosophical and sociological parameters with regard to cultural identity and spiritual expression.

I shall discuss some of the perceptual issues that arise from both inside and outside the rhythmic tradition in the Yoruba cultural group, paying particular attention to music and movement. Before we discuss the nature of our rhythmic experience, we need to look at our assumptions about space and time to deconstruct how we encounter our immediate surroundings and the priorities we use to represent our perceptions of the world around us (Taiwo 1998, 163).

Perceptions of space–time

In these changing times, the concepts of 'time and space' are being re-examined. That is, how we perceive time and space in our inner world and how they are encountered in the outer. We have all experienced how time seems to speed up and slow down depending on our level of bliss or anxiety, yet we dismiss these subjective phenomena as unimportant. Why? Surely we can deduce that our 'bliss factor' and 'anxiety factor' play an important role in transforming our relationship with time and similarly space?

Bliss is important not just for our own creativity connected to a perceptive relationship of space–time, but for a whole community of witnesses. It is a chance to galvanize the group, opening vistas of experience for everyone, creating a shared point of reference. Bliss has a greater role than feeling good; it is about feeling divinity. The bliss factor is a term I use to describe that which generates an inner glow, which in Yoruba culture is seen as a gift from the universe giving us the motive force for our endeavours. It is an expression of our transformative libido. Bliss opens playful energies, it mushrooms creative possibilities, it originates from developing personally what we really want to achieve, feeding our ability to 'unfold' effort by unconsciously creating a positive feedback loop (van Nieuwenhuijze 1998). As we approach the end of the second millennium, Newton's linear, fixed perception of time appears to have reached its limits, and new models are being and have been constructed. Some of these models place what we have dismissed as 'subjective' (our personal point of view) into equations dealing with our perceptions regarding the structure of matter in time–space. Einstein's 'relativity' and Neils Bohr's 'quantum mechanics' are two such examples. The implication of these theories suggests that our unique individual viewpoint provides us with the initial window into our perceptual apparatus, an important factor that affects how we measure observed events that occur in space–time. Artistic expression enables us to bridge the gap between the self (passion, bliss) and active participation (agency) in the 'creation' of our physical world and our society (as defined by space–time). This is a great responsibility, due to the layered complexity that is inherent from self, family, society, ethnicity, nationality as well as what is increasingly becoming known as the global village. Within traditional Yoruba society this complexity is further increased by the unseen presence of the ancestor and the unborn.

Artists, in trying to reflect the perspective of their contemporary surroundings, have to journey paradoxically both internally and externally to create an enduring piece of work, which is often an apprehensive and painful process. Creating is like giving birth, the pain and awesome fearfulness of the process is not a sign in itself that something is wrong, but simply that we have entered the heat of the underworld, that we are engaging with the savage undertow of birthing, of creating. In traditional Yoruba culture this responsibility is taken very seriously, time and space are experienced, not as a singular absolute condition, but as a series of continuous coexistent states. Wole Soyinka expresses this clearly in his essay, 'The fourth stage', when he suggests that: 'Continuity for the Yoruba operates both through the cyclic concept of time and the animist interfusion of all matter and consciousness' (1993, 30). This means that space–time is not seen as separate from matter and consciousness, but as a whole that unfolds like an onion in concentric spheres. According to Soyinka, this idea stretches to incorporate the notion of temporal existence, where the world of the living (the present) is seen, in a metaphysical sense as sharing the same spatial and temporal context as the world of the ancestors (the past) and the world of the unborn (the future). The differences between these worlds are dimensionality, phase and frequency.

Robert Lawlor discusses a third perception of time that emerges when contemplating logarithmic spirals. Traditional geometers named these geometric patterns, *Spira mirabilis*, miraculous spirals, because they were so rich in geometric and algebraic harmonies. Lawlor calls this third perception of time 'gnomonic time', which I consider provides an insight into Yoruba perspectives surrounding personal encounters with spatial–temporal reality. He is referring here to the phenomenon Greek mathematicians called *gnomon*, which is the basis of a type of growth called gnomonic expansion. Lawlor discusses Hero's mathematical definition of a gnomon:

> Hero of Alexandria defines it as follows, 'A gnomon is any figure which, when added to an original figure, leaves the resultant figure similar to the original.' The contemplation of this figure leads to an understanding of one of nature's most common forms of growth, growth by accretion or accumulative increase, in which old form is contained within the new. This is the way the more permanent tissues of the animal body, such as bones, teeth, horns and shells, develop, in contrast to the soft tissue which is discarded and replaced. (Lawlor 1982, 65)

The visibility of the past within the present through the rhythmic pulsation of spiralling growth offers fascinating notions about the nature of time.

Predominant in Western notions about time are two main ideas with many variations. First is the idea that the present moves, like an arrow, forward sequentially through time towards an unknown future, leaving behind a dissolving past that is immortalized by written records and memory. The second notion is of an all-embracing, absolute, universal and mystical time that is a direct result of a single creator. Lawlor continues:

> The gnomonic principle adds a third description of time. This is time as an expanding growth upon growth, an evolution, one might say, belonging to the conscious energies which transcend their transitory forms and substances. As Chinese wisdom says, 'The whole body of spiritual consciousness progresses without pause; the whole body of material substance suffers decay without

> intermission.' In such a model, past time remains present as form, and the formation grows through pulsating, rhythmic gnomonic expansion. (1982, 71)

Ritual expression through music, art and movement acting together can bridge the differences between dimensionality, phase and frequency, for the individual by inviting us to partake in the co-creation of gnomonic space–time within the context of the community. These ritual expressions manifest culturally through mythology, music, art, and dance, by individuals actively participating in drumming, masquerading (mask) and dancing, as a result reaching states of trance collectively, through the constant momentum of rhythmic cycles (Soyinka 1993, 30). Partake means to participate, to interact, to exchange. So each participant with their inherent coexistent states (ancestors, living and unborn), combines to create a we-ness that is galvanized by an agreed or stated return beat (Soyinka 1993, 32). When I say that art can bridge the gap, I need to qualify a distinction. There is a distinction to be made between a 'piece of Art', i.e. an interaction between expression-instinct with analysis-craft resulting in an object or event, and 'art', i.e. the process of making and becoming. It is the latter definition of art that bridges the gap since the focus is not on the finished object, though this is important, but the spiritual process of making which concentrates and transforms our immediate experience of the living moment.

As human beings we have the ability to change and project ourselves in space–time, using storytelling to re-enact, communicate and transform myths about our ancestry along with our divinities. Our ability to be virtual has always been with us. Ritual is about the virtual being embodied within the actual revealing itself through the living moment. Only three hours of ritual has the weight to create a harmonic balance with longer periods in life. By this I mean that within a theatrical, ritualistic space there is a concentration of mental and emotional energy that is actively created by the attention of all those involved. Those involved are not to be seen with the western dualistic notion of audience and spectator, but should be perceived as ritually inhabiting the same space with degrees of participation (Soyinka, 1993, 30). This dense collective focus can then balance out the more mundane, lighter experience of everyday life.

These sentiments bring us to the concept of artistic expression as utility, which as a process, falls under 'design' rather than 'Art for Art's sake'. In design there is always a tension between form and function. What is produced is a result of this tension. The design process is closely linked to, and encoded by the prevailing culture and its tacit or silent knowledge. The stratagems adopted in these design processes emerge from this tacit, presumed knowledge. These design processes are then maintained by and reinterpreted by each generation. This is the wisdom of our ancestors, which motivates our elders to encourage the present generation to embody the design processes within culture, our ancestral inheritance, and reinterpret these tendencies in the world of the living. So it is not the mask as object, divorced from anything that has major significance, but the mask as subject connected to a ritual life that has social value. The second view embodies the design tendencies within a living context while the first view distances and objectifies these tendencies within the context of a gallery or museum (Soyinka 1993, 164–5). The direct experience of the living moment is vital for the Yoruba individual and community. This enables us to become active agents in rhythmic phase, participating with the coexisting complexities that constantly unfolds in numerous pulsating patterns, as a unified cosmic event. To sum up then, the perception of space–time is likened to a dynamic substance that unfolds holistically in minute fragments while, simultaneously, being a unity.

Yoruba cosmology

The Yoruba language is full of parables and sayings that are poetic in nature. It is part of the culture's desire to transmit the essence of an experience and not just the substance and form. So the role of myth and stories within Yoruba society serve as allegories and metaphors for the transmission of moral and paradoxical values. To some traditional Yoruba people, Ile Ife is the place where the world began. Others suggest that we as a people migrated from the east led by a celebrated king named Oduduwa and that Ile Ife was where he first settled. Currently, Ife is a city situated in the southwestern region of Nigeria. There are many myths and stories surrounding this king named Oduduwa. We need to clarify a point at this junction, when we say myths we mean stories that have become folklore, mixing historical facts with a symbolic imagination. These myths become virtual sites where heaven (the group imagination) and earth (the group reality) meet. Oduduwa is said to have created the earth at Ile Ife after climbing down a mythical cord. He is the root ancestor of the Yoruba kings.

Another of our Yoruba myths states that Oduduwa is the younger brother of Orish-nla (also called Obatala). His older brother, Orish-nla is responsible for sculpting human beings, after the world was created. All the dynasties of kings in the different regions of southwestern Nigeria, the Oni' of Ife, the Alaafin of Oyo and the Oba of Benin, claim to have spiritually descended from Oduduwa, the brother of Orish-nla.

Within Yoruba traditional belief, there is only one Supreme Being, called Olodumare. It is impossible to approach this impersonal being with our normal human psyche, so one has access through 'agents' or, philosophically speaking, through an aspect of Olodumare. These agents or Divinities are called Orishas and are both processes of the creator and the created – they are regarded as different faces of the one Supreme Being.

When Gert Chesi, a journalistic traveller, visited Susanne Wenger in Oshogbo in Nigeria, she commented on St Theresa's theological perspective to communicate how she perceived the Orishas. She remarks that St Theresa uses a metaphor placing God at the centre of a mansion containing many rooms indicating that life is the mansion. She suggests that we Yorubas equate Olodumare as 'the centre' and the Orishas as the many rooms of the mansion (Wenger and Chesi 1983, 23). There are many Orishas, all of which represent particular forces that have lateral connections through all aspects of nature, the cosmos and the spirit. Susanne Wenger uses words like transcendental pregenetic, procreation and metaphysical to describe the ancestral nature of the Orishas (Wenger and Chesi 1983, 81). When we experience the metaphysical reality of the Orisha we come in touch with dimensions of life that are the animating force behind all living matter. (In a Yoruba context matter is considered to be imbued with life.) We can use *ashe* to signify the ethereal substance or life's own energy, known to the Chinese as *Chi*. *Ashe* is the essential substance, which is sacred to the Orishas and everything that lives (Wenger and Chesi 1983, 84). Some Orishas existed before and during the creation of space-time, while others are humans who have become Divinities. The number of Orishas differs depending on cultural points of view. Some say 401, others 601. Whatever the real number, the religion is a celebration of complexity and difference. Each Orisha can be considered as a room in one's own psychological mansion. We will consider a few of these rooms in a little more detail.

Orish-nla, also known as Obatala is the supreme Orisha, the sculptor divinity who is responsible for creating the inner and outer forms of matter in existence. His essence is transcendental and benevolent. He has the ability to change into any form (Wenger and Chesi 1983, 88). Orish-nla is likened symbolically to Christ and Buddha in that they all embody truth, purity and are associated with the colour white, the summation of all the colours.

Ifa is the Orisha associated with oracles and with divination. He is of great importance to the Yoruba. Ifa's system is underpinned by a metaphysics that is contextualized by the dynamic order that runs through organic and inorganic matter manifested in the forest-savannah. There are a vast number of poems called *odu*, which the priest has to learn verbatim, so that it is part of his subconscious mind. Each poem is linked to a geometric pattern. There are 4,096 symbolic poems. When the priest throws 16 cowry shells on his divining tray, the configuration that comes up triggers one of the poems from the *odu* corpus.

Oya is the fierce fiery goddess who inspires tornadoes. She is present when the River Niger is active as well as near the awesome stillness of graves. Originally she was Ogun's wife until Shango's electric personality appealed to her more. With her roaring passion, her experience in magic and medicine, she is highly respected within the Yoruba pantheon.

Ogun is the divinity associated with Iron. He represents the qualities needed for the hunt. He is said to be clothed in fire and wearing a garment of blood. Traditionally worshipped by blacksmiths, hunters and palm wine collectors, i.e. people who harvest palm wine by climbing a palm tree to collect the sap from the top in a gourd where it ferments into wine. He is now also associated with motor car drivers, mechanics and barbers. The kill is sacred to Ogun as life and death perform the eternal dance while the soul transforms from one dimension to another. This is similar to the symbolism of creation and destruction embodied by Shiva in Hinduism.

Shango is the Orisha associated with thunder and lightning. He was the fourth Alaafin (King) of Oyo who had the reputation of being tyrannical. He was given a charm that could control the forces of lightning which inadvertently caused the death of his wife and family. Guilt, remorse and the condemnation of his subjects drove him to hang himself. But they never found his body, just the rope. From that moment on he became the Orisha of swift action, divine retribution. One of his symbols is the double-headed axe. His devotees today associate him with electricity.

Oshun, the Orisha of beauty and sacred waters, represents the supreme sacred mystery behind water. She has a famous shrine dedicated to her in Oshogbo in Nigeria. She represents the paradox of beauty along with moody stillness and intense unpredictability, and in this way is similar to Venus-Aphrodite.

Eshu is the trickster Orisha who sometimes carries out Olodumare's wishes but is not bound by the supreme deity. He is associated with the road and people do not pray to this Orisha directly, but to avoid the things that he might do potentially. This would be done before embarking on any long journey. Offerings to Eshu are made to pacify his tricks and for him to give the traveller plenty of warning. In the Yoruba translation of the Bible, the devil is translated as Eshu. This gives the wrong impression. He really represents the restless urge, the catalytic interference and the principle of uncertainty. His presence contributes to that which breaks us from the comfort zone of certainty.

Traditional Yoruba worship revolves around these Orishas, and in parts of Brazil and Cuba is fused or layered with Catholicism (see the chapters in Clarke 1998). There are different dance steps and rhythms associated with each Orisha designed to create the right state for the particular Orisha to inhabit the devotee. These ritual celebrations are performed mostly in secret societies and contribute to the movement culture of the Yoruba community.

The creation myth tells us how the Supreme Being gave specific tasks to each Orisha to perform according to his or her strengths and that after the universe, earth and humans were created, and there was an 'Eden' where the presence of the Orishas communed with humankind. In effect, heaven and earth were one. Something happens to annoy the Supreme Being. Some Yorubas say that 'man drank too much of the sacred palm wine and threw up in heaven', others say that 'man stole something from heaven'. The result was that Olodumare separated heaven from earth. (It is interesting to note how fluid the stories are, leaving gaps for different groups and generations to fill.) This meant that the only entrance for humans into heaven was through death. Wole Soyinka makes an important observation here when he suggests that the Orishas suffered as well, as a result of this act of severance, inasmuch as the Orishas were barred from communing with humankind. It is these divinities who re-established the link between heaven and mankind after a period of time (Soyinka 1993, 30). Knowing that the Orishas wanted and want to re-contact has major implications for spiritual development within the tradition. It implies that a devotee has to open up to their chosen Orisha and contact will be made aided and facilitated by the Orisha's rhythm.

The return beat: a key for transmission

In Yorubaland and throughout the Yoruba Diaspora, the return beat plays a key semiotic role in the transmission of cultural codes, ideas and sensibilities. The transmission of knowledge in traditional Yoruba culture occurred mostly through story telling using an integration of drama, art, songs, music and dance. But during colonial Nigeria, great pains were taken to produce a written form of the language using the English alphabet with a view to protecting the oral tradition.

Now as we head towards a new millennium, information about our culture has another major channel for transmission, which is in its embryonic stage, the Internet. There are networks of websites, which link shrines in Ife, Nigeria, and New York to the rest of the world. As an interactive, non-linear, multi-dimensional and interdisciplinary medium the Internet suits the transmission of Yoruba ideas and sensibilities. But without a relationship to the return beat in the plethora of Yoruba rhythms, one misses a major part of the communication, the non-verbal messages and its subtle nuances.

This cultural landscape is ostensibly non-verbal (proxemic and kinesic relations that belong to the particular region and tribe), as well as verbal. There is an interesting phenomenon to be observed, that is, rhythms from the Yorubas maybe structurally different from that of the Ibo or Hausa peoples, but the return beat that underpins them all, will feel the same. The importance of the return beat is present not only when passing coded messages from person to person, as well as from one generation to the next, but also when passing coded information across large distances in the present. When we as Yoruba people have embodied the return beat at an early age a whole virtual terrain opens up. It is of major importance for a young child to embody the return beat, so that it becomes embodied knowledge. This embodiment happens through a process of osmosis, which occurs by being exposed to the rhythms at parties, at home, in religious ceremonies and other social gatherings (Taiwo 1998, 163). For a child growing up in traditional Yoruba society, one of these regular social gatherings is called the '*Egungun* masquerade', which emerges out of the cult of the ancestors. These masks are seen as the ritualistic evocations of the ancestors as they celebrate with the world of the living. There is excitement and fear when seeing an *Egungun*. Men with large twigs play 'dare' with the crowd, as the *Egungun* parade passes (Drewal 1992, 91). This kind of social event, be it festive, ceremonial or ritualistic, gives the child non-verbal access into the main web of our culture. This exposure helps the child to feel and realize those important connections vital for decoding non-verbal signifiers in the process of communication. Paul Gilroy highlights this point beautifully when he talks about the need for new analytical models. He says:

> It also requires a different register of analytic concept. This demand is amplified by the need to make sense of musical performances in which identity is fleetingly experienced in the most intensive ways and sometimes socially reproduced by means of neglected modes of signifying practice like mimese, gesture, kinesis, and costume. (Gilroy 1993, 78)

'Identity . . . experienced in the most intensive ways' brings us to notion of the return beat as a shared temporal reference point, which creates a shared temporal moment horizon. This temporal horizon point becomes a point of reference for those who want to understand and embody the patterned matrix within a particular Yoruba rhythm, by taking part in the dynamic drive (tempo) of the return beat. Similar to the way signals are transmitted exponentially via carrier waves in radio through space–time, the return beat within a basic and cross-rhythmic pattern, acts as carrier waves for a signal to be sent by a master drummer (Taiwo 1998, 164). The return beat can be considered the primary rhythmic cycle, which augments the basic and cross-patterns or secondary rhythmic cycle. The solo signal will then be the voice sailing through the unfolding waves of the primary and secondary cycles. The combination of the primary and the secondary cycle constitutes the personality pattern of the rhythm and produces the basic feeling, which differs from rhythm to rhythm, i.e. Juju, jazz, blues, samba, hip hop, etc. (Taiwo 1998, 161).

In traditional Yoruba music, the personality cycle can be made up of one single instrument or a series of complex cross-patterns usually played on a combination of the Bata drums, talking drums and Dun-dun (referring to the bass drum). The Bata drums are tall two-headed cylinder drums, which lie horizontally across your lap so that you can play the heads with both hands. Traditionally in a classic ensemble there will be three drums: the father, mother and baby drum. In rituals this trio is used to call the Orisha (Wilson 1992, 114). The talking drum, used in Juju music, is shaped like an hourglass with the two heads connected by strands of skin or rope. When tension is applied to the strands the pitch on the heads moves higher. It is important to note that drum lore belongs traditionally to a particular family, so that verbal and non-verbal details can be passed from one generation to the next holistically. Whatever the structure, a rhythmic space is constructed with the personality rhythmic cycle sustained by the primary cycle pulsating an energy state within it. What is created is a rhythmic environment where individuals can solo (improvise), communicate (call and response 'antiphony') or just maintain the rhythmic architecture of the temporal space by playing or dancing to the basic pattern. Any rhythmic environment that we Yorubas create, evolves and expands internally and externally without changing its inherent rhythmic structure, enabling the world of the ancestors to be perceivable in the world of the living and the unborn. This is crucial to the understanding of rhythm as communication and transformation. Paul Gilroy adds:

> Antiphony (call and response) is the principal formal feature of these musical traditions. It has come to be seen as a bridge from music into other modes of cultural expression, supplying along with improvisation, montage, and dramaturgy, the hermeneutic keys to the full medley of black artistic practice. (1993, 78)

Within the Yoruba experience of music and dance, improvisation occurs inside a shared rhythmic environment, with a shared socio-cultural history.

Improvisation displays the creative ability within our culture's context, to respond to changing circumstances that are at once psychological, physiological and spiritual. This is the essence of Yoruba improvisation.

The nature of the return beat can be summarized as a perception that paradoxically enables an individual to share a rhythmic environment, finding his or her rhythmic voice without disturbing but embodying the frequency drive or tempo of the community (Hart 1990, 198).

The return beat in contemporary culture

The presence of the organic return beat within Western culture has had a controversial history. By organic I mean rhythmic sensibility that is produced and maintained solely by the direct use of human hands, mouth, with or without an instrument. Morris, Irish, Scottish and Welsh dancing in the traditional sense, rely on an organic return beat for their cultural manifestations. As with African music and dance, they too have suffered the cultural snobbery of classical and modernist sensibilities. So the presence of the organic return beat in Western culture has a political dimension, the politics of aesthetics and, in the case of Africans taken from Africa, the politics of human rights and liberation. It is ironic that the presence of the African aesthetic sensibility has such a high profile within Western contemporary culture. This is especially so as Africans were originally denied the right to play their traditional drums when they arrived as slaves in the Americas and the Caribbean. This denial caused Africans in bondage to find other ways of expressing, articulating and maintaining ancestral rhythms with the distinctive aesthetics of sub-Saharan sensibility. For music there are forms like samba from Brazil, jazz, rhythm and blues from the USA, reggae and calypso from Jamaica and Trinidad, respectively. For dance there are forms like Capoeira from Brazil, Jitterbugging and the Lindy Hop from the USA, Scanking from Jamaica. All these forms emerge from a deep spiritual need to express gnomonic time which, as explained earlier, is the living rhythm of spiralling growth where the past (world of the ancestors) coexists with the present (world of the living) and the future as potential (world of the unborn).

Sule Greg Wilson examines the political and cultural impact African drumming has had in the United States of America from a ritualistic perspective. Historically, the white slave owners lived with the fear of the African drum and the power it has for communication. He says:

> In South Carolina they lived with it and feared it. They experienced the power of the spirit-calling drum. That's why in 1740, after the Stono Rebellion, the South Carolina colonial assembly outlawed hand drums. In some areas Europeans were outnumbered by Africans five to one. (And don't mention the Native Americans.) With the across-the-mile communication that talking drums gave Africans, those who rose up against slavery and utilised that technology stood a good chance of success. To destroy that military power, Europeans said drums – all drums – had to stop. Maryland, then other colonies, quickly followed suit with similar 'no-drumming-in-public' laws. (Wilson 1992, 21)

But the return beat continued and the rituals were secretly maintained. He continues:

> In the 1930's Amer-Africans told government interviewers from the Works Progress Administration about doing their ritual with hand drums. How did they do it, if drums were outlawed? Simple; take your everyday mortar or barrel, put a rim and a skin on it, and there's your drum, anytime you need it. And, for safety's sake, it was instantly dismantlable. Others buried their drums in the earth after use. (Wilson 1992; 21)

In the 1970s and 1980s, King Sunny Ade and Fela Kuti dominated the Yoruba music scene, fusing traditional musical forms with jazz as well as rhythm and blues. This unique blend of Yoruba and African-American sensibilities produced an interesting polarization in the politics of post-colonial Nigerian music. As Nigeria embraced capitalism, both these artists enjoyed international fame and success. King Sunny Ade continued the rich tradition of Juju music with Yoruba praise lyrics that didn't rock the political views of the new super-rich in the Nigerian establishment. Whereas Fela Kuti's brand of Afro-jazz, who employed lyrics spoken in pidgin English, communicated his own style of spiritual socialism with revolutionary zeal. Fela's audiences were mainly the working class, student and socialist sympathizers around the nation. Both artists were firmly rooted within the spiritual aesthetics of the organic return beat and both contributing to the globalization of Yoruba sensibility and to a degree, spirituality. But where they differ, is in their respective ideologies.

The relationship between African ritual fighting dance and Capoeira throws up some strong issues dealing with spirituality, because there are clear cultural threads that run structurally and historically through both, even though their socio-cultural, political and spiritual contexts are different. African ritual fighting dances emerge out of a rooted historical sense of self and community, with shared verbal and non-verbal codes. Capoeira, on the other hand, emerged out of a necessity for spiritual, personal and political liberty, in the context of slavery. Capoeira as an African martial/dance–art form evolved from rituals of war cultivated for over 400 years in Brazil. Africans taken to Brazil by the Portuguese in the sixteenth century kept Capoeira alive as an African art form. While few would disagree that Capoeira has a distinctive flavour derived from Africa, others might dispute the claim that Capoeira is an African art form, saying instead that it is a fusion of all the cultural forms that existed in Brazil at that time. This martial art took the form of community dance in order not to reveal its true intentions. The movements are sinuous and graceful ranging from bound, sustained movement qualities to lithe, fast dynamic kick combined with acrobatics. These movements or martial techniques were practised to the point of precision, until the dancer became a fighting embodiment of the spirit integrated with the mind. What is important about this assertion, 'a fighting embodiment of the spirit integrated with the mind', is that the dancer embodies both 'form' and 'improvisation', while dancing in rhythmic (gnomonic) time. In its original form Capoeira is played on the streets of Salvador, Bahia in Brazil. Capoeira is today practised as an accepted national sport all over Brazil. Its popularity is such that it is now practised in North America and Europe (Hart 1990, 221).

Conclusion

I have tried to communicate the complexity of Yoruba culture and spirituality. It is not based on an 'epistemology' emerging from literary text, but on 'phenomenology' that emerges from poetic experience. I want to stress that our culture is as diverse as any other and that it is not and has not been static. The Yoruba culture has always incorporated influences from other cultures while retaining its Yoruba-ness, which in itself is diverse. When we embody the curved spatial experience facilitated by the return beat, through music, movement and art, we can then understand the subtle para-linguistic, non-verbal codes are rooted in the body. This means placing the 'body' in a reverential position and not as the site for sin. This is an important point, because Yoruba spirituality is expressed through the body, which manifest emotionally as passion, bliss and ecstasy. This is diametrically different to Christianity whether Orthodox, Catholic or Protestant, in that passion, bliss and ecstasy are seen to be the province of the snake, which in their 'Old Testament' was responsible for the downfall of humanity.

I have talked about some of the developments in 'art' and 'science' in the twentieth century and how some of their implications have parallels in traditional Yoruba philosophy and perception. There is scope here for more research, as I have only touched on this subject. When we look at the nature of space–time and ideas surrounding quantum mechanics, we see a perspective that contradicts the static view of the universe. Instead, we see a dynamic flux with probability states that underpin an apparently fixed condition. When in the Yoruba tradition we assert that everything has its own life and is under the jurisdiction of a particular Orisha, it is tempting to make parallels between the 'quantum' realm and *ashe* which, as stated above, signifies the ethereal substance or life's own energy.

I would like to end with a quote from Olaudah Equiano's autobiography, first published in 1789. In its day Equiano's narrative was a very successful publication. Being an ex-slave, his autobiography played a major part in the abolition of slavery. He was an Ibo man. The Ibo tribes are situated in the eastern region of current Nigeria. In this quote he is recalling the time before he was forced into slavery:

> We are almost a nation of dancers, musicians, and poets. Thus every great event, such as a triumphant return from battle, or other cause of public rejoicing is celebrated in public dances, which are accompanied with song and music suited to the occasion. (Equiano 1989, 4)

Even though he is of a different tribal group, this sums up the essence of Yoruba spiritually.

12. The unwieldy promise of ceremonies: The case of the Jakalteko Maya's Dance of the Conquest

Charles D. Thompson, Jr.

> And in the belly of this story the rituals and the ceremony are still growing.
> (Silko 1977, 2)

Ceremonies, particularly indigenous ceremonies that have arisen from colonialist predicaments, are far from static traditions held onto by people removed from world history. On the contrary, ceremonies and the people who perform them must respond to history in order to remain alive. As historical circumstances change, as is always the case, even in remote areas, ceremonial performances must also change in order to remain relevant. However, the past need not die out as present realities are added or grow, as Silko says.

For the same reason that 'we never write on a blank page, but always on one that has already been written on' (de Certeau 1984, 43), ceremonies are layered with the contributions of others from the past. This is true of every song sung again, every story retold, every dance danced anew. While performances connect people to their senses of identity, and though often those senses of identity are rooted in stories of the past, performances must also make sense to people who witness them in the present. When this happens, ceremonies become ways of bridging pasts and presents, and ceremonies remain alive and fecund, even when the world shifts violently. Without this relevance, the ceremonies die off completely, or become anachronisms that people cling to for reasons of folkloric nostalgia. Ceremonies that cannot account for life's unwieldiness have no present.

Ceremonies that have no present have no future. They exist only in the past tense, gradually losing both power and devotees.

In order to remain alive and responsive to change, ceremonies must grow. To grow, as with all living things, ceremonies must remain unfettered. Yet, because they are unfettered, ceremonies guarantee no particular outcome. In fact, ceremonies may reveal or foretell entirely undesired futures never dreamed of by their originators. Once a ceremony is released, it is out of the originator's control, and like a word spoken, it cannot be recalled:

It's already turned loose.
It's already coming.
It can't be called back. (Silko 1977, 138)

Ceremonies are therefore much more than repetitions of the predictable, 'habit-memory', or mere re-enactments of the already extant (Connerton 1989, 23). The setting, the time, and the human performers all undergo transformations with each performance. A ceremony is a practice that 'can only be grasped in action' (Bourdieu 1980, 92) by human agents (Bell 1998, 209), even though it stems from a precedent. Hence, through ceremonies, futures and pasts coexist in the present progressive tenses of performance, a tense that is always becoming.

In realms of colonial dominance, ceremonies often contain evidence of multiple layers of interpretations in a single image or performance. Past, present, and future layers of interpretation may dwell in a single ceremony. This provides evidence of the growth and change of ceremonies. Ceremonies such as the Dance of the Conquest (*Baile de la Conquista*) as performed in San Marcos Huista (which is examined below), contain images of both conquistador and *indígena*. They tell stories of terror and fear, and at the same time a story of hope that inheres in change itself.

Dancing conquest

The *Baile de la Conquista,* first taught to the Jakalteko Maya in Guatemala by the conquering Spaniards in the sixteenth century, demonstrates today how a ceremony intended for a singular purpose of Conquest has grown and changed since priests 'turned it loose'. Though the Spaniards intended the performance to teach one lesson and one lesson only, generations of new performers have added to it and adapted it to their lives, thereby changing its tone and its historical significance dramatically. However, the change represents no mere opposite of what was intended; no mere resistance to dominance. Rather, the Dance of the Conquest in San Marcos' ceremony side-steps singular or unilinear interpretations that attempt to fence it into confining nomenclature, whether syncretism, conquest, resistance, or folklore. Ceremonies such as the indigenous dancing their own conquest defy neat encapsulations. In such a context we can only speak of layers of interpretation, layers that will probably be added to in the future, and this is perhaps all that is predictable about it.

Outside their cathedral in San Marcos, stone-faced musicians play a slow drum cadence and a simple melody from the kazoo-like *chirimia* throughout the day for the grand day honoring of their patron. They accompany young men, teenagers, and children, as the troupe interprets Cortes's and his lieutenant Alvarado's entry into Aztec and Maya territory and the Spaniards' bloody vanquishment of the indigenous people of Mesoamerica. In other words, the Maya enact the Conquest. Though Alvarado never ventured this deep into the Cuchumatán mountains to this region called the Jacaltenango *municipio*, the colonialism he introduced certainly did. And here in San Marcos, a Jacaltenango Maya *aldea*, he is remembered in a ceremony.

The young dancers don intricately carved masks representing the Spaniards and *indígenas*. Wearing elaborate costumes of red, blue, and yellow velvet covered with sparkling tassels and mirrors, they proceed in well-rehearsed circular and linear formations, choreographed over generations, danced again and again on the quadrangle next to the centuries-old whitewashed cathedral in the center of town. At appointed times, the drumming ceases, and the dancers halt and stand stiffly as the oldest participants among them hold forth with lengthy though muffled speeches spoken from inside rigid wooden masks. These speeches are triumphal, and are often sarcastic in their portrayal of might and pomposity (Morales 1988, 11). The themes of military onslaught, confrontation, surrender are all present.

Yet, here in this dance there is much more that is present at first glance, evidence that the ceremony has grown and changed a great deal since the triumphal entry of Spaniards into Maya territory. Though this is true, we must ask the obvious question: why does a dance ostensibly representing their own conquest remain important to the Jakaltekos today? Most importantly, how did Spanish triumph come to mean Maya commitment? By looking more deeply into the layers of the ceremony since the Conquest, and even before, we find some possible answers.

To residents of San Marcos, the Dance is worth hefty expenditures of both time and money. The costumes must be rented from San Francisco del Alto located nearly five hours away, for as much as 500 quetzales, or nearly

85 dollars per participant, more than several months' wages for many of the town's residents. Participation requires of the dancers at least nine months of weekly practice, usually every Sunday. Yet, the expense is accepted by the faithful in San Marcos Huista because, as with other *costumbres,* it is an offering, a way of staying true to God and to the ancestors, and a way of paying tribute to San Marcos, both the saint and the town.

If this were all there is to the *Baile de la Conquista,* then it seems an ironic choice of offerings, for the theme of the dance – bloody conquest – was far from convivial for the Maya ancestors who succumbed to military defeat and to colonial rule. Dancing is a ritual often chosen by the victorious, not the vanquished. The Maya dance their own defeat? An even more basic question to ask is why this dance of conquest has remained a Maya *costumbre* outlasting any obvious coercion by Spaniards, and enduring many changes of history, culture, and religion, centuries since Spaniards with armor and swords, led by Gonzalo de Alvarado, lived their last days upon Guatemalan soil?

It is apparent that the ironies portrayed in the Dance of the Conquest contradict any answers claiming that indigenous forms rely upon sharp cultural divides and bordered places, or upon the eliding or synthesizing of two or more dialectical histories into a third. The dance defies singular interpretations. Instead the ceremony stems from histories of conflict as different life-worlds have come to share the same places. Here overlapping histories reflect conflicts and even uncontrollable releases of power, repeated mixing, unceasing commentary on the less-than-clear divisions between Maya and Spaniard, between Maya and the state, and finally, the unwieldy forces of change.

Also, the dance's relevance to the Jakaltekos today seems to lie in its capacity to convey the realities of a multiplicity of interpretations of histories, of cultures and religions that all inhere in uncanny ways in this ritual. It is not that the ceremony harks back to a distant past, but that it brings to light the fact that the history of the oppressed, as Walter Benjamin tells us, has never ceased to be present (Benjamin 1968, 257). The dance conveys an interplay between a complexity of narratives that overlap one another, defying a singular or unilinear reading of history, of power, and of resistance, of states and localities, of the indigenous and their conquerors. The Dance of the Conquest presents layers of a story that is not only about Spanish military victory and a counter-narrative of an indigenous group that has weathered Conquest and its legacies, but also about their coexistence in the present.

The dance tells neither a one-sided story of direct confrontation nor of passive acceptance. Rather, the Dance of the Conquest tells a story of people who have lived through the tragedies and triumphs of overlapping histories, sometimes weathering or suffering from these layerings, and sometimes incorporating these new narratives into their own life-worlds. In this dance and among the Jakalteko Maya in general, we find layers of histories and cultures and religions from various origins, all of them now intermingled, all of them present. We find symbols laden with double meanings and dissonances, of realities that fail to divide into clear categories of victor and vanquished, of indigenous and foreign powers clashing. Rather, the dance represents uncanny juxtapositions. The layers are immediately apparent when one recalls that under masks of a Spanish victor, the Maya, those presumed vanquished and even vanished, are the ones who dance.

These juxtapositions of histories become apparent when one realizes that there are actually four different dances performed during the San Marcos fiesta: *El Baile de la Conquista* (the Dance of the Conquest), *El Baile de los Moros* (the Dance of the Moors), and *El Baile de los Monos* (the Dance of the Monkeys) and *El Baile del Venado* (the Dance of the Deer). Each is choreographed separately, though all the characters flow in and out of each of the dances, or at least stand nearby as others dance. And all are part of the collective performance involving nearly all the characters at once. The monkeys and the Moors are never far from the conquistadors, often dancing on the perimeter, though the particular characters move to the front as their dance is played. At times, the Moors, the monkeys and the deer and the conquistadors seem to dance together, creating wild possibilities for interpretation. All of the dancers dance what is now called *El Baile de la Conquista*, but in actuality they represent the coexistence of overlapping pasts within the present.

The Jakalteko people talk of all of these dances as their own, the Moors and well as the monkeys. They describe them all as depictions of history and as *costumbres*. They also readily point out that there are several dances intertwined here. The deer and the monkey dances are not Spanish in origin, yet the dancers who perform the dances from Spain intermingle with those who dance stories of animals. All the characters become part of one drama.

There are other dissonances. The presentation of history with the Spaniards dressed in exaggerated finery along with wigs of long flowing blond hair are amusing, though, of course, the history the characters portray is anything but a joke. The people who dance, and the spectators, know the history of conquest and its ramifications. They know that thousands of Maya people in the Cuchumatanes mountains died at the hands of the Spaniards. Jakaltekos have spoken to me on several occasions about Maya victims of Spaniards, of the Maya valiantly fighting back, and, then, perhaps most interestingly, of the Jakaltekos meeting the Spaniards with their intelligence rather than by brute force (Thompson 1997, 163). The dances are about all of this and more.

More than folklore

San Marcos Huista is not unique in its observance of the Conquest dance. A number of studies have documented the spectacle of the Dance of the Conquest in other towns in Guatemala (see, for example, García Escobar 1987; Rodríguez Rouanet 1992; Hanvik 1994). Unfortunately these studies have concentrated on the intricacies of the amazing costumes or the folkloric aspects of the performance and thus fit under the rubric of artistic and cultural appreciation, and even scenes for tourists. Yet, for interpretive purposes we must turn to histories of the dance, as well as histories conveyed by the dance, even as we are mesmerized by their sheer spectacle. Indeed, some of these studies provide important observations of the dance's historical importance, particularly the Dance of the Conquest's connections to Spain. Italo Morales, for example, traces the Dance of the Conquest to Spanish origins (1988, 11). He shows that the Dance of the Moors, still practiced along with the Dance of the Conquest in San Marcos Huista, originated in Spain during the *Reconquista* and was brought to the New World as the Moors dance.

In Spain the dance depicts the Moors as the vanquished in Europe, along with the Christian victors who are often led by St George, the patron of the Crusaders (Epton 1968, 43), or sometimes as Saint James often seen riding on a white stallion (Epton 1968, 144). The Spanish version of the dance retells, in intellectually simplistic, though visually glorified, form, the exploits of the Crusaders in Spain, sometimes even borrowing from the mythology associated with Charlemagne in France. According to Joan Amades, during the sixteenth and seventeenth centuries, the *Baile de los Moros* was practiced over the entire Spanish peninsula (1966, 71). Even in the 1990s the dance was still performed in dozens of small towns in various regions of Spain, where it is often called the '*Baile de Moros y Cristianos*' (Urgoti 1996, 27–9). These dances are characterized by caricatures and pantomimes of the Moors. A Moor, for example, may be a giant wearing a turban who repeatedly blows a single note on a bugle (Epton 1968, 144). Significantly, the Christians' *Reconquista* of Spain and their banishment of the Moors concluded in 1492.

The Spanish priests and soldiers who came to what is now Guatemala and to the rest of the New World knew first-hand the history of the *Reconquista* and applied what they had assumed about the universalities of paganism to their new enemies, the indigenous peoples of Meso- and South America. Not surprisingly, the conquering Christians brought the dance along to teach the common theme of Spanish conquests to the Maya too (La Farge and Byers 1931, 99). What applied to the defeat of the Moors, according to the Spaniards, easily could be retrofitted onto pagan Maya *costumbres*. Their goal in using the dance was to teach both religion and restraint, to inculcate in the Maya a unilinear history of Spanish superiority and Indian subservience. The dance also offered the Maya, at least as the Spaniards saw it, an emotional release and solace during this time of crisis. For the Spaniards, the dance was an ideal means of religious education because it replaced Maya ceremonial dances and used a traditional means of conveying information while at the same time it taught a different means of viewing the world. Of course, to correlate Maya military defeat with Catholic moral and religious victory was also an effective tool of evangelization.

The Dance of the Moors and the Conquest were intended to replace the Maya rituals prohibited by the Spanish, and, as Morales says, 'to mend the widening fault created by their prohibition' (1988, 11, my translation). In addition to the dance's pedagogical uses, there is also ample evidence that the dance was a way of encouraging pious practice among the newly-made Catholics (Morales 1988, 8). For the Spaniards, this means of teaching Catholicism was effective in that it allowed history and religion to be acted out ritually and did not require the difficult translation from Spanish to the Maya languages.

We do not know exactly when the Spaniards, using the *Baile de los Moros* as their template, first began to tell with dance the story of Cortes's exploits in Mexico and later, Alvarado's conquest of Guatemala. What is clear, however, is that the dance from Spain – telling of an otherwise unrelated history – soon became two dances in the New World. We can deduce that one dance was used in connection with the other, in part, because both dances are part of the same ceremony in towns such as San Marcos today. Hence, it is incorrect to say that the Dance of the Moors from Spain was replaced by its New World counterpart. Rather, it is more accurate to say they overlapped one another and became layers of ceremonies practiced simultaneously. Though the dance of the Mesoamerican Conquest can only be considered a reinterpretation, or a translation, of the Dance of the Moors, what is most interesting about this translation is that both versions continue to be present in the same place. In other words, though the Dance of the Conquest is another version of the Moor portrayal in Spain, the new version did not supersede the old. Rather, both dances exist together simultaneously, and otherwise disparate histories overlap during fiesta here on this Guatemalan town square.

Today the representation of the European dances together with the indigenous American, the Muslim with the indigenous. Uncannily, the Moors who never set foot there, as far as we know at least, arrive as dance characters in San Marcos every year. Hence, the histories of the Moors and Spaniards mix with the history of the Aztec and the Maya conquests and all encircle the quadrangle in a choreographed amalgam of histories.

Because the deer and monkeys are also characters in the dances today, the Dance of the Moors and the Conquest did not replace the Maya ceremonies as the Spaniards had attempted, neither did they lull the Maya into forgetting their old dances after all. Instead what we witness today in San Marcos Huista is the Spaniard and the Moor dancing with deer and monkey tricksters. Also playing a role in the dance are the first father and mother of the Jakaltekos, Jich Mam and Jich Mi, who are invoked as part of the offering of the deer. The dance presentation resonates with what Michael Taussig, following Walter Benjamin, calls a 'juxtaposition of dissimilars' or 'montage' (Taussig 1992, 45). In this case, the dissimilars of history, religion, culture, and even continents dance together in one place to the beat of the same drummer. This is simultaneousness, but not syncretism. The present has become an arena of performance for many histories as they have collided and bled into one another.

Friars as dance teachers

Documentation of the missionaries' arrival to the Jakalteko region and their subsequent work is sketchy, and thus it is difficult to say when, and how, a priest taught the dances to the Jakaltekos for the first time. What we do possess today are written records of the travelling representatives of the Church and the Crown as they passed through the *municipio*. A number of travel reports were archived in the Jacaltenango convent and remained there over the centuries, and today these records are housed in the Maryknoll hospital in Jacaltenango. By perusing these archives, anthropologist Anne Cox-Collins discovered that priests came to this high mountain region as early as the 1550s and that the Mercedarian convent in Jacaltenango was established in 1567. She found that the friars followed the common pattern of *reducción* and persuaded, or forced, the Jakaltekos to move closer to the town center and thus to the church. The move also allowed the priests to change Jakalteko housing patterns, family structure and the like. During this painful *reducción* period in the highlands, music and dancing were often employed in an attempt to diminish the sadness of removal (Cox-Collins 1980, 141–8).

We can surmise that the Dance of the Moors and the Conquest came to the Jacaltenango *municipio* early in the history of these missionaries' presence there. There is the alternate possibility that the Jakaltekos learned the dance from people in neighboring towns, especially given the conglomerate of meanings that inhere in the dance today. Regardless of how the dance first arrived in Jakalteko territory, however, we can be reasonably certain that the dances were first introduced to the region by Spaniards, perhaps Mercedarians, who had some familiarity with *Reconquista* history in Spain.

We do know from official reports from representatives of Church and Crown that by the eighteenth century, after the Mercedarians had been present in Jacaltenango for over two centuries, Maya beliefs coexisted and intermingled with Catholic rites and doctrine. When Cortés y Larraz visited Jacaltenango in 1770, for instance, itinerant friars serving the region told him that the Indians burnt copal incense in the church, though he tells us the friars had made no moves to eradicate this practice (Cox-Collins 1980, 164). Perhaps due to the missionaries' tolerance of other religious practices, perhaps the dances of the Moors and the *Conquista* could have merged with the *Venado* and the Monkey dances during this period. This was certainly possible for, as Warman shows, by the eighteenth century, many dances of the Moors had become Indian celebrations in Mexico (Warman 1985, 100, quoted in Taylor 1994, 159).

Apparently a number of Maya rites were resurrected during this period, for in the year 1800, only 30 years after Cortés y Larraz's visit, a crown official known as the *Alcalde Mayor* found practices there he abhorred (Cox-Collins 1980, 164). The *alcalde* claimed to eradicate some of the practices. He also claimed to destroy a pagan temple in nearby Concepción. If he was referring to the site of Yulá, the burial site of the first mother and father of the Jakaltekos located near Concepción, as I suspect, he was far from successful. The tombs exist today and were refurbished in 1995.

Certainly Spanish Catholicism was carried to Jacaltenango and to some extent the Maya accepted this new presence, some of which they probably welcomed. Yet it is also clear that the Jakaltekos did not, as a result, eradicate their observance of other rituals as they accepted new traditions. This was particularly true during the years, sometimes decades, between the official *visitas* when Jakaltekos were able to layer the new with the old.

Despite the fact that official *visitas* to the Jakalteko *municipio* were sporadic following the departure of the Mercedarians, who abandoned their convent in the late eighteenth century, some church authorities were relentless, even during their short visits, in their continuing attempts to conquer Jakalteko 'paganism'. For example, in 1815, some 300 years after the Guatemalan conquest, a non-Mercedarian priest returned to

Jacaltenango, and following one of the lengthy periods of the region's neglect by the church, to find what he termed 'idolatry' rampant among the Jakaltekos. As a result, the priest, standing in the middle of Jacaltenango, excommunicated, with one decree, the entire population of the region (Cox-Collins 1980, 164).

Independence from Spain in 1821 ended this official church involvement in the municipality and 'cut short whatever results the . . . clergy might have produced with respect to the extirpation of paganisms' (Cox-Collins 1980, 165). After 1821 the use of the convent and mission declined until re-occupied by the Maryknolls in the 1940s. This of course does not imply that local Jakalteko religious activity, including their version(s) of Catholicism, declined during these periods of official Catholic neglect. In fact, it is clear that in the absence of the friars certain religious practices, including the dances, continued to remain significant to the Jakaltekos, and perhaps even to grow in importance.

During these alternating periods of religious rigidity and laxity from the officials, the Dance of the Conquest must have persisted. While copal burning was questioned and so-called pagan ritual centers were being alternately re-employed and destroyed in sites scattered around the mountains, the dance seems to have found a place in the various mixes of old and new *costumbres* among both the Jakaltekos and the visiting Catholic officials. This is most likely true because the dances are never mentioned in official records and hence, their absence from the literature probably means they were tolerated to some extent. After all, they were, ostensibly at least, Spanish dances and taught docility and subservience. One key to the dances' longevity, then, could be their approval by Crown and Church officials during their visits, along with their acceptance as Jakalteko rites during official absences. Layering of histories may have meant their ability to weather the ebb and flow of various influences.

After Guatemalan Independence in 1821, the Jakalteko Maya Catholics had over a century to reinvent new and combined rituals and structures of identity, before new challenges to their indigenous authority, at least in their local town, would surface. Of course, *hacienda* expansion and various government forms of forced labor procurement during this period prevented indigenous people from working or living as they pleased (La Farge and Byers 1931, 81; Thompson 1997, 87). One can claim only that the absence of official interventions in terms of religion provided room for some additional freedom of thought and interpretation of these realities of economics and violence.

Rituals such as the Dance of the Conquest change when they are not forcibly held in check by powerful individuals, and, even when held in check, they may change to suit the needs of the performers in subtle ways. Change occurs at times simply because a ritual becomes irrelevant in the present and does not survive the test of the passage of generations. This is true particularly if people who perform the rituals must leave their homes for long periods as the Jakaltekos have had to do. During the Jakaltekos' long treks to the coast to work on plantations, the Dance of the Conquest had to remain pertinent to their lives in order to continue as part of their ritual observance, particularly during the periods of Church neglect. In short, in the absence of coercion, people do not persist in their ritual practices unless they find them to befit their quotidian world.

Of course one may argue, following Foucault, that coercion may be internalized and inhere in discourses even in the absence of power as exhibited in Jeremy Bentham's panopticon. But, I argue that if this were the case, we would find only Spanish symbols and rituals, the rituals of coercion, among the Jakaltekos today. If people practiced the Dance of the Conquest only out of coercion, then why has it been combined with the Dances of the Monkey and the Deer? And why, for example, have Maya sites once thought to be eradicated come back to life?

Sedimentations of dance

The *cofradia* members who participate in the Dance of the Conquest said in 1996 that through their sacrifice of time and money they are doing all they can to remain faithful. Through their sacrifice, the whole town demonstrates its remembrance of all that is important in this life. There is a connection between their observance of the *costumbres* and rainfall for their corn and coffee, and in general there is connection between ritual observances and a bountiful crop yield, between an observance of the *costumbres* and the overall health and well-being of parents, children, and livestock.

As the *dueños* (owners) of the hills where the crops grow, including Jich Mam and Jich Mi are pleased with the observance, dancing the conquest is also a means of demonstrating one's commitment to being part of the *aldea* of San Marcos in the *municipio* of Jacaltenango, and to being a Jakalteko Maya *indígena*. By performing the dance year after year, the participants carry out the wishes of the *antepasados*, the ancestors, who fought so hard to claim and to hold to this land.

Surrounding the *aldea* the hills are covered with small agricultural plots from where much of Jakalteko sustenance has been taken. Hence we must include this crucial ground in this scene where the dance is performed. As steep and marginal as this place is, it is still Maya soil belonging not to the Spaniards who conquered it, but, within the dominant borders of Guatemala, to the Jakaltekos themselves (Stadelman 1940, 102, in Lovell 1992, 33).

These words about land, if unexamined, could invoke images of people who have remained separated from global histories. All that Jich Mam and Jich Mi and the deer and monkeys represent may appear to be the antithesis to modernity and globalism where an indigenous group maintains its customs far from Western influences. Jakaltekos and other indigenous peoples have endured eras of conquest and oppression; they have not avoided them. Therefore, Jakalteko history includes Spanish conquest. Their places are saturated with epochs of dominance. They have long worked on small plots to carve a living from steep slopes, while they have worked on plantations on the coast, travelling to distant places in order to live. But this is not survival that conjures people who are somehow immune to the realities of history, where they live not through layerings but through separation from history. Closeness to land must be seen within the context of layers of histories, not as separation from history. Land tenure in the Jakalteko context is never naïve attachments to old traditions, but rather deep awareness of contested space, of marginalization, of dominance, and of conquest.

Of course there is traditionalism in San Marcos. There are also new innovations and changes. There are small *milpas* (cornfields) and there are jobs in the USA. Though there is a collision of forms here and elsewhere due to the Maya diaspora, this does not mean necessarily that the *costumbres* are being lost. Interestingly, those most ardent in their desire to preserve them are the intelligentsia of Jakaltekos, those who have travelled farthest: the school teachers, the artists, the professors in the United States, and also the *cofradia* members who study how to regain some of the old performances. Others in exile in Florida have also resurrected ceremonies on different soil.

The Jakaltekos exile began in 1982. Jakaltekos were attacked in their homes and fields by death squads. Helicopters circled overhead and dropped charges along the river. Numerous people, most of whom had never met a guerrilla, were killed and tossed into the river below San Marcos for being potential threats to power. The survivors fled beyond the borders of their town and then their nation. In 1996 many Jakaltekos were just returning. When I asked over 40 Jakalteko families who had been refugees in Mexico for various periods this simple question: can you be Jakalteko in Mexico or the United States, I received direct and unanimous answers: of course, we just did that. Through this survey and other experiences I determined that Jakaltekos' concepts of their identities were far from something attached to simple places or fixed and unmoving in other ways. Instead, their concepts of identities have come about and continue to exist within contested spaces.

Indigenous identities must be attributed to much more than the fact that Indians were not fully dispossessed of their land by the Conquest as some have argued (see, for example, Warren 1978, 41). These identities must arise, in part, from the tremendous pressures of conflict that bear upon this land and its people. It is the land where Spaniards created servants, where priests created adherents, and where the Maya have managed to remain both what their ancestors were and something else at the same time. In this context of contested history, and where cornfields now coexist with stereos from Los Angeles, where Jich Mam vies for attention with Chuck Norris films, a highlight of the present-day fiesta at San Marcos, the dance continues.

Conclusion

When I last attended the Dance of the Conquest in 1996 only a few years had passed since military troops swept over this landscape strafing houses with machine-gun bullets. Some of the exiles of violence and economic hardship were just beginning to return. From these exiles I learned that being Jakalteko now has much more to do with these realities of the history of oppression, of confrontation, of contestation than with being part of any particular place. During my fieldwork, refugees taught me that reverence for *costumbres* may increase due to separations and returns, to layers of habitations and exiles, rather than simple attachments. I began to realize that the Dances of the Conquest were about layers of space and time. They tell the story of thousands of people who have weathered countless onslaughts of soldiers, priests, and other would-be conquerors over generations. The realities of this history have not faded, the dances say, but neither have Jakaltekos.

As I watched the dance, I talked with one of the *cofradia* captains, Don León, who explained to me that the masks worn for the dance contain some uncanny characteristics. Some of the masks were blood red. 'To represent (stereotypical) indigenous skin?' I asked. 'No,' he replied, 'The red is for blood.' It represents bloodthirstiness.

In such subtle ways, ceremonies contain multiple symbols of conflict and negotiation, of commentaries on violence and bloodshed, on resistance, on the influence of the nation–states upon localities. Within the dance is commentary without reductionism. Within overlapping, interweaving symbols coming at the viewer from the Maya past, the Moors, the *Venado*, the violent present, the exit and entrance of numerous forces and contingents, is a lack of resolution that speaks powerfully as the truth. This presentation leaves us with numerous layers of interpretations of histories, of layers sedimented upon a landscape like soil, all of them present in one place, none leading to a final breakthrough.

Particularly in the Guatemalan highlands, past atrocities of colonialism have never completely become the past, but the present often replays themes of the conquest in everyday life. This continual awareness of replayed histories is what Benjamin refers to as the 'tradition of the oppressed' (1968, 257). 'Tradition' in this materialist sense bears much weight; it is not about travelling backwards in time and space in order to view the past through 'folklore'. Rather, this tradition is about making the past resonate with the present so that neither epoch seems removed and irrelevant to the others. This is what is meant by pasts layered, one upon the other. The indigenous must bear them, all of them, in the present, in order to be indigenous.

Within Jakalteko ceremonies, *costumbres*, responses to history have to be subtle and layered. Yet, the fact that they are layered teaches us that performances may be means to embrace the past, preventing its atrocities from going unrecognized in the present. Indeed, to attempt to persevere without acknowledging the cold realities of conquest, whether through ceremony or other means, would be to allow the past to become unrelated to the here and now, and perhaps to forget that these layers of history exist at all.

Because the Dance of the Conquest addresses these clashes of culture and history, there is some comfort in knowing such a ceremony is 'loose' in the world and is 'still growing'. In the unwieldy promise of such ceremonies dwells a special source of hope for those whose futures, and pasts, are not entirely their own. For the colonized, a ceremony that is free in its interpretation of entrapment can be liberating, even if the change it portrays is uncertain, perhaps even fearful. At least the performance is their own, and their interpretations have not ceased to be present.

13. Rites of passage among the Lohorung Rai of East Nepal

Charlotte E. Hardman

The notion of ritual is widely used and has become central to studies of religion and society. The meaning of the term, however, is multifaceted. It can describe highly elaborate ceremonial occasions and yet because it describes the performance of actions, it can also imply repetitive, excessive behaviour as in describing someone ritually walking their dog every three hours on the hour. It can even be used to mean 'empty, meaningless' behaviour – 'it's just a family ritual'. More commonly, however, it is used to describe religious behaviour. Rituals are seen as connected to belief systems and myths so that for neo-Tylorian intellectualists like Horton, ritual has primarily to do with belief in and communication with the supernatural (Horton 1982; see Morris 1987, 304). Yet even among anthropologists there is disagreement. Many have suggested a wider definition which brings out either the performative or the prescriptive aspect of ritual behaviour and the notion that it can be connected to non-religious behaviour. Beattie, in a key article (1966), distinguished between the expressive and the functional aspects of ritual language and, focusing on ritual as symbolic, stressed its ability to make metaphorical statements about the world. Tambiah (1968), in contrast, sees ritual as performative; it is not just describing a state of affairs, it is trying to bring something about. And for Pocock (1975, 175, 177), too, rites are not just re-enactments of beliefs or myths but 'say' things; 'rites ... are actions that *do* things which words cannot', such as indirectly focusing on values and reinforcing forms of classification. A very broad definition emphasizing the prescriptive aspect describes ritual as 'behaviour prescribed by society in which individuals have little choice about their actions' (Hendry 1999, 66). In this sense we can call greetings a form of ritual.

Whether we are talking about rituals in Western society or in the rest of the world, clearly there is a wide range of forms or types of ritual. The ones we are concerned with here are those rituals which mark basic and irreversible turning points in life. The obvious ones are birth, puberty, marriage and death. We all go through most of these key life events and not surprisingly, then, in almost all cultures the entry of a new member of society is celebrated with rites, as is the transition from being single to married. Likewise the distinction between 'being a child' and 'being an adult' is crucial, and to mark it and initiate those making the transition, rituals are performed. These events, traditionally seen as evoking tension and anxiety, are often referred to as 'crises of life'.

The classic study of 'life crisis' rituals was written by Arnold van Gennep in French in 1908 but not translated into English until 1960. He was a contemporary of Émile Durkheim and like many of the *Année Sociologique* was interested in comparing sociological phenomena across a wide range of cultures. His interest focused on what those rituals which mark life crises have in common.

In this chapter one of my aims is to look at van Gennep's analysis and how it helps to make sense of some 'transition' rituals held by people who call themselves Lohorung Rai. They are subsistence agriculturalists and a sub-tribe of a much larger tribe of Rai who inhabit the middle hills of East Nepal. The Lohorung Rai live in an area bound by the Arun Kosi to the West and the Sabhaya river to the east. (For an ethnographic study of the Lohorung Rai see Hardman forthcoming.)

What struck van Gennep was that in many societies any change that can be thought of as a passage from one state to another is ritualized, whether changes in seasons, changes of location or status. Although Durkheim gave attention to rituals to do with social relations and changes in social status, van Gennep was the first really to see the significance of these rites:

> The life of an individual in any society is a series of passages from one age to another and from one occupation to another ... every change in a person's life involves actions and reactions between sacred and profane ... a man's life comes to be made up of a series of stages with similar ends and beginnings, birth, death, social puberty, marriage, fatherhood, advancement to a higher class, occupational specialization, and death. For every one of these events there are ceremonies whose essential purpose is to enable the individual to pass from one defined position to another which is equally well defined. (1960, 2–3)

Van Gennep argued that underlying all such transition rituals was a pattern (*schéma*) or sequence, a tripartite structure, which could be subdivided into three phases. The first he called *séparation* (separation), the second *marge* (transition) and the third *agrégation* (incorporation). In rites of separation the person or group is cut off from their previous condition, separated from a previous world. The rite may consist of 'cutting hair', purification or scarification and the individual during the rite removed from the rest of the community and placed in what Durkheim called the realm of the 'sacred'.

In rites of transition the person or group is in an 'in-between' phase, has no identity and goes into a liminal, marginal period when one stage has been left behind but the new one has as yet not been entered. The individual is as if on the threshold. Neither in nor out, the person may be seen as symbolically dead. There are often taboos or restrictions, the body may be painted white or red, the colours of the dead. The rites symbolically place the person 'outside' of the society and to do so, van Gennep comments that the normal rules of society are often suspended. Victor Turner expanded on the significance of these liminal rites (1967, 1969) and the symbolic aspect of ritual. He saw liminality as being frequently likened to death, to being in the womb, to invisibility, to darkness, to bisexuality, to wilderness and to an eclipse (1969) and that those in such rites are often passive and submissive yet as a group often develop among themselves intense friendships. The characteristics of liminality are an expression of what Turner calls 'communitas' which he described as being the opposite of social structure: liminal ritual has an anti-structural function offering dynamic alternatives to conventional institutions. Though weakened in one sense, those in the liminal phase, because of their marginality, are creative, they can express potential alternatives. Such states, he noted, are a seedbed of innovative forms. We only have to look at the creativity of Western sub-cultures, those marginal groups which set themselves up against the mainstream, to appreciate the relevance of Turner's comments on liminality.

The final rites as described by van Gennep are those of incorporation and are rites that integrate the person into their new condition, status or role. Their new status is either created or confirmed by social recognition. In such rites the restrictions of the previous phase are lifted.

In addition to looking at the Rai material in the light of van Gennep's schema, the further aim to this chapter is to illustrate Durkheim and van Gennep's view of ritual as being primarily of social importance to indigenous societies. Whereas for many Westerners rites of passage have to do with individuals and not society, I will demonstrate in this chapter the way in which rites of passage, for an indigenous religion, accomplish social purposes and at times almost ruthlessly ignore the individual. It is crucial to realize that van Gennep, like Durkheim, was mainly interested in this aspect of the rites and in the dynamics of society; that is, how society deals with groups of people at particular stages, as much as how they deal with individuals. Looking at indigenous religions Émile Durkheim suggested that ritual was one of the crucial mechanisms for maintaining solidarity in 'primitive societies', as he called them. Such societies, he reasoned, are held together by *conscience collective* (translated as either 'collective consciousness' or 'collective conscience'), a set of supra-individual sentiments and mechanisms, like religion and ritual, which integrate society. More 'civilized' societies, he argued, achieve cohesiveness through other means such as the division of labour and interdependence, and are led to reject obsolete mechanisms like ritual. We shall see in this chapter the extent to which the meaning of the rites are intricately bound up and dependent on traditional ideals, beliefs and world views. Rebelling against these rites is hence one of the surest ways of undermining the traditional society but in the process of rejection other important functions of the rites may be lost, such as the significance of the psychological impact of these rites in changing the identity of the individual.

In the sections that follow I will examine these two aspects of rites of passage in relation to ethnographic material among the Lohorung Rai. At the same time we will see how the rites can be analysed in terms of the stages noted by van Gennep.

Lohorung Rai birth rites

Unlike many cultures, Lohorung Rai society does not emphasize the separation of a woman during pregnancy. Moreover, although for the birth itself she is set apart, in formalized ritual terms the focus is on van Gennep's transitional phase and on final rites of re-incorporation into society. For this group of sedentary agriculturalists who place as much emphasis on their relations with their ancestors as on relations with other human beings, the significant transition is after the birth, when restrictions on the mother are gradually withdrawn and she can be reintegrated into society in her new status as a mother and a new clan member can be introduced to society. Until the baby has been introduced to the ancestors, it is not considered 'a person'.

When a woman goes into labour men are supposed to keep away; they shouldn't see the birth – it's woman's work. She usually calls upon her mother-in-law, sister-in-law, or any woman from her own father's clan living nearby, to give her assistance. They prepare the verandah at the side or back of the house where women commonly wash the dishes, store their pots of fermenting beer and give birth. In terms of location the woman giving birth is located away from parts of the house connected to ancestors. Connections with the spiritual world at this time are avoided at all cost.

A piece of smouldering rag gives off strong-smelling fumes to keep away harmful spirits or ghosts of the dead. The ghosts of women who have died in childbirth wander alone unless they can befriend the spirit of another woman who dies in childbirth, so they hover around labouring women hoping to attack. The women in attendance speak words of warning to the spirits, at the same time circling round the pregnant woman, throwing rice over her, putting some into the pocket of her blouse to feed and appease any approaching spirit, *chap*. These are rites to protect the mother and child. As van Gennep said (1960, 45), protective rites are often confused with rites of passage, explaining why the latter are often not given their due importance. Though these are clearly rites of protection – women in labour are particularly vulnerable to attack from the spirits – they indicate the necessity for the separation of the woman from the rest of society. She is both in danger and dangerous. Any indication of further weakening of the woman or any desire to sleep is dealt with vigorously. Non-Lohorung ancestral spirits, *bayu* (N.), are said to crave the blood. The women repeat over and over the words: 'the cloth is burning, don't come and give us trouble, you have died, so now you must follow that path, now go.' She is dangerous in that her condition has attracted ghosts of the dead.

The principal separation of the infant from its previous environment is expressed in the rite of cutting the umbilical cord. As soon as the baby has emerged and the cord has stopped pulsating, it must be cut by the oldest woman present with her scythe, the knife she carries for cutting maize and other crops. So important is this task that the woman must be given a piece of newly woven cloth in appreciation of her services in safely delivering the baby. To indicate the lineage's collective as well as the individual family's gratitude, it is said that if she is not given cloth, the whole lineage will remain forever in her debt.

To delineate the special status of the new mother, her 'liminal' status, the mother remains in the verandah area separated from the main arena of household life. Food rules are a mechanism for emphasizing her special position, as well as improving the physical strength of mother and child. The mother must eat 'hot' food, such as chicken, meat, eggs, honey and rice, as much as possible for fifteen days. She must drink hot chicken broth, distilled liquor and hot millet beer, known to make the afterbirth come quickly and make good milk for the child. And a new mother should eat four times a day if possible instead of the normal two. Prohibited 'hot' foods include pork, buffalo meat, chillies, and also hot spicy food not easily digested. For a month after the baby is born a woman avoids any cold drink. All beer is warmed and liquor (*raksi*) is only drunk while still hot. Though these food rules emphasize that the mother is not a 'normal' member of society, they are also a reflection of the Lohorung understanding of the physiology of the body. Like others in Nepal, Rai groups conceptualize food into two categories, 'hot' and 'cold' not referring to temperature but to a symbolic force. Most foods are innately 'hot' or 'cold' though some, like rice or lentils can be made 'hot' through cooking. A person's strength depends upon maintaining a balance between the two. 'Cold' food makes a baby retreat into the womb and after birth women are vulnerable to 'cold' air and food. Hence the importance of eating 'hot' foods before and after the birth.

The restriction of mother and child during these first few days, a state called *suksi khedu*, can easily be understood in van Gennep's terms as a state of liminality. Mother and child are without status. In their indeterminate condition both are submissive and yet also dangerous and must remain on the side verandah of the house or in a corner of the house as far from the household shrine as possible. If the shrine is in the back storeroom, the woman is allowed to sit on the lower side of the house, near the fire to keep the baby warm. No one is allowed to touch her, and the mother is forbidden to touch the hearth; she is forbidden to have any contact with the ancestors, and kept away from those parts of the house with *saya*. Some authors talk of restriction in terms of her being *jutho*, N. 'ritually unclean' or 'polluting', a Hindu influence (Gaenszle forthcoming). The more indigenous Lohorung attitude is one of extreme care not to arouse the anger or displeasure of any ancestor, especially before the infant has been introduced to the house ancestor. The ceremony, performed five days after the birth if the baby is a girl and six days after if a boy, is regarded as the most important in a person's life. It is the rite in which the child leaves the liminal stage and gains personhood. The child's future health and success may rest on it. For this reason no other ancestral (*sammang*) ritual is performed by *any* other household of the same clan from the time of the new baby's birth until after the *khimpie* or *lataba* ceremony, introducing the child to the house ancestor, has been performed. One woman explained the ceremony as being like a person's first marriage – the marriage of the child to the *sammang* ancestors. Another woman put it, 'previous to the *khimpie* or *lataba* ceremony, as far as the ancestors are concerned the child is not in the house. They do not exist.' After the rite, from then on, the infant has begun its relationship with the ancestral world.

The rite (*saya pokme*) performed as part of this 'first marriage' rite acts to raise the 'ancestral soul' (*saya*) and restore links with the ancestors which for the mother have been severed during her separation from society. It is from this moment on that the child is considered to be a clan member and the mother reintegrated to society with a new status. As van Gennep stresses (1960, 46), what we see here is the mother's social return from childbirth as opposed to her physiological return which happens to coincide with the social. The force of the ancestors, and particularly the 'house ancestors', in Lohorung lives, their domination over traditions and prevalence in everyday normal life are apparent in both the social purpose of the birth rites and the forms that they take. I shall return later to this dominant force in Lohorung lives.

Lohorung Rai marriage rites

Marriage among Lohorung Rai is not an event but a process. For many Westerners marriage focuses on a single ceremony: the transition from single to married occurs in the marriage rite itself, with the optional 'engagement' as the only step towards it. In contrast, Lohorung marriage traditionally involves a ten-step process. Although the number is more metaphorical than actual, a marriage in practice involving many more than ten steps, it demonstrates the complexity of a process of negotiation between two social groups. As van Gennep emphasized, rites of passage of all kinds are a means by which a society reaffirms its classifications and its values, and we can see this in Lohorung marriages. They are not just a significant passage for an individual boy and girl from single to 'married' status. Lohorung marriage emphasizes the degree to which a person is embedded in a complex network of relationships as a member of a village, clan, and lineage and is one of the most important ways in which alliances are made with other clans and other villages and with other ancestors. Lohorung marriage is exogamous up to seven generations in the paternal line and three generations in the maternal. Residence is virilocal and inheritance is patrilineal. Marriage brings with it new rights and obligations relating to relationships with both sides of the alliance. Van Gennep says:

> Marriage constitutes the most important of the transitions from one social category to another, because for at least one of the spouses it involves a change of family, clan, village, or tribe, and sometimes the newly married couple even establish residence in a new house. (1960, 116)

Not surprisingly, Lohorung prefer 'arranged marriages' (*ngakme*, literally 'request') so that marriage is not left to the whim of the individual. About 70 per cent of Lohorung marriages are arranged and include full-scale ritual and ceremonial exchanges. These are either first time marriages or men's second marriages. The second marriages of men are mostly of widowers who want to offer the most formal kind of marriage to their new wives, in spite of the cost. The other forms of marriage are 'persuasion' (*leme*), 'theft' (*khume*), 'elopement' (*sepmimpa*). These show much less clearly the three stages suggested by van Gennep.

The complex rites surrounding arranged marriages may be identified as follows:

1. First talks: request.
2. Mediation.
3. The gift.
4. The wedding itself.

First talks: request

The first rites involve unofficial talks, in which the chosen girl's parents are presented with a gift of liquor (*raksi*) and told about the boy, his village, wealth and attractions. The boy's parents find a relative of the girl (MB, FZH, or eZH)[1] who will act to convince the girl's parents of his worth since it is they who decide if the boy is suitable. The 'talks' traditionally begin metaphorically. 'The *suwa* creeper (i.e. the girl) is soft, but to dig out the roots (i.e. to take her from her natal home) is hard.' The emissary talks quietly about the request, sympathizes with the difficulty of giving away a daughter, using the images of creepers, roots and blooming flowers. 'Although I could not scrape the domesticated creeper from the ground or dig up the wild creeper in the end I managed to take their white seed.' When the answer from the girl's side is initially negative, another mission is sent. To see if it is a favourable match a Brahmin looks at the astrological chart of the proposed couple. Generally the girl's parents are initially reluctant and several trips are made. Refusals are expressed by returning the liquor untouched. If the girl's parents agree to a match then they accept by drinking the liquor and telling the emissaries how much meat they will need and how to distribute the meat that must be offered to the bride's side.

These ritual negotiations, which may be seen as initial rites of separation, take place late in the evening or very early in the morning: no one else should know about them, in case an agreement cannot be reached. Too many rejections known by everybody would 'throw away the nose' and threaten the health and vitality of the boy's parents, but are also bad for the girl and her parents, gaining a reputation of people who don't want their daughter to marry. Nowadays the girl's consent is also sought though Lohorung women talked of how when they were young their own consent was not needed for the marriage to proceed.

Mediation

Initial gifts are taken by two or three elders (*yakuchepa pasing*) and a go-between (*bangapa*) – the same person who went to request the girl. *Bangapa* means both 'first gifts' and 'the messenger or intermediary who takes it'. As one Lohorung said, 'It's not really a gift because it's not given freely; you *have* to give. It's payment. It's a real custom.' With great insight he saw the prescriptive nature of these rituals; in theory the gifts are voluntary but as Mauss (1970, 1, 3) said in his classic book, 'in fact they are given and repaid under obligation' and are part of 'a system of *total prestations*' (sic). The first gift consists of liquor (*raksi*) and the meat required by the girl's family, which might be one buffalo and five pigs but at least one pig (*sachep ngachep*) for the bride's father and father's brothers – one haunch to the father and one to his brothers. Other lineage members each receive smaller pieces of meat indicating their involvement in the contract and at least some compensation for the loss of a member of their social group.

A short time later a further visit is made with liquor and meat or fish and includes the rite of 'examining the path' (*lamphu aksi tadhami*) in which the seriousness and legality of both the alliance and the 'envoy' are expressed in a ritual conversation between the clan elders and the groom's father. We see here how marriage acts for Lohorung as a rite of initiation. Marriage itself acts as an indication of the boy's 'grown-up' status – social recognition that he has become a man. The boy's father reminds the clan elders how his son has reached a 'ripe age'. In ritual language he describes the 'wanderings' of his son, now returned with vivid descriptions of the girl he has found, 'just like gold she dazzles, just like silver she dazzles . . . shall I pluck her by the hand or bring her down by the foot?' Continuing in ritual conversation the father persuades the son against theft marriage (catching her foot) and agrees to collect the necessary prestations (meat, fish and liquor) for an arranged marriage. The social purpose of this rite seems to be threefold; to emphasize the 'civilized' and moral nature of an arranged marriage as opposed to the possibility of theft marriage; to persuade the elders that the marriage is not incestuous or prohibited in any way and finally, that it is the right time for the boy to marry. The boy is at the right age to change his status and it should be done in this way.

This rite initiates the first of several journeys in which clan elders and *bangapa* leave for the girl's house each time bearing gifts, some 'compensation' for the bride's household. As van Gennep says 'These "ransoms" always coincide with rites of separation to such an extent that, at least in part, they may be considered rites of separation in themselves' (1960, 119). Each time the bride's family accept more gifts they go one step further in separating from their daughter.

The gift

Called by Lohorung *huksok*, 'the gift', the rite is the formal handing over of a live pig, rice and liquor needed for the wedding day and marks the pledging of the girl, the final 'ransom'. From this point on the marriage must take place and the girl has been 'given'. Even if her mother died so that her father's household needed her, the marriage would still take place. If the groom dies, his brother can claim the girl (a custom called levirate). If the girl dies, her sister should be given (sororate). In one marriage during fieldwork a younger sister was taking the place of her elder sister who had eloped.

We see the extent to which these rites of passage are not about two individuals but about contracts between two lineages. We also see the degree to which the marriage rites signify loss for one lineage and gain for the other. Lohorung say when parents lose a daughter they're losing both heart and liver. The loss is not only emotional, it is economic since they lose a productive member and the ritual on the wedding day describes the repayment needed for their multifaceted loss. But alliances are crucial and Lohorung say parents know better than their children – they have more knowledge – which alliance is best. Modern 'love' marriages are few and deeply disapproved of when they occur, recognized as undermining fundamental aspects of their society. Girls who elope are called 'leaves that flap in the wind', without morals or strong kinship ties. They 'throw away the noses' of the father, threatening his standing, his pride and even his strength. The kind of extreme 'individualism' which has become basic to 'modern society' (see Macfarlane 1978) is alien to the systems of marriage and descent to be found in cultures like that of the Rai in Nepal. (For a further discussion of the notion of the person in Nepal, see Hardman (1981) and McHugh (1989) and for a detailed account of marriage and descent among the Rai see McDougal (1979).)

The wedding itself

The wedding goes on all night and involves the rites of incorporation as well as much feasting and fanfare. The groom is accompanied to the bride's house by the *hanglisa*, that is his cousin, his father's sister's son. The relationship of father to daughter is said to be the same as the relationship of a man to his sister's son and thence the *hanglisa* is the symbolic equivalent of the bride and the right person to accompany the boy to meet his bride. To understand this it is important to add that for Lohorung cross-cousin marriage is considered incestuous. The son of a woman can never gain any of his mother's father's property. It lies in the hands of his mother's brother and is inherited by his cousin. Lohorung daughters do not inherit land from their fathers (inheritance is patrilineal). But maternal uncles are aware of the imbalance and on their son's wedding day they will try to give some moveable goods or land to their sister's son, just as the bride's father will try to give some goods, a cow or utensils to their daughter. As mentioned earlier, rites of passage emphasize key values and the relationship between brothers and their sisters is crucial. On the day of his mother's brother's son's wedding the *hanglisa* is treated like a king (*hang*) and given whatever his mother's brother can afford, usually cash, clothes or animals. It is a gesture to equalize the disparity in inheritance. On the way to the bride's home and village the *hanglisa* leads the way.

Central to the rites of incorporation are rites performed by the local priest (*yatangpa*). Prior to the departure to the bride's house a pig, raised in the village, is shot in the heart with a bow and arrow from the right-hand side and offered to the ghosts of the dead (*chap*) and to Maruhang and Paruhang, whom Lohorung recognize as their founding ancestors. Just as the *saya* (ancestral soul) of the baby was raised in order for it to be recognized as a person, so now the boy is 'grown up' it is raised again, for him to be accepted by ancestors with a new status. The *yatangpa* recites the ritual words: 'fathers, mothers I have now grown. Today is the auspicious moment for my marriage. How is my *saya*? (*apa amachiba kanga dia'wepoking. Kangam lagana, kam saya manthole'e?*)' and he cuts a piece of ginger, dips one side into ash and cuts off the knob to see which way it falls. If it falls clean side up with no ash then the marriage will be a success, if on the ash side there will be problems. When good fortune is indicated, the groom's strength is ensured, there are shouts of 'hah, hah' and the ginger is tucked in his turban. If it falls on the wrong side, the groom is teased about future problems with his wife. The rite, *mangkringma teme*, is a rite of passage from boyhood to manhood, which in Lohorung terms is synonymous with marital status. Whether his predicted fortune is good or bad the rite raises the *saya* of the groom, revitalizing the links between the groom and the ancestors thence giving him strength, the vitality to stand with 'his head held high', and resist insults. Lohorung said if the *mangkringme* rite was not performed, the groom would become sick and dizzy, a man without vital force, a force which is obtained from links with the ancestors.

The significance of the rite in changing the identity of the groom is such that a similar rite is again performed after the two sides have met, this time with two chickens and the *yatangpa* divines from the blood of the chickens. The cock and hen are killed with heavy blows on their backs. If the cock vomits a large globule of blood the groom jumps up, shouting 'hah' since the signs are good: from his side the marriage will be a success. The blood from the hen is examined in the same way. These rites are central and introduce the couple to the ancestors and as such can be seen as rites of incorporation.

Without going into all the complex details of the wedding day I will focus on the crucial gathering in the bride's house, a rite in which final payments to the bride's parents are made along with a vivid ritual re-enactment of the process whereby a daughter is 'given', all spoken by elders in ritual language and clearly another 'rite of separation'. (Allen (1987) looks at a similar kind of dialogue amongst the Thulung Rai.) The rite begins when the bride's elders play ignorant of what the groom's side is doing:

> What on earth, what are you saying? they have laid out gold, they have laid out good cloth. We only offered you a sleeping place while we thought you were looking for your rivals at the border. And now look what they are doing!

The elders from the groom's side remind the bride's parents they have already offered compensation with the witness of those parts of the house where ancestors come to reside, reminding them that an agreement has been reached which is why the people have congregated together. For food and drink the groom makes a formal repayment of 50 peisa (this has ritual not economic value); for the lodging space made available a further 50 peisa is laid down; for 'the ten springs of mother's milk' which over the years have been given to the bride and as if now drunk by the groom's side, the repayment is Rs1; and for their loss, 'for taking tomorrow your heart and liver', Rs1. 'Father and mother I hold your hand, I hold your foot' (as the groom does to the bride in theft marriage), that is, they are tied and must proceed. But the ritual exchange continues.

The bride's side protest sterility and tell the groom to find a Tibetan wife of whom there are many of good character who are skilful weavers. The groom's side knows about such skilful women but their customs don't mix and he doesn't want his son to marry elsewhere. 'Even though I cry when you kick me with your right foot, when you kick me with your left foot; I hold', i.e. they want to proceed.

The bride's side suggest rich Khambu Rai women from the other side of the Arun, then Limbu girls, but the groom's side repeat their insistence.

In metaphorical terms the groom's side repeat the obstacles, the fallen paths, the landslides they have had to overcome and how the bride's parents have helped them so that in the end the bride's side has to admit the suitor is brave. But will they treat the bride well? When she is useless will they dry her in the sun, in the moon, starve her? The groom's side offers reassurance to all their doubts as if re-enacting what was said throughout the negotiations. Finally they protest 'forgive me but a gift given is a gift for life!' She has been given.

The ritual ends with the bride's side accepting gold (or cash of Rs 44), the clothes, silver bangles and necklace (the traditional symbols of marriage). 'These are my signs; tomorrow, father and mother you will give me your daughter and with these I will recognize her. Tomorrow I will go with this crowd of people. When I go, for the porters carrying my luggage ...' and 8 peisa is laid down. 'Please don't hinder my way' and 50 peisa is laid down.

At one wedding in Lingkhim where more Nepali is spoken than the tribal language the mother of the bride, clearly bemused by all the ritual talk said, 'Oh get on with it – stop pretending, we're going to give her to you anyway!'

Following this, the bride and groom in turn offer liquor given by the groom's family in bowls to the bride's family – known as *saino peme*, 'the establishing of the relationship' – signifying how their relationship has changed by using the new terms of address and can be seen as the initial rite of incorporation.

There are numerous smaller rites many of them recent Hindu additions (see Allen 1987). What is significant though is that although the girl has been 'given' and the rites of 'incorporation' performed so that she now formally belongs to the groom's family, she still has not finally 'separated' from her parents and natal village. Though on the day after the wedding she goes with the groom to his parents' house, accompanied by some selected friends from her own village, on the third day there is a procession (*duran* N.) in which she returns with her companions to her natal home. Along with her goes more liquor and meat for the bride's parents and for all the father's brothers. Sixteen days later the bride should return to the groom's house, though again only for a few days.

The wedding has established a ritual alliance but the sexual and economic rights over the girl are not exercised for some time. Though the new couple may spend short lengths of time together, living in whichever household needs their labour, for much of the time they are apart. Moreover, although the girl is 'given' to a boy, she returns to her everyday behaviour much as before, notwithstanding the increasing pressure for her to live up to her new status.

It may be as long as a year before the girl finally leaves her natal home to live with her husband and even then, the final rite of separation is only performed, in a rite called *sangchame,* many years later, usually after she has a child. She returns to her natal home and receives from her brothers whatever they can give her in the way of moveable goods. At this point they say 'now be off with you', her separation from her natal home is complete.

Conclusions

Van Gennep's work on rites of passage suggested that such rites involve a transition that begins with separation from a previous existence, leads through a liminal stage and ends with incorporation into a new social world. Van Gennep also noted that all *rites de passage* express the core values sacred to any society.

What we have seen emphasized here in the birth and marriage rites of the Lohorung Rai are, amongst others, those Lohorung values and ideas developing from their understanding of the human person and their relationship of trust and exchange with the superhuman world. For them rites of passage are not just about changes in individual status and the dynamics of human society, but also about the dynamics of their relations with ancestors. Changes in the membership of a clan or changes in the identity of one of its members are considered as much the concern of ancestors as it is of the groups and individuals concerned. It is striking the extent to which relations with ancestors in these rites resemble those with the living, reaffirming that frequently they extend their social world to include the dead. Just as gifts to the bride's family, the 'ransom' for the girl, consist of liquor and meat, so too gifts to ancestors when introducing them to the infant in the rite of incorporation and when seeking affirmation of the groom's new status consist of liquor and meat. It makes sense that such rites to ancestors form a key part of the rites of passage. The dividing cloth between the two worlds of the dead and the living is so fine we can appreciate the interdiction against showing fear in such rites lest someone's soul is not strong enough to prevent them being swept into the other world. The social networks of Lohorung extend beyond that of the human world to that of the ancestors and key changes in the human world must be recognized by their ancestors. In both the birth rites and the marriage rites, the main rite of incorporation, the acceptance of the new identity of a member of the clan, involves a rite renewing links with the ancestors, the rite of *saya pokme*, raising the soul which is an internal link with the ancestor.

It is hard perhaps to appreciate the extent to which in indigenous societies such as that of the Lohorung Rai control of the world lies less with the individual and more with society and ancestral tradition. The person acts as an agent but not always as an 'individual' agent as in the West. The focus of their actions is not the self but rather the household or the lineage. If rites of passage, as van Gennep shows, are about protecting society from the whims of the individual, ensuring continuity of knowledge and behaviour, then when a society places emphasis on the individual, then personal beliefs, desires will naturally take precedence over organized pre-established ritual. The fate of rites of passage in Western cultures illustrates the effects of secularization and individualization. Individuals have increasingly wanted to distance themselves from such Western rites of passage as baptism and formal church weddings, seeing them as unnecessarily binding the participants to a particular doctrine or involving beliefs they no longer hold, and hence seeing them as a waste of time and money. But we can see that these rites have a function beyond that of re-asserting the values and dominant beliefs of society, Durkheim's 'collective consciousness'. These rites, as both actions and statements, also have significance psychologically and legally, allowing those involved to absorb and experience new identities, their new roles in society and in affirming a new legal status. Perhaps it is these aspects of rites of passage which help to explain the recent renewed interest in them in the West. New religious movements like Paganism and the New Age (Bloom 1990; Harvey 1997) have started to develop their own rites of passage as have non-religious bodies like the Family Covenant Association. Increasing numbers of people want to celebrate, for example, the birth of a child, give a welcome to a new member of the family and society, celebrate the giving of a name as well as celebrating the solidarity and commitment needed for bringing up a child. Individuals are creating their own rites of passage. Maybe it is just that this modern 'individualism' has become our Western *conscience collective*.

Note

1. MB = Mother's Brother; FZH = Father's Sister's Husband; eZH = elder Sister's Husband.

14. Gifts for the sky people: Animal sacrifice, head hunting and power among the Naga of Burma and Assam

Mark R. Woodward

The overwhelming majority of the inhabitants of the Southeast Asian world are followers of one of the great transcultural religious traditions: Hinduism, Buddhism, Christianity or Islam. In more remote sections of the region – the uplands of the mainland nations of Burma, Thailand, Laos and Vietnam and in the more remote portions of the insular states of Malaysia and Indonesia – indigenous peoples continue to practice religions that are variants of what Quaritch Wales described as the 'Southeast Asian Megalithic Complex' (Wales 1997). The central elements of this complex are communal feasts in which cattle, water buffalo or *mithan* (Asiatic bison) are slaughtered and offered to the inhabitants of the sky world, and, in areas where warfare is endemic, headhunting. (On the *mithan* and its role in the religions and economies of tribal peoples of South and Southeast Asia, see Simoons and Simoons 1968.) This chapter focuses primarily on the Naga of the Assam-Burma border region. Comparative materials on the feasting systems of other indigenous people are included to illustrate the range of variation in the region and the ways in which the megalithic complex has been transformed in colonial and post-colonial contexts.

Sacrifice: theoretical considerations

The category sacrifice has been used to describe ritual acts ranging from the Catholic Mass to Aztec rites in which the hearts of living victims were offered to the gods. In most cases it entails the death or destruction of a valued being or object which is presented to non-human beings in return for immaterial gifts of blessing, power, or grace. Theoretical reflection on these acts (see Henninger 1987) focuses on their origin and intent. Explanations of sacrifice offered by anthropologists, historians of religion and theologians range from Tylor's theory that the intent of sacrifice is to bribe non-human beings to Durkheim's sociological interpretation, according to which sacrifice is the means through which the individual recognizes his or her own social position. It is, however, extraordinarily difficult to come to general conclusions concerning the meaning of such diverse modes of ritual action. A significant problem in the analysis of sacrifice, and of ritual more broadly, is that it is all too often conducted without considering the systems of cosmological and metaphysical postulates within which ritual and other modes of human action are located.

The analysis of sacrifice among the Naga and other indigenous peoples of Southeast Asia presented here is predicated on the assumption that the meanings of sacrifice and other modes of ritual action are determined by the cosmological and social orders in which they are located. Cosmology and social order cannot, however, be taken as irreducible cultural categories. They are, rather, among the theoretical constructs employed by anthropologists, historians of religion and others in the study of cultures. As such, they do not necessarily correspond with the ways in which nonwestern and nonmodern peoples organize and explain experience. The Naga and other indigenous peoples of Southeast Asia understand what scholars refer to as cosmology and social structure as elements of a system of social relations including living humans, certain animal species, most commonly cattle and tigers, the ancestors and other people of the sky and underworld. These systems of social relations are based on more abstract metaphysical postulates. Several recent studies of Southeast Asian and Melanesian cultures have pointed to the importance of understanding indigenous metaphysical thought as a precondition for the analysis of social and ritual action. Godelier put it this way:

> The relation between the conceptual and the nonconceptual in the real world cannot be construed as the relation between a reflection and the reality reflected. Thought does not reflect; it gives meaning to situations born of causes and forces whose origins do not lie solely in the conscious or the unconscious. Thought invents and produces this meaning by constructing systems of interpretation which engender symbolic practices ... It would be simple if thought could confine itself to reflecting or representing society, but the whole difficulty of scientifically analyzing the conceptual factor in the real world stems from the fact that thought not only represents society but itself contributes to the production of society. (1986, 232)

Lehman (1977) makes a similar point arguing that in the indigenous cultures of Southeast Asia 'social categories' cannot be taken as 'primes' and that their construction is informed by 'metaphysical considerations'. The same is true of sacrifice and other modes of ritual action. It is futile to seek for *the* meaning or purpose of sacrifice.

In the case of the Naga and other indigenous peoples of Southeast Asia, sacrifice is simultaneously religious, social and economic action. Gifts are presented to ancestors and/or non-human persons, who in return bestow potency and power on the sacrificer, his family and community. The ability to acquire these spiritual gifts establishes or reconfirms his social and political status. It also establishes his position in the ancestor world, for when he dies, a feast giver reclaims the sacrifices he has offered. Sacrifice is economic action in two senses. It is the source of the spiritual potency that is believed to lead directly to the acquisition of wealth. At the same time it redistributes acquired wealth within the community of living humans. This points to two primary conclusions. The first is that for purposes of social and ritual action the Naga and other indigenous peoples of the region do not distinguish clearly between living humans and other social persons. The second is the categorical distinctions between religion and economy and religion and politics common in Western cultures since at least the time of the Enlightenment are not elements of Naga ontologies. Rather, they see these acts as elements of a single system, the purpose of which is to establish the prosperity of human groups both in this world and in the life/lives to come.

Metaphysical postulates

Fertility and prosperity are the central concerns of the indigenous religions of Southeast Asia. Fertility is acquired through sacrifices to the inhabitants of the sky world, who may be either ancestors or human-like beings. This concern with fertility motivates animal sacrifice and head hunting. Hutton describes these concerns as follows:

> the fertility of the crops and the prosperity of the village are closely associated with the dead, whose life-substance is conceived of as forming a continuous cycle of reproduction, passing from men to cereals sown, and thence back through grain eaten, or through the flesh of animals that have eaten it, to man again. It is this theory that forms the philosophic basis of head hunting. (1921, 414)

The earth, the sky world and the underworld are inhabited by humans, or human-like beings who lead lives very similar to those of humans.

Mills describes the sky world and underworld of the Lhota Naga as follows:

> The Land of the Dead (*etchili*) lies under our world and has the bottom of our world for a sky, just as our world lies under the world of the *potsos*. The dead live exactly as men live here, those who have done good deeds being rich and happy, and those who have done evil deeds being poor and miserable. As the sun passes under the earth every evening their day is our night. (1922, 119)

> [The *potsos*] live in a world like ours, of the earthly floor of which our sky is the underside. The world of the *potsos* in turn has another sky which supports yet another *Potso* world, and so on for an unknown number of layers. The only *Potsos* which affect us are those in the world immediately above our sky. They resemble men in appearance and have host of attendants who are sometimes regarded as their servants and sometimes as their relations. (1922, 113)

This understanding of the cosmos is common throughout the region. There is, however, considerable variation about the details. Some groups, including the Kachin of Burma, believe that the sky is home to god-like beings as well as ancestors; others populate the underworld with spiritual beings and place ancestors in the sky; still others place their own ancestors in the sky and those of their enemies in the underworld. (For general discussion of indigenous Southeast Asian cosmologies see Loeffler 1968.)

There is a categorical distinction between culture and nature. The worlds are divided between the natural world, the jungle, and the human world, the village. Tigers and/or leopards are often believed to be lords of the jungle in the same sense that humans are lords of the village. They are also believed to have souls and can be understood as non-human persons. Felines cannot be sacrificed, but can be sent to the ancestor world with head hunting rites. The largest domestic animal is also believed to have a soul and to make the journey to the ancestor world. Cosmogonic myths describe the separation of culture from nature as well as the origins of the three worlds. Relationships between the two realms are generally understood as being hostile (see Woodward 1996).

Relationships between the three worlds are based on the principle of generalized exchange. Lévi-Strauss describes generalized exchange, known in much of the subsequent literature as asymmetric alliance, as a system of reciprocity characterized by the inequality of exchange partners. The superior/inferior distinction, which is also described as male/female, has been most clearly described in studies of kinship and marriage alliance (see Leach 1954; Lehman 1970). Most of the kinship systems of the region are based on exogamous patrilineal clans. A distinction is made between clans from whom one receives wives and those to whom one gives wives.

Material goods, cattle, ornaments, trade-goods and cash pass from wife-taker to wife-giver. Status and spiritual power move in the opposite directions. The status of a clan or lineage, and consequently the bride price it can demand for its women is determined by the amount that was paid for their mothers. A Kachin proverb describes this relationship as follows:

> The *mayu* (wife givers) are the breath of life; the *mayu* are the main source of our children; the *mayu* are the source of refreshment, and by making marriage we are refreshed. The *dama* (wife-takers) are those who put wealth in the hand. (quoted in Woodward 1989a, 129)

With respect to the human realm, the sky is a superior exchange power and the source of spiritual potency. The Ao Naga of Assam refer to this potency as *aren*, the literal meaning of which is 'to increase' (Clark 1911). *Aren* is understood to be a nonmaterial substance possessed by the ancestors, sky people and wealthy and powerful humans. It is believed to be responsible for the fertility of crops, animals and humans. Mills reports that the primary purpose of sacrifice is to acquire *aren* and that it is conveyed to the fields in agricultural ceremonies (Mills 1922, 380–1). Bourdieu saw spiritual potency as a form of 'symbolic capital'. He suggested that in many premodern societies the concept of spiritual potency is employed to disguise economic exchanges as pure gifts and that the rituals in which such concepts are employed can be understood as symbolic statements about social relations (Bourdieu 1977, 182–91). It is true that sacrifices and marriages are among the primary means through which material goods are exchanged in the indigenous cultures of Southeast Asia. It is, however, incorrect to describe these rites as symbolic reflections of social order. In indigenous ontologies, spiritual potency is as real, and as highly valued as material goods. The rituals through which they are acquired are pragmatic attempts to ensure agricultural and other forms of prosperity.

Spiritual potency is obtained by establishing and renewing relationship with the skypeople. Sacrifices of cattle, water buffalo or *mithan* are the primary means through which this is accomplished. In almost every case these sacrifices are adorned with feathers and other sky symbols. Sacrifice generally involves the erection of large wooden posts or stone megaliths through which the animal is sent to the heavens. Rites for captured heads center on a tree that is the center of the village (Woodward 1989a).

While spiritual potency comes from the sky world, the prosperity to produce it rises from the earth. Cane shoots and smooth round stones are common symbols of relationships with the underworld. At the Ao Naga *mithan* sacrifice prayers are recited asking that the feast giver and his children 'grow and flourish like a cane shoot which can push its way up past sticks and stones' (Mills 1922, 372). The Ao, Lhota and other Naga tribes consider smooth round stones, known as *oha* among the Lhota, to be signs of their relationship with the underworld. They are sometimes said to be found in the stomachs of sacrificed *mithan*. They are kept in granaries, the communal men's house and at the foot of the head tree. Mere possession of the stones is believed to result in prosperity. They sometimes multiply spontaneously, resulting in even greater wealth for their owners. When a new village is founded it is considered to be essential to steal one of these stones to establish a relationship with the underworld (Mills 1922, 166).

Sacrifices are never offered to the people of the underworld. Rather, they are summoned and ordered to ensure the fertility of the crops. Among the Lhota, the people of the underworld are known as *rangsi*. At the beginning of the agricultural season each cultivator builds a field house where he and his family will spend much of their time until the harvest. He then calls the name of every variety of rice he knows asking the *rangsi* to provide it. In return they are offered a small amount of pork and beer. These offerings are similar to the meals provided to inferior human exchange partners in return for their services at sacrificial feasts. Immediately prior to the harvest the *rangsi*, including those obligated to others, are called upon to bring loads of rice to the field house (Mills 1922, 55).

Metaphysical postulates and cosmological variation

In a study of the Atoni of the Indonesian island of Timor, Schulte Nordholt argues that a common set of structural principles, or what I have termed metaphysical postulates, can be interpreted in variant ways and give rise to related, but distinct and even contradictory surface structures (Schulte Nordholt 1971, 15; Woodward 1989b, 22–30). It is perhaps for this reason that Naga cosmologies range from systems such as that of the Lhota in which the most important non-human beings are god-like creatures, to that of the Rengma for whom both the sky and the underworld are populated by ancestors. In many cases the ethnographic data indicate that many of the Naga are uncertain of exactly where their ancestors are and who it is that populates the sky and the underworld (see Woodward 1989a, 127; and Lehman 1977). This variation and ambiguity suggest that what is important is not 'where the ancestors are' or 'who the non-human persons are', but rather that there are sky people to whom sacrifices can be offered and underworld people from whom wealth can be extracted. The animal sacrifices and head hunting rites of the various Naga tribes are remarkably similar despite this cosmological variation.

Animal sacrifice

In most of the indigenous religions of Southeast Asia, the sacrifice of the largest domestic animal plays an important role in the quest for spiritual potency and fertility. Sacrifice also serves as a means of establishing or validating social status and of distributing accumulated surpluses of grain and meat. The Ao Naga *mithan* sacrifice is representative of this mode of ritual action.

The *mithan* sacrifice culminates a graded series of feasts of merit which are the basis of the Ao status hierarchy. It can only be performed by married men who have performed a series of preliminary feasts in which gifts of meat, grain and beer are presented to affinal relations, wife-givers and the sky people. These preliminary feasts are themselves not sacrifice because the souls of the animals are not sent to the sky world.

The sky people may attempt to prevent the sacrifice. The reason for this is that the *mithan* is believed to be one of the souls of a sky person. Its sacrifice results in the death of the person whose soul it is. Similarly, the *mithan* of the sky people are the souls of humans. When they are sacrificed, the human whose soul they are dies. This is illustrative of the tension between inferior and superior exchange partners in systems of asymmetric alliance. The inferior partner depends on spiritual potency that can only be acquired by sacrifice or payment. The superior receives wealth in return, but may be reluctant to enhance his inferior's position in the status hierarchy. To fool the sky people, it is announced that the sacrifice will be performed a day before the actual date.

On the second day of the ceremony the *mithan* is adorned with ropes made from cane and sword beans, both of which represent the fertility that will rise through the earth as the result of the sacrifice, and with feathers of the Great Indian Hornbill, a symbol of the upper world. These feathers can be as much as two feet long and are the most common symbol of relationships with the sky world among the indigenous peoples of mainland Southeast Asia. The next day a forked post carved with images of hornbills is erected in front of the feast giver's house. The *mithan* is tied to the post and greeted by all the men and women of the clan. It is presented with offerings of rice, salt and beer. The sponsor of the feast then calls the *aren* of his ancestor and tells the *mithan* that it should find his father when it arrives in the land of the dead. After the beast is killed the men of the sponsor's clan dance all night with women from the wife-giving clan.

In the morning the meat is divided after two of the sponsor's agnatic relatives climb to the roof of his house and cry out like hornbills to announce the sacrifice to the ancestors. The *mithan's* skull is cleaned and placed in the village men's house where it remains until the next harvest. Then it is moved to the sponsor's house, where the offerings and prayers for *aren* performed at the sacrifice are repeated. The *mithan* continues to serve as a source of potency throughout the feast giver's life. When he dies and travels to the land of the dead he reclaims the beasts from his kinsmen.

The *mithan* sacrifice is among the most important sources of social status in Ao society. It is, however, a communal as well as an individual rite. The feast giver and other village dignitaries are obligated to share the *aren* they have acquired with the community at large. This is accomplished by means of planting rituals. Before the fields are planted seed is collected from the richest men in the village. It is mixed together and planted in a special plot just outside the village gate. The purpose of this rite is to attract *aren* to all of the village fields. If no one in the village has performed the *mithan* feast in the past year, the village as a whole sacrifices a bull to ensure the fertility of the fields.

Head hunting or 'stealing ancestors'

Prior to the establishment of European administration in the late nineteenth and early twentieth centuries head hunting was widely practiced among the indigenous peoples of Southeast Asia. Some of the Dyak tribes of Kalimantan still preserve ancient skulls. There are frequent reports of incidents of head hunting in Kalimantan and in the more remote areas of the Assam Burma border area. The practice is based on the same metaphysical postulates as the sacrificial cult, so much so that captured heads are often decorated with the horns of sacrificed animals. The fact that head hunting rituals can be performed for (other people's) *mithan* and tigers also suggests that the two death ceremonies should be understood as part of a single ritual system.

The link between sacrifice and head hunting is clearly articulated in the Ao harvest ceremonies. New rice and salt are offered to *mithan* and human skulls. The *mithan* are instructed to bring others of their kind to the village. A man instructs the heads he has captured as follows: 'I am rich, I can feed all who come. Call Semas, Lhotas, Sangtams, Aos to my house. Call your parents and children. I will feed them' (Mills 1926, 205, 387).

Among the Rengma the association of head hunting was so strong that in 1933 leaders of the tribe asked the British Assistant Resident James Mills for permission to raid 'just a little bit', or at least that they be allowed to serve as transport coolies in a punitive expedition into unadministered territory (Mills 1937, 161).

Ao head taking rituals are particularly well described. When a head is taken it is brought back to the village where it is first placed on the village drum, which is carved in the shape of a stylized hornbill, and which is beat vigorously. The beating of the drum is recognized as being among the means of communicating with the sky people. When a new drum is carved, a head and the blood of animals sacrificed on the occasion are placed on it and the following prayer recited:

> Oh moon, sun, to you we are speaking indeed; children good let there be born in deed; rice plenty let there grow in deed, foreign heads, Ao heads let there be got in deed; tigers, elephants let there be got indeed, wild boars, hornbill cocks let there be got in deed.

In some villages a young boy killed a chicken, smeared its blood on the drum and called to the men of other villages to come to be killed (Mills 1926, 108).

All of the men who participated in killing the victim are entitled to a piece of the head and to participate in the rituals. First, the head is divided. Each man takes his portion to his house where his wife feeds it rice and beer saying: 'I am feeding you. Bring your father and your mother and your sons and your daughters here. My husband is a warrior' (Mills 1926, 204). The head is then placed on the end of a long bamboo and leaned against the head tree near the center of the village. An old man addresses it, explaining that it was taken because of the sins of its village and imploring it to provide more heads, bumper crops and prosperity in the days to come. It remains in the head tree for six days, after which its owner takes it to his own residence. Like the skulls of sacrificed *mithan* it is fed and invoked annually at harvest ceremonies. In periods of scarcity, human and *mithan* heads are taken out of the village and placed on a path leading to the fields to renew their fertility.

Fertility cults and Christian conversion

Prior to the establishment of colonial rule the Naga and most of the other indigenous peoples of Southeast Asia had limited contact with the world beyond their own villages. While there were complex trade networks linking tribal communities with Hindu, Muslim and Buddhist communities, conversion seems to have been relatively rare. Nor did the premodern Southeast Asian states attempt long-term occupation of the uplands of the mainland or the interiors of many of the Indonesian Islands. This situation changed dramatically in the late nineteenth and early twentieth centuries. In the interest of fixing colonial boundaries and enforcing uniform administration, British, French and Dutch administrations established direct control of many indigenous communities and regions.

Missionaries followed hard on the heels of soldiers and administrators. By the middle of the twentieth century the majority of tribal people had become at least nominally Christian. The Naga are a clear example. Today at least 90 per cent are self-described Christians. Eaton has argued that three factors contributed to the conversion process: the elimination of head hunting and military activity; an increased awareness of a larger world and desire to participate in it; and the congruence of Christian and Naga understandings of a 'high god' (Eaton 1984). Here, I will be concerned only with the religious aspect of Naga Christianities and those of other tribal people of the region.

Many of the indigenous religions of Southeast Asia hold that a high god was ultimately responsible for creation, but that he has only a minor role in the day-to-day lives of humans. The high gods of the Nagas, for example, do not figure directly in the fertility cults that are the most pressing religious concerns. Eaton's argument is that Christianity came to be understood as a new way of acquiring spiritual potency, from the previously neglected high god. Given the changing social context, 'conversion' was a reasonable option and it led to the establishment of Christianity as an 'indigenous Naga religion' (Eaton 1984).

This raises the question of exactly what is meant by the categories 'religion' and 'indigenous'. Morrison has suggested that many Native American Christianities are rooted in indigenous metaphysical postulates, in other words, that the meanings of Christian stories and symbols are informed by structural principles rooted in indigenous cultures (Morrison 1992b). An alternative model of conversion is one in which the metaphysical postulates change, and local traditions are interpreted in terms of structural principles derived from a larger, text-based tradition. The choice between these two models cannot be made on the basis of theoretical criteria. It is an empirical question, to which different communities and individuals respond in different ways.

Naga, Chin and Kachin Christians with whom I have discussed this issue have offered a variety of solutions. Some clearly see the world from the perspective of Christian assumptions and regard the traditions of their ancestors as having been simply wrong. Others distinguish between those parts of the traditional wealth/fertility complex that Christians can maintain, such as the custom of paying bride prices, and those that involve interaction with non-Christian spiritual beings that must be rejected. There are widely varied attempts to find parallels ranging far beyond the high god analogy proposed by Eaton. The crucifixion of Christ is sometimes compared with the *mithan* sacrifice. Missionary activity can be understood as 'winning souls' and as such compared with head hunting.

The range of creative adaptations that individuals in a single community may employ can be significant. In 1996 I attended a mortuary sacrifice in a Toraja village on the Indonesian island of Sulawesi. The Toraja are Christian, but unlike most of the Naga, have continued the practice of offering sacrifices to or for the ancestors. One finds graves marked with crosses littered with small offerings to the spirit of the ancestor. Megaliths are erected and water buffalo are sacrificed at Protestant funerals. Of the Torajan people I interviewed two stand out. One was an *adat* (customary law) specialist who was responsible for distributing pork and buffalo meat to various classes of relatives. He explained that the Christian god is important but that, at least in the Toraja country, he works through the spirits of the ancestors. We subsequently had a lengthy discussion of spirits and the Toraja kinship system. The Calvinist pastor who preached at the funeral saw things differently. He had been educated in the United States and explained Toraja custom in terms of Calvin's doctrine of election. He explained pigs and water buffalo were 'visible signs of election' and that the fact that the deceased man's family were capable of giving so much food to the 'visible Church' was a sign that he was among the elect of God. We subsequently had a long conversation about Calvin's *Institutes of the Christian Religion*. I left Toraja convinced that the *adat* specialist interpreted his world based on metaphysical postulates derived primarily from Toraja culture, but that the pastor's world view was more closely related to Calvin's Geneva than to the land of his birth.

15. Characteristics of African indigenous religions in contemporary Zimbabwe

James L. Cox

In this chapter, I shall focus on indigenous religious expressions in Zimbabwe. I contend that the main characteristics of African indigenous religions persist in and through the variety of Christian denominations and movements found throughout the country, in syncretistic new religious movements and through contemporary expressions of traditional observances. Christianity and traditional religions in Zimbabwe have influenced each other for nearly 150 years and thus neither is practised in the same way today as at the time of first contact during the middle to late nineteenth century. (For a history of mainline Christian missionary activity in Zimbabwe, see Weller and Linden 1984.) Traditional beliefs and rituals, although maintaining many of the characteristics of the original religions, have been altered by Christian teachings about God, the Bible, sin and redemption. In like manner, Christianity in Zimbabwe has incorporated many indigenous perspectives into its beliefs and practices.

The dynamic or cumulative development of religion in Zimbabwe, of course, is nothing new. The religious expressions of Zimbabwean peoples have always changed just as societies have changed; they have adopted different forms as contact has been made with other African peoples and as economic modes and power structures have evolved. The term indigenous, therefore, does not refer to some static African religiosity but designates what we are able to know historically about the religious life and practices of Zimbabwean societies, both prior and subsequent to extensive encounter with the West and through a study of those practices which persist among contemporary Zimbabwean peoples. The indigenous religions of Zimbabwe, just as in other parts of Africa, are known through a combination of historical and phenomenological methodologies.

Over half of Zimbabwe's current population of 10 million adheres to some form of Christianity, but religious allegiances are flexible. Many who would call themselves Christians join mainline Christian denominations but continue to consult traditional religious practitioners, participate in rituals prescribed by the practitioners and, if the need is evident, seek the mediation of prophets in African Initiated (Independent) Churches (Lan 1985, 39–43). The largest single Christian denomination today in Zimbabwe is the Roman Catholic Church. Just less than 1 per cent of the population is white, however, meaning that the vast majority of the people are influenced in large measure by indigenous religious practices (Berens 1988, 3, 44).

General characteristics of African indigenous religions

In his contribution to a book examining African traditional religions in Zimbabwe (ter Haar *et al.* 1992, 22–7) and later published in the South African *Journal for the Study of Religion* (1993, 29–48), J. G. Platvoet of Leiden University identifies the essential features of African indigenous religions, which I have summarized under the following seven points.

1. African indigenous religions are co-extensive with their societies; religion is an undifferentiated part of social life. Social life includes not only the living, but also what the community understands to be a variety of spiritual forces, foremost the ancestors.
2. The visibility of African indigenous religions is low due to their being co-extensive with society. It is difficult for outsiders to recognize religious as opposed to public ceremonies.
3. Religion is complex due to the multi-stranded nature of thought. By multi-stranded, Platvoet means that it consists of ideas, feelings, norms and symbolic representations which have been formed in past interaction processes into complex patterns which for members of the society are unsystematic and for Westerners unanalytical. For this reason, believers in indigenous religions can develop innumerable explanations for misfortune and ritual responses to it.
4. African religions are pragmatic. They perform rituals and seek explanations to deal with what Platvoet calls 'tangible salvific goods in this life only' (1993, 40). Another way of putting it is that African indigenous religions concern themselves with means of providing benefits which are largely material and which promote the harmony of society. Communication with the spirits in rituals is intended to achieve this end.

5. Reciprocity between the community and the spirits marks the central core of indigenous religious activity. Generally this means that the community must provide gifts to the spirits, often in the form of sacrificed animals or through the pouring of libations, as a sign of respect and remembrance. In return, the spirits provide protection and material beneficence for the community.
6. Beliefs are not articulated, but remain implicit. Hence, there are no doctrines, theologies, claims to truth or factional disputes between sects. African indigenous religions are non-missionary in their intent.
7. African indigenous religions are adoptive and adaptive. They have an open mind towards other religions and import the deities and practices of other peoples readily, integrating them into their own complex systems. They are also able to accommodate new factors, including the modernization process, without losing their essential identity.

If Platvoet's list accurately encapsulates the essence of African indigenous religions, including their expressions in Zimbabwe, on my thesis, I would expect to find the same emphases, to a lesser or greater extent, in all forms of Zimbabwean religions, whether in missionary-founded churches, African Initiated Churches, new religious movements or the practice of traditional rituals. My argument is not ideological in the sense of affirming the ethical or ontological priority of indigenous religions over contemporary Zimbabwean religions. My approach is fully methodological. I am arguing that by identifying the central characteristics and core elements within African indigenous religions, a student of religion is provided with the key for analysing the multiple expressions of religion in Zimbabwe. This is much the same method advocated by Andrew Walls, a noted historian of Christianity in Africa, who regards the core elements in African indigenous religions, what he calls 'African maps of the universe', as instrumental for achieving an understanding of African forms of Christianity.

> Christianity has ... necessarily inherited all the old goals of religion; in particular, the association with protection and with power is undiminished. The operating maps of the universe provide for the frequent interventions of the transcendent world in the phenomenal world; for the operation of spiritual forces, whether acting independently or directed by human malice, or indicating neglected familial or social duty. The effectiveness of the Christian faith, or any particular manifestation of it, is accordingly open to the test of whether it gives access to power and prosperity or protection against natural or spiritual enemies (purposes to which much traditional practice was directed) and satisfactorily enforces familial and social duty. (1996, 189)

Clearly, it is beyond my ability to test this thesis within the limits of this chapter since it would involve a detailed study throughout Zimbabwe among a wide variety of Christian communities, new religious movements and expressions of traditional religions. However, in order to draw attention to the way contemporary religious practices retain the core elements of indigenous concerns, I want to relate two cases drawn from my own research in Zimbabwe. The first describes my consultations with a spirit medium in 1992, and the second relates the phenomenon of Ambuya Juliana, whose movement reached its apex in 1995 by weaving Christian beliefs into traditional Zimbabwean observances.

An interview becomes a possession

In March 1992 I interviewed Mrs Shumba (pseudonym), a traditional spirit medium operating in the region of Chief Chingoma (among the Karanga in the Zvishavane District). I was accompanied on the interview by my MA student in the University of Zimbabwe, Douglas Dziva (also son of Chief Chingoma) and by his mother (the wife of the Chief). Also present were Mrs Shumba's daughter and her granddaughter of around two years of age.

Mrs Shumba was a woman of approximately 50 years who was the chosen medium of her deceased father. People in the region came to her, just as they would to any traditional healer (*n'anga*), for diagnosis of problems such as illness or death in the family, prognosis and treatment. Her method was to enter into possession in the presence of the enquirers and allow her father to speak through her. In this way, she would convey what was causing a particular problem and how to resolve it.

When I encountered Mrs Shumba, it was around 4:30 p.m. She was seated outside of her hut with her daughter and granddaughter. She was wearing a simple dress and a sweater. After some initial formalities, greetings and general conversation, I paid her a small amount of money and began to interview her. I asked her how she helps people. She relayed to me that people come to her with many different problems such as sickness, poor crops, death, infertility and difficulties at school. She indicated that her deceased father had chosen her to be his voice. When people come to her, he speaks to them through her and tells them why they are having problems and what they have to do about it. I asked her how long she had been a voice for her father. She replied that it had been for about three years. She had experienced a long illness which no one could cure. Then, during a special ritual prescribed by a *n'anga*, she became possessed by her father. After that, she recovered completely. Since that time she has helped other people when they come to her.

I then asked her how her father's spirit takes control of her. She seemed a bit confused by this question and simply replied that he does. I was curious to know if her father (as an ancestor) has special knowledge that he did not have when he was alive, and that if he was in communication with other ancestors. Again, Mrs Shumba seemed confused by this question and began to appear uncomfortable by turning away and shaking a little. I enquired if her father carries messages to higher ancestor spirits, and if they carry them to Mwari (God). Mrs Shumba was now becoming visibly uncomfortable and muttered something to her daughter which none in our party could understand. Finally, I asked if any people come to her because they are victims of *varoyi* (witches).

When I asked about witches, Mrs Shumba let out a very loud belch and began to shake. Her daughter rushed to her and spoke to her in a low voice. Her daughter informed us that Mrs Shumba was now possessed and that she needed to put on her clothes. Her daughter took her into the hut near to where we were sitting, no more than five feet away. From inside the hut a deep voice could be heard, apparently addressing Mrs Shumba's daughter. The voice asked, 'Who are these people?', 'Why are they asking my daughter such hard questions?', 'Have they paid money?'

When Mrs Shumba returned with her daughter from the hut, she was no longer the simple village woman but the spirit of her father. She was wearing a skirt of animal skins, a hat of eagle feathers, a black cloth draped over her shoulders and around her waist. She had rattles tied on the side of her legs. She was carrying a dark walking stick, approximately three feet high with designs on the top. She approached us from the hut walking with heavy steps like a man and spoke to us in a deep voice. She squatted in front of us with her legs bent like a man and began to talk with us. I posed further questions about what life is like in the world of the ancestors, but I was told these are questions which cannot be answered. I then presented her with a practical problem, and the atmosphere suddenly became quite relaxed. The tension evoked by my theoretical questions dispelled almost immediately.

The problem I posed resulted from a chance occurrence. On my trip to Chief Chingoma's region a few days earlier, my wallet had been lost. I noticed that it was missing the first morning after I had arrived at the Chief's house where I was staying. As soon as I discovered that my wallet was not in my room, I relayed the problem to the Chief's son, who immediately told his father. The Chief called together his entire household to discuss the problem. After an extensive search, it was apparent that the wallet was not at the Chief's home.

I posed the problem of my missing wallet to the spirit medium while she was under possession. When this issue was introduced, she stood in front of us and began dancing. The sun, which was lowering in the western sky, cast a bright light across her body. She raised her walking stick in the air several times in an up and down motion. She then told us in a dramatic presentation what had happened to the wallet. She said that I had stopped at a shop on the way to the Chief's home. My wallet was in my back pocket. There were many people in the shop. Someone in the crowded shop spotted my wallet and said to himself, 'Ah, *murungu* (white person)! I will be rich.' The person slipped the wallet out of my back pocket and disappeared from the shop. When he looked in the wallet, however, he was extremely disappointed, because there was very little money in it. He then threw the wallet in some red soil beside the road. Another person came along and spotted it. He also thought, 'Ah, I will be rich!' When he found no money in it, he threw it back into the red soil. That is what happened, said the spirit medium, and the wallet will never be found. During the whole time that the medium was telling this story, she was acting it out. She showed how the man had slipped the wallet out of my back pocket, how he hurriedly left the shop, how he had opened it and expressed disappointment before throwing it alongside the road.

When the medium had finished, she sat down again among us with her legs crossed like a man. Mrs Shumba's granddaughter, who was about two years old, climbed on the medium who held the child quite naturally. The conversation was very relaxed and the situation homely. Then the medium stood up and the voice of the spirit announced that he had to return to a mountain near Great Zimbabwe. At that, he said goodbye and went into the hut. Shortly afterward, Mrs Shumba reappeared in her former simple dress and sweater. She sat down with us. I asked her if she remembered being possessed by her father. She said she did not remember anything.

Interpretation of the spirit possession

My consultation with Mrs Shumba was intended as an interview with a practising *n'anga* in Chief Chingoma's region. I knew that she employed spirit possession as her means of diagnosis and treatment of people's difficulties. Nevertheless, I had not expected that she would become possessed in my presence.

From a believer's perspective, there is no doubt that Mrs Shumba does become possessed by the spirit of her deceased father and that she acts as a medium for communication with him. Moreover, those who consult Mrs Shumba believe that her father's spirit is able to discern the causes of misfortune and to prescribe the proper remedy. It is safe to conclude at one level, therefore, that Mrs Shumba would have regarded my meeting with her as one among many consultations aimed at alleviating people's problems. This is evidenced by the fact that she disclaimed any memory of what went on during the time she was possessed.

Mrs Shumba's possession in my case, however, was markedly different from other consultations. I was an outsider interested in talking with her about what she experienced under possession and how that could be understood in a larger framework of ancestor spirits. I was not a part of the community and could not be regarded as a believer. It was for this reason that initially I did not approach her with a specific problem. My questioning created an uncomfortable emotional atmosphere and seemingly it was this that prompted her to enter into a possessed state.

Moreover, the normal inducements to possession were lacking in my situation. No drumming, singing, clapping, ululating or taking of snuff occurred. As I asked the most sensitive question, that of witchcraft, Mrs Shumba let out a huge belch as an indication that she was becoming possessed. I regard this as self-induced and as a response to the discomfort she felt with my interview. It was in fact the most poignant answer she could provide.

What Mrs Shumba was telling me by becoming possessed is that the purpose of possession has nothing to do with revealing knowledge of the other world nor with constructing a systematic diagram of the relationships between ancestor spirits. In other words, the religious experience she displayed was not undertaken to reinforce religious doctrines, nor to translate structural hierarchies of spirits into a kind of African systematic theology. The purpose of possession is entirely practical, the aims of which are to resolve specific problems facing people. The ancestor speaks through her, not to tell others of the nature of the afterlife, but to alter directly the balance of the community's experience in favour of health and well-being.

This does not mean that Mrs Shumba's responses to me were irrational; indeed, she illustrated the type of rationality characteristic of the indigenous religions of Zimbabwe. For example, when the spirit was about to depart, he indicated that he was going to a mountain in the region of Great Zimbabwe. This would be quite unusual since the spirit was neither that of a chief nor even a messenger of the chief in the Mwari (high god) cult. Although the Mwari cult is now situated in the Matopos Hills, tradition relates it in earlier days to Great Zimbabwe (Mukonyora 1993, 49–51). It would not have been unusual for the spirit to go to a mountain, but one so far away and so steeped in traditional legend would be. This further underscores that the issues relating to the ordering of the spirit world are largely irrelevant. Indeed, this may have been Mrs Shumba's oblique answer to my questions about how the spirits relate to one another. She was confirming that there is communication in the spirit world; messages are carried to other, probably higher, spirits, but this is incapable of being constructed on a consistent theoretical model. Thought in Zimbabwean indigenous religions, as Platvoet notes, remains unsystematic, multi-stranded and largely inarticulate.

The Ambuya Juliana movement

From 28 to 30 July 1995, I conducted another series of interviews with people in the district of Chief Chingoma in the Mberengwa region (also see Cox 1998, 141–6). My intention in returning briefly to the area was to determine how the persistent droughts were being interpreted by those I had interviewed in 1992. The Chief and the spirit medium I interviewed then largely attributed the lack of rain to the failure of those in government to follow traditional rituals and to respect the authority of the chiefs.

On this visit, however, I encountered the unexpected influence of Juliana, who throughout the sixteen chieftaincies of the Mberengwa region had made a substantial change in the way rain rituals were being conducted. Although I was unable to reach Juliana personally during my brief visit, I interviewed five people who had attended one of her large gatherings held in November 1994 in Chief Chingoma's region and one person who had attended a meeting she conducted in June 1995 in the Garenyama Area of Mberengwa. These five were Fana Tazvi, Headman of Chief Chingoma and attendant to VaEmpty, the spirit medium for the Dunda territorial spirit; Christopher Hove, ex-teacher at Gwai School; Dhiriza Dziva, Headman of Chief Chingoma and one of the custodians of Juliana's rain-making village at the base of the Imbahura Mountain; Nelson Shumba, subsistence farmer in the Garenyama Area; Miclot Dziva, who is Chief Chingoma; and Douglas Dziva, a PhD student at the University of Natal, Pietermaritzburg and son of Chief Chingoma.

According to those I interviewed, Juliana, who is Karanga having been brought up near Chivu, reports that she was taken by an *njuzu* (sometimes translated as a mermaid or water spirit) at around the age of seven. Mawere and Wilson (1995, 254) report that originally Juliana claimed to have come from Mt Darwin in the northeast region of Zimbabwe, but that later she admitted to Gurli Hansson (1994, 286) that she originated near Chivu in central Zimbabwe. She spent approximately ten years under the water where she was instructed by the water spirit in African customs and the Bible. (Hansson 1994, 5, relates that Juliana told her that she had spent four years with the *njuzu*. It is possible that as the story of Juliana spread among the people, her time spent with the *njuzu* increased.) She also learned church songs there.

In an interview with the Swedish researcher Gurlie Hansson, Juliana related her experiences with the *njuzu*:

> We lived like crocodiles, ate soil and mud. I was very skinny and pale when I returned from her. When you stay with the *Njuzu* you learn to be humble and well behaved. I was also taught about the Bible there. There is everything down there. When I left I had a *Shanga* – reed, growing on my head. (Hansson 1994, 5–6)

When she emerged from her instruction, she went to the Matopos Hills at Matonjeni and apparently became an *mbonga* or virgin attendant in the Mwari cult. This corresponds to what Mawere and Wilson (1995, 286) refer to as one who is 'based out of the shrines, who in the case of women must be virgins', and to what Leslie Nthoi (1998, 70) calls the *wosanna* whose main duty at the shrine 'is to dance and sing to the High-God during rain ceremonies'.

Sometime in 1992, after the failure of the rains to come, Juliana began a mission to the people of Zimbabwe by going out from the shrine at Matonjeni to various regions, largely across the south-central areas. Subsequently, she has constructed a number of sacred enclosures, called *Majacha Emapa* or rain-making villages, generally at the base of sacred mountains. I visited two of these, one at the foot of the Imbahura Mountain, under the care of the Chingoma spirit, and one in the Garenyama Area. At Imbahura (on 29 July 1995), I interviewed Mr Dhiriza Dziva, Headman of Chief Chingoma and one of the custodians of the *Jacha* which had been constructed at the base of the sacred mountain.

The interview I conducted with Mr Dziva took place in the company of Chief Chingoma and, as before, in the presence of the chief's son, Douglas Dziva. Before entering the enclosure, we were all required to remove our shoes and watches. As we entered the grounds, each one of us clapped our hands and uttered a praise word to Musikavanhu (the creator of people). At the Garenya *Jacha*, we offered praise to Shoko (monkey), the totem of the Mwari cult (Mawere and Wilson 1995, 286). The interview was conducted on some raised boulders on the right side of the enclosure under some trees. Mr Dziva told me that it was a traditional custom to sit in this place to discuss any matters of concern. He told me that just in front of this spot Juliana had conducted a *Mutoro* (rain) ritual in November 1994 personally supervising the distribution of traditional beer and meat.

He reported that over 2,000 people attended, all fitting within the enclosure. He reported that, although Juliana used no microphones, she spoke in her normal voice during the ritual and could be heard clearly by everyone.

The primary teachings which Juliana conveyed to the people at the ritual, as reported to me by Mr Dziva and confirmed by the others I interviewed, are as follows:

1. Mwari (God) is above all creation, including people and ancestor spirits.
2. Mwari is responsible for providing rain and will do so when the people return to their traditional practices and honour him.
3. The possession of spirit mediums by territorial ancestor spirits is strongly discouraged (if not forbidden) at *mutoro* rituals. (Mr Fano told me that if anyone started to become possessed during the ritual, Juliana would shout out commanding them to stop.)
4. The people should not work on Wednesday or on Sunday.
5. No wild animals should be killed, including snakes.
6. No sexual intercourse should take place on mountains or in forests.
7. When the people dip for water in wells, they should not use metal containers but rather should employ traditional gourds.
8. Promiscuity should be avoided; women especially should take care not to accept the casual advances of men.

Although Juliana does not claim to be a Christian, she acknowledges the importance of Christianity in her teachings. She knows the Bible from memory, since, as she claims, she was taught it by the *njuzu* spirit. The chief's wife, Mrs Dziva (herself a schoolteacher), confirmed to me that Juliana is indeed illiterate since she is teaching her how to form English and Shona letters. During the rituals she conducts for rain, Juliana also uses church songs, again which she claims were taught to her by the *njuzu* during her long period of instruction. In these ways, Juliana has assimilated aspects of two religious traditions by combining them for two clear purposes: the renewal of the land and its resources and the preservation of traditional culture. According to my informants, she sees herself involved in a mission to redeem the people from their persistent suffering due to repeated droughts. Juliana is reported by Hansson (1994, 6) as having described her mission as follows: 'I have been sent by Tshokoto shrine to save the people of Zimbabwe. They have to listen to Musikavanhu, the Creator and also observe respect for the *Vadzimu*, our ancestral spirits.'

Implications of the Juliana movement

Recent reports I have received from Zimbabwe indicate that Juliana has receded in importance among the people, partly due to power struggles with the Mberengwa chiefs. However, I want to draw attention to three components in her movement which shed light on an understanding of how indigenous religions and African Christianity are mutually dependent.

First, it is clear from the outset that we see in Juliana what Walls refers to as the magnification of the God component (1996, 192–3) beyond what would probably have been present in the indigenous religions of the area prior to Christianity. This is witnessed by the emphasis on God as creator and on the discouragement of possession by lesser spirits at Juliana's rituals for rain. The 'God factor' is complicated, however, because Juliana is related to the Mwari cult of the Matopos Hills with its complex system of messengers coming from chieftaincies throughout southern Zimbabwe (Daneel 1970; 1998). No agreement has been reached on how significantly Mwari, as the Shona High God, has been redefined due to the widespread influence of Christianity (Cox 1995).

This, however, need not be resolved here, since it is clear that Juliana uses Mwari in very much the same way indigenous religions would understand territorial spirits. God operates in Juliana's presentation as one who provides health, in this case through rain, or who withholds it as a punishment for failing to maintain a proper reciprocal relationship with him. The misfortune of the drought results, as is common in indigenous perspectives, from failing to respect traditional customs. The way to restore benefits to the community is to adopt once again the attitude of respect toward tradition, shown through ritually honouring God and the ancestors and by conforming to traditionally acceptable social behaviour. In this sense, God, like all ancestor spirits in Zimbabwe, communicates through misfortune in order to rectify the negligence of the people toward him and to correct their deviance from traditional norms of behaviour (Cox 1996).

Second, Juliana could be called a prophetess of indigenous practices in Zimbabwe. She received a message from the spirit world, as communicated in the traditions of the *njuzu*, which the people need to hear and respond to if further calamities are to be avoided. Because she later became associated with the Mwari shrines and now reportedly can actually assume the 'Voice of Mwari', she communicates directly to the people what Mwari wants the people to know (Daneel 1970, 49–50). This can be interpreted as a Christian influence; the original ancestor (the creator of the people) comes near through his mediator. This is just the role assigned to Christ in many forms of African Christianity. Walls notes:

> the Christian impact has greatly intensified the sense of the immediacy of the presence of God, particularly in the figure of Christ. God's interventions in the phenomenal world need no longer be attributed to refractions of his existence, . . . or sought through intermediaries; he speaks directly. (1996, 197)

Here again, however, we see that this is not something new, but an extension of the widely practised mediation of traditional healers and religious specialists throughout Zimbabwe. Communication with the spirit world provides the hinge on which the whole well-being of the society depends. As a result, spirit mediums are widespread. They become possessed of ancestors and other spirits in order to communicate directly to the people. Other forms of communication from the spirit world, such as through mechanical means or through dreams, perpetuate the traditional practice of direct contact with the spirits. The 'Voice of Mwari' in Matonjeni reflects a consistent pattern with what is done in every village throughout Zimbabwe. Juliana, therefore, as a prophetess with a direct message from Mwari, is fully indigenous in her representations to the people. Her negative attitude towards possession in the rituals under her control probably represents her view of the hierarchy of spirits which she enforces as her direct authority from Mwari over lower spirits.

Finally, the scope of Juliana's message could be regarded as reflecting the universalistic tendencies of Christianity. Her call for a return to tradition has been interpreted by some that I interviewed as applicable beyond the boundaries of Zimbabwe. It was reported to me, when I was seeking an interview with her, that she had just returned from Mozambique where she 'preached' the value of tradition. Some people suggested that she might even regard herself as a prophet to Europe, where her message would be for Europeans to discover and return to their indigenous traditions to avoid the many ills plaguing modern societies in the West.

A close examination of the content of Juliana's message, however, shows that it is quite culture-specific, complex and multi-stranded. Her emphasis on the water spirits as becoming offended by the building of modern dams and even the drilling of bore holes complicates the explanations for the drought. Water spirits are perceived as living in pools, some of which are found at the top of mountains where they never become dry. Connecting the pools are innumerable underground streams through which the spirits travel. It would be clear that disturbances to the ground would also disturb the spirits (Ranger 1995, 239.) Yet, any endeavour to construct a systematic explanation as to how that relates to Mwari or other ancestors and their grievances is bound to be artificial and probably meaningless to those who receive Juliana's message. Thought is complex and, from Western perspectives, unanalytical. Moreover, Juliana's emphases on the use of traditional instruments for gathering and drinking water, from a Western point of view, do not fit into a strict logic. References to refraining from sexual intercourse in natural settings reflect the widespread belief that prophets and followers of African Initiated Churches engage in promiscuous behaviour on mountains or in forests. (This information was conveyed to me in two interviews I held on 15 August 1995, one with Lillian Dube, Lecturer in Theology and Women Studies in the University of Zimbabwe, and the other with Dr Tabona Shoko, Lecturer in African Traditional Religions, University of Zimbabwe.) The content of Juliana's message, therefore, represents a specific context and its multi-stranded nature marks it as indigenous without universal applicability despite similarities to Christian universalistic motives.

Conclusions for the study of religions in Africa

Through the cases of Mrs Shumba and Ambuya Juliana, I have tried to show how the general characteristics of indigenous religions identified by Platvoet apply in contemporary Zimbabwean contexts. The possession of Mrs Shumba by her ancestor father underscores the pragmatic, unanalytical and multi-stranded nature of indigenous religiosity. Her possession demonstrates in a concrete way that the well-being of society depends on a reciprocal relationship between the community and the ancestor spirits, although beliefs about this remain implicit rather than articulated.

In the Juliana movement, the Christian God has been assigned primarily the role of an ancestor in protecting the people against misfortune and by maintaining a reciprocal relationship with them. Christ has been apportioned the same function as a spirit medium, such as Mrs Shumba, who conveys messages directly from the spirit world. The potentially universal message of Juliana, calling all peoples to return to traditional practices, is reduced to a complex, multi-stranded and culturally specific pattern of thought.

If my analysis is correct, the cardinal significance of indigenous religions for the study of religious practices in Zimbabwe, and by extension in many other parts of Africa, becomes apparent. The starting-point for such a study emanates from and is located within the very indigenous roots which receive, adopt, adapt and eventually transform how religion appears in contemporary African contexts.

16. Spirituality, values and boundaries in the revitalization of a Mi'kmaq community

Raoul R. Andersen, John K. Crellin and Misel Joe

This chapter focuses on one way in which spirituality functions in cultural revitalization. The scene is the small Mi'kmaq reserve at Conne River, Newfoundland, Canada. The three authors, two from outside the community (R.R.A. and J.K.C.) and M.J., who is both the traditional and the elected chief of the Conne River Band, have collaborated on various ventures for some time. The present account is a combined effort, but it seemed only appropriate to rely heavily on recently tape-recorded reminiscences of Misel Joe. As an architect of cultural revitalization, he constantly expresses in words and intonation aboriginal spirituality and its values. Not only does he illustrate what other commentators have said about revitalization – the 'blending' of pan-Indian and Mi'kmaq traditions – but he also shows how traditions (or the values that underpin them) are, or may be, ultimately woven into the fabric of community development. Moreover, the blending embraces the values of various non-aboriginal institutions such as the Christian Church.

We sketch first some history of the Mi'kmaq band and Misel Joe's awakening spirituality amid a time of challenge, bordering on personal crisis. Finally, we look at the revitalization of his community and the role of spirituality and values. There, we see that spirituality has no hard and fast boundaries. Its plastic, pervasive and utilitarian facets contribute much to community development. The two authors from the outside community believe that this deserves close attention from other communities, aboriginal and non-aboriginal.

Mi'kmaq in historical and cultural perspective

Newfoundland Mi'kmaq are the most easterly extension of Algonquian-speaking peoples in North America. Their primary historical identity in Newfoundland, as a hunting and trapping people, contrasts with that of Newfoundland's white European people in shore and offshore commercial fisheries. In this century, the decline of the fur trade, industrialization, and non-native competition have reduced Mi'kmaq dependency upon the land, and they have entered occupations like forestry, construction, mining and even commercial fishing.

Confederation with Canada in 1949 brought Newfoundland's aboriginal peoples – Mi'kmaq, Inu, and Inuit – citizenship and eligibility for federal support as aboriginals. However, official recognition of Newfoundland Mi'kmaq as aboriginals began only in the early 1970s. In the 1980s, the Conne River Mi'kmaq gained a direct federal relationship, registered aboriginal status, and reserve community status under Canada's Indian Act.

By the early 1900s, Conne River was the major settlement and perhaps last refuge of the island's traditional Mi'kmaq people (see Jackson 1993). Today the Conne River Band of around 700 occupies a small reserve about 30 miles inland from Newfoundland's south coast in Bay d'Espoir. It is a historic summer camping place and access point to the island interior's rich hunting and trapping grounds, and nearby waters abound in marine game and waterfowl.

Conne River Mi'kmaq remember well a history of church and Newfoundland government actions that stigmatized and nearly obliterated their aboriginal cultural identity, abolished their designated community under the Newfoundland government in the 1930s, and attempted to assimilate them – albeit as a marginalized people – into Newfoundland and Canadian non-aboriginal society.

Today, Conne River Mi'kmaq maintain relations with mainland Mi'kmaq bands in Nova Scotia, New Brunswick and eastern Quebec. This reflects historical connections and understandings that Newfoundland Mi'kmaq originated on the mainland. The island–mainland relationship is part of the process of an ongoing search for, discovery, re-invention and consolidation of Mi'kmaq cultural identity and religious and spiritual life. Misel Joe's personal story exemplifies this ongoing search because of his roles as chief, but this is only one case among a people whose traditions permit and encourage spiritual self-discovery and harmony.

Chief Misel Joe

Misel Joe was born at Conne River in 1946. His family worked at seasonal hunting, trapping, and logging. Although he learned little of the Mi'kmaq language from his family, he grew up on traplines, knew wigwam life, living on the land, and identified strongly with his own patrilineage group or clan. He learned, too, that the natural world was invested with forces and beings, and that animals and nature must be shown respect. He heard stories of Mi'kmaq and other aboriginal people, some described as 'witches', believed to have the power to cast harmful spells when betrayed or disrespected.

Such traditional cultural matters were often left undiscussed and unquestioned, partly from fear created by church teachings that demonized and suppressed the Mi'kmaq language, spiritual beliefs, and practices. At Conne River the Roman Catholic priest was 'the ultimate power'. Father St Croix served the area parish from 1916 to 1946 and strictly enforced the use of English in school. St Croix had children strapped if they spoke Mi'kmaq, and he banned its use in church, just as he ridiculed and objected to Mi'kmaq spiritual beliefs and religious rituals as superstition, the devil's work (Jackson 1993, 163–5). It seems fair to say, as Jackson observes, that the Christian Church 'fractured [Mi'kmaq] ethnic identity and accelerated cultural deterioration' (1993, 161; see also Anger 1983; cf. Prins 1996).

At age sixteen Misel Joe left to explore life off the island. He worked on mainland farms, ranches, at mining and commercial fishing, and became a skilled heavy equipment operator. His life became a gruelling cycle of seasonal migrant work, cash payoffs, sharing resources with companions, alcohol abuse, unemployment and handouts, lost personal dignity, and loneliness. Misel Joe recalls no particular interest in spirituality or traditional healing during the many years he lived away from Conne River; however, he did meet aboriginal people who took pride in their identity despite stigmatization (see Anger 1983, 95–6).

In 1973 Misel Joe, now married, left a job at Sudbury, Ontario, to return to Conne River to stay. 'I wanted to be able to smell the woods again, to walk on the bogs again, go hunting and trapping again, to taste my mother's cooking again. All those things called me back.' Only later did he form conscious links with these early experiences as roots of spirituality and commitment to healing.

The years between 1973 and 1983 were turbulent years, personally and for the community itself. The Conne River people were awakening to the political and cultural issues occurring widely among aboriginal people; there was growing resistance to their marginalization in Canadian society. Significant divisions erupted locally in the mid-1970s over whether or not to pursue re-establishing the community as a reserve, this time under the Indian Act. Some 'traditionalists' and others urged this course (see Anger 1983).

An unexpected spiritual intervention

In 1983, in the heat of the struggle for political and cultural autonomy, Chief Joe had a spiritual experience that brought out many inner feelings. When police forced him and his followers out of the government offices that they had seized in St John's, in defiance of the provincial government which had withheld federal funds owed to the band, it seemed they were beaten. They retreated to the Catholic Action Centre, where Misel Joe remembers:

> I locked myself in a room all night and I said there has got to be answers. That's when spirituality started to happen. All over the Action Centre there were pictures of Christ and there was one on the wall in this little kitchen that I locked myself in.
>
> All night I tried to pray to this picture and nothing happened. But every time I did that, this picture, this vision of a Mi'kmaq person, Roddy Stevens, would come. I prayed to the vision of this face, not one with the beard, but one with the crew cut and the glasses and the round face.

Stevens, an older, wise and gentle person, approached the Chief in ways that expressed a strong sensitivity to personal values, especially respect for others. At the time it gave Misel Joe the strength to decide he and his followers would fast resolutely. Very soon, the government freed their band funds.

Victory and retreat

In 1985 the band wrested control over schooling from the Catholic Church. In 1986 the reserve was formally recognized and band members became registered Indians under Canada's federal Indian Act. New funding agreements with the federal government followed. However, community unrest continued and Misel Joe was ousted from office as elected chief in 1988; he remained traditional chief and saw that role as having a responsibility to foster native spirituality. He turned to the Grand Chief in Nova Scotia for advice in conformity to their 'traditional form of government'. This resulted in a plan to march to Ottawa. It included some fifteen or sixteen Conne River Mi'kmaq men who believed themselves disenfranchised or 'taken over' by 'non-traditionalists,' even by 'non-Indian' people who had taken control of their government.

The march fostered a sense of healing and spiritual renewal when, together with mainland Mi'kmaq, the Conne River participants were introduced to sweet grass, sweat lodge and other ceremonies and their spiritual meaning. Marching and talking together, they soon determined that they could heal themselves without continuing to Ottawa. They returned home to 'discover' traditions such as the sweat lodge.

Nowadays, Chief Joe continues to seek the 'proper' way to conduct various ceremonies. He still believes that what he does may not always be historically correct, but what matters, in spiritual terms, is the practice:

> We all need something to lean on, something to believe in. If the Church has not done it, the treatment centres have not done it, then there's spiritualism, there's the sweat lodge where you can talk openly about how you feel about alcoholism, family abuse or whatever. It becomes an important crutch that you can lean on and, after you get to the point where you want to go back and be your same old self again, you know that there's always the sweat lodge and I can go back. There's always going to be people there in a circle that do care about me and do care if I survive or not and do care for my family.

The responsibility for spiritual leadership, inherent in his role as traditional chief, led Misel Joe to re-examine and seek out what many aboriginal people regard as a fundamental spiritual tradition, the personal vision quest. After a year of preparation he undertook a fast near to his grandfather's trapline. On the second night in his wigwam:

> I was alone inside with the fire going and every once in a while this white figure would come in through the flap of the wigwam, stir the fire with a little stick, and stare at the fire.
>
> Finally, before daybreak, I figured, well, this is the time I am going to find out what this is all about. I want to see a face this time. But next time, when the figure came to the door, there was no face. It was just like a hood, a dark hole, and I looked all the way down, looking at the feet, and there were no feet. It was caribou hooves. And right away I got scared. The devil, mindu, it was here to get me! As soon as I realized this is not mindu, because this thing had been keeping me warm all night, it disappeared. In the morning I decided I have to figure this thing out. He didn't turn and go out, he didn't do anything, he was just gone. That same night I was sitting by the fire outside, and looking at me through the woods was a pure white caribou, even the eyes were pure white, the antlers, everything, and that too disappeared after I realized I had seen it. At daybreak I searched around the island, but there were no caribou tracks.

At the time, my vision of the white caribou didn't mean very much to me. It wasn't until two years later that I decided that I wanted the Mi'kmaq name. I was tired of being called Mike or Michael or whatever. It was an English name. I decided I was going to visit Talking Eagle, an elder and medicine man in New Brunswick, to ask for a Mi'kmaq name.

So we sat around a table and he spoke in Mi'kmaq for a long time, not to me, not to anyone. Sometimes he would look at the sky, sometimes all around. Finally, he said White Caribou. And he prayed some more and talked to people around him, and he said your name is White Caribou. It took a long time to go through the ceremony. While he was praying I was having visions of my own, what I wanted to be and, of course, everybody wants to be some kind of relation to the eagle. If not the eagle, then the hawk. But the caribou fed our people for thousands of years, and it is clothing, medicine; the antlers and the bones are weapons and tools. So the name had as much significance or magnificence as the eagle itself. I walked away feeling pretty proud of myself.

Spirituality and its boundaries

Misel Joe's understanding of spirituality, his readiness to share it, not impose it, and the mantle many people (perhaps even more from without the community than from within) bestow on him as a healer, all serve his roles as administrative chief as much as traditional chief.

Cultural revitalization involves a general, albeit often selective, restoration of a people's ethnic traditions and identity. However, in a situation such as we describe, many members of a community may not see this as necessarily part of native spirituality, for promoting such traditions as history and language, trapping skills, herbal knowledge and crafts can be viewed as largely secular and utilitarian. For some people, revitalization involves solely economic development that brings employment and activities to the community. For others, it is much more. In Conne River, a variety of community initiatives are vehicles for native spirituality and values, albeit in a restrained manner that leaves spiritual meanings, if they are seen, up to each individual community member.

Before mentioning some of the community initiatives, we must comment on the central role of the sweet grass purification ceremony. Within the past ten years or so, there has been increasing use of the ceremony in various community activities and regular use within the Band administration building. The pleasant sweet grass aroma in the building often prompts positive comments from visitors. For many people, like Misel Joe, sweet grass is essential to native spirituality: 'Like a door, it allows people to enter.' If members of the community have become accustomed to the sweet grass purification – perhaps through respect rather than acceptance of the beliefs it represents, just as many respond to national anthems – many also see it as a symbol of roots. Sweet grass has become recognized as a core part of First Nation traditions and values that arm cultural renewal, such as the sweat lodge, the sentencing circle, and the powwow (see Anger 1983, 245).

As among other First Nation peoples, not all community members of Conne River are enthusiastic about trends to revitalization. However, in Conne River, where the Catholic Church of St Anne's has just been rebuilt with Band Council financial support, there is a growing curiosity about traditional practices. Moreover, a sense of values, especially that of respect – respect for people, the land and the environment in general – is increasingly evident. No one claims that this sense of values is unique to First Nation people, but in Conne River values pervade significant community programmes, as we now relate.

Respect for the elders and for children is wonderfully displayed in the yearly calendar of the Band Council. This year-round tribute displays photographs and names of all the community elders. Moreover, it singles out the eldest and the youngest newborn in the community, thus making a spiritual connection between them.

The place of values in the range of health and social services is perhaps less tangible, though they are part of a 'holistic' care philosophy. According to Misel Joe:

> We have come a long way from when my grandmother died of tuberculosis for which she received very little care except from the family around her. But we are still not a healthy community in the sense, for instance, that we still don't know why there is a high level of cancer. We still don't know why there is still such a high level of diabetes. We still don't know why all these things are happening to us.
>
> Nevertheless, what we are doing is to develop programmes. For example, around elders who live alone, we ensure that there is a programme in place that allows someone to go in to visit them, talk with them, do basic cleaning and cook good meals for them. That not only gives them good service, but also personal contact with people. And we provide meals for older couples and elders who live alone that don't always cook good meals.
>
> Several years ago we identified that a number of elders living alone had special dietary requirements as a result of diabetes and hypertension. Presently these elders receive two cooked meals a week suited to their diet from the Clinic's nutrition centre.
>
> We also provide meals to people who have alcohol or drug problems. Alcoholics, for instance, don't always have good meals, and, in some cases, just need someone to talk to. So we provide a service for them. We also have a drug and alcohol counselling service and home visits for those who don't want to come into a clinic setting, but want to talk at home.

It's so easy to be lonely, so easy to get sick from loneliness, so we maintain contact. We know when birthdays roll around or when it is a special day for elders; we make sure that there is a postcard or a birthday card going out to elders to maintain that contact. Our staff, during Christmas season, take Christmas presents around to elders, and right after I make my visits people from the clinic will go around with gifts for them. There will be people from the school, people from other departments, who do the same thing. And it doesn't only apply to elders, but also to anyone who lives alone. It could be a sixteen-year-old to a ninety-five-year-old. If you are living alone, there's a helmet of loneliness that you must go through, so if there's a contact out there, that's fulfilling some basic need. To me it's a form of healing in itself.

In a community of people, we are all linked together

We are not individuals in one sense, for, in a community of people, we are all linked together, we are all part of the same family. So, when my neighbour hurts, I hurt. I have to play a role in making sure that he stays healthy as long as he can. If there's something that I have that he needs to ensure his health – whether it be just a regular visit to talk to them – then that's my role.

Sometimes it's left to the individuals; some may want to live in seclusion and not want the Chief or anyone else to visit; but we make certain that he's sure that if the time comes when he wants to talk to me or to anyone else, that the opportunity is there. He is never turned away. We have a system whereby the Clinic itself will make regular calls to individuals' homes; for instance, if we know that a person has a history of alcoholism, and locks himself in his house, someone will check every day to make sure everything is as it should be. And to ensure that at the end of the week or at the end of the day that there's someone offering good nutritious meals for that individual and also to encourage them to leave that helmet behind. In a sense, to get out to work within the community system. The Clinic's mission statement is to address the health, social and survival needs of the residents of the reserve in a manner 'that teaches self-reliance, strengthens families and promotes community values of mutual support, sharing and togetherness'.

We provide jobs. We don't ask them, 'Do you want to go to work?' We have a lady that calls on a regular basis to say, 'Well, I found another job for you.' It may be working at the warehouse, it may be working with the garbage collection system, it may be with the security system, it may be with something else within the band that this individual could fit into. But it's his choice.

Leaders and healers in the community

We know through our own history how we should be looking after elders. We know that if you take an elder from the community into some clinic or hospital away from his family, that, in some regards, it may kill him or her altogether. So, as a community, as leaders and healers in the community, we need to take control of that and ensure that we do everything we can within the community system itself, that every service possible will be provided for them to ensure that they stay there. And every health concern that he has, if we can, we will try and cover, including cooking meals, once or twice a week, to ensure that there is someone who will visit on a regular basis.

Treatment is far more than just handing out pills

Treatment is far more than handing out pills. It's the way the doctor *hands* you those pills, it's how he receives you in his waiting room, it's how he receives you in his clinic, it's how he is able to talk to make you feel comfortable, how he is able to relate to some of the things you are talking about.

It may not be that I've got a sore finger, but that I've got something in here that's bothering me as well. He's got to be able to deal with the finger, but he's also got to deal with what's in here in a nice and friendly way. And when I walk out through the door, I need to feel healthier, to have things under control, including my sore finger.

And it is important to be able to walk out into a community that supports you. We are not only dealing with physical health, but with the spiritual health of individuals as well. That spiritual help comes from a number of sources, from the clinic, from the community, from the leaders of the community, from different lay-people.

When an elder walks through the door he has swallowed a lot of pride to do so

The big problem we have been having, like all types of institutions that start to get bigger and broader, is to bring along the staff at the same speed, to make them sensitive to know that when an elder walks through the door he has swallowed a lot of pride to do so. And when he gets in the door, he has got to feel comfortable. He knows full well that when he gets to see the doctor, he is meeting someone that should be given a lot of respect, but he also has to feel comfortable in that building.

We have put in place what we call a 'spiritual building'

We have just put in place what we call a 'spiritual building' which will enable our staff from the Clinic, our people from the administration, band members, to get together in this little building – free from politics, free from the everyday hangups that we may have. I may not like the colour of your coat or I may not like the way you look, but once we walk into this little building, then you hang what you call your monkey on the nail outside. There's no place for it inside. And very simply, the building is small enough where we can sit across from each other and talk to each other without having to raise our voices. The central fireplace is the focal point of the building itself. The lighting is such that it's not directly on your face, but on your back. It will be comfortable. We will be encouraging everyone to come into the building, to use the building at storytelling time, to have children come into the building to sit with elders and listen to their stories.

We hope people will use this building to unload and have a healthier family, a healthier lifestyle; indeed, to become a healthier worker that's going to be able to make a long-lasting contribution to the overall health of all of us.

Child and family services

In the same building as the clinic we have Miawpukek Child and Family Services, which provide programs to both elders and children. For instance, we bring children in from the school. In fact, when we were building the Clinic, we had the children paint designs on the basement walls. Inside the building we have a fully functioning playroom for children. And it's not uncommon for adults to walk in and take part in the services that we provide and to play with the children. I go down some days and get involved with some of their discussions and play. And it's very humbling and very rewarding at the same time.

We don't just want to feed you bologna

It's customary for us, when we invite people into the community, to provide a meal, as an invited guest. Now, we wouldn't want to bring you into our community and give you food that's no good for you – we don't want to feed you bologna, although I think bologna is a good food! So our staff prepare meals based on a guide that's high in nutrition and not by any means fatty food that sometimes we have been known to eat. So the Clinic itself provides that service – for a fee of course. And they also provide different functions throughout the year to band members. For instance, they will find out ahead of time who are they catering to. If you have allergies that may not allow you to eat the foods that we eat, then we'll make sure that a special plate is provided, muffins, perhaps, without chocolate or without raisins. Or something instead of red meat. So it is a unique service outside the Clinic and it also runs a nutrition building with staff year-round – nutrition workers that's been trained and certified to deal with foods and to cook, not only for elders and people that live alone, but on occasions for the whole band when we come together.

Closing comments

A full account of the recent development of the community requires much more space than is available here. However, we hope we have shown a range of activities and programmes that provide opportunities to raise an awareness of traditional values that, in turn, encourages curiosity about First Nation traditions, spirituality and values. That this has come with improved economic circumstances is also a significant factor in prompting interest. On the other hand, the fact that the majority of the community has not yet expressed open interest reveals that the recovery of native spirituality faces many hurdles. However, Misel Joe and others in the community are not in a hurry.

Time will be the test of their approach, which is one of example and of promoting traditional values through various community activities and programmes. The absence of fixed boundaries to spiritual values – indeed, one might say there are no boundaries – can well be described as a significant community development model. By 1998, much has been put in place. We close with more comments by Misel Joe on yet a further activity that has aroused community enthusiasm, the building and first journey of a traditional Mi'kmaq birch bark canoe. Perhaps even more than such traditions as the sweat lodge and the use of a talking circle for healing and sentencing, the canoe has fired the imagination and raised questions about spirituality:

> Some years ago, I visited the Glenbow Museum in Alberta. Once I saw the Mi'kmaq canoe there it was like touching a fork to an electrical outlet – you get sparks, all kinds of things happening. My mind was going a thousand miles an hour. The things we could do! I thought about how we could raise awareness by taking this canoe out of the museum – if I could get my hands on it. But it would be crazy to try and steal the canoe! We just had to raise our awareness in other ways. Build our own canoe. Some of us sat night after night talking about things we needed to do. The canoe project was always a part of our discussion, and the more we talked about it, the more we realized that it wasn't just a dream.
>
> And the main thing, when we watched the canoe being built, was realizing that a lot of what we were doing is going to bring us in touch with the spirits, especially at the landing place at Cape Ray. I took a friend of mine there and when I went near the water there was all kinds of things happening; the hair on my neck was standing up, sparks went up my arm and I realized it was the perfect place, an ideal and a true place, for landing, either starting from or coming back to. We knew that we had to leave from there, and once we took the canoe there, there was going to be spirits all over the place.
>
> From the beginning it was a kind of spiritual project to me, though that wasn't as clear at first as it was later on. But it was still a spiritual journey that I

was taking as part of my own understanding of what I was going through and needed to do. As we got further into the project it became a spiritual one for the builders, at least some of the builders anyway. I know one for sure. Maybe it was a little easier for me because I knew what was happening and why it was happening.

Like the people in Maui, where I was honoured to have a ride on a traditional double-hulled canoe, we consider a Mi'kmaq canoe very much a spiritual craft, spirits of the ancient people. When we started our canoe project it did the same thing to us and without even trying to go after that kind of thing, just happening. Every time you saw the canoe, every time you spoke to people you realized that there were some pretty clear thoughts about the canoe – magic, dreams.

Our Stonehenge is the canoe. Our Stonehenge is our wigwam, our whole history, and our use of the land, our claim to be protectors of the land, all are spiritual, all are our Stonehenge. Without those we would be nothing at all.

The whole idea of building something like this for any community is that it can be a way of pulling a community together because it is such a challenge. It has never been done before, at least not in living memory. At least they are aware that this is a craft that had been built by our people. And it is part of our visual history, it has links to the past.

And there is appreciation for the craft by people themselves. It was unbelievable to watch them sit and work on their paddles, the kind of art-work that they used on their paddles. There was pride in what they were doing and it showed in their faces, it showed when they did the sea trial with the canoe, it showed in the people around them, like their friends and family. It showed in the kids who greeted them. It all came together in that regard. And the community really did get involved with this, which was what we wanted anyway.

In August 1999 the canoe was safely paddled from Newfoundland to Nova Scotia.

Bibliographic note

Most literature on the Mi'kmaq concerns those on the mainland. Information on Newfoundland Mi'kmaq is scattered, largely among unpublished and archival sources (see the bibliography on the Newfoundland Mi'kmaq Government's web site at http://www.geocities.com/CapitolHill/2071/bibl.htm). Much of this information is devoted to establishing the prehistory and history of Mi'kmaq in Newfoundland (see e.g. Anger 1983 and Wetzel 1995), and their rights struggles (e.g. Anger 1983 and Stone 1997).

17. Touching the past, teaching ways forward: The American Indian powwow

Teri Brewer

In the older traditions, time is not passing around the people; we are time.
(Kenneth Lincoln)

Powwows are periodic short festive events which American Indians organize for social and celebrative, competitive, educational, political, benevolent and sometimes commercial purposes. They have developed gradually from many and diverse models of older spiritual, ceremonial and political traditions unique to individual tribes. The religious and spiritual aspects of powwow are variable today, but remain a constant quiet presence in even the most determinedly secular and competitive events.

Like someone else's giant family reunions, powwows may at first seem like vast chaotic picnics or parties to the visitor from outside the native community, but the fact that there are underlying similarities of structure and content as well as deeply significant spiritual and political overtones to the powwow will quickly becomes evident to most visitors, whether or not they appreciate the history or can interpret the nuances of what they see and hear.

Whenever we find an activity which is much discussed but little explained, often attended, rife with symbolism, apparently proliferating and obviously elaborating, it will well be worth exploring, and so it proves with powwow. In this chapter, we will look at some of the historical background to powwow as an important and complex contemporary phenomenon of the American Indian peoples which has developed out of religious ceremonial forms and which continues to embed characteristic elements of Native American spirituality as well as acting as a site of negotiation in the melding of traditional forms of spirituality with elements drawn from broader American popular culture.

Powwow season is roughly from Memorial Day weekend in late May through until Labor Day in the September. During this period, as many as 2,000 special gatherings will be scheduled throughout the United States and Canada, mostly on weekends, each sponsored by a particular tribe or region or in some cases by centers and organizations which support urban Native American and Canadian native communities. Wherever powwows are held, the set-up will be similar in many respects, and while they are primarily meant as gathering-ins for the Indian community, in most, all are made welcome, whether from other tribes, non-Indians, or foreign visitors.

Characteristics of the powwow

Even the most secular and commercial of powwows begins with the creation of a sacred space. Very ordinary places may be chosen. A high school gymnasium, city park, sports ground, church hall, athletic stadium or farmer's field is consecrated to this special use with a blessing by elders, usually of the tribe hosting the powwow. While the powwow ground is sacred, it is not necessarily the territory of any one particular faith. Traditionalists, Catholics, Protestants of various denominations, all acknowledge the special 'set aside' of the powwow ground.

Typically there will be a circular arena set up for dancing, with room for spectators and possibly seating for contestants. On one side of the circle will be the hosting elders, an announcer and judges. The breath of the powwow is the rhythmic accompaniment of great drums, marking a beginning, beckoning the audience, punctuating time, the heartbeat of the dancing and signaling the close.

On opening day, the drums invite all present into the circle to join together in a grand opening ceremony. Outside the arena in bigger powwows a virtual village will already have sprung up for the duration of the powwow, which may last a weekend or longer.

If the powwow is aimed at an audience beyond the purely local, a camping area for contestants and perhaps a separate one for spectators is typically provided, and there will be an organized concession district – stalls set up to supply food (Indian tacos and fry bread are perennial favorites, but you can expect to find anything from hot dogs and hamburgers to regional or tribal specialities). Soft drinks, iced tea and juices, coffee, herb teas and bottled water are all available. Alcohol is almost always banned at powwows.

As well as the food vendors there may be stalls for craft specialists and providers of clothing (Indian produced usually, and including anything from elaborate handmade dance costumes and special occasion wear such as ribbon shirts and Seminole patchwork through to mass-produced Indian-themed clothing like T-shirts with slogans). Some stall-holders specialize in other accoutrements of tribal ceremony, handmade wooden flutes, tobacco pipes, gourd rattles and drums for instance. Book stalls, music stalls, specialist purveyors of beads, feathers, tanned deer-hides, special fabrics and bells, all the things needed to make powwow costumes.

Around this temporary village wander the diverse crowds including painted and costumed dancers, spectators who dress in traditional tribal clothing for the occasion, and many who wear ordinary commercial clothing, with jeans, pearl snap buttoned western shirts, cowboy boots and hats being common.

Once the grand opening has begun, the drummers have found their rhythm and the arena is full of slowly moving dancers in a massed opening procession. Many of the audience will join in, and the sound of low chanting by the dancers will rise from the arena. This is a powerful time, and one for which serious powwow visitors will always be present. Then there is the national anthem and a blessing and moment of prayer. An announcer who acts as master of ceremonies for the powwow will now explain the order of things, often reminding people of correct rules of behaviour at the powwow, thanking organizers and participants and letting everyone know how far people have come from and who has helped.

The role of this announcer is a very important one. In many powwows, the announcer will give short talks on individual and community responsibility, right thinking, morality, self-improvement, etc. The announcer may also fill a role like that of a minister or self-help group leader. The homilies, advice and exhortations of the announcer may be spiritual and metaphysical in tone, but in some powwows they take on the air of secular social and individual improvement programmes, some resembling mainstream American 12 step programmes such as Alcoholics Anonymous.

The focus of the arena then becomes a series of dance competitions alternated with 'friendlies', non-competitive social dances. Most of these are based on the circling of the arena, rather than on dancing in couples or in small groups. While all dancers may circle the arena together, in competitive dances the skill, presence, costuming and general style of individual dancers are on display and under consideration.

While the present article is a more general description of powwow and its religious elements, the elaborated tradition of competitive and social dance which is developing is a whole fascinating subject in itself. Susan

Power's novel *The Grass Dancer* (1994) provides an accessible experiential introduction. An excellent photo essay on powwow which illustrates the importance of costume is Michael Parfit and David Harvey's (1994) article 'Powwow'. Another element common in many powwows which is worth analysis in itself is the tradition of Indian rodeo. An introductory discussion forms part of Peter Iverson's (1990) *When Indians Became Cowboys*.

The history of an incrementally re-invented tradition

The term *powwow* comes from the Algonquin languages spoken in the north-east of the what is now the United States and the south-east of Canada. In Algonquin dialects *Pau wau* is the term for a spiritual leader and healer, and early European settlers among the Algonquin peoples sometimes witnessed the dances which would take place in conjunction with the work of such a leader, apparently mistakenly thinking that it was the ceremonial dance which was the *Pau wau*. The term was adapted for use by various immigrant groups and in the nineteenth century by Anglo (non-Indian) community organizations as well, and came to signify not only ceremonial dances, but any kind of social gathering or conference. The term was applied not only to Indian gatherings and dances, but eventually by extension to certain kinds of gatherings amongst the immigrant communities of the eastern seaboard.

> Popular cultural expression took a new route in the development of Indian themes with the establishment of elaborate Indianized societies ... This visible use of Indian metaphor transferred to the proliferating social and civic clubs so common to the growth of smaller communities ... [such as] The Improved Order of Red Men, with its powwows, victory dances, braves and princesses. (Green 1988, 83–5)

This phenomenon was part of a widespread fashion for fraternal and social orders based on antiquarian enthusiasm for the ancient and the exotic and it seems to have returned from settlers to the Indian community at some point although there is little information on this transfer. Ceremonials, gatherings and social dances of course continued to take place throughout Indian America in the late eighteenth and early nineteenth centuries although the borrowed term powwow would not have been used for these occasions by most until much later.

As a linked class of event, religious ceremony and social dance across tribal boundaries were proscribed by official edict when the committee which steered government control of Indians affairs was packed with Christian missionaries by 1880. Under the terms of legislation introduced in 1883 by Interior Secretary Henry Teller:

> 4. *Offenses* – For the purposes of these regulations the following shall be deemed to constitute *offenses*, and the judges of the Indian court shall severally have jurisdiction for the same when committed within their respective districts.
> a) Dances, etc. – Any Indian who shall engage in the sun dance, scalp dance or war dance or any similar feast, so called, shall be deemed guilty of an offense, and upon conviction thereof shall be punished for the offense by the withholding of his rations for not exceeding ten days or by imprisonment for not exceeding ten days; and for any subsequent offense under this clause he shall be punished by withholding his rations for not less than ten days nor more than thirty days, or by imprisonment for not less than ten nor more than thirty days . . .
> c) Practices of medicine men – Any Indian who shall engage in the practices of so-called medicine men, or who shall resort to any artifice or device to keep the Indians of the reservation from adopting civilized habits and pursuits, or who shall adopt any means to prevent the attendance of children at school, or shall use any arts of the conjuror to prevent Indians from abandoning their barbarous rites and customs, shall be deemed to be guilty of an offense, and upon conviction thereof, for the first offense shall be imprisoned for not less than ten nor no more than thirty days*: Provided*, That for any subsequent conviction for such offense the maximum term of imprisonment shall not exceed six months.

(For a full account of the relationship between the US Federal government and the Indian nations see Prucha (1985), a brief overview, or (1984) for a more comprehensive and technical account. A more popular treatment is found in Josephy 1996.)

Development of the syncretic powwow tradition as well as the widespread Indian adoption of the term itself almost certainly began in earnest after 1920 when the crusading social reformer John Collier organized very public resistance to this ban on Indian ceremonial and religious activities both public and private which had been in place effectively by then for more than 40 years. Collier was fighting against entrenched attitudes which increasingly saw the survival of any ceremonial or social tradition as a sign of inadequate assimilation and a need for the exercise of greater paternalistic control. An example is seen in this extract from a letter written by Ernest Jermark, superintendent of the Fort Berthold Indian Agency in 1922:

> It is realized that Indians, as well as whites, must have recreation and amusement, but it is also realized that such recreation and amusement, in

order not to become a nuisance or detrimental to the best interests of the Indians must not be carried to excess.

With the idea of curtailing and to control these dances it is deemed advisable to make certain special rules, which it is my understanding, the Council approves:

1st. Permission for Indian dances must be obtained in writing from the office, such permission to show the date and the place.

2nd. Dances are to be limited to legal holidays.

3rd. Citizens attending Indian dances to be required to observe the same rules as non-competent Indians. [Indians who were not citizens and thus judged unable to make decisions about property etc.]

4th. No presents to be exchanged or gifts to be made at the dances.

5th. Big feasts and donations of foodstuffs for dances to be discontinued, except on special occasions and with special permission.

6th. No men under 21 or girls under 18 years of age to be permitted to dance or to wear costumes at the dances.

7th. Promiscuous running from one dance hall to another must be stopped.

Dances are to be conducted in the evening only. No dancing later than 2 A.M. and all Indians to return home not later than the following morning. (Hurtado and Iverson 1994, 379–80)

It was just under a century after the Teller legislation that the terms of the American Indian Religious Freedom Act theoretically and specifically extended the same freedom of religious expression to Native Americans that was constitutionally guaranteed to others. This came after an organized campaign which grew out of a vision of political action for American Indian self-determination with roots in Collier's 'Indian New Deal' during the presidency of Franklin Roosevelt. However, the activist pan-Indian movement in the 1960s and 1970s in the United States borrowed some very contemporary and trans-ethnic techniques of social and political action making common cause with the Civil Rights movement, adopting political street theater, organized marches, sit ins, seizure of symbolic sites and federal or state facilities and other techniques for generating interest in and discussion of issues facing Native Americans, by then a largely invisible minority to most Americans.

Forging a stronger sense of collective identity and common cause between members of disparate tribal groups and disenfranchized individuals from urban areas in the United States and Canada involved a variety of teaching events as well as protest activities. An interesting consequence of this movement was the strengthening of certain older traditions which had been shared in common by a number of tribes. The increased development of intertribal collaboration in ceremonial and social gatherings as well as the tradition of lobbying and political collaboration which had become established became the basis for 'pan-Indian' activism. In the parlance of the day, powwows were a useful form of consciousness raising as well as a political fund-raiser and get together. Amongst young Native American activists there were all the elements of a spiritual revitalization movement present in the activities of overtly political organizations such as AIM (the American Indian Movement) and the powwow became in part the vehicle of some of that spiritual quest.

Contemporary powwow

Today the term powwow is widely used to designate various kinds of public gathering, but is most often used for a type involving ceremonial dancing even by tribes far from the region of the Algonquins. Powwow is not just one tradition enacted the same way all over North America, rather, it has become a classificatory term which highlights the commonalities of gatherings which are both regionally distinctive and evolving, and which are gradually coming closer together through cross-participation. Based on ancient traditions, then, the powwow as such is an invention of the twentieth century, reflecting and reinforcing the changing culture, both secular and spiritual, of contemporary American Indians.

The practical logistics of powwow are managed by designated committees, advertising is common, and most tribes sponsoring powwows nowadays make sure that their events are included on the sophisticated grapevine which the Native American community has developed using the Internet and the World Wide Web. The endeavors and plans of individual communities are meshed together by these means into a relatively well-organized and defined powwow high season and spread through the calendar to facilitate the existence of a potential powwow trail, composed from the available events in any given season by individuals with the means and inclination to turn their interest in powwows into an occasion of annual pilgrimage to multiple sites and events. Key nationally alluring events on this trail may include Crow Fair and the Gathering of Nations, but also big regional and urban powwows.

Awareness of powwows in the Indian community is augmented by attractive pitches to participation by non-Indian tourists such as the 'Indian Territory' brochure produced by the Nevada tourist board. The front of this brochure is a photo profile of a young Indian man in an elaborate headdress and dance costume. The text of the brochure exhorts the traveler to 'Make it a point to take in one of these joyous tribal Pow Wow celebrations while traveling through Indian Territory. You won't be disappointed.' The text of the rest of the brochure is woven through a series of images of colorful powwow costume, landscapes and depictions of crafts. No mention is made of the spiritual dimension of any of these things.

Spirituality and powwow

For Native Americans, powwows are integrated events which incorporate all these social, political, competitive, charitable and commercial incentives to participate as well as embodying particular spiritual aspects. It is important to understand that for most Indian participants these elements are idealized as fully integrated, and inextricably intertwined. Spiritual life and religious understanding are not a sphere separable from the everyday in the ordinary sense, and in fact when something happens in a powwow that needs purely religious commentary or liturgical handling, there is often a sense in which the participants suddenly break out of this integrated frame very briefly to handle the issue, and there is an understanding that during this break there will be no photography or discussion. Events then resume without further comment. An example of this comes from the description of the first Northern Cherokee powwow. When a dancer dropped a feather, the announcer quietly signaled a pause during which time the feather was retrieved, a short blessing pronounced and the dancing resumed (Coviello 1992).

Contrary to much of the popular misinformation in circulation, thinking of American Indian's religious beliefs as essentially similar is a mistake. Just as there are many distinct tribal cultures, there are many distinctive traditional religious and spiritual belief systems amongst the indigenous peoples of the Americas. Some of these are still practiced in a traditional form by some individuals and groups, some are combined with elements of Christianity or other imported faiths. Some Native Americans turn their back on traditional tribal spirituality and may be members of mainstream Christian churches, atheistic or agnostic in their thinking.

There are, however, certain features which are common amongst many, if not all, of the traditional belief systems. One is a habit of mind. Religion or the spiritual aspect of life is seldom categorically separated from the day-to-day business of living. The emphasis of Native American spiritual thought, if we have to generalize, is on the acquisition of an integrated understanding of the relationship between a particular landscape, its human, plant and animal inhabitants as well as on the acquiring of wisdom which leads to the ability to understand and possibly control the invisible power which is immanent in all things, animate and inanimate.

Recent revitalization of powwow

In a sense, then, powwow is the result of developments in the internal cultural politics of Native America over the course of this century. It may be as much or more a secular as a spiritual phenomenon from the perspective of participants as well as of those interested in comparative theology, but the occasions of powwow serve well as a point of introduction to Native American social and theological thought, reflecting accurately the diversity of experience and interpretation, the intricate shifting interplay of individual motivation, tribal identities and intertribal relations as well as the changing mutual gaze between Indians and non-Indians.

American Indians have been through several centuries of rapid forced cultural change in which there have been dramatic population swings, threats to their many distinctive languages and cultures as well as loss of self-determination in the seventeenth and eighteenth centuries. This has been followed by gradual reassertion of tribal and ethnic identity in the later half of the twentieth century, just as many people thought that the indigenous peoples and cultures of the Americas would disappear. One of the reasons why the Native American community has a strong sense of collective identity today is that it is very much a contemporary phenomenon. Treated as a relatively undifferentiated mass for centuries by outsiders, eventually tribal leaders began to act increasingly in concert, putting aside differences of language and tribal identity. The religious expression and spiritual dimension of life show this partial shift to pan-Indian thinking too.

Powwow pilgrims

Movement between areas of resettlement and tribal lands (return of urban residents to reservation) and the existence of an increasingly well advertized and carefully scheduled season of powwows has encouraged the development of a pilgrimage aspect to the powwow, and some people – whether or not they are competing as dancers – now go on the powwow 'highway' or 'trail' annually, organizing time and travel to permit participation in as many powwows as possible in any given year. For the powwow pilgrim, motives may be single or many, bearing witness, having fun, seeking visions, competing for cash, any and all of these.

For the Northern Band of Cherokee, their first experience of holding a powwow came in September of 1991. The Northern Band are a group of families from Central and Southern Missouri and Northern Arkansas who are descended from Cherokee who migrated into the area in the late eighteenth century. Their descendants have had no legal recognition as a tribe from the United States government for complex historical reasons although there are recognized Cherokee tribal groups further west in Oklahoma as well as in their original homeland in North Carolina. After years of planning and discussion, the Northern Band were at last going through the initial stages of making a formal petition for federal acknowledgement, a process involving the collection of detailed documentation, the writing of an historical account of the group showing a continuous connection to an identified tribe, continuity of tribal political influence or authority recognized by members of the group etc. (See the Code of Federal Regulations 43 fr 39361, Sept. 5 1978: 'Procedures for Establishing that an American Indian Group exists as an Indian Tribe'.) The petition submitted by the Northern Cherokee still awaits a decision at the time of writing.

During band council meetings over a period of years the idea of holding a powwow was proposed, the first one that members of the band would be involved in organizing. In 1991 Chief Elva Beltz was an enthusiastic supporter of the idea, hoping that the powwow would bring people from the band together in increased appreciation of their heritage, attract the support of neighboring tribes and possibly raise some money for depleted tribal coffers and the cultural heritage center that the band had been planning (Coviello 1992).

Many other powwows started in ways similar to the Northern Cherokee powwow. A very assimilated tribe on the East Coast whom David Kerzer refers to as the 'Monhegan' had similar motives:

> stressing the rites and symbols that identified them as Indians and as Monhegans. The most important of these rites is the annual powwow. Each year widespread publicity goes out to announce the event. The hosts invite Indians from other, better established tribes to join with them and, before a large crowd of non-Indian neighbors and tourists, the Monhegan perform native dances, parade in Indian clothing, display Indian crafts and recount their history. (Kerzer 1988, 20–1)

The small powwow that asserts the Indian identity of disenfranchized groups or of remnant or assimilated communities and which has relatively little sacred character exists on a continuous spectrum of possibilities for the sacred/social/political/fund-raising mix in powwow schedules.

Another distinctive type of powwow is the large urban pan-Indian powwow which acts as a point of contact for dispersed families settled in urban areas. These powwows, like the Monhegan and Northern Cherokee events, develop a strong strain of what Joan Weibel-Orlando has called 'ethnic theatre' (Weibel-Orlando 1991, 132). That is to say that making manifest an Indian identity which may not be outwardly visible in daily life is a particularly important aspect of such powwows. In addition, with the dispersed urban Indian populations, negotiating a common identity not vested in the language and customs of any particular tribe will be important in the larger urban powwows.

The Southern California Intertribal Powwow held annually at the Orange County Fairgrounds is a good example of this particularly syncretic event. In 1997 this powwow attracted performers from both the extended conurbation of Southern California, but also from many other parts of the country. The audience was mostly Indian, but there were many spectators from outside the Indian community. The competitive dancing was tightly organized and the dancers often displayed a great deal of professionalism or specialist knowledge in their exhibitions. Commercial adjuncts in the shape of the adjacent Indian marketplace were extensive and properly organized to feed, entertain, instruct and lighten the pockets of the many thousands of participants over three summer days.

In big intertribal powwows like this one the distinction between an event particular to the Indian community and the tradition of county fairs widespread over the United States begins to blur, particularly when the powwow is held in a County Fairground. On the surface the similarities are so great that non-Indian visitors may treat the powwow as the largely passively experienced and secular booster spectacle that the County Fair will be. Only careful attention in the sacred circle of the dance ring and close examination of the wares in the marketplace allow attention to the spiritual testimonial present even in such a powwow.

Conclusion

Over the course of the past century, a variety of dances associated with different ritual and social activities originally done at different times during the year – or to precede a hunt or a war party, etc. – have tended to be telescoped into the period originally associated with the summer ceremonial cycle of the Plains Indians. Why would the cycle and rituals of one region come to dominate modern patterns of Indian life through the whole country? Probably for several reasons. Plains ceremonials were relatively public large-scale events. There has been some continuity in their observance by a critical mass of people. Starting after the First World War many families from Plains reservations migrated into the cities of the urban west where they established a modified version of the summer ceremonial cycle which had been characteristic of their region.

Picking out patterns from the activity on the modern powwow highway, we can make some tentative conclusions. Despite occasional protests to the contrary, clearly an element of the sacred remains an important if understated (and often specifically denied) aspect of powwow culture. However, powwow is continually changing and adapting to shifting circumstances and new needs, and the style of spiritual expression present in any given powwow will vary depending on organizers and participants. Traditional Indian practices such as the giveaway and honoring ceremonies will sometimes incorporate tropes and rhetorical styles which are borrowed from other traditions. For example, the group support and affirmation of familiar American mainstream institutions such as twelve step programmes, the casseroles and salvation ethos of evangelical Protestantism, or the civic religion of American citizenship.

People from the Native American community themselves distinguish between the various types of powwows which dot the summer season, as well as sometimes dividing themselves notionally into categories of participant. Perhaps the most important distinction is between:

1. The reservation powwow, scheduled annually and attended mostly by people whose Indian identity is integral to their everyday lives, and where the level of personal acquaintance, shared experience and values with other participants may be very high. In Mary Douglas' terms, events which demonstrate high grid and group markers. The spiritual aspects of the powwow may be both taken for granted and central to the occasion in such a situation.
2. The intertribal regional powwow where political, competitive and commercial elements of the occasion may dominate and where tribal identities may be particularly overtly performed, sometimes paradoxically considering the pan-Indian identity which may develop implicitly in these powwows. Intertribal regional powwows are often a real tourist attraction, welcoming many non-Indians as spectators and occasionally as participants.
3. The ethnic theater of the urban powwow which may play down or frame spiritual elements very differently than the above, and which will usually be scheduled specifically to avoid conflict with relevant reservation powwows wherever possible. In some urban areas like Los Angeles these powwows may be organized by clubs and held on a monthly schedule throughout the year. In urban powwows key roles in drumming, dancing and singing will often be taken by people from Plains tribes. It is in the urban powwow tradition that non-Indian hobbyists most often take some active role. Indians make a distinction between hobbyists who are comfortable with their own ethnicity and spirituality

and what are usually called 'Wanabes' (Want to be Indians): individuals who either feel such an affinity that they wish they were Indians, adopting hairstyles, etc. or claiming spurious or undemonstrated Indian ancestry.

4. The revitalization powwow where a marginalized and possibly assimilated group adopts the powwow tradition as a way of building common identity and performing it explicitly to non-Indian audiences as well as seeking acceptance by established groups.

Native American scholar Kathleen Glenister Roberts has proposed that we think of powwows and the expressive behaviors which form part of them (not just dance, but the attention to costume, music, etc.) in terms of their aesthetic functions of *extension* and *expression*. She suggests that extension flows naturally out of traditionality, that in powwows on reservations for instance, a powwow is attended mostly by people from the local tribe or tribes, that it is not in itself the focus of their identity, but an integrated working face of the total system (Glenister Roberts 1998).

Expression, on the other hand, can be seen as characteristic of urban powwows or perhaps the initiatory powwows previously discussed. In these there will often be a more explicitly educational agenda, and the audience may in fact be largely non-Indian. The competitive dancing of the extensive powwow may be absent or less elaborated. There may be more of an emphasis on re-enactment, on 'authenticity' and on public declarations of Indian identity or identification with Indians by a non-Indian audience.

Glenister Roberts warns us not to assume that powwow is always the form of personal choice for either expression or extension among contemporary Indians, quoting one Hopi woman who said: 'I just can't stand powwows. I'm Indian every day – don't need to pack it up and take it on the road.'

Although the points that Glenister Roberts makes were in the context of a discussion of powwow regalia, they are equally useful in thinking about the spiritual side of powwow. In the extensive powwow the spiritual element may be particularly understated or implicit as the audience and participants are amongst relatives, friends and neighbors with a high level of cohesion and mutual understanding. The spiritual politics of expressive powwow, on the other hand, may be extremely complex as audience and participants seek to identify and situate one another.

An extreme form of expressive powwow is sometimes found in Europe as a relatively small number of Native Americans may be invited to be part of a programme which perhaps combines education on issues confronting indigenous peoples with fund-raising for particular causes. The audience for this sort of 'powwow' (to use the term pretty loosely) are often well intentioned 'cultural primitivists'. Actively aware of the problems of their urban lives, isolated in nuclear families and often living away from ancestral communities they may project onto indigenous people their romanticized longing for unmediated and authentic experience. This projection can take interesting forms, often in a very strong identification with a particular version of Indian spirituality.

There is a fast-growing and sometimes bitterly satirical commentary on such longings, with contributions from widely respected Indian writers such as Vine Deloria, Ward Churchill and Sherman Alexie. 'The idea that spiritual knowledge now belongs to any non-Native who happens to desire it is the new version of Manifest Destiny ...' (Root 1996, 93–4). For a superb overview of this subject see Ward Churchill's (1994) attack on well intentioned cultural appropriation: *Indians are Us? Culture and Genocide in Native North America*. Hugh Honour (1975) explores contemporary romantic primitivism directed at American Indians by European 'wanabes' or hobbyists. *Cannibal Culture* by Deborah Root (1996) also offers a thoughtful analysis of problems in well intended cultural appropriations.

Finally, powwows form part of a living tradition, embedded in the very contemporary Native American communities which enact them, whether reservation based, urban weekend get-togethers, symbolic new beginnings for reviving tribal communities or transcontinental intertribals like the Gathering of Nations annual powwow at Albuquerque, New Mexico. All the best are full of hope and negotiation, dreams as well as competition, ironies and dislocations, visions and connections. All offer a varied experience for audience, visitors and participants alike. All offer the human experiences which connect the power manifest in place, community and culture. The great drums are the heartbeat of each powwow, and the secular pilgrimage of the powwow trail offers a path to wisdom as well as a spectacle for those with eyes to see.

Bibliography

Ajayi, J.F.D. and Smith, R. (1964) *Yoruba Warfare in the 19th Century* (Ibadan: Ibadan University Press).

Akrofi, C.A. (no date) *Twi Mmebusem: Twi Proverbs, with English Translations and Annotations* (Accra: Waterville Publishing House).

Albanese, C.L. (1990) *Nature Religion in America: From the Algonkian Indians to the New Age* (Chicago: University of Chicago Press).

Allen, N.J. (1987) 'Thulung weddings: the Hinduisation of a ritual cycle in East Nepal', *L'Ethnographie*, LXXXIII, 100–101, pp. 15–33.

Amades, J. (1966) *Las Danzas de Moros y Cristianos* (Etnología Valenciana 4. Valencia, Spain: Institución Alfonso el Magnanimo).

Anderson, K. (1993) 'Native Californians as ancient and contemporary cultivators', in T.C. Blackburn and K. Anderson (eds) *Before the Wilderness*. Menlo Park, CA: Ballena Press, pp. 151–74.

Anderson, K. (1996) *Changing Woman: A History of Racial Ethnic Women in Modern America*. (Oxford: Oxford University Press).

Anger, D.C. (1983) 'Putting it back together: Micmac political identity in Newfoundland', unpublished MA thesis (Anthropology), Memorial University of Newfoundland.

Anger, D.C. (n.d.) *Where the Sand Blows: Vignettes of Bay St. George Micmacs* (Port au Port, Newfoundland: Bay St. George Regional Indian Band Council).

Aquili, E.G. d', Laughlin, C.D. and McManus, J. (eds) (1979) *The Spectrum of Ritual: A Biogenetic Structural Analysis* (New York: Columbia University Press).

Ardener, E.W. (1970) 'Witchcraft, economics, and the continuity of belief', in M. Douglas (ed.) *Witchcraft Confessions and Accusations* (London: Tavistock), pp. 141–60.

Arewa, O. (1978) 'Zande ultimate reality and meaning', *Ultimate Reality and Meaning* 1.4, pp. 240–50.

Arnold, D. (1989) 'Kinship as cosmology: potatoes as offspring among the Aymara of Highland Bolivia', in D. McCaskill (ed.) *Amerindian Cosmology* (Brandon: *Canadian Journal of Native Studies*; Edinburgh: Traditional Cosmology Society), pp. 323–37.

Atkinson, J.M. (1989) *The Art and Politics of Wana Shamanship* (Berkeley, CA: University of California Press).

Atkinson, J.M. (1992) 'Shamanisms today', *Annual Review of Anthropology* 21, pp. 307–30.

Balzer, M.M. (1990) *Shamanism: Soviet Studies of Traditional Religion in Siberia and Central Asia* (Armonk: M.E. Sharpe).

Barlow, C. (1991) *Tikanga Whakaaro: Key Concepts in Maori Culture* (Auckland: Oxford University Press).

Barnes, B. (1974) *Scientific Knowledge and Sociological Theory* (London: Routledge and Kegan Paul).

Barnes, S.T. (ed.) (1997) *Africa's Ogun: Old World and New* (Bloomington: Indiana University Press).

Bartle, P.F.W. (1978) 'Forty days: the Akan calendar', *Africa* 48, pp. 80–4.

Basso, K. (1996) *Wisdom Sits in Places: Landscape and Language among the Western Apache* (Albuquerque: University of New Mexico Press).

Beattie, J. (1966) 'Ritual and social change', *Man* I, pp. 60–74.

Beidelman, T.O. (1981) 'The Nuer concept of thek and the meaning of sin: explanation, translation, and social structure', *History of Religions* 21.2, pp. 126–55.

Beit-Hallahmi, B. (1985) *Prolegomena to the Psychological Study of Religion* (Lewisburg: Bucknell University Press).

Belich, J. (1986) *The New Zealand Wars and the Victorian Interpretation of Racial Conflict* (Auckland: Auckland University Press).

Bell, C. (1998) 'Performance', in M.C. Taylor (ed.) *Critical Terms for Religious Studies* (Chicago: University of Chicago Press), pp. 205–24.

Bell, D. (1998) 'Aboriginal women and the religious experience', in M. Charlesworth (ed.) *Religious Business* (Cambridge: Cambridge University Press).

Benjamin, W. (1968) *Illuminations*, edited by Hannah Arendt, translated by Harry Zohn (New York: Schlocken Books).

Berens, D. (ed.) (1988) *A Concise Encyclopedia of Zimbabwe* (Gweru: Mambo Press).

Berkhofer, R.F. (1978) *The White Man's Indian: Images of the American Indian from Columbus to the Present* (New York: Knopf).

Bird-David, N. (1999) '"Animism" revisited: personhood, environment, and relational epistemology', *Current Anthropology* 40, pp. 67–91.

Black, M.B. (1977) 'Ojibwa power belief system', in R.D. Fogelson and R.N. Adams (eds) *The Anthropology of Power* (New York: Academic Press), pp. 141–51.

Blackburn, T.C. (ed.) (1975) *December's Child: A Book of Chumash Oral Narratives* (Berkeley, CA: University of California Press).

Blackburn, T.C. and Anderson, K. (eds) (1993) *Before the Wilderness: Environmental Management by Native Californians*, Ballena Press Anthropological Papers 40 (Menlo Park, CA: Ballena Press).

Blake, A. (1997) *The Land Without Music: Music, Culture and Society in Twentieth-Century Britain* (Manchester: Manchester University Press).

Blake, W. (1793) 'The marriage of Heaven and Hell', in J. Bronowski (ed.) (1958) *Blake* (London: Penguin), pp. 93–109.

Bloom, W. (1990) *Sacred Times: A New Approach to Festivals* (Findhorn: Findhorn Press).

Boddy, J. (1989) *Wombs and Alien Spirits: Women, Men, and the Zar Cult in Northern Sudan* (Madison: University of Wisconsin Press).

Bordewich, F. (1996) *Killing the White Man's Indian: Reinventing Native Americans at the End of the Twentieth Century* (New York: Anchor Books).

Bourdieu, P. (1977) *Outline of a Theory of Practice* (London: Cambridge University Press).
Bourdieu, P. (1980) *The Logic of Practice* (Stanford, CA: Stanford University Press).
Bowie, F. (1985) 'A social and historical study of Christian missions among the Bangwa of South West Cameroon', unpublished DPhil thesis, University of Oxford.
Bradley, J. (1988) *Yanyuwa Country: The Yanyuwa People of Borroloola Tell the History of their Land* (Richmond: Greenhouse Publications).
Braidotti, R. (1994) *Nomadic Subject* (New York: Columbia University Press).
Brain, R. (1967) *The Bangwa of West Cameroon* (London: University College).
Brain, R. (1970) 'Child witches', in M. Douglas (ed.) *Witchcraft Confessions and Accusations* (London: Tavistock), pp. 161–79.
Brain, R. (1977) *Kolonialagent* (London: Faber and Faber).
Brain, R. and Pollock, A. (1971) *Bangwa Funerary Sculpture* (London: Duckworth).
Brett, M.G. (ed.) (1996) *Ethnicity and the Bible* (Leiden: E.J. Brill).
Bright, W. (1957) *The Karuk Language* (Berkeley, CA: University of California Press).
Buckner, M. (1995) 'Modern Zande prophetesses', in D.M. Anderson and D.H. Johnson (eds) *Revealing Prophets: Prophecy in Eastern African History* (London: James Currey Ltd), pp. 102–21.
Bunge, R. (1984) *An American Urphilosophie: An American Philosophy BP (Before Pragmatism)* (Lanham, NY: University Press of America).
Bunting, R. (1997) *The Pacific Raincoast: Environment and Culture in an American Eden, 1778–1900* (Lawrence, Kansas: University Press of Kansas).
Burns, A.F. (1993) *Maya in Exile: Guatemalans in Florida* (Philadelphia: Temple University Press).
Callicott, J.B. (1989) 'American Indian land wisdom? sorting out the issues', *Journal of Forest History* 33.1, pp. 35–42.
Camaroff, J. (1985) *Body of Power, Spirit of Resistance: The Culture and History of a South African People* (Chicago: University of Chicago Press).
Castaneda, C. (1968) *The Teachings of Don Juan: A Yaqui Way of Knowledge* (Berkeley, CA: University of California Press).
Castillo, A. (1994) *Massacre of the Dreamers: Essays on Xicanisma* (Albuquerque: University of New Mexico Press).
Charlesworth, M., Morphy, H., Bell, D. and Maddock, K. (eds) (1984) *Religion in Aboriginal Australia* (St Lucia: University of Queensland Press).
Churchill, W. (1994) *Indians are Us? Culture and Genocide in Native North America* (Monroe: Common Courage Press).
Clark, E. (1911) *Ao Naga Dictionary* (Calcutta: Baptist Mission Press).
Clarke, P.B. (ed.) (1998) *New Trends and Developments in African Religions* (Westport, CT: Greenwood).
Classen, C. (1993a) *Inca Cosmology and the Human Body* (Salt Lake City: University of Utah Press).

Classen, C. (1993b) *Worlds of Sense: Exploring the Senses in History and Across Cultures* (London: Routledge).
Clendinnen, I. (1987) *Ambivalent Conquests: Maya and Spaniard in Yucatan, 1517–1570* (New York: Cambridge University Press).
Clifford, J. (1988) *The Predicament of Culture: Twentieth Century Ethnography, Literature, and Art* (Cambridge, MA: Harvard University Press).
Clifton, J. (1990) *The Invented Indian: Cultural Fictions and Government Policies* (New Brunswick: Transaction Publishers).
Cohen, J.H. (1993) '*Danza de la Pluma*: symbols of submission and separation', *Anthropological Quarterly* 66.3, pp. 149–58.
Comaroff, J. and Comaroff, J. (eds) (1993) *Modernity and its Malcontents: Ritual and Power in Postcolonial Africa* (Chicago and London: University of Chicago Press).
Connerton, P. (1989) *How Societies Remember* (Cambridge: Cambridge University Press).
Cook, N. (1998) *Music: A Very Short Introduction* (Oxford: Oxford University Press).
Coviello, E. (1992) The Northern Cherokee of Missouri and Arkansas, unpublished BSc thesis, University of Glamorgan.
Cox, J.L. (1995) 'Ancestors, the sacred and God: reflections on the meaning of the sacred in Zimbabwean death rituals', *Religion* 25.4, pp. 339–55.
Cox, J.L. (1996) 'Methodological considerations relevant to understanding African indigenous religions', in J. Platvoet, J. Cox and J. Olupona (eds) *The Study of Religion in Africa* (Cambridge: Roots and Branches), pp. 155–71.
Cox, J.L. (1998) *Rational Ancestors: Scientific Rationality and African Indigenous Religions* (Cardiff: Cardiff Academic Press).
Cox-Collins, A. (1980) 'Colonial Jacaltenango, Guatemala: the formation of a closed-corporate community', PhD dissertation, Tulane University.
Crumrine, N.R. and Halpin, M. (1983) *The Power of Symbols: Masks and Masquerade in the Americas* (Vancouver, BC: University of British Columbia Press).
Daneel, M.L. (1970) *The God of the Matopos Hills* (The Hague: Mouton).
Daneel, M.L. (1998) 'Mwari the liberator: oracular intervention in Zimbabwe's quest for the "Lost Lands"', in J.L. Cox (ed.) *Rational Ancestors* (Cardiff: Cardiff Academic Press), pp. 94–125.
Davidson, D. (1980) *Essays on Actions and Events* (Oxford: Oxford University Press).
Davidson, D. (1984) *Inquiries into Truth and Interpretation* (Oxford: Oxford University Press).
de Certeau, M. (1984) *The Practice of Everyday Life* (Berkeley, CA: University of California Press).
Deloria, V. (1995) *Red Earth, White Lies: Native Americans and the Myth of Scientific Fact* (New York: Scribner).
de Rosny, E. (1985) *Healers of the Night: A French Priest's Account of his Immersion in the World of an African Healer* (Maryknoll, New York: Orbis Books).

Detwiler, F. (1992) 'All my relatives: persons in Oglala religion', *Religion* 22.3, pp. 235–46.

Diallo, Y. and Hall, M. (1989) *The Healing Drum* (Rochester, NY: Destiny Books).

Douglas, M. (ed.) (1970a) *Witchcraft Confessions and Accusations* (London: Tavistock).

Douglas, M. (1970b) 'Thirty years after witchcraft, oracles and magic', in M. Douglas (ed.) *Witchcraft Confessions and Accusations* (London: Tavistock), pp. xiii–xxxviii.

Douglas, M. (1975) 'Heathen darkness', in M. Douglas, *Implicit Meanings: Essays in Anthropology* (London: Routledge and Kegan Paul), pp. 73–82.

Douglas, M. (1980) *Edward Evans-Pritchard* (New York: Viking).

Douglas, M. (1992) *Purity and Danger: An Analysis of Concepts of Pollution and Taboo* (London: Routledge).

Dreardon, E. (1997) 'Matua Whakapai tou Marae, ka Whakapai ai I te marae o Tangata: first set in order your own marae before you clean another', *Te Komako: Social Work Review* (New Zealand Association of Social Workers) 8.1, pp. 6–8.

Drewal, M.T. (1992) *Yoruba Ritual, Performers, Play, Agency* (Bloomington: Indiana University Press).

Duff, A. (1991) *Once Were Warriors* (Auckland: Tandem Press).

Dunstan, E. (1965) 'A Bangwa account of early encounters with the German colonial administration', *Journal of the Historical Society of Nigeria* 3, pp. 403–13.

Durie, M. (1998) *Te Mana: Te Kawanatanga: The Politics of Maori Self-Determination* (Auckland: Oxford University Press).

Eaton, R. (1984) 'Conversion to Christianity among the Nagas 1876–1971', *Indian Economic and Social History Review* 21, pp. 1–44.

Elam, K. (1993) *The Semiotics of Theatre and Drama* (London: Routledge).

Eliade, M. (1964) *Shamanism: Archaic Techniques of Ecstasy* (New York: Pantheon).

Elkin, A.P. (1977 [1945]) *Aboriginal Men of High Degree* (St. Lucia: University of Queensland Press).

Epton, N. (1968) *Spanish Fiestas* (London: Cassell and Company).

Equiano, O. (1989) *The Life of Olaudah Equiano* (London: Longman).

Erdoes, R. and Ortiz, A. (1984) *American Indian Myths and Legend* (New York: Pantheon).

Evans-Pritchard, E.E. (1929) 'The morphology and function of magic: a comparative study of Trobriand and Zande ritual spells', *American Anthropologist* 31, pp. 619–41. Here cited as reprinted in J. Middleton (ed.) (1967) *Magic, Witchcraft, and Curing* (New York: Natural History Press), pp. 1–22.

Evans-Pritchard, E.E. (1937) *Witchcraft, Oracles and Magic Among the Azande* (Oxford: Oxford University Press).

Evans-Pritchard, E.E. (1956) *Nuer Religion* (Oxford: Clarendon Press).

Evans-Pritchard, E.E. (1962) 'Zande theology', in E.E. Evans-Pritchard (ed.) *Social Anthropology and Other Essays* (New York: Free Press), pp. 288–329.

Evans-Pritchard, E.E. (1965) *Theories of Primitive Religion* (Oxford: Clarendon Press).

Evans-Pritchard, E.E. (1976) *Witchcraft, Oracles and Magic among the Azande*. Abridged version (Oxford: Clarendon Press).

Evens, T.M.S. (1996) 'Witchcraft and selfcraft', *Archives Européennes de Sociologie* 37.1, pp. 23–46.

Evers, L. and Molina, F. (1987) *Yaqui Deer Songs Maso Bwikwan: A Native American Poetry* (Tucson: University of Arizona Press).

Fiensy, D. (1987) 'Using the Nuer culture of Africa in understanding the Old Testament: an evaluation', *Journal for the Study of the Old Testament* 38, pp. 73–83.

Fienup-Riordan, A. (1983) *The Nelson Island Eskimo: Social Structure and Ritual Distribution* (Anchorage: Alaska Pacific University Press).

Fisiy, C.F. (1990) *Palm Tree Justice in the Bertoua Court of Appeal: The Witchcraft Cases*. Working papers No. 12 (Leiden: African Studies Centre).

Fogelson, R.D. and Adams, R.N. (eds) (1977) *The Anthropology of Power: Ethnographic Studies from Asia, Oceania, and the New World* (New York: Academic Press).

Foster, H.M. (1995) 'Lost women of the matriarchy: Iroquois women in the historical literature', *American Indian Culture and Research Journal* 19.3, pp. 121–40.

Foucault, M. (1977) *Discipline and Punish: The Birth of the Prison* (Harmondsworth: Penguin Books).

Franz, M.-L. von. (1995) *Creation Myths* (Boston: Shambhala).

Frisbie, C. (1987) *Navajo Medicine Bundles, or Jish* (Albuquerque: University of New Mexico Press).

Fulbright, J. (1992) 'Hopi and Zuni prayer sticks: magic, symbolic texts, barter, or self-sacrifice?' *Religion* 22.3, pp. 221–34.

Gaenszle, M. (forthcoming) 'Raising the head soul – a ritual text of the Mewahang Rai', *Journal of the Nepal Research Centre* 10.

Gale, F. (ed.) (1983) *We are Bosses Ourselves* (Canberra: Australian Institute of Aboriginal Studies).

García Escobar, C.R. (1987) *Talleres, Trajes, Danzas Traditionales de Guatemala* (Guatemala: Universidad de San Carlos).

Geertz, C. (1973) *The Interpretation of Cultures* (New York: Basic Books).

Gennep, A. van. (1960) *The Rites of Passage*. Translated from the French by M.B. Vizadren and G.I. Caffee (London, Routledge and Kegan Paul).

Geschiere, P. (1997) *The Modernity of Witchcraft: Politics and the Occult in Postcolonial Africa* (Charlottesville and London: University Press of Virginia).

Gifford, P. (1998) *African Christianity: Its Public Role* (London: Hurst & Co).

Gilbert, K. (1987) 'Kevin Gilbert', in D. Green and D. Headon (eds) *Imaging the Real: Australian Writing in the Nuclear Age* (Sydney: ABC), p. 83.

Gill, S.D. (1977) 'Prayer as person: the performative force in Navajo prayer acts' *History of Religions* 17.2, pp. 143–57.

Gill, S.D. (1981) *Sacred Words: A Study of Navajo Religion and Prayer. Contributions in Intercultural and Comparative Studies*. No. 4 (Westport, CN: Greenwood Press).

Gill, S.D. (1982) *Native American Religions: An Introduction* (Belmont, CA: Wadsworth Publishing Company).

Gill, S.D. (1987a). *Mother Earth: An American Story* (Chicago: University of Chicago Press).

Gill, S.D. (1987b) *Native American Religious Action: A Performative Approach to Religion* (Columbia, SC: University of South Carolina Press).

Gill, S.D. and Sullivan, I. (1992) *Dictionary of Native American Mythology* (New York: Oxford University Press).

Gillies, E. (1976) 'Introduction', in E.E. Evans-Pritchard *Witchcraft, Oracles and Magic among the Azande* (Oxford: Clarendon Press), pp. vii–xxxiii.

Gilroy, P. (1993) *The Black Atlantic* (London: Verso).

Glenister Roberts, K. (1998) 'Beauty and identity values in powwow dress', paper presented at the American Folklore Society Annual Meetings, Portland, Oregon.

Godeleir, M. (1986) *The Making of Great Men* (London: Cambridge University Press).

Goldman, I. (1975) *The Mouth of Heaven: An Introduction to Kwakiutl Religious Thought* (New York: John Wiley & Sons).

Goodman, F.D. (1972) *Speaking in Tongues: A Cross-cultural Study of Glossolalia* (Chicago: University of Chicago Press).

Goodman, F.D. (1981) *The Exorcism of Anneliese Michel* (New York: Doubleday).

Goodman, F.D. (1988) *How About Demons? Possession and Exorcism in the Modern World* (Bloomington: Indiana University Press).

Goodwin, G. (1939) *Myths and Tales of the White Mountain Apache*. Memoirs of the Apache Society 33 (New York: J.J. Augustin for The American Folklore Society).

Goreng Goreng, T. (1997) 'Time for the world to receive the message: Aboriginal Dreaming wisdom', *The Silver Cord*, July, p. 23.

Green, E.C. (1999) *Indigenous Theories of Contagious Disease* (Walnut Creek: Altamira Press).

Green, R. (1988) 'Poor Lo and Dusky Ramona', in J. Becker and B. Franco *Folk Roots, New Roots: Folklore in American Life* (Lexington: Museum of National Heritage).

Grinde, D. and Johansen, B.E. (1991) *Exemplar of Liberty: Native America and the Evolution of Democracy* (Los Angeles: UCLA Press).

Gunther, E. (1926) 'An analysis of the First Salmon ceremony', *American Anthropologist* 28, pp. 605–17.

Haar, G. ter. (1992) *Spirit of Africa: The Healing Ministry of Archbishop Milingo* (London: Hurst).

Haar, G. ter., Moyo, A. and Nondo, S.J. (1992) *African Traditional Religions in Religious Education. A Resource Book with Special Reference to Zimbabwe* (Utrecht: Utrecht University Press).

Hackett, R. (1996) *Art and Religion in Africa* (London: Cassell).

Halifax, J. (1979) *Shamanic Voices: A Survey of Visionary Narratives* (New York: Dutton).

Hallowell, A.I. (1926) 'Bear ceremonialism in the Northern Hemisphere', *American Anthropologist* 28, pp. 1–175.

Hallowell, A.I. (1975) 'Ojibwa ontology, behavior, and world view', in D. Tedlock and B. Tedlock (eds) *Teachings from the American Earth* (New York: Liveright), pp. 141–78.

Hallowell, A.I. (1992) *The Ojibwa of Berens River, Manitoba: Ethnography into History*, (ed.) J.S.H. Brown (Fort Worth, TX: Harcourt Brace Jovanovitch).

Hamilton, M.B. (1995) *The Sociology of Religion: Theoretical and Comparative Perspectives* (London: Routledge).

Hamilton, W. (1966) 'American theology, radicalism and the death of God', in T.J.J. Altizer and W. Hamilton (eds) *Radical Theology and the Death of God* (New York: Bobbs-Merrill), pp. 19–23.

Hammond, D. (1970). 'Magic: a problem in semantics', *American Anthropologist* 72.6, pp. 1349–56.

Hansson, G. (1994) 'Religious innovation in Zimbabwe: Mbuya Juliana Movement', unpublished paper presented at the Conference Christians and Muslims in Contemporary Africa: Religious, Social and Political Perspectives, Uppsala, 25–28 August.

Hanvik, J.M. (1994) 'Mayan Culture is rescued through dance', *Dance Magazine* November, pp. 40–4.

Hardman, C. (1981) 'Conformity and self-expression', in P. Heelas and A. Lock (eds) *Indigenous Psychology: The Anthropology of the Self* (London: Academic Press), pp. 161–80.

Hardman, C. (forthcoming). *Other Worlds: Self and Emotion among the Lohorung Rai of East Nepal*.

Harner, M. (1982) *The Way of the Shaman* (New York: Bantam).

Harrington, J.P. (1932) *Tobacco among the Karuk Indians of California* (Washington, DC: US Govt. Print Office).

Harrod, H.L. (1987) *Renewing the World: Plains Indian Religion and Morality* (Tucson: University of Arizona Press).

Hart, M. (1990) *Drumming at the Edge of Magic* (San Francisco: Harper).

Harvey, G. (1997) *Listening People Speaking Earth: Contemporary Paganism* (London: Hurst & Co).

Harvey, G. (forthcoming) *Animism* (London: Hurst).

Heizer, R.F. and Elsasser, A.B. (1980) *The Natural World of the California Indians* (Berkeley, CA: University of California Press).

Henare, M. (1988) 'Nga Tikanga me Nga Ritenga o Te Ao Maori', *The Royal Commission on Social Policy* 3.1: *Future Directions*. Wellington (April).

Henderson, D.K. (1987) 'Winch and the constraints of interpretation: versions of the principle of charity', *Southern Journal of Philosophy* 25, pp. 153–73.

Hendry, J. (1999) *An Introduction to Social Anthropology: Other People's Worlds* (London: Macmillan).

Henninger, J. (1987) 'Sacrifice', in M. Eliade (ed.) *The Encyclopedia of Religion* 12 (London: Macmillan), pp. 544–57.

Heusch, L. de. (1981) 'Possession and shamanism', in L. de Heusch (ed.) *Why Marry Her? Society and Symbolic Structures* (Cambridge: Cambridge University Press).

Hiatt, L.R. (1997) 'A new age for an old people', *Quadrant*, June, pp. 35–40.

Hillman, L. and Salter J.F. (1997) 'Environmental management: American Indian knowledge and the problem of sustainability', *Forest, Trees and People* 34, pp. 20–6.

Hillman, L. (1997) 'Variations between Euro-American and Native American Thought and Perception'. Paper presented to International Conference on Creativity and Innovation in Grassroots Sustainable Resource Management, Ahmedabad, India.

Hollenback, J.B. (1996) *Mysticism: Experience, Response, and Empowerment* (University Park, PA: The Pennsylvania State University Press).

Honour, H. (1975) *The New Golden Land: European Images of America from the Discoveries to the Present Time* (New York: Pantheon).

Hoppál, M. (ed.) (1984) *Shamanism in Eurasia* (Göttingen: Herodot).

Horton, R. (1971) 'African conversion', *Africa* 41.2, pp. 85–108.

Horton, R. (1975) 'On the rationality of conversion', *Africa* 45.3, pp. 219–35; 45.4, pp. 373–99.

Horton, R. (1976) 'Professor Winch on safari', *Archives Européennes de Sociologie* 17.1, pp. 157–80.

Horton, R. (1982) 'Tradition and modernity revisited', in M. Hollis and S. Lukes (eds) *Rationality and Relativism* (Cambridge, MA: The MIT Press).

Horton, R. (1993) *Patterns of Thought in Africa and the West: Essays on Magic, Religion and Science* (Cambridge: Cambridge University Press).

Hultkrantz, A. (1983) 'The concept of the supernatural in primal religions', *History of Religions* 22, pp. 231–53.

Hultkrantz, A. (1992) *Shamanic Healing and Ritual Drama: Health and Medicine in Native North American Religious Traditions* (New York: Crossroad).

Hume, L. (1994) 'Delivering the word the Aboriginal way: the genesis of an Australian Aboriginal theology', *Colloquium* 25.2, pp. 86–95.

Hume, L. (1996) 'The rainbow serpent, the cross and the fax machine: Australian Aboriginal responses to the Bible', in M.G. Brett (ed.) *Ethnicity and the Bible* (Leiden: E.J. Brill), pp. 359–79.

Hume, L. (1997) *Witchcraft and Paganism in Australia* (Melbourne: Melbourne University Press).

Huntsinger, L. and McCaffrey, S. (1995) 'A forest for the trees: forest management and the Yurok environment, 1850 to 1994', *American Indian Culture and Research Journal* 19:4, pp. 155–92.

Hurtado, A. and Iverson, P. (1994) *Major Problems in American Indian History* (Lexington: D.C. Heath & Co).

Hutchinson, S.E. (1996) *Nuer Dilemmas: Coping with Money, War, and the State* (Berkley, CA: University of California Press).

Hutton, J. (1921) *The Angami Nagas* (London: Macmillan).

Irwin, L. (1992) 'Contesting world views: dreams among the Huron and Jesuits', *Religion* 22.3, pp. 259–69.

Irwin, L. (1994) *The Dream Seekers: Native American Visionary Traditions of the Great Plains* (Norman, OK: University of Oklahoma Press).

Irwin, L. (1998) 'Native voices in the study of Native America religions', *Critical Review of Books in Religion* 11, pp. 97–147.

Isasi-Diaz, A.M. (1996) *Mujerista Theology: A Theology for the Twenty-First Century* (Maryknoll: Orbis).

Iverson, P. (1990) *When Indians Became Cowboys* (Norman, OK: University of Oklahoma).

Jackson, D. (1993) *On the Country: The Micmac of Newfoundland* (St. John's: Harry Cuff Publications).

Jacobs, J. (1994) 'Earth honouring: Western desires and indigenous knowledges', *Meanjin* 53.2, pp. 305–14.

Jaimes, M.A. (1992) 'Re-visioning Native America: an indigenist view of primitivism and industrialism', *Social Justice: A Journal of Crime, Conflict, and World Order*, Special Issue on Columbus on Trial: Myth-Busting and New Perspectives 19.2, pp. 5–34.

Johnson, D.H. (1994) *Nuer Prophets: A History of Prophecy from the Upper Nile in the Nineteenth and Twentieth Centuries* (Oxford: Oxford University Press).

Jones, R. and Jones, S. (1976) *The Himalayan Woman* (Paolo Alto: Mayfield Publishing Co.).

Josephy, A.M. (1996) *500 Nations* (New York: Knopf).

Jung, C. (1939) *The Integration of Personality* (New York: Farrar and Rinehart).

Jung, C. (1963) *Memories, Dreams, Reflections* (London: Routledge).

Kapferer, B. (1991) *A Celebration of Demons: Exorcism and the Aesthetics of Healing in Sri Lanka* (Oxford: Berg).

Katz, R. (1982) *Boiling Energy: Community Healing among the Kalahari Kung* (Cambridge, MA: Harvard University Press).

Kawagley, O. (1995) *A Yupiaq World View: A Path to Ecology and Spirit* (Prospect Heights, ILL: Waveland Press).

Kawharu I.M. (1980) 'Traditional Maori Worldviews', lecture department of Anthropology and Maori Studies. Massey University, New Zealand.

Keen, I. (1986) 'Stanner on Aboriginal religion', *Canberra Anthropology* 9.2, pp. 26–50.

Keen, I. (1994) *Knowledge and Secrecy in an Aboriginal Religion* (Oxford: Oxford University Press).

Kelley, H.J. (1978) *Yaqui Women: Contemporary Life Histories* (Lincoln: University of Nebraska Press).

Kendall, L. (1985) *Shamans, Housewives and Other Restless Spirits: Women in Korean Ritual Life* (Honolulu: Hawaii University Press).

Kerzer, D. (1988) *Ritual, Politics and Power* (New Haven: Yale University Press).

Kohák, E. (1991) 'Speaking of persons' *Personalist Forum* 7, pp. 41–58.

Kohák, E. (1993) 'Speaking to trees', *Critical Review* 6, pp. 371–88.

Laban, R. (1966) *Choreutics* (London: Macdonald).

La Farge, O. and Byers, D. (1931) *The Year Bearer's People* (New Orleans: Tulane University Department of Middle America Research).

Lagae, C. (1926) *Les Azande ou Niam-Niam* (Bruxelles: Vromat).

Lakoff, G. and Johnson, M. (1980) *Metaphors We Live By* (Chicago: University of Chicago Press).
Lan, D. (1985) *Guns and Rain: Guerrillas and Spirit Mediums in Zimbabwe* (London: James Currey; Berkeley and Los Angeles: University of California Press).
Landes, R. (1968) *Ojibwa Religion and the Midewiwin* (Madison: University of Wisconsin Press).
Lang, J. (1994) *Ararapikva: Creation Stories of the People* (Berkeley, CA: Heyday Books).
Lau, G. (1997) *Adults in Wonderland* (New York: Serpent's Tail).
Laue, Th. H. von. (1975) 'Transubstantiation in the study of African Reality', *African Affairs* 74, pp. 401–19.
Laue, Th. H. von (1976) 'Anthropology and power: R.S. Rattray among the Ashanti', *African Affairs* 75, pp. 33–54.
Lawlor, R. (1982) *Sacred Geometry* (London: Thames and Hudson).
Lawlor, R. (1991) *Voices of the First Day* (Rochester: Inner Traditions).
Leach, E. (1954) *Political Systems of Highland Burma* (London: Beacon Press).
Lee, D. (1959) *Freedom and Culture* (Englewood Cliffs, NJ: Prentice-Hall).
Leeming, D. and Leeming, M. (1994) *A Dictionary of Creation Myths* (Oxford: Oxford University Press).
Lefebvre, H. (1994) *The Production of Space* (Oxford: Blackwell).
Lehman, F.K. (1970) 'On Chin and Kachin marriage regulations', *Man* (ns) 5.1, pp. 118–25.
Lehman, F.K. (1977) 'Kachin social categories and methodological sins', in W. McCormack and S. Wurm (eds) *Language and Thought: Anthropological Issues* (The Hague: Mouton), pp. 229–49.
Lerner, B.D. (1995a) 'Winch and instrumental pluralism', *Philosophy of the Social Sciences* 25, pp. 180–91.
Lerner, B.D. (1995b) 'Understanding a (secular) primitive society', *Religious Studies* 31, pp. 303–9.
Lerner, B.D. (1998) 'Winch and instrumental pluralism: a response to my critics', *Philosophy of the Social Sciences* 28, pp. 312–20.
Lévi-Strauss, C. (1969) *The Elementary Structures of Kinship*. Translated by R. Needham (Boston: Beacon Press).
Lewis, H.T. (1993) 'Patterns of Indian burning in California: ecology and ethnohistory', in T.C. Blackburn and K. Anderson (eds) *Before the Wilderness* (Menlo Park, CA: Ballena Press), pp. 55–116.
Lewis, I.M. (1986) *Religion in Context: Cults and Charisma* (Cambridge: Cambridge University Press).
Lewis, I.M. (1989) *Ecstatic Religion: A Study of Shamanism and Spirit Possession* (London and New York: Routledge).
Lex, B. (1976) 'Psychological aspects of trance', *Journal of Altered States of Consciousness* 2, pp. 109–22.
Lex, B. (1978) 'Neurological bases of revitalization', *Zygon* 13, pp. 276–12.

Lex, B. (1979) 'The neurobiology of ritual trance', in E.G. d'Aquili, C.D. Laughlin and J. McManus (eds) *The Spectrum of Ritual* (New York: Columbia University Press), pp. 117–51.

Lienhardt, G. (1961) *Divinity and Experience: The Religion of the Dinka* (Oxford: Clarendon Press).

Lincoln, K. and Slagle, A. (1987) *The Good Red Road: Passages into Native America* (New York: Harper and Row).

Lockhart, V. (1994) *A Social-Historical Study of Social Change among the Bangwa of Cameroon*, occasional papers No. 52 (Edinburgh University: Centre for African Studies).

Loeffler, L. (1968) 'Bird, beast and fish: an essay in South-East Asian symbolism', in *Folk Religion and World View in the Southwestern Pacific* (Tokyo: Keio University Institute of Cultural and Linguistic Studies), pp. 21–33.

Loftin, J.D. (1986) 'Supplication and participation: the distance and relation of the sacred in Hopi prayer rites', *Anthropos* 81, pp. 177–201.

Lokensgard, K. (1996) 'Medicine bundle persons: Blackfoot ontology and the study of Native American religions', unpublished MA thesis, Arizona State University.

Lovell, W.G. (1992) *Conquest and Survival in Colonial Guatemala: A Historical Geography of the Cuchumatán Highlands, 1500–1821* (Montreal: McGill-Queen's University Press).

Luckert, K.W. (1975) *The Navajo Hunter Tradition* (Tucson, AZ: University of Arizona Press).

Ludwig, A. (1967) 'The trance', *Comprehensive Psychiatry* 8, pp. 7–15.

Ludwig, A. (1968) 'Altered states of consciousness', in R. Prince (ed.) *Trance and Possession States* (Montreal: R.M. Buckle Memorial Society), pp. 11–24.

Ludwig, A. (1972) 'Introduction', in Ch.T. Tart (ed.) *Altered States of Consciousness* (New York: Doubleday), pp. 1–6.

Lyons, O. and Mohawk, J. (eds) (1992) *Exiled in the Land of the Free: Democracy, Indian Nations, and the U.S. Constitution* (Santa Fe: Clear Light).

Macfarlane, A. (1978) *The Origins of English Individualism* (Oxford: Blackwell).

Machin, N.P.F. (unpublished). Understanding the natives: the life of R.S. Rattray.

MacLaine, S. (1984) *Out on a Limb* (New York: Bantam).

Malony, H.N., Newton, H. and Lovekin, A.A. (1985) *Glossolalia: Behavioral Science Perspectives on Speaking in Tongues* (Oxford: Oxford University Press).

Mander, J. (1991) *In The Absence of the Sacred: The Failure of Technology and the Survival of the Indian Nations* (San Francisco: Sierra Club Books).

Mankiller, W. and Walls, M. (1993) *Mankiller: A Chief and Her People* (New York: St Martin's Press).

Marcus, J. (1988) 'The journey out to the centre: Ayers Rock and cultural appropriation', in A. Rutherford (ed.) *Aboriginal Culture Today* (Copenhagen: Dangaroo Press), pp. 305–14.

Marcus, J. (1996) 'New Age consciousness and Aboriginal culture', *Thamyris* 3.1, p. 41.

Margolin, M. (1994) *Living in a Well-Ordered World: Indian People of Northwestern California* (Berkeley, CA: Redwood National Park; Heyday Books).
Marsden, M. (1992) 'God, man and universe: a Maori view', in M. King (ed.) *Te Ao Hurihuri: The World Moves On* (Auckland: Octopus Publishing Group).
Marsden, M. and Henare, T.A. (1992) 'Kaitiakitanga: a definitive introduction to the holistic worldview of the Maori', paper in response to the Resource Management Act 1991. Auckland: self-published.
Martin, C. (1987) 'The metaphysics of writing Indian-White history', in C. Martin (ed.) *The American Indian and the Problem of History* (New York: Oxford University Press), pp. 27–34.
Martinez, D. (1996) 'First people: firsthand knowledge: the wisdom of Native Americans', *Sierra* 81.6 (Nov–Dec), pp. 50–4.
Masuzawa, T. (1998) 'Culture', in M.C. Taylor (ed.) *Critical Terms for Religious Studies* (Chicago: University of Chicago Press), pp. 70–93.
Mauss, M. (1970) *The Gift*, trans. I. Cunnison (London: Cohen and West).
Mawere A. and Wilson, K. (1995) 'Socio-religious movements, the state and community change: some reflections on the Ambuya Juliana Cult of southern Zimbabwe', *Journal of Religion in Africa* 25.3, pp. 252–87.
McDougal, C. (1979) *The Kulung Rai: a study in kinship and marriage exchange* (Kathmandu: Ratna Pustak Bhandhar).
McHugh E. (1989) 'Conceptions of the person among the Gurungs of Nepal', *American Ethnologist* 16.1, pp. 75–86.
Mead, S.M. (1969) 'Imagery, symbolism and social values in Maori chants', *Journal of Polynesian Studies* 78.3, pp. 378–404.
Mead, S.M. (1997) *Landmarks, Bridges and Visions: Aspects of Maori Culture* (Wellington: Victoria University Press).
Meeker, M.E. (1989) *The Pastoral Son and the Spirit of Patriarchy: Religion, Society, and the Person among East African Stock Keepers* (Madison: University of Wisconsin Press).
Merchant, C. (1980) *The Death of Nature* (San Francisco: Harper & Row).
Metge, J. (1998) 'Time and the art of Maori storytelling', *New Zealand Studies* 8.1, pp. 3–9.
Mihesuah, D.A. (ed.) (1998) *Natives and Academics: Researching and Writing about American Indians* (Lincoln: University of Nebraska Press).
Miller, W.H. (1955) 'Two concepts of authority' *American Anthropologist* 57, pp. 271–89.
Mills, A. (1994) 'Introduction', in A. Mills and R. Slobodin (eds) *Amerindian Rebirth* (Toronto: University of Toronto Press), pp. 3–14.
Mills, A. and Slobodin, R. (eds) (1994) *Amerindian Rebirth: Reincarnation Belief among North American Indians and Inuit* (Toronto: University of Toronto Press).
Mills, J.P. (1922) *The Lhota Nagas* (London: Macmillan).
Mills, J.P. (1926) *The Ao Naga* (London: Macmillan).
Mills, J.P. (1937) *The Rengma Naga* (London: Macmillan).
Moore, A.C. (1995) *Arts in the Religions of the Pacific: Symbols of Life* (London: Cassell).

Morales H.I. (1988) *La Persistencia de la Tradición Carolinga in Guatemala y Centroamerica* (Guatemala: Instituto Indigenista Nacional, Ministerio de Cultura y Deportes).

Morgan, M. (1995) *Mutant Message from Down Under* (London: Thorsons).

Morris, B. (1987) *Anthropological Studies of Religion* (Cambridge: Cambridge University Press).

Morrison, K. (1992a) 'Beyond the supernatural: language and religious action', *Religion* 22, pp. 201–5.

Morrison, K. (1992b) 'Sharing the flower: a non-supernaturalistic theory of grace', *Religion* 22, pp. 208–20.

Mukonyora, I. (1993) 'The fulfilment of African religious needs through the Bible', in I. Mukonyora, J.L. Cox and F.J. Verstraelen (eds) *'Rewriting' the Bible: The Real Issues. Perspectives from within Biblical and Religious Studies in Zimbabwe* (Gweru: Mambo Press), pp. 249–62.

Munn, N.D. (1984) 'The transformation of subjects into objects in Walbiri and Pitjantjatjara myth', in M. Charlesworth *et al.* (eds) *Religion in Aboriginal Australia* (St. Lucia: University of Queensland Press), pp. 57–82.

Ndobegang, M.A. (1983) *Our Cultural Heritage (1): Lebang Chiefdom* Privately printed in Cameroon.

Needham, R. (1972) *Belief, Language, and Experience* (Oxford: Blackwell).

Nelson, R. (1983) *Make Prayers to the Raven: A Koyukon View of the Northern Forest* (Chicago: University of Chicago Press).

Newcomb, S. (1994) 'Traditional native law: a path to an ecologically appropriate life', *Turtle Quarterly* 6.1, pp. 20–3.

Nieuwenhuijze, D.O. van (1998) 'The simplicity of complexity', paper at 14th World Congress of Sociology, Montreal.

Noonuccal, O. and Noonuccal, K.O. (1988) *The Rainbow Serpent* (Canberra: Australian Government Publishing Service, unpaginated).

Nthoi, L.S. (1998) 'Wosana rite of passage: reflections on the initiation of Wosana in the cult of Mwali in Zimbabwe', in J.L. Cox (ed.) *Rites of Passage in Contemporary Africa* (Cardiff: Cardiff Academic Press), pp. 63–93.

O'Gorman, E. (1961) *The Invention of America: An Inquiry into the Historical Nature of the New World and the Meaning of its History* (Bloomington: Indiana University Press).

Orbell, M. (1995) *The Illustrated Encyclopedia of Maori Myth and Legend* (Christchurch: Canterbury University Press).

Pals, D.L. (1996) *Seven Theories of Religion* (Oxford: Oxford University Press).

Pandian, J. (1997) 'The sacred integration of the cultural self: an anthropological approach to the study of religion', in S.D. Glazier (ed.) *Anthropology of Religion: A Handbook* (Westport, Connecticut: Greenwood Press), pp. 505–16.

Paper, J. (1988) *Offering Smoke: The Sacred Pipe and Native American Religion* (Moscow, ID: University of Idaho Press).

Parfit, M. and Harvey, D. (1994) 'Powwow', *National Geographic Magazine*, June, pp. 88–113.

Parkhill, T.C. (1997) *Weaving Ourselves Into the Land: Charles Godfrey Leland, 'Indians', and the Study of Native American Religions* (Albany: State University of New York Press).

Pattel-Gray, A. (1990) 'Aboriginal Australian presentation on JPIC', *Justice, Peace and the Integrity of Creation: Sermons and Speeches*, 53.1, p. 2.

Pere, R.T. (1991) *Te Wheke: A Celebration of Infinite Wisdom* (Gisborne: Ao Ako Global Learning New Zealand).

Pere, R.T. (1994) 'The mother energy', in W. Ihimaera (ed.) *Visions Aotearoa* (Wellington: Bridget Williams Books), pp. 166–76.

Pflug, M.A. (1992) '"Breaking Bread": metaphor and ritual in Odawa religious practice', *Religion* 22/3, pp. 247–58.

Pflug, M.A. (1998) *Ritual and Myth in Odawa Revitalization: Reclaiming a Sovereign Place* (Norman, OK: University of Oklahoma Press).

Philipps, J.E.T. (1926) 'Observations on some aspects of religion among the Azande (Niam-Niam) of Equatorial Africa', *Journal of the Royal Anthropological Institute* 56, pp. 171–88.

Phillips, D.Z. (1981) *The Concept of Prayer* (Oxford: Blackwell).

Platvoet, J.G. (1973) 'Verschuivingen in een West-Afrikaanse godsdienst: hekserijbekentenissen en de opkomst van de "beul"-goden in de godsdienst van de Ashanti', *Bijdragen: Tijdschrift voor Filosofie en Theologie* 34.1, pp. 15–39.

Platvoet, J.G. (1979) 'The Akan believer and his religions', in P.H. Vrijhof and J. Waardenburg (eds) *Official and Popular Religion* (The Hague: Mouton).

Platvoet, J.G. (1982) *Comparing Religions: A Limitative Approach. An Analysis of Akan, Para-Creole and IFO-Sananda Rites and Prayers* (The Hague: Mouton).

Platvoet, J.G. (1983) 'Verbal communication in an Akan possession and maintenance rite', *Nederlands Theologisch Tijdschrift* 37.3, pp. 202–15.

Platvoet, J.G. (1993) 'African traditional religions in the religious history of humankind', *Journal for the Study of Religion* 6.2, pp. 29–48.

Platvoet, J.G. (1996) 'The religions of Africa in their historical order', in J. Platvoet *et al.* (eds) *The Study of Religion in Africa* (Cambridge: Roots and Branches), pp. 46–102.

Platvoet, J.G. (1999) 'Seeds of destruction: European Christianity abroad in the late 20th century', *Africana Marburgensia* 31, 1998, no. 1.

Platvoet, J.G., Cox, J. and Olupona, J. (eds) (1996) *The Study of Religion in Africa: Past, Present and Prospects* (Cambridge: Roots and Branches).

Pocock, D. (1975) *Understanding Social Anthropology* (London: Hodder & Stoughton).

Polanyi, M. (1958) *Personal Knowledge* (London: Routledge and Kegan Paul).

Pomare, M. and Cowan, J. (1987) *Legends of the Maori* (Auckland: Southern Reprint).

Pool, R. (1994) *Dialogue and the Interpretation of Illness: Conversations in a Cameroon Village* (Oxford and Providence: Berg).

Popov, A.A. (1936) 'Tavgiytsy [The Tavgy]', in *Trudy Instituta Antropologii i Etnografii*, vol. I, pt 5, Moscow and Leningrad.

Power, S. (1994) *The Grass Dancer* (New York: G.P. Putnam's Sons).

Powers, W.K. (1986) *Sacred Language: The Nature of Supernatural Discourse in Lakota* (Norman, OK: University of Oklahoma Press).
Prigogine, I. (1984) *Order Out of Chaos* (New York: Bantam Books).
Primack, J.R. and Abrams, N.E. (1998) '"In the Beginning ..." quantum cosmology and kabbalah', *Tikkun* 10.1, pp. 66–73.
Prince, R. (ed.) (1968) *Trance and Possession States* (Montreal: R.M. Buckle Memorial Society).
Prins, H.E.L. (1996) *The Mi'kmaq: Resistance, Accommodation, and Cultural Survival* (Toronto: Harcourt Brace College Publications).
Prucha, F.P. (1984) *The Great Father: The United States Government and the American Indian* (Lincoln: University of Nebraska Press).
Prucha, F.P. (1985) *The Indians in American Society* (Berkeley, CA: University of California).
Rainbow Spirit Elders (1997) *Rainbow Spirit Theology* (Blackburn, VIC: Harper-Collins Religious).
Ranger, T. (1995) 'Religious pluralism in Zimbabwe', *Journal of Religion in Africa* 25(3), pp. 226–51.
Rasmussen, K. (1929) *The Intellectual Culture of the Iglulik Eskimos* (Copenhagen: Gyldendalske).
Rattray, R.S. (1923) *Ashanti* (Oxford: Clarendon Press).
Redfield, R. (1952) 'The primitive world view', *Proceedings of the American Philosophical Society* 96, pp. 30–6.
Reichel-Dolmatoff, G. (1971) *Amazonian Cosmos: The Sexual and Religious Symbolism of the Tukano Indians* (Chicago: Chicago University Press).
Reichel-Dolmatoff, G. (1975) *The Shaman and the Jaguar: A Study of Narcotic Drugs among the Indians of Colombia* (Philadelphia: Temple University Press).
Ridington, R. and Hastings, D. (In'aska) (1997) *Blessing for a Long Time: The Sacred Pole of the Omaha Tribe* (Lincoln: University of Nebraska Press).
Ridington, R. and Ridington, T. (1975) 'The inner eye of shamanism and totemism', in D. Tedlock and B. Tedlock (eds) *Teachings from the American Earth* (New York: Liveright), pp. 190–204.
Rockwell, R. (1998) 'Real peace is elusive in Guatemala', *Baltimore Sun* Sunday, 8 November, 4c, column 1.
Rodríguez Rovanet, F. (1992) *Danzas Folklóricas de Guatemala* (Guatemala: Subcentro Regional de Artesanías y Artes Populares, Ministerio de Cultura y Deportes, Organización de Estados Americanos).
Roesch Wagner, S. (1996) 'Is equality indigenous? The untold Iroquois influence on early radical feminists', *On the Issues*, Winter: 21–5.
Root, D. (1996) *Cannibal Culture: Art, Appropriation and the Commodification of Difference* (Boulder, CO: Westview Press).
Rose, D.B. (1996) *Nourishing Terrains* (Canberra: Australian Heritage Commission).
Rosendale, G. (1989) 'Reflections on the Gospel and Aboriginal spirituality', *The Occasional Bulletin of Nungalinya College*, Darwin, 42, pp. 1–7.
Rowlands, M. and Warnier, J.-P. (1988) 'Sorcery, power and the modern state in Cameroon', *Man* (NS) 23, pp. 118–32.

Ruel, M. (1974) *Leopards and Leaders* (London: Tavistock).
Salmond, A. (1991) *Two Worlds: First Meeting between Maori and European 1642–1772* (Auckland: Penguin Books).
Samarin, W.J. (1972) *Tongues of Men and Angels: The Religious Language of Pentecostalism* (New York: Macmillan).
Sanchez, V. (1998) '"As long as we dance we shall know who we are": Cross-cultural communications in Ohio traditional powwows', paper presented at the American Folklore Society Annual Meetings, Portland, Oregon.
Schneider, L. (1970) *Sociological Approach to Religion* (New York: John Wiley and Sons).
Schulte Nordholt, H.G. (1971) *The Political System of the Atoni of Timor* (The Hague: Martinus Nijhoff).
Schultes, R.E. and Hofmann, A. (1979) *Plants of the Gods: Origins of Hallucinogenic Use* (London: Hutchinson).
Schwimmer, E. (1966) *The World of the Maori* (Wellington: Reed).
Scott, J.C. (1990) *Domination and the Arts of Resistance: Hidden Transcripts* (New Haven: University of Connecticut Press).
Seligman, C.G. and Seligman, B.Z. (1932) *Pagan Tribes of the Nilotic Sudan* (London: Routledge).
Shirokogoroff, S.M. (1935) *The Psychomental Complex of the Tungus* (London: Kegan Paul).
Shirres, M.P. (1994) *Tapu: Te Mana o Nga Atua: The mana of the Spiritual Powers: A Maori theological understanding of Tapu* (Auckland: Te Runanga o te Hahi o Katorika ki Aotearoa/The Catholic Church of New Zealand).
Shiva, V. (1997) *Biopiracy: The Plunder of Nature and Knowledge* (Boston: South End Press).
Sierra (1996) 'Native Americans and the environment', 81 (November/December), p. 6.
Siikala, A-L. (1978) *The Rite Technique of the Siberian Shaman* (Helsinki: Academia Scientiarum Fennica).
Silko, L.M. (1977) *Ceremony* (New York: The Viking Press).
Simoons, F. and Simoons, E. (1968) *Ceremonial Ox of India: The Mithan in Nature, Culture and History* (Madison, WI: University of Wisconsin Press).
Singelton, M. (1972) 'Theology, "Zande Theology" and secular theology', in A. Singer and B.V. Street (eds) *Zande Themes: Essays Presented to Sir Edward Evans-Pritchard* (Oxford: Basil Blackwell), pp. 130–57.
Slobodin, R. (1994) 'The study of reincarnation in indigenous American cultures: some comments', in A. Mills and R. Slobodin (eds) *Amerindian Rebirth* (Toronto: University of Toronto Press), pp. 284–98.
Smith, J.Z. (1998) 'Religion, religions, religious', in M.C. Taylor (ed.) *Critical Terms for Religious Studies* (Chicago: University of Chicago Press), pp. 269–84.
Smith, P.S. (1913, 1915) *The Lore of the Whare Wananga* (New Plymouth: Polynesian Society) (Memoirs 3/4).

Smith, T.S. (1995) *The Island of the Anishnaabeg: Thunderers and Water Monsters in the Traditional Ojibwe Life-World* (Moscow, ID: University of Idaho Press).

Soyinka, W. (1993) *Art, Dialogue and Outrage* (London: Methuen).

Spencer, H. (1882) in Henderson L.J. (1917). *The Order of Nature* (Cambridge, MA: Harvard University Press).

Stadelman, R. (1940) 'Maize cultivation in Northwestern Guatemala', *Contributions to American Anthropology and History* 6, no. 33, pp. 91–125 (Washington, DC: Carnegie Institution).

Stanner, W.E.H. (1979) *White Man Got No Dreaming* (Canberra: ANU Press).

Stanner, W.E.H. (1998) 'Some aspects of Aboriginal religion', in M. Charlesworth (ed.) *Religious Business* (Cambridge: Cambridge University Press), pp. 8–9.

Stone, H. (1997) 'Since time immemorial: Newfoundland Mi'kmaq struggles for rights recognition', unpublished proceedings, Canadian Historical Association Conference, June.

Strehlow, T.G.H. (1971) *Songs of Central Australia* (Sydney: Angus & Robertson).

Sugirtharajah, R.S. (1996). 'Orientalism, ethnonationalism and transnationalism: shifting identities and biblical interpretation', in M.G. Brett (ed.) *Ethnicity and the Bible* (Leiden: E.J. Brill), pp. 419–30.

Swain, T. (1989) 'Dreaming, whites and the Australian landscape: some popular misconceptions', *Journal of Religious History* 15.3, pp. 345–50.

Swain, T. (1992) 'Reinventing the eternal: Aboriginal spirituality and modernity', in N. Habel (ed.) *Religion and Multiculturalism in Australia* (Adelaide: Australian Association for the Study of Religions), pp. 122–36.

Swan, J. (ed.) (1991) *The Power of Place: Sacred Ground in Natural and Human Environments* (Bath: Quest Books).

Swezey S. and Heizer, R. (1993) 'Ritual management of salmonid fish resources in California', in T.C. Blackburn and K. Anderson (eds) *Before the Wilderness* (Menlo Park, CA: Ballena Press), pp. 299–327.

Taiwo, O. (1998) 'The return beat', in J. Wood (ed.) *The Virtual Embodied* (London: Routledge), pp. 157–67.

Tambiah, S. (1968) 'The magical power of words', *Man* 3, pp. 173–208.

Tanner, A. (1979) *Bringing Home Animals: Religious Ideology and Mode of Production of the Mistassini Cree Hunters* (New York: St Martin's Press).

Tart, Ch.T. (1972) *Altered States of Consciousness* (Garden City, NY: Doubleday).

Tauroa, H. and Tauroa, P. (1986) *Te Marae: a Guide to Customs and Protocol* (Auckland: Reed).

Taussig, M. (1992) 'Violence and resistance in the Americas: legacy of the conquest', in M. Taussig, *The Nervous System* (New York: Routledge).

Taussig, M. (1998) 'Transgression', in M.C. Taylor (ed.) *Critical Terms for Religious Studies* (Chicago: University of Chicago Press), pp. 349–64.

Tawhai, T.P. (1988) 'Maori religion', in S. Sutherland, L. Houlden, P. Clarke, F. Hardy (eds) *The World's Religions* (London: Routledge), pp. 854–63.

Taylor, J.E. (1992) 'Steelhead's mother was his father, salmon: development and declension of Aboriginal conservation in the Oregon Country Salmon Fishery', unpublished MA thesis, University of Oregon.

Taylor, M.C. (ed.) (1998) *Critical Terms for Religious Studies* (Chicago: University of Chicago Press).

Taylor, W.B. (1994) 'Santiago's horse: Christianity and colonial resistance in the heartland of New Spain', in W.B. Taylor and F. Pease (eds) *Violence, Resistance, and Survival in the Americas: Native Americans and the Legacy of the Conquest* (Washington, DC: Smithsonian Institution Press), pp. 153–89.

Tedlock, D. and Mannheim, B. (eds) (1995) *The Dialogical Emergence of Culture* (Urbana and Chicago: The University of Illinois Press).

Tedlock, D. and Tedlock, B. (eds) (1975) *Teachings from the American Earth: Indian Religion and Philosophy* (New York: Liveright).

Thomas, G.T. (1987) 'The land is sacred: renewing the dreaming in modern Australia', in G.W. Trompf (ed.) *The Gospel is not Western: Black Theologies from the Southwest Pacific* (Maryknoll, NY: Orbis Books), pp. 90–4.

Thomas, N. and Humphrey, C. (eds) (1994) *Shamanism, History and the State* (Ann Arbor: University of Michigan Press).

Thompson, Jr., C.D. (1997) 'Borders bleed: refugees, repatriates, religion, and the Jacalteco Maya', PhD dissertation, University of North Carolina, Chapel Hill.

Thompson, L. ([1916] 1991) *To the American Indian: Reminiscences of a Yurok Woman* (Berkeley, CA: Heyday Books).

Thwaites, R.G. (1959) *The Jesuit Relations and Allied Documents*, 73 vols (New York: Pageant Book Co).

Trask, H.K. (1993) *From A Native Daughter: Colonialism and Sovereignty in Hawai'i* (Monroe: Common Courage Press).

Trigger, B. (1991) 'Early Native North American responses to European contact: romantic versus rationalistic interpretations', *Journal of American History* 77, pp. 1195–215.

Turner, V. (1967) *The Forest of Symbols: Aspects of Ndembu Ritual* (Ithaca, NY: Cornell University Press).

Turner, V. (1969) *The Ritual Process* (London: Routledge and Kegan Paul).

Tylor, E. (1871) *Primitive Culture: Researches into the Development of Mythology, Philosophy, Religion, Language, Art, and Custom* (London: John Murray).

Urgoti, M.S.C. (1996) *El Moro Retador y el Moro Amigo: Estudios Sobre Fiestas y Comedias de Moros y Cristianos* (Grenada: University of Granada).

Vecsey, C. (1980) 'American Indian environmental religions', in C. Vecsey and R. Venables (eds) *American Indian Environments: Ecological Issues in Native American History* (Syracuse, NY: Syracuse University Press), pp. 1–37.

Vitebsky, P. (1993) *Dialogues with the Dead: The Discussion of Mortality among the Sora of Eastern India* (Cambridge: Cambridge University Press).

Vitebsky, P. (1995a) *The Shaman* (London: Macmillan; Boston: Little Brown).

Vitebsky, P. (1995b) 'From cosmology to environmentalism: Shamanism as local knowledge in a global setting', in R. Fardon (ed.) *Counterworks* (London: Routledge).

Vizenor, G. (1994) *Manifest Manners: Postindian Warriors of Survivance* (Hanover: University Press of New England).
Vrijhof, P.H. and Waardenburg, J. (eds) (1979) *Official and Popular Religion: Analysis of a Theme for Religious Studies* (The Hague: Mouton).
Walens, S. (1981) *Feasting with Cannibals: An Essay on Kwakiutl Cosmology* (Princeton, NJ: Princeton University Press).
Wales, H.Q. (1997) *The Universe Around Them: Cosmology and Cosmic Renewal in Indoanized South-East Asia* (London: Probsthain).
Walker, A. (1983) *In Search of Our Mothers' Gardens: Womanist Prose* (New York: Harcourt Brace Jovanovitch).
Walker, R. (1990) *Ka Whawhai Tonu Matou, Struggle Without End* (Auckland: Penguin).
Walker, R. (1996) *Nga Pepa a Ranginui/The Walker Papers* (Auckland: Penguin).
Walker, S. (1972) *Ceremonial Spirit Possession in Africa and Afro-America* (Leiden: E.J. Brill).
Wallace, A.F.C. (1966) *Religion: An Anthropological View* (New York: Random House).
Wallace, A.F.C. (1980) 'Alfred Irving Hallowell', *National Academy of Sciences, Biographical Memoirs* 51, pp. 194–213.
Walls, A.F. (1996) 'African Christianity in the history of religions', *Studies in World Christianity. The Edinburgh Review of Theology and Religion* 2.2, pp. 183–203.
Walsh, R.N. (1990) *The Spirit of Shamanism* (Los Angeles: Tarcher).
Ward, M.C. (1999) *A World Full of Women* (Boston: Allyn and Bacon).
Warman, A. (1985) *La danza de los Moros y Cristianos*. 2nd edition (Mexico City: Fondo de Cultura Económica).
Warren, D.M. (1974) 'Disease, medicine, and religion among the Techiman-Bono of Ghana: a study in culture change', unpublished PhD thesis, Indiana University.
Warren, K. (1978) *Symbolism of Subordination: Indian Identity in a Guatemalan Town* (Austin, TX: University of Texas Press).
Weaver, J. (ed.) (1998a) *Native American Religious Identity: Unforgotten Gods* (Maryknoll, NY: Orbis).
Weaver, J. (ed.) (1998b) 'From I-hermeneutics to we-hermeneutics: native Americans and the post-colonial', in J. Weaver (ed.) *Native American Religious Identity* (Maryknoll, NY: Orbis), pp. 1–25.
Weber, M. (1966) *The Theory of Social and Economic Organisation* (New York: Glencoe Free Press).
Webster, P. (1979) *Rua and the Maori Millennium* (Wellington: Price Milburn, Victoria University Press).
Weibel-Orlando, J. (1991) *Indian Country, L.A.: Maintaining Ethnic Community in Complex Society* (Urbana: University of Illinois Press).
Weller, J. and Linden, J. (1984) *Mainstream Christianity to 1980 in Malawi, Zambia and Zimbabwe* (Gweru: Mambo Press).
Wenger, S. and Chesi, G. (1983) *A Life with the Gods: In their Yoruba Homeland* (Wörgl: Perlinger Verlag).

Wetzel, M.G. (1995) 'Decolonizing Ktaqmkuk Mi'kmaw history', unpublished MLL thesis, Dalhousie University, Halifax, Nova Scotia.

Williams, N. (1986) *The Yolngu and their Land* (Canberra: Australian Institute of Aboriginal Studies).

Wilson, B.R. (ed.) (1970) *Rationality* (Evanston, ILL: Harper & Row).

Wilson, S.G. (1992) *The Drummer's Path* (Rochester: Destiny Books).

Winch, P. (1964). 'Understanding a primitive society', *American Philosophical Quarterly* 1, pp. 307–24.

Witherspoon, G. (1977) *Language and Art in the Navajo Universe* (Ann Arbor: University of Michigan Press).

Wittgenstein, L. (1966) *Lectures and Conversation on Aesthetics, Psychology and Religious Belief* C. Barrett (ed.) (Berkley, CA: University of California Press).

Wittgenstein, L. (1979) *Remarks on Frazer's Golden Bough* trans. R. Rhees (Nottinghamshire: The Brynmill Press).

Witthoft, J. (1949) 'Green Corn Ceremonialism in the Eastern Woodlands' *Occasional Contributions from the Museum of Anthropology of the University of Michigan*, 13 (Ann Arbor: University of Michigan Press).

Wood, J. (ed.) (1998a) *The Virtual Embodied* (London: Routledge).

Wood, J. (1998b) 'Redesigning the present', in J. Wood (ed.) *The Virtual Embodied* (London: Routledge), pp. 88–101.

Woodward, M.R. (1989a) 'Economy, polity and cosmology in the Ao Naga Mithan feast', in S.D. Russell (ed.) *Ritual, Power and Economy: Upland Lowland Contrasts in Mainland Southeast Asia* (Dekalb: Northern Illinois University Center for Southeast Asian Studies), pp. 121–42.

Woodward, M.R. (1989b) *Islam in Java. Normative Piety and Mysticism in the Sultanate of Yogyakarta* (Tucson, AZ: University of Arizona Press).

Woodward, M.R. (1996) 'Ritual as cosmogony: village founding rites of the Lhota Naga', in N. Tannenbaum and C.A. Kammerer (eds) *Merit and Blessing in Mainland Southeast Asia in Comparative Perspective* (New Haven: Yale Southeast Asia Studies), pp. 134–58.

Wright, K. (1999) 'First Americans', *Discover: The World of Science magazine*, February issue, pp. 53–62.

Young, E.V. (1994) 'Conclusion: the state as vampire: hegemonic projects, public ritual, and popular culture in Mexico, 1600–1990', in W.H. Beezley, C.E. Martin and W.E. French (eds) *Rituals of Rule, Rituals of Resistançe: Public Celebrations and Popular Culture in Mexico* (Wilmington, Delaware: SR Books), pp. 343–7.

Index of Subjects

Index of Authors

Index of Nations, Peoples and Groups